AF560159

The Early Cultural Relations of India and Iran

This book deals with the cultural relations between India and Iran. It evaluates the cultural heritage which bequeathed upon each one of them as a collective phenomenon or individually and the indigenous growth, in each case actions and interactions of ideas and conceptions and determining influences to which they were subjected.

In the first two, chapters cultural backgrounds of both countries and the growth of civilization in the neighbouring region of Iran has been examined. An analytical study of the Indus culture with all its aspects has elaborately been done in the chapter three concluding that its original roots are Iranian. The chapters from IV to VIII cover the cultural history of Aryans from the Indo-Europeans to the Indo-Aryans. The most controversial point of original home of Aryans has been touched pinpointing, the region extending from Hindukush to Pamir. The comparison of all Indo-European languages has been constituted in respect of vocabulary, syntax and formation of sentences, substantiating that Sanskrit is the mother of all Indo-European languages which preserved original words and original meanings. It includes the facts that Iranian Aryans and Indian Aryans were once one and the same people speaking the same language, worshipping the same gods and following the same social customs and traditions. The close affinity between Sanskrit and Avesta has elaborately analysed proving it is so great in syntax, vocabulary, diction and general style that by mere application of phonetic laws whole stanzas may be translated word for word into Vedic mantras so as to produce verses correct not in form but in poetic spirit. In dealing with the Indo Aryan culture, the author, first of all, adequately emphasized the place of the Rigveda which contains the original feelings, the oldest thoughts and primitive ideas of undivided Ayrans. In this field no substantial work has been done, whatever has been done is not free from bias and prejudices and national sentiments have been allowed to colour the facts. The Semitic religious beliefs and the legends which crept in the religions of Avesta and Rigveda have been ingeniously traced.

Dr. G.A. Qamar is a retired Assistant Superintending Archaeologist from Archaeological Survey of India, Government of India. He did his Ph.D. from the Agra University on the subject entitled "The Comparative Study of Cultural Evolution in India and Iran from the Earliest Time to the Later Vedic Period" and obtained the degree of Fazil from Dar-Ul-Uloom, Deoband, U.P.

He has good knowledge of medieval Indian archaeology. He deciphered numerous coins of medieval period and deciphered inscriptions recorded on monuments in Arabic and Persian. He Possesses a great insight in the Indo-Islamic architecture, especially in Mughal architecture. He studied the Lucknow architecture thoroughly and wrote a research paper namely "Monumental Glory of Lucknow" which received great appreciation.

The author was appointed at Taj Mahal as caretaker to which he was attached for more than 25 years. By virtue of being placed at this world famous monument, visited by tourists from every nook and comer of the world, the author got a good opportunity to come in contact with the people of different countries, consequently he acquired and accumulated profound knowledge and penetrating insight in various cultures of the world.

He attended national and international seminars and conferences and delivered lectures on the Agra Monuments. He has authored several research papers, the research paper entitled, "The Lesser Known Monuments of Agra" is much appreciated.

The Early Cultural Relations of India and Iran

G.A. Qamar

DEV PUBLISHERS & DISTRIBUTORS
New Delhi

Published by:
DEV PUBLISHERS & DISTRIBUTORS
2nd Floor, Prakash Deep,
4735/22, Ansari Road,
Darya Ganj,
New Delhi-110002
Phone : 011-43572647, 9810236140
e-mail: devbooks@hotmail.com
website: www.devbooks.co.in

ISBN 978-81-920752-0-4
First published 2011

Printed in India

To the memory of
My Revered Mother
Smt. Bhuri Begum

Contents

Preface

This book originally formed part of my thesis entitled "the Comparative Study of Cultural Evolution in India and Iran from the earliest time to the later Vedic period", which the Agra University approved in 1976 for the degree of Ph.D. It includes an evaluation of the cultural heritage which bequeathed upon each one of them as a collective phenomenon or individually and the indigenous growth in each case actions and interactions of thoughts and concepts and the determining influences to which they were subjected.

Chapter I is introductory to the study. It deals with the pre-historic cultural background of India. Chapter II seeks to study the growth of civilization in India and Iran since the New Stone Age and the influences which were mutually exchanged. During the Chalcolithic period India came very nearer to Iran. It appears that during this period the region in between India and Iran was culturally homogeneous. In this chapter sufficient light has been shed on the obscure phases of the Indian culture. Chapter III gives an appraisal of the evolution of the Indus Valley civilization. It appears that Iranian influence was more determining in its formation than that of Summer, though in fact, it was largely of an indigenous growth. This has been studied from the point of view of almost all aspects of culture, viz., religion, town-planning and architecture, terracottas, pottery, ornaments, seals and miscellaneous objects of usage. Chapter IV is devoted to the study of the Aryans. The great controversy as to their original home has been touched. Primitive Indo-European culture has been studied in chapter VI from the socio-religious point of view. The original religious beliefs and social conditions of the undivided Aryans have been reconstructed on the basis of a critical study of comparison in regard to cults, conceptions, gods, myths and social customs prevalent among the various Aryan branches and many controversial points have been taken up. Chapter-V studies the linguistic affinity between Sanskrit and Avesta vis-a-vis the stock of the Indo-

European languages. As a mater of fact Sanskrit occupies unique position among the Indo-European languages and it appears to be their mother. Sanskrit is the chiefest witness as what was the original word and its original meaning. In the light of new researches this chapter seeks to champion the real cause of Sanskrit. Indo-Iranian culture has been taken up in Chapter VII. No doubt the Indo Iranian is the most important branch of the Aryans. The Indo-Iranian people developed a distinct culture of high order. It is also fairly certain that the Indo-Iranians inherited the largest share of the common heirloom and preserved it very zealously. They advanced further in the path of civilization than any other Aryan Nation. They developed a highly sublime conception of Rta which is beyond the reach of any other people in such a remote past. Chapter VIII deals with the Indo-Aryans culture. In this chapter the place of the Rigveda has been adequately emphasized. It is an undoubted fact that the Rigveda represents the primitive Aryans in its all aspects. Of course, the Rigveda contains the original feelings, the oldest thoughts and primitive ideas of the undivided Aryans. In this field no substantial work has been done, whatever has been done is not free from bias and prejudices and national sentiments have been allowed to colour the facts. Hence attempts have been made in Chapters VII and VIII to present the subject in its true perspective. Chapter IX summaries the various conclusions.

Without doubt, it was an extremely difficult and complicated work. The data which is available is not only in fragments, it is also mutually conflicting and there are more controversies than conclusions. The archaeologists have studied only from the point of view of a world culture and no aspect-wise consistent and intensive study has been made so far, least from an Indian point of view Surprising is the fact that the Rigveda which is the source book of Aryan culture has not been given the importance which it deserves and without which a proper study of the Indo-Europeans vis-a-vis the Vedic people and their brothers in Iran, cannot be pursued with profit. The study was particularly handicapped by the non-availability of the books, and but for the kind help. I received from various Institutions, particularly the Iran Society, Calcutta and Heras Institute of Indian History and Culture, Bombay, this work could not have been completed.

These difficulties which at times appeared to be insuperable beset the pursuit of this subject which was originally registered for the degree of Ph.D. at Agra University in 1968. The Vice-Chancellor of Agra University in view of its great magnitude and the handicaps, has been kind enough to grant me three extensions, one after the other, enabling me to complete this work to my satisfaction and that of my learned supervisor Professor G.L. Mukerji and to submit it 1975. I have no words to express my gratefulness to the Vice-Chancellor, Agra University. I am also immensely thankful to Dr. M.C. Gupta, Registrar, Dr. R.A. Sharma and Shri R.K. Bansal, Agra University for their kindly looking into the matter from time to time for their encouragement and whole hearted assistance.

I feel grateful to my supervisor Professor G.L. Mukerji whose learned guidance has helped me to understand this difficult work. He has taken a great interest and pain to guide me in order to find out new facts. He has guided me with fatherly affection and love which cannot be expressed in words.

I am also thankful to Dr. R. Nath whose scholarship and deep knowledge of the medieval Indian History impressed me of Indian History and gave me a great incentive to work on this difficult topic. He has personally seen my work and made valuable suggestions.

I express my gratitude to my daughter and son-in-law namely—Kishwar Nahid M.A. (Sanskrit), M.A. (Sociology) and Falak Mohammad Meo (Advocate) in Delhi High Court who gave me a great incentive and encouragement to work on this difficult topic. In spite of insurmountable family problems and hardships of their personal life, they have taken a great pain and exertion to get this book published. All credit goes to Mr. Falak, who, much to his inconvenience, with his hard perseverance, with his whole hearted devotion and with his persistingly engaged attachment to the pursuit, has rendered this form and shape of this book.

I am also beholden to my elder son, Sarfraz Ahmad Khan who checked the typed and printing material and made necessary corrections at his great inconvenience and a busy life.

I have no words to express my gratitude to Dr. Ram Bilas Sharma, Retired Director of K.M. Institute, Agra, one of the greatest linguists of the country, who not only gave me valuable guidelines on the chapter on linguistic affinity and discussed the various points but also checked it up word by world, much to his inconvenience. But for his help, I am afraid this chapter could not have come to its present standard. I am also greatly obliged to Dr. Y.D. Sharma, Ex-Superintending Archaeologist, Dr. S.C. Ray, then Superintending Archaeologists, and Shri J.S. Nigam, Deputy Superintending Archaeologist, Archaeological Survey of Indian for their constant help which they have kindly extended to me in preparation of this thesis.

I am grateful to Mr. P.D. Jhamb, then Assistant Librarian, Central Archaeological

Library, and Mr. G.N. Uniyal, then Assistant Librarian, Northern Circle, Agra, Archaeological Survey of India and Mr. S.A. Tripathi, then Librarian, Agra College, Agra and Mr. D.K. Samuel Raj, then Librarian, St. John College, Agra, for library assistance which constitutes a major part of this study. I am also greatly thankful to Dr. Anthony d'Costa, St. Xavior College, Bombay and Mr. K.M. Yusuf and Mr. M.A. Majid, Iran Society Calcutta, for all assistance they have kindly extended to me during these years.

I feel extremely grateful to Shri A. Majid and Shri K.K. Nagar, caretaker, Taj Mahal, Archaeological Survey of India, who always extended their cooperation in my work and rendered their help whenever I needed it. Mr. Nagar, who had been working with me for several years at Taj Mahal, has provided great assistance in typing work and in other respect.

I cannot forget to pay my gratitude to Shri B.B. Sur, Draftsman, Archaeological Survey of India, who has rendered a valuable assistance in my work. All the diagrams, maps and sketches given in this thesis have been prepared by him.

I also pay my gratefulness to Shri T.R. Suyal, Conservation Assistant, Shri A.N. Dubey, Stenographer and Sarva Shri Balbir Singh, Mohan Singh, R.K. Kapoor, K.V. Subrahamaniam, M.U. Khan, Aqueel Ahmad, Sita Ram, R.P. Sharma, Chandan Singh, H.K. Kathpal, A.K. Goswami, L.D. Cs, Shri Banwari Lal of the Archaeological Survey of India, who rendered help in my work.

I feel extremely thankful to Shri Harun of Photo Centre studio and to Shri Ram Sanehi, Chopra Studio, Agra, who prepared the photographs and to Shri K.K. Gupta who has typed this thesis very carefully.

Lastly, I owe a deep sense of gratitude to my wife, Mrs. Quresh Khanum who gladly rendered whole-hearted assistance and I acknowledge that without her co-operation this work could not possibly have been done. She has scarified all her ambitions and desires and shared moments of anxieties and troubles of hard life with little grumble and murmur.

With profound respect I dedicate this back to the memory of my late mother in token of the inrepayable debt I owe to her.

Dr. G.A. Qamar

12th October, 2010
2/8, Siddhi Darwaza
Tajganj, Agra - Uttar Pradesh (India)

Abbreviations

SK	*Sanskrit*
IE	*Indo-European*
II	*Indo-Iranian*
Rv	*Rigveda*
AV	*Avesta*
Ibid	*In the same book or passage*
Lo-cit	*Locally cited*
Op-cit	*Opposite cited*
Cf	*Carried forward*
ie	*Compare*
eg	*Example gratia that is to say*
viz	*Namely, that is to say*
Ch.Up	*Chhandogya Upanishad*
Scyth	*Scythian*
Hitt	*Hittite*
Nir	*Nirubta*
SB	*Shatpatha Brahmana*
TS	*Taitariya Samhita*
JAOS	*Journal of Asian Oriental Society*
Yas	*Yasna*
AB	*Aitariya Brahmana*
TA	*Taitariya Aranyaka*
Ken-Up	*Kena Upanishad*
Mun-Up	*Manduka Upanishad*
KB	*Kena Brahmana*
TB	*Taitriya Brahmana*
V	*Vendidad*
Khila	*Explanatory treatises on Vedas*
Scot	*Scotland*
Teu	*Teutotonic*
Ugr	*Ugro-Fins*

JGOS	*Journal of German Oriental Society*
ABS	*Archaeological Society of Bombay*
JRAS	*Journal of Royal Asiatic Society*
ERE	*Encyclopedia of Religion and Ethics*

1

Introduction

The Birth of Civilization

(a) The Earliest Man—The origin of man has been ascribed to different regions. Asia was considered to be the most probable birth-place of the first man. Of course, certain fossil remains discovered from the Siwaliks indicate man's early evolution in India.[1] In the light of the new researches, however, it has now been established that Africa was the cradle of the first man.[2]

Geological evidence tends to show that man evolved out from primate (Fig. 1). The first appearance of man is marked with the dawn of the Pleistocene which is the last period of Cenozoic era in the geological reckoning of time. Several thousands of years elapsed before man grew to his distinctive physical and mental capacities. The primate evolution shows its several different stages from the tree shrews up to the Hominidae, which includes other intermediate stages of the primates such as lemurs, tarsiers, monkeys and apes. The fossil remains, scattered all over the world, show that the earliest known primates were wide-spread during the Eocene period. In the Oligocene period the various species of apes emerged out in Africa. In the succeeding Miocene period, the apes further diversified. By this time an important ape known as Proconsul appeared. It was more human than the modem man. Proconsul is believed to have been ancestral to both ape and man. The fossil remains indicate that before the close of Miocene period these diversified species of apes migrated from Africa to other parts of the world. Many species of these apes are traced to have lived on the Siwaliks in India at this time. Another species of apes, Oreopithecus, lived in southern Europe during early Pliocene, which is believed to be a fully evolved hominid. Our true hominid was the first group of Paleaoanthropus, the man of the Palaeolithic age, which marks the dawn of culture.

The Australopithecine or ape-man who inhabited several localities of Africa was very primitive and is assignable nearly to a million years[3] ago. He was small and stood to about the size of modern pigmy and seems normally to have walked upright.[4] A complete skull of Australopithecine assigned to the middle Pleistocene has been discovered in Oldoway George, Tanganiyaka.[5] Oldoway man is known as Zinjanthropus which is claimed to be half-way between the Australopithecine and the hominid.[6] By this time nowhere except in Africa the true hominids were seen. During the middle Pleistocene a new species of Palaeoanthropus which was somewhat more advanced than Australopithecine and known as Pithecanthropus, was found living in south east Asia. He was half-brained man and walked upright.[7] The fossil remains also show their presence in Africa, Java, China and in the north west India. The Choukoutien cave of China revealed that the Pithecanthropus was a true genus Homo, the first tool maker and the inventor of fire.[8] They must have lived in the middle Pleistocene or about 5,00,000 BC Later on in the upper Pleistocene the Neanderthals who had highly developed-brain appeared in Europe. They were the last group of Paleaoanthropus in Europe, Africa and western Asia during c. 5,00,000 to 50,000 BC. They were full brained-man. They were the authors of famous cave paintings of Spain and France.[9] They were the first to give ceremonial burials to their dead and also to entertain the religious ideas of the Palaeolithic man.[10]

It is commonly believed that all the Paleaoanthropus species disappeared suddenly near the close of the last Ice Age (c. 50,000 BC) and our own species the Homo sapiens emerged.[11] The scholars have divergent views about the ancestral line of the Homo sapiens.[12] As a matter of fact, in the present state of knowledge a satisfactory solution of the problem of emergence of Homo sapiens is not an easy task. It has, however, been generally admitted that Australopithecines, then Pithecanthropus and finally Homo sapiens represent three main stages of man's evolution in the Lower, Middle and Upper Pleistocene periods respectively.

(b) Formation and Diversification of Races—During the period from the Pleistocene to the Late Pleistocene (c. 40,000 to 8,000 BC) the whole old world and probably America were peopled by Homo sapiens. During this period Homo sapiens began to be diversified into different races. Many factors were responsible for ethnological variations: "Sun and frost, forest and plains, humidity and dryness, height and latitude, diet and water content, a variable inheritance from the remoter past and the chance movement of the peoples, all united during these millennia to give our single species the differences of height and proportion of facial structures and skin colours of shade and texture of hair, which make the rich variety of mankind."[13]

During Late Pleistocene period, the formation and diversification of races appeared clearly, first of all, in Africa. By this time the African population showed two distinct divisions. One is Australoid and the other Bushmanoid. Bushmen who were once widespread in Africa during pre-historic times, were pushed southwards towards the tip of the continent. The Australoid element is found in aborigines of Australia and in the population in the Hadramaut, throughout the East Indies, the Pacific Islands and, in south and south-east India. Now this region of India is inhabited by the Dravidian stock, who most likely had descended from the pre-Caucasoid aborigines of India with a racial admixture of Australoids.[14]

The Negroid race appeared during the post Pleistocene period. The centre of differentiation of this race is probably Sudan. The Negroid people are found on both sides of the Equator in Africa. The Negroid element is suspected in the population that appeared in Europe after the extinction of Neanderthals. The forest pygmies of Australia, Tasmania, Philippines; 'the 'Malay peninsula, the Andaman Islands and India are genetically related to Negroid of Africa.[15]

The Mongolian race emerged in the eastern Asia during the Late Pleistocene. This race is genetically related to the inhabitants of Choukoutien cave of China.[16] The Polynesian-Micronesian race that inhabits Islands of Pacific, is believed to have grown from a mixture of Mongolian people with Australoid population of East Indies and Philippines. The Caucasoids, the major racial group, are found in Europe, north and north east Africa, western Asia, India and Ceylon. The Semites, the African Watusi, the Indian Brahmans and the European Danes belong to this race. The Mediterranean race originated in the region, east of the Mediterranean during the Upper Palaeolithic period.[17] Of course, this race dispossessed the Neanderthals in Europe. In the Mesolithic period in the south-east Asia the Mediterranean race diversified into Semitic and Hamitic stocks, the Semitic stock inhabits, now the south-west Asia and north Africa and the Hamitic, people cover the region south of the Semitic population. Another stock, limited; to the cool and temperate zone in the north and west Europe is Nordic. The Alpine race that originated over the great mountain backbone of the old world entered Europe after last glaciations. The last group is Eskimo.

(c) Evolution of Culture—There is little doubt that the early man or hominid was, for several thousands of years, one among. other species, who gathered their food from the nature. When he began hunting is not exactly known. Perhaps by natural instinct, the early man learnt the use of stone or stick to protect himself from wild animals. Gradually he learnt to shape ston, bone and wood as tools, which marks the beginning of culture. This is the dawn of culture which took place in the Lower Pleistocene period.

The cultural history of man of the Pleistocene period has been reconstructed on the evidence of his implements and fossil, remains which have been found scattered all over the world. The stone tools had been, made by the Paleaoanthropus (Australopithecines, Pithecanthropus and Neanderthals) show different techniques and stages of development during, the Palaeolithic period.

The stone tools of Palaeolithic period scattered in many parts of the world show two techniques of tool making. One is known as core-tool industry in which a block is chipped to the desired form. The other is the flake-tool technique in which a large flake is detached from a block of stone and the flake is then worked out into the finished tool. The core-tool tradition originated in. Africa and flake-tool mainly in eastern Asia. These techniques of tool-making divide the, Old World into two principal cultural divisions. The chopper-chopping tools of flake industry made of rough flakes have been found in Java, Burma, China, Europe and in north central India. Abbevillion and Acheulian hand axe evolved from the core Industry in Africa, Europe, peninsular India and in the region from eastern Mediterranem to the Black Sea. Thus we find the two cultural traditions mingling and overlapping at some places and mutually influencing each other in Europe and India.

Africa was not only the home of the early man and the Homo sapiens, but also of the first tool maker as is proved by the discovery of the implements. They are made of quartz and water-worn pebbles of lava. These pebble-tools have been classified into two different cultures-viz., the Kafuan and the Oldowan. Kafuan tools are no longer regarded as man-made tools. The Oldowan pebble tools of Sterkfontein are sure proof of origin of the oldest stone tools in Africa.[18] In this culture pebbles were flaked on both the faces. The pebble tools of the Oldowan culture were fully rounded. The characteristic tools of its early phase are scrapers, chopping and cutting implements. The tools of the latest Oldowan phase were chipped from both sides to form oval bifacial tools. They have been found in the Sterkfontein cave, the Vaal Valley, the Oldoway Gorge and at Kanam in Kenya in the deposits dating back to a later phase of the Lower Pleistocene period.[19] It is generally held that the bifacial pebble tools of the Oldowan culture are ancestral to the true Abbevillion hand axe culture. It has been established that the core-tool culture of hand-axe had evolved into the full Abbevillion culture in central Africa. The Abbevillion tradition shows increasing elaboration and clarity of purpose. Its tools are peer-shaped but a tongued-shaped tool having point at one end is most common. The Acheulian is the immediate successor of the Abbevillion tradition.

At the dawn of Pleistocene, the tool making communities are nowhere traceable outside Africa. No doubt second Interglacial age witnessed the tool-making communities at three centres outside Africa. The first was the Flake Industry in India. The second culture, Anyathian developed in Burma; and, lastly. the Choukoutien culture was established in China. These industries are related to the chopper-chopping tools complex. The most elementary workmanship of these stone tools indicates that Palaeolithic man entered Asia already as a tool maker. It is most probable that the first hominids entered Asia from Africa with the practice of battering stones to get cutting edge on rough points. In Africa this basic tradition steadily developed into that of the bifacial pebble tools and ultimately hand-axe, while the people in Asia remained backward, and failed to develop much beyond this basic tradition.[20]

(d) Flake Industry in North India—During the second Interglacial the Soan culture developed in the north-west India.[21] The Early Soan culture presents

two series of tools; one comprising of massive pebble tools made from rounded pebbles which are unifacial and bifacial choppers and are comparable to the Oldowan Palaeolithic deposits in the south-east Africa.[22] The flake tools of the subsequent phase of Early Soan culture are large, thick, flat formed-flakes and cortexed-sided. It reflects Cloctonian industry corresponding with "Cloctonian" family of flake tools of the Old World.[23] Later on the Late Soan culture developed a tortoise core technique popularly termed "Levalloision" culture identical with that of Africa, Europe and western Asia.[24] The flake tools of the Late Soan culture presents varying shapes. The chief characteristic of these tools is fairly pronounced 'bulb of percussion.' The tools of the Late Soan culture unearthed in the lower levels at Sanghao cave in North-West Frontier province and in the Punjab have close affinities with the Levallois-Musterians of this technique in Iran.[25]

The general survey of Soan culture shows the folk movement from Africa to India through Arabia before the second Interglacial period. Soundarajan confirms the view, ". . . the Punjab pebble industries by themselves, do not show any independent physical evolution . . ."[26] He further adds, "Thus in the Palaeolithic, the generic affinities of India are, literally speaking, more with Africa and to much less extent with Europe, but none too significantly with East Asia.[27] This view gets an additional support from the discovery of tools identical with the Soan culture, in the south Arabian area around the Persian Gulf.[28] It indicates the direction of folk movement and its determining influence on the pebble industry. It confirms that the Soan culture of the Punjab was an off-shoot of the flake industry of Africa.

(e) Core Industry in South India—The core tools of hand-axe are found commonly in the area of Soan culture itself, in the central and western India and abundantly in south east India, chiefly in Madras, hence the nomenclature of this family is 'Madras Industry.' Undoubtedly the Madras industry is related to the Abbevillion-Acheullian hand-axe culture of south Africa. The striking similarity subsists between Madras industry and hand-axe of Africa. Both in India and Africa whereas cleavers are totally absent in the Abbevillion stage; the cleavers of a distinct type are common in Acheullian stage.[29] The ovates and the 'S' twist in the hand axe are noticeable both in South India and Africa in the Mid-Acheul stage.[30] The upper culture in Stellenbosch in Africa shows the Vall technique and the Victoria west type of hand-axe which developed in India also at Madras, Bombay and in the central India.[31] Many examples from Madras are comparable to the Victoria West type.[32] Lowe recognizes the identity of the two cultures, "An entire assemblage of atrifacts of the old stone from Madras is literally indistinguishable from one Stellenbosch."[33] We know that in Africa transition from Abbevillion to Acheullian is an archaeologically proven fact. India presents no credentials of Abbevillion stage of Acheullian hand-axe culture and moreover no evolution of Abbevillion-Acheullian culture is traceable. It stands to reason

to conclude that during second Interpluvial when in Africa Acheullian evolved from primitive Abbevillion stage producing very fine and well proportioned tools; the people with this tradition entered India from the west. The folk movement with the tradition of this culture from Africa to India is also established by Tayacian finds in Palestine.[34] These finds are identical with the flake implements of Acheullian phase at Khandivle in India.[35] This view is supported by the finds of the Acheullian hand-axe uncarthed in Arabia and Iraq.[36] Hawkes asserts, "The Acheullian must be presumed to have reached India by a narrow corridor north of Persian Gulf and south of Iranian Highlands."[37]

(f) *The Upper Palaeolithic Culture*—The cultural story traced hitherto falls into the span of Lower Palaeolithic (from c. 400,000 to 10,000 BC). The Upper Palaeolithic period dawned with a revolutionary stage pregnant with crucially momentous events in the cultural progress that marks the first crystallization of the blade culture which is prelude to the birth of civilization. The provenance of the culture is no longer speculative. Archaeology accredits Western Asia to be the region where the culture originated. The industries of blade culture take their origin from three centres during the last Ice Age. Of these industries, Early Aurignacian that diffused mainly early European blade culture originated at Aldun in Lebanon.[38] The second Aurignacian which is believed to have evolved in the Iranian plateau.[39] This culture extended to Iraq and Afghanistan and reached as far as western Europe.[40] Gravettian is the third that evolved in Iraq.[41] It spread to Spain, France, Italy, the south Russian plains and the central Europe.[42]

India presents several sites of the Upper Palaeolithic cultures. The Indian tradition is closely associated with the Upper Palaeolithic cultures of the West Asia. The parrot-beak type and angle burins discovered at Khandivli near Bombay recall analogies in West.[43] A similar industry is discovered at Kurnool.[44] The upper Palaeolithic culture in North and South India in its final phase, is exactly identical with the Asiatic Aurignacian.[45] The blade and burin tools unearthed at Kurnool and Khandivli show close similarities with those of Tayacian in Palestine.[46]

(g) *Mesolithic Culture*—During the post glacial time the blade and burin culture developed in west Asia, Africa and Europe into a culture known as the Mesolithic. This culture shows a marked tendency to reduce blade tools to small dimensions giving usually geometric forms. Natufian site in Assyria provides the best example of the Mesolithic culture. In fact this culture originated in West Asia. Sickle and other stone implements have been largely discovered in the Natufian site. The people of this culture used wild cereals and knew how to grind them with stone grinders. Crude storage stones have also been found [47] which indicates a step forward towards Neolithic advancement. Persia also presents two famous true Mesolithic sites at Caves Hotu and Belt.

Except the Punjab plains, Bengal, Assam, Nepal and Kerela,[48] the Microlithic implements have been found all over India. These sites are later rather than contemporaneous with the Assyrian examples. On the basis of new Microlithic finds at Kurnool, however, Sankalia claims higher antiquity for the Indian blade and burin culture.[49] The scholars are of the view that this culture owed its spread in India to the West Asia.[50] Piggot remarks, "The fact that the microlithic industries of India seem to represent the arrival of new people, probably from the West, rather than the fact that they are an evolution out of more or less non-existent Upper Palaeolithic blade industry, relates them more to those cultures which follow them than to those supersede."[51] Drummond points out that in its final phase, the Indian Mesolithic culture is similar to the Aurignacian of south west Asia; both Burkitt and Todd confirmed it on the basis of Mesolithic finds at Kurnool and Bombay.[52] Krishna Swami asserts that the Mesolithic industry of India is intimately related to Wilton culture of south Africa.[53]

References

1. W. Theobald, "The Siwalik Group of the Sub–Himalayan Region," *Royal Geological Survey of India*, XIV, pt. 1, pp. 122, 1881.
2. J. Hawkes, *History of Mankind*, Vol. I, p. 60, fn. 1. (London, 1963).
3. C. Gabel, *Man Before History*, p. 11, (edited by Graham Clark).
4. Graham Clark, *The Dawn of Civilization*, "The hunters and gatherers of the stone Age," p. 35, edited by Piggott (London, Edinburg, Harvard, 1961).
5. V.P. Yakimo, "Discovery of Bone Remains of New Representative of Australopithecus in East Africa" *Voprasi anthropologi*, 1960, No. 4, pp. 151–54.
6. J. Hawkes, *History of Mankind*, Vol. I, pt. I, p. 43, (London, 1963).
7. Graham Clark, op.cit., pp. 21, 36; W.E.Le Gros Clark, *Antiquity*, XIX, 1945, pp. 1–5.
8. Graham Clark, op.cit., pp. 21, 36.
9. W.E. Le Gros Clark, *Antiquity*, XX, 1946, pp. 8–12.
10. Graham Clark, op.cit., p. 37.
11. C.S. Coon, *The Prehistory of Man*, pp. 26–27, (London, 1954).
12. Graham Clark, op.cit., p. 36.
13. J. Hawkes, op.cit., p. 54.
14. M. Nesturkh, *The Races of Mankind*, p. 12 (Moscow, 1966).
15. J. Hawkes, op.cit., p. 53.
16. M. Nesturkh, op.cit., p. 75–88.
17. M. Nesturkh, op.cit., p. 73.
18. A.J.H. Goodwin, *Method in Prehistory*, (Cape town, 1953), p. 58, 2nd ed., The South African Archaeological Society Handbook Series No. 1.
19. J. Hawkes, op. cit, p. 66.
20. J. Hawkes, op.cit., p. 68.
21. H.De Terra, Preliminary Report on the Yale North Indian Expedition, *Science*, LXXVII, pp. 497–500 (Lancaster, 1965).
22. H.L. Movious, *Early Man and Pleistocene, Stratigraphy in Southern and Eastern Asia* (Papers of Peabody Museum Harvard, 1944).
23. V.D. Krishna Swami, loc cit., p. 24.
24. J. Hawkes, op.cit., p. 70–71.

25. B. Allchin, *The Birth of Indian Civilization*, p. 74 (Suffolk, 1968).
26. K.V. Soundarajan, *Ancient India*, No. 17, (Delhi, 1961), p. 75.
27. Ibid., p. 79.
28. G.C. Thompson, "*Some Palaeolithic from Arabia*" Proceeding Prehistoric Society, N.S. 19 No. 9 (1953), p. 215.
29. V.D. Krishna Swami, "Stone Age in India," *Ancient India*, No. 3, (Delhi, 1947), p. 41.
30. Ibid.
31. M.C. Burkitt and L.A. Canniade, "Fresh Light on the Stone Ages in S.E. India" *Antiquity*, IV, pp. 327–29, 1930.
32. KRU. Todd, "Prehistoric Industries of Bombay" *Journal Anthropological Institute Of Great Britain and Ireland*, LXIX, pp. 297, 272.
33. Cf. A. Aiyappan, The Manely Collection of Stone Age Tools, Memoir, *ASI*, No. 68, p. 14, fn.l (Delhi, 1942).
34. D.A.E. Garrod, "The Stone Age of Palestine," *Antiquity*, Vol. VIII, 1934, p. 133.
35. D.A.E. Garrod, The Upper Palaeolithic in the Light of Recent Discovery, *Proceeding Prehistoric Society*, No. IV, pp. 1-26, (Cambridge, 1936).
36. S. Piggot, op.cit., p. 33; D.H. Gordon, *Prehistoric Background of Indian Culture*, pp. 6-7 (Bombay, 1958).
37. J. Hawkes, op.cit., p. 82.
38. D.A.E. Garrod, *Proceeding of Prehistoric Society*, Cambridge, No.4, 1938, "Upper Palaeolithic in the light of Recent Discovery," pp. 1–26.
39. V.G. Childe, *New Light on the Most Ancient East*, (London, 1952), p. 19; S. Piggot, op.cit., p. 34 (1950).
40. Grahame Clark, op.cit., p. 37.
41. V.G. Childe, *New Light on the Most Ancient East*, (London, 1952), p.19.
42. Grahame Clark, op. cit, p. 37.
43. KRU. Todd, op. cit., pp. 257–72.
44. V.D. Krishna Swami, op. cit., p. 41.
45. De Terra, H. Teilhard, D. Chardin, P. and Paterson, T.T., Joint Geological and Prehistoric Studies of Later Cenozoic in India, *Science*, LXXXII, pp. 233–36, (Lancaster, 1936).
46. D.A.E. Garrod, "The Upper Palaeolithic in the light of Recent Discovery," *Proceeding of Prehistoric Society*, No. IV, pp. 1–26, (Cambridge, 1936).
47. D.A.E. Garrod and D.M. Bate, *The Stone Age of Mount Cramel*, Vol. I (London, 1937), pp. 9–16, 30–40, 119.
48. H.D. Sankalia, *Prehistory and Protohistory in India and Pakistan*, p. 129 (Bombay, 1968).
49. H.D. Sankalia, U.N.I., Times of India, 22.8.72.
50. S. Piggot, op. cit, p. 36 (1950).
51. Ibid.
52. V.D. Krishna Swami, op. cit., p. 41.
53. Ibid.

2

India and Iran since the New Stone Age

The Dawn of Civilization

Some eight or nine thousand years ago a revolution ushered a new economy on the scene which is known as Neolithic or New Stone Age culture. Neolithic economy is, as a matter of fact, a significant event in the history of mankind, inasmuch as it opened a new vista to the civilization. The marked difference between Neolithic and the Old Stone culture is the farming and domestication of animals in the former as opposed to food-gathering and hunting during the latter. The secondary traits of this culture are polished stone tools, manufacture of pottery and village settlements.

(a) Neolithic Culture

By definition the first mark of the full Neolithic culture is the practice of settled farming. Certain scholars hold that farming started in North Africa or in Abyssinia. But it has now been archaeologically proved that the earliest centres of both farming and domestication of animals started in south-west Asia.[1] Botanical and Zoological researches have also confirmed the view that Neolithic culture originated in West Asia. It was there that wheat and barley were first experimented for cultivation,[2] and where they originally grew wild.[3] It was also the home of animals suitable for domestication.[4] The Archaeological evidence has also now established with more or less certainty that the region extending from Iranian plateau and the Anatolian Highlands to central Arabia[5] was the land of origin of the Neolithic culture.

It has already been observed that the Natufian though a Mesolithic culture transformed into the Neolithic economy. In fact Jericho in Palestine and Jarmo Qalat in Iraq reveal the signs of culture developing into a full Neolithic farming during the 8,000 BC and 6,500 BC respectively.[6] Persia also presents two important settlements of farming origins, i.e. the Hotu and Belt Caves. At the Belt Cave the people, in the beginning of the sixth millennium, BC, first of all, domesticated animals.[7] It led the scholars to conclude that farming is likely to have originated in the region extending from Jericho to Jarmo and Belt Cave.

Another important trait, of the Neolithic culture is pottery, which first of all appeared in this area at Cave Belt about 5500 BC.[8] the recent excavations at Catal Hayuk on the Anatolian Highlands have yielded pottery which is assignable to c. 7000 BC.[9] and pushed its antiquity to two centuries back. It stands to reason that pottery originated in the region extending from the Anatolian Highlands to Persia. Later on the Hassuna culture evolved in Mesopotamia advanced a little from that of Jarmo inasmuch as its people made painted and incised wares of a finer quality.[10] This culture did make its impact on the neighbouring area. The other most important culture which is noted for its remarkable pottery is known as Samarra culture and is believed to have flourished somewhere to the south of Hassuna. This was more widespread than the Hassunian. The characteristic feature of the Samarran painted pottery is its basketry pattern and stylized animal figures[11] another culture known as the Halafian is also distinguished by its remarkable pottery. This came into being at Tel-Halaf lying at the head-waters of Khabur about 5000 BC. Its inhabitants were pre-eminently potters, who used kiln for baking pottery.[12]

In Persia Tanga Pabda and Bakun are very early Neolithic settlements. Another Persian site, Sialk is a truly Neolithic site[13] this culture occupies a very important place in the west Asian Neolithic complex. Its first phase is assigned to 5,000 BC.[14] Next comes the Ubaid culture which originated on the head of the Persian Gulf at about 4,000 BC. This culture revolutionized the whole course of human civilization. Its pottery was certainly derived from the highlands of Persia.[15] In due course the Ubaidian culture became so strong and dominating that it overtook and supplanted the Halafian from the region extending from Persia to the Mediterranian. Its spread completed the full achievement of the Neolithic culture. At about 3500 BC the Uruk culture developed in Sumer. It shows a highly advanced stage of its precursor. It is noted for the beautiful temple complex architecture, the picture writing, the delicately made vessels, the striking, 'Scarlet Ware,' and sensitive and elaborate geometrical designs on the painted pottery.[16]

From its cradle land the Neolithic culture spread rapidly into far-flung regions. No doubt the Neolithic set-up of society in Europe, North Africa, Turkestan and in India was either directly influenced by folk movements or by diffusionary impulses from south-west Asia. That the farmer communities penetrated from south-west Asia east-ward towards India is borne out by the fact that the painted pottery unearthed at most of the Neolithic sites has a very close link between the Indian farmers and those of Iraq and Iran.[17]

(b) *Neolithic India*

The fact that the farmer communities came to Baluchistan during Neolithic period appears most probable on the evidence of painted pottery distribution in this region.[18] The excavations conducted by Casal at Mundigak and Nad-i-Ali in Afghanistan and Kili-Gul-Mohamad in India have yielded the material that proved the folk movement from Persia via Afghanistan to India.[19] The Indian settlements show strikingly close relationship with Sialk, Giyan and Hissar in Iran.[20]

Of course, the Indian Neolithic culture poses a problematic situation. Piggot observes, "The origin of these Neolithic cultures is unknown though they are more likely to be the result of folk movements from the west than of independent invention."[21] It is, however, certain that the Indian Neolithic culture positively assimilated different traits arriving in different orders.

The Neolithic polished and ground stone tools have been found all over India. Bellary is considered to be real focus of the Neolithic culture in south India.[22] A full blooded Neolithic culture is also recognised at Brahmgiri in central India[23] The Neolithic settlement at Burzahom in Kashmir is of high antiquity.[24] Paterson divides Indian Neolithic culture into several stages, the earliest being the Proto-Neolithic which was established at Sukkar and Rohri in Sind.[25] Three principal regions of the Neolithic culture, viz., Northern, Eastern and Southern have been recognised.

(i) Northern Culture—A culture of remarkable features has been discovered at Burzahom in Kashmir. The culture renders foreign traditions of the pit-dwellings, bone implements, stone rings and the rectangular perforated stone knife. The pottery is coarse grey or black burnished, in many cases with mat marked base.[26]

The culture discovered at Burzahom exhibits the typological similarity of certain tools notably harvester with those of contemporaneous China and Japan.[27] The use of bone implements, the rectangular perforated stone knife, pit-dwelling and the burial of animals especially the placing of domestic dogs with their masters in their graves, are also common in both cultures.[28] This leads us to look towards north China for diffusionary impulses.[29] But the Burzahom pottery is entirely different from those of the Chinese Neolithic caves. As a matter of fact Burzahom presents a sort of hunting-based culture which corresponds with that of the Neolithic hunting people of central Asia.[30] Recent discovery of bone tools in Iran by Braidwood impressed Sankalia to conceive Iran the most likely source to Burzahom culture.[31]

(ii) Eastern Culture—The Eastern Neolithic culture flourished in the north-east region of India and has been sub-divided into the Bengal-Bihar-Orissa Culture and the Assam Culture Complexes. This culture has yielded the stone implements of wide variety in shapes.[32] Its pottery is coarse or fine black-and-red but considerably varied in shape.[33]

The origin of this Neolithic culture is speculative. Dani has advocated that it owed its origin to the south east Asia.[34] His theory is based on common existence of rounded butt-axe, shouldered-celt, bar-celt and chisel with a triangular section in both cultures.[35] F.R. Allchin remarks that rounded butt-axes and identical metallic technique of certain tools recall to anticipate cultural inspiration from China.[36] Splayed axe, pointed butt-axe, facetted-tool or 'square-cut' axe impressed Anderson to look towards China for diffusionary impulses.[37] Worman also conceives that the culture is indebted to China.[38] It is pertinent to note that pottery of the east India finds no similarity in China or the south-east Asia. The lipped-bowls, the perforated-pots and the black-and-red wares discovered at Sonpur in Gaya, Rajar Dhipi in Burdwan recall similar forms discovered at Piklihal, Navdatoli and west India.[39] Moreover, identical form of wedge-shaped axe has been found at Nevasa and Maskiy,[40] shouldered celt in central India,[41] splayed axe at Jorwe, Newasa[42] and Navdatoli,[43] rounded-butt axe and axe with broad cutting edge at several sites of south, north and west India,[44] and the comparable specimen to the shouldered tools and shoe-last-celt at Navdatoli and Sangankallu[45] in Deccan respectively. The most interesting feature is that some of these forms are true copy of the tools of copper hoards discovered in the Gangetic valley and Nagaur.[46] Hiene Geldern has proved that these copper hoards owed their origin to Iran.[47] Such similarities show that the East Neolithic culture is also related to the cultures of Deccan. The distribution of the black-and-red pottery in India poses a difficult problem, [48] but it is certain that it originated in Iran.[49] It appears that the perforated vessels and the black-and-red wares show slow diffusion from Iran, Baluchistan, Afghanistan and west India.[50] It has nearly been established that the Neolithic cultures of Afghanistan, Baluchistan and Deccan had strong Iranian influence. Hence Iran is also a source directly or indirectly to the Neolithic culture of the east India. It appears that the Neolithic culture of the east India was not homogeneous but received inspirations from different directions.

(iii) Southern Culture—Excluding Kashmir and the eastern India we have a very little knowledge of a pure or full Neolithic culture in the sub-continent.[51] Worman goes to this extent that India had no such culture as can definitely be called Neoithic.[52] As a matter of fact no sharp distinction is envisaged between the Neolithic and the Chalcolithic cultures because these very often overlapped and intermingled and it has become difficult to draw a dividing line. In the majority of cases, the sites in the southern, western and central India present the Neolithic-Chalcolithic phase of the culture that will be discussed in the succeeding pages.

In the south the Neolithic tools have been obtained from several important sites.[53] the pottery is either hand-made or wheel-turned with black-and-red wares. It shows a wide variety of shapes such as perforuted vessels and spouted and channel-spout-pots.

The origin of the southern Neolithic culture baffles archaeologists. Krishna Swami argues for indigeneous origin.[54] Sankalia remarks that entire south-east of the Indian peninsula seems to have been the home of Neolithic culture.[55] The scholars single out Langhnaj as holding out greater possibilities for change from Mesolithic to Neolithic for indigenous origin. But it is more indicative than conclusive. Braidwood observes that the Neolithic economy is now almost universally believed to have developed in Western Asia.[56] The pointed-butt axes lead Haimendorf to postulate eastern affinities.[57] The typology of tools convinces Worman the derivation of the culture from the south east Asia.[58] Wheeler asserts that the axes came to India from Iran via China.[59] F.R. Allchin points out that in India there is no evidence of any evolution of stone-working-techniques, flaking, pecking and grinding; and believes in the derivation from the Neolithic stone working techniques of Iran.[60] The use of tabular basalt, grey ware, perforated vessels and spouted and channel-spout pots and the close similarity in potting technique found at Shah Tepe and other sites of Iran and at Piklihal in India impressed Allchin to argue for Iranian origin.[61] (Fig. 12) The skeleton remains discovered at several sites in south India infer its relationship to the Neolithic population of Iran.[62] Its pottery form, stone-working techniques and skeleton remains show the folk-movement from Iran to India via southern Baluchistan through Sistan.

(c) *Chalcolithic Culture*

It is worthwhile to recall that Neolithic economy culminated in a stage of progress which Wolley has defined in inimitable words—"man in time adopted a different solution to the problem of existence, that of adapting his environment to himself; by the control of fire, by the use of shelters and clothing, by the use of tools fabricated by himself, he could to some extent disregard the change of climate, and instead of having to live where food abounded he made it abound where he lived. That revolution had been effected during the Neolithic period."[63] Indeed, the inventions of metallurgy and potter's-wheel, which ushered a new era known as the Chalcolithic culture, were epoch-making events and marked the important steps towards the crystallization of urban civilization.

The Chalcolithic revolution, too, set out in western Asia.[64] We have sufficient material to trace its course since its beginning. The invention of metallurgy is reasonably claimed for highland zone of Anatolia and Iran,[65] the only region in western Asia for metals.[66] It is well evidenced by the finds of copper pins as early as level XXIII at Mersin[67] and the earliest hammered copper awls and pins in the late phase of Sialk I and Sialk II.[68] It is also in Mesopotamia that the Halafians[69] knew metal which was intelligently worked[70] by casting, the example of which are found in Al-Ubaid. In the Uruk period smiths knew to alloy[71] copper with lead and could cast in cire perdue technique.[72] It was the stage when the art of intelligent[73] metallurgy had been grasped and professional potters[74] and smiths were established. On the evidence of the new finds in the excavation at Catal Hayuk and Sialk II the technique and style of painted pottery too may be claimed to have been devised on the highlands of Anatolia and Iran.[75]

At the end of Early Chalcolithic period, the Western Asia is marked to have secured marvellous discoveries of metallurgy, potter's wheel, wheeled-vehicle, harnessing of animals for motive power, bricks and seals. All the conditions for crystallization of civilization were available by c. 5,000 BC and ultimately in their cumulative effect ushered in great civilization of Ur and Elam.

(d) Iranian Sites of the Chalcolithic Age

The Chalcolithic culture evolved in Iran at the ancient site of Sialk. In the" last phase of Sialk I the people stepped into the Chalcolithic age.[76] At about 4,000 BC the pise houses were replaced by mud-brick constructions.[77] Sialk II presents unique craftmanship of painting which is not traceable in any contemporary site. It suggests that Iran was the origional home of the painted pottery.[78] The Silak III registered a great advance in architectural technique.[79] The painted pottery exhibits a realistic approach to designs and natural figures are depicted with life and movement.[80] That the art of intelligent metallurgy had been mastered in this phase, is amply borne out from the traverse axes, adzes and mid-rib dagger cast in closed mould.[81] The use of button seal also became common.[82] The terracotta figures, precious stone jewellery and copper mirror appeared [83] in this phase point out the high order of the culture.

This advanced stage of the culture discovered at Sialk was remarkably ripe to shape the urban civilization. But the Iranian plateau with its difficult terrain and extremely unfavourable environments, could not have been an ideal site for this development.[84] This, however, did not fail to inspire the neighbouring plains where better resources and favourable conditions were available.[85] Hence the urban civilizations of Susa and Elam in south-west and south Iran, and of Ur and AI-Ubaid in Iraq emerged.[86] Sialk III also had its impact on the urban civilization of Hissar and Giyan in northern Iran.[87] Another prehistoric site of the same affinity in southern Iran is Tal-i-Bakun.[88] Similar culture have also been traced in eastern Iran.

(e) Indian Sites of the Chalcolithic Age

The achievements discussed in the preceeding pages diffused to India before 3,000 BC and probably due to this inspiration, the urban civilization of Indus Valley arose. So far Indian Chalcolithic culture is concerned, it falls, into four groups i.e., (i) Peasant settlements of Baluchistan, Makran and Sind, (ii) Harappan culture, (iii) Post Harappan settlements, and (iv) Neolithic-Chalcolithic culture of south India.

(i) Peasant Settlements of Baluchistan, Makran and Sind—The Neolithic settlements of Baluchistan have already been discussed. In the Cholcalithic age the village cultures were flourishing at different centres. Five such cultures have been distinctly recognised in this age. They are Zhob, Quetta, Amri, Nal and Kulli cultures. The Iranian influence made it felt in all these settlements before 3,000 BC. Piggot observes, "It must be noted that all evidence is in consistence with the ultimate derivation of the prehistoric culture of north-west India from Iran."[89] McCown ingeniously discovered in Iran the contrasted distribution of Red Wares and Buff Wares, the former in the north and the latter in the south.[90] Piggot connected these cultures with those of India and observed that this typical distribution traditionally persisted in Baluchistan where he discovered red ware in the north and the buff in the south.[91] It leads to infer that there were two folk movements: one north-eastern from Hissar and the other south-eastern from Sialk, Giyan and Musyan to Baluchistan.[92] The Zhob culture in the north Baluchistan is related to the Red Ware culture and Kulli, Arnri, Nal and Quetta cultures in the south exhibit the traits of the Buff Wares culture of Iran.[93] There is no reason to disbelieve Gordon who claimed, ". . . that with the exception of the bull and pipal motifs, the whole of repertoire of the painted pottery of the Indo-Iranian border originated in Iran."[94] He, however, challenged the orthodox view of hard and fast separation of red and buff wares in Baluchistan and conceived a certain degree of overlapping, if not interconnection.[95] On the evidence of certain painted pottery motifs he goes on to assert that early Iranian cultures of Sialk and Giyan reached Quetta, Loralai and Amri in Baluchistan and entered India from the Kerman-Sistan-Kandahar route; southern approach to south Baluchistan and further into India was made from the Iranion centres of Kerman and Shiraz through Halil Rud-Bampur-Makran route.[96] (Fig. 3) Whatever may be the nature and scope of Red and Buff Ware distribution which is a controversial matter, it is certain that the peasant settlements of Baluchistan were influenced by the Iranian culture. This is the crux of the present study. This influence is noticed abundantly and extensively in all the above referred five cultures of this age in Baluchistan. The respective points of simiarity of these cultural centres with their counterparts in Iran are as follows :

(A) Zhob Culture—The culture developed in the north Baluchistan extended from the valley of Zhob to the Pishin-Lora region. (Fig, 24-I; Fig. I6-II-III; Fig. 20- IX-XI-XII-XIII; Fig. 26-I).

(1) The vertical elongation of legs and horns in the frieze of stylized animals on the pottery of Loralai II and III corresponds exactly with the pot decoration in northern Iran.[97]

(2) A six-spoke wheel pattern reveals close relations between Bakun A IV and Duki and Rana Ghundai in the Zhob culture.[98]

(3) Some fragments of pottery with hatched zone found at Periano Ghundai recall Sistan sherds.[99]

(4) The identical tradition of post-cremation burial in pots as discovered at Sialk in Persia persists at Rana Ghundai site of this culture.[100]

(5) Scale pattern of painted pottery also establishes a close relationship between Sialk III and Bakun B in Persia and Surjangal in India.[101]

(6) The painted pottery of Rana Ghundai II is identical in form, technique and decoration with that of Hissar.[102] The wheel-made vases are decorated with stylized animal in the Hissar manner with the only difference, that the bull is preferred to panther or ibex at the Indian site.[103]

(7) The registers of animal motif of Rana Ghundai and Moghul Kila seem to have been derived from Sialk, Giyan, Hissar and Musyan in lran.[104] it is interesting to note that the lines under the belly in the case of oxen of Lorali appear to be similar to those under the ibex of Hissar showing the outline of exaggerated Genital.

(8) The pottery of Loralai is generally akin to that of Sistan in Iran.[105] Likewise the footed bowls of Hissar IC and Surjangal show a close affinity both in shape and decoration.[106] The beakers also have a strong family resemblance in both cultures.[107]

(B) Quetta Culture—This culture developed in the Quetta Valley. (Fig. 23-II -III-VII; Fig. I2-III; Fig. 3-II; Fig-15-I).

(l) Quetta wares exhibit striking similarity with those of Bakun A, Susa I, Giyan V and Sialk III.[108]

(2) Chevrony zigzag pattern of Tal-i-Iblis and Chah Husaini painted pottery persists in similar form on the Quetta ware.[109]

(3) Stepped triangle with a zigzag dividing line on a Quetta beaker show interesting similarity with a motif of Bakun A, Giyan V C and Susa I, which also shows a band of sigmas having zigzag dividing lines.[110]

(4) The fragment of a goblet found at Quetta shows that the reconstruction is the exact replica of the goblets of Sialk I1I-7 and Giyan VD-IV.[111]

(C) Amri Culture—The geographical distribution of the Amri Culture includes south Baluchistan and certain sites in Sind. (Fig. 24-I; Fig. 16-II-III; Fig. 19-XXXVI; Fig. 27-I-II-III; Fig. 9).

(1) Though the Amri wares are generally akin to the Jamdet Nasr ware of the Sumer culture and this affinity is unmistakably perceptible, the former appears more to be Iranian in origin on the basis of similar findings in Fars.[112]

(2) The clay figurine of bull found at Kot Diji in the Amri culture exactly corresponds with the bull painted on the Scarlet Wares of Susa.[113]

(3) The scale pattern on the painted pottery of Chaure suggests a definite link between Amri culture and Sialk III and Bakun B.[114]

(4) Sigmas which are used on the Rudbar[115] and Bampur[116] pottery have also commonly been used on the Sistan vessels. At Amri this motif was very popular. It is also frequently found as space filler in the designs of Kulli.[117] pottery.

(5) The beakers found at Sialk III 5-7, Giyan C, Ram Rud and Sistan appear in Amri and Loralai cultures in similar form.[118]

(D) Nal Culture—The culture developed in the Nal valley and extended up to Nundara is designated as Nal Culture. (Fig. 28-XIII; Fig. 19-XXXVII-XXXVIII; Fig.7).

(1) Though the early Dynastic Sumerian influence is easily discernible from the drawings of animals at Nal and Nundara,[119] the tradition seems to have come through Iran, more affirmatively than from Sumer.

(2) In respect of the use of vertical zigzags in painted pottery certain Iranian and Baluchistan sites show traces of Tal-i-Iblis influence,[120] A strange bird pattern from Tal-i-Iblis which is found at other Iranian sites, e.g., Nurabad,[121] Susa, Giyan, Damin and Khurab, is also met with in" recognizable form at Nal.[122]

(E) Kulli Culture—This culture is confined to south Baluchistan in the region which is touching eastern Iran border. (Fig.30-II, IV, VII; Fig.16-III; Fig.30- V; Fig. 17- I; Fig-30-VII; Fig.16-II; Fig.30-II-VII; Fig. 16-I-III; Fig.4-VI-XII; Fig. 12-IV; Fig. 7-1-11; Fig. 30-I-IX-X, IV-V; Fig. 20-V-VIII; Fig. 19-XXVI-XXVIII).

(1) The 'landscape with animals' frieze is found on the Kulli pots.[123] A distinctive style depicting the animals standing between the trees in a landscape which is occasionally crowded with geometrical designs or small birds or beasts recalls the similar design of Susa D and Khuzistan in Iran.[124]

(2) The compartmented seals of Shahi Tump corresponds with the similar form at Susa.[125]

(3) The files of animal figures on Kulli ware are surprisingly identical to Musyan pot style.[126]

(4) At Mehi there are small cylindrical pots divided into four compartments, some of which are decorated with fine engraved pattern of chevron and hatched triangles. Sistan and sites near Bampur present similar analogies.[127] (Fig. 14), (5) A disc mirror discovered at Mehi has its parallel at the earliest cemetery at Susa.[128]

(6) The figurines of humped bulls discovered in the Kulli culture are similar to those fround at Susa.[129]

(7) The characteristic exaggerated circular rendering of the eye painted in

a war-chariot drawn by an ox on a pot of Scarlet-Ware of Susa and its style of depiction are identical to that of Kulli pot-painters.[130]

(8) The paintings on the pottery exhibiting long files of the goat or ibex figures in the abbreviated 'shorthand' yielded in Kulli culture are analogous to those on the pots of Susa.[131]

(9) The hard grey ware with channelled incisions in straight lines and zigzags discovered at Shahi Tump in the Kulli culture are akin to the similar fragments found at Sistan and at other parts of Iran.[132]

(10) Raised wavy bands between cordons on vessels, row of stylized buck or ibex, tree motif and an occasional naturalistic large scale animal, are some of the designs which are common both in Mushkai-Kalwa region in the Kulli cultures and at Bampur and Sistan in Iran.[133]

(11) Vessels with a high shoulder found at Mehi correspond with the pots of similar form unearthed at Khurab cemetery near Bampur in Iran.[134]

(12) A typical style of a stone vase of the Kulli culture is akin to the stone vase found in a grave situated between Bakun and Shahi Tump.[135]

(13) Quite parallel to Susa I, the Kulli culture yielded wide open dishes, tall tumblers, small squat pots and ovoid jars.[136]

(14) Swastika and Maltese squares again relate the Kulli culture with Susa. [137]

(15) The zones of ibex or other animals on painted pottery, which is one of the most characteristic features of Iran and is abundantly found at Sialk III-5 and 6, Hissar I-C, Giyan V-D and Bampur[138] are also met with in the Kulli culture.[139] The ibex horns which appear as a repetitive motif in a zone at Tal-i-Pir, Tal-i-Bakun, Herraj,[140] Shahi Tump and Khurab[141] in Iran are also found in the Kulli culture and at other sites of Baluchistan.[142]

(16) Likewise the tree motif with fringed branches is one of the most characteristic features of the painted pottery of Bampur.[143] It has also been used in a more stylized form at Kulli and with upturned fringes at both Kulli and Mehi.[144]

(ii) Harappan Culture—Archaeologically named as the Harappan culture is popularly known as Indus-Valley culture, the sites of Indus civilization are widely scattered in north-west and western India. The most interesting feature of this culture is that while it is quite parallel in generalization with its western contemporaries, it abundantly differs from them in details.[145] This provides an interesting and a useful study which shall be made elaborately in the following chapter.

(iii) Post Harppan Chalcolithic Cultures—After the disappearance of the Harappan culture we find the various Chalcolithic cultures flourishing at several centres in the Deccan, the south-eastern and central India. The hand-made or wheel-turned pottery of these cultures is characterised by black-and-red ware, but generally black-on-red ware is more common which shows wide variety in shapes including bowls of various shapes, spouted, lipped or lugged bowls, channel-spouted bowls, hollow-footed bowls, carinated bowls, handled pots, bell-shapped jars, jars with broad, narrow, wide or open mouths, legged-stands, perforated vessels, goblets with high neck, shallow dish with broad flat rim and high-concave-walled up with bulging bottom, dish-on-stand and bowl-on-stand. Strangely, these cultures hold no probabilities to show their relationship with the Indus civilization and seem to have been directly inspired from Iran.[146] They may be classed–as follows :

(A) Banas Culture
(B) Central Indian Chacolithic Culture.
(C) Northern Deccan Culture.

(A) Banas Culture—The new cultural relation between India and Iran is borne out by the culture discovered at Ahar.[147] The centre of the Banas culture was south east Rajasthan in the valley of the Banas. Ahar and Gilund are its most important sites known so far. The main points of similarity are as follows : (Fig. 31-1; Fig. 21-I-V).

(1) The pedestalled grey-ware-bowls, the unique chandelier-like dish-on-stand and animal handled lids found at Ahar bear close similarity with the pots from Hissar, Shah Tepe and Geoy Tepe in Iran.[148]
(2) The dish-on-stand in the red and black-on-red, the high necked-jar and basin with cut-spout in the red ware, and lipped basin and vase with strap handle in the burnished grey ware found at Gilund exactly correspond with the similar finds from west Asia, especially from Iran.[149]
(3) A bowl-on-stand, in burnished grey ware with the hollow type of stand was found in the Ahar culture. This typical bowl corresponds with similar hollow based bowl-on-stand in grey ware from Hissar in Iran even in its feature and shape.[150]
(4) The incised ornamentation of the pattern such as chevrons, zigzag arches, row of arches and the figure of stylized stag occurring on terracotta beads, and on copper bangle and rings found in this culture, are similar to those of decorated beads of central Asia.[151]

(B) Central Indian Chalcolithic Cultures—This culture developed in the Narmada valley, Navdatoli, Maheswar, Nagda, Eran and Tripuri are its important sites. The findings at Navdatoli reflect an unambiguous Iranian influence. (Fig. 11, PI. VII-VIII-IX; Fig. 10; Fig. 12-V; Fig. 21-I-V; Fig. 12-II-XIII; Fig. 12-V-XIII-XIV).

(1) The dancing human figures on a white-slipped pottery bear a close similarity with the motif of painted pottery from Sialk and Hissar in Iran.[152]

(2) The narrow-necked vessels with dish-like top, round bowls decorated with hollow circles filled with dots, pedestalled champagne, channel and pinched-spouted bowls, low and high footed bowls and goblets discovered at Navdatoli mark incontrovertible influence from Iran.[153]

(3) The geometric pattern, birds, animals and human painted motifs are analogues[154] to those of Iranian sites.

(4) The channel-spouted bowls of Navadatoli correspond exactly with the similar forms from Nicropolis of Sailk and Tepe Giyan I.[155]

(5) The pedestalled-bowls, footed-cups or goblets with ringed or footed base from Navdatoli recall similar finds in Western Asiatic Neolithic or Chalco lithic culture[156] particularly those from Hissar III.[157]

(6) A bowl in fine white slip found at Navdatoli exactly corresponds with a similar pot from Sialk I in Iran.[158]

(7) A teapot-like bowl without a handle has been unearthed at Navdatoli. A hole at the junction of the spout and the body of the bowl or other vessels in order to control the flow of the liquid recalls similar contrivance notable in the bowls from Iran and other cultures of the south-west Asia.[159]

(8) The channel-spouted bowls of Navdatoli bear close resemblance with those from Tepe-Giyan.[160]

(9) The spouted vessels of Navdatoli and those of Iran are strikingly identical.[161]

(10) A thin buff ware of the Banas culture and certain examples found at Navdatoli recall similar ware from Iran.[162]

(11) The tubular spout having painted band of Tepe Giyan also occurs at Navdatoli.[163]

(12) The peculiar conoid cups and concave sided cups of Navdatoli and those from Sialk and Hissar, are strikingly identical.[164]

(13) The cream slipped-ware with painting in black found at Navdatoli is similar to those from Khurab and Bampur in Iran.[165]

(14) A dagger-pendent found at Maheshwar recalls similar triangular tops, perforated and similar conception of shape of a pendent from Tepe Hissar in Iran.[166]

(15) The tiny steatite disc beads discovered at Navdatoli are favourably compared to those found in Iran and other south-west Asian sites.[167]

(c) Northern Deccan Chalcolithic Culture—The geographical distribution of this culture was confined in the valleys of the Godavari and Pravara rivers. Nasik, Jorwe, Dhoki, Chandoli, Kogargaon, Pravara, Sangam, Nevasa, Girnar, and Bahal sites belong to this culture. (Pl.-VII, XI; Fig. 12-XI).

(1) A striking style depicting the animals with elongated and hatched bodies

on a white-slipped ware unearthed at Daimabad remainds the similar motif on Sailk pottery.[168]

(2) The chisels, adzes, packers and the flat axes, with slightly tappering sides and straight convex or flaring edges are comparable with those from western Asia and more akin to their counterpart in Iran.[169]

(3) Certain designs like the spotted tiger, with its neck turned back and crane-like birds among reeds and bushes of Prakash pottery bear similarity with those from Sialk.[170]

(4) The cups or bowls with the high multi-legged-stands recently found at Chandoli are similar to those from Tepe Giyan.[171]

(5) A dagger with mid-rib found at Chandoli and a fragment of a bronze dagger with raised mid-rib discovered at Navdatoli recall west Asian analogies.[172]

(6) A theriomorphic pot (bull) from Chandoli is akin to that of the west Asian examples of the Early Dynastic and later period.[173]

(iv) Neolithic—Chalocolitic Settlements of the Deccan—This culture was found flourishing in the region extending from Andhra-Karnatak to Maharastra. The culture has been discovered at Brahmigri, Maski, Bellary, Piklihal, Prakash and Sangankallu. (Fig. 12-I-II-V-XII-XIII; Fig. 21-VII-XVIlI, PI. VII).

(1) The cups or bowls with ringed or footed base found at Brahmgiri and Piklihal recall identical forms in west Asiatic Neolithic and Chalcolithic cultures.[174]

(2) Some of these cups or bowls mentioned above have the high multi-Iegged-stands exactly correspond with those from Tepe Giyan.[175]

(3) The legged stands, the perforated or the handled pots, the bell-shaped jars, the lipped spouted or channel spouted bowls and wide-mouthed jars with flaring rim found at Brahmgiri, Maski, Sanganakallu and Piklihal remind the identical vessels from Sialk, Giyan and Shah Tepe in Iran.[176]

(4) The similar potting technique, the perforated vessels, the spouted or the channel spouted pots and the grey wares show close relationship between Shah Tepe and Giyan in Iran and Piklihal and Brahmgiri in India.[177]

(5) There also seems to be a correspondence between burnished grey ware of Brahrngiri and grey ware complex of Iran.[178]

This brief survey of the dawn and development of the various cultures in India in the Chalcolithic age leads to the following conclusions :

(1) The peasant settlers of Baluchistan (c. 3000 - 2000) were not indigenous but directly influenced by the Iranian cultures.

(2) The Iranian influence appears to be the greatest and the most intensive

in the Kulli branch of this culture. Its site was no doubt nearer to Iran than any other culture of Baluchistan. Kulli was also situated on the southern route from Iran to India which was most probably the easiest inroad of inter-communication and consequently of cultural influence.

(3) The Quetta and Zhob branches also betray deep impact of Iranian culture.

(4) The Ahar, Navdatoli and Brahmgiri sites do not show any connection with their Indian precursor, viz., the Harappan culture, but the extraneous influence preferably Iranian, is distinctly discernible. The nature and degree of this inspiration, however, has to be ascertained.

(5) The view that Northern Neolithic culture of Burzahom was inspired exclusively by China is not tenable as there is sufficient evidence to show that Iran also had enormous influence in shaping this culture. Likewise the Eastern Neolithic culture was not only influenced by China and the south-east Asia, but also by Iran through Deccan.

References

1. J. Hawkes, op. cit., p. 220.
2. R.J. Braidwood and B. Howe, *Prehistoric Investigation in Iraqi Kurdistan*, pp. 73, 75 (Chicago, 1907).
3. U. Peake, *Journal of Royal Anthropological Institute*, London, LVII, 1927, p. 22, ff; Antiquity, VII, 1933, p. 73 ff.
4. G.C. Ewart, *Proceeding Highland and Agricultural Society*, XXV, 1913, p. 160 ff.
5. J. Mellaart, *'The beginning of village and urban life,"* The Dawn of Civilization, p. 59, (London, 1960).
6. D.A.E. Garrod and D.M Bate, *The Stone Age of Mount Cramel*, Vol. I, pp. 9-16, 30-40, 119 (Cambridge, 1937); R.J. Braidwood, *Antiquity*, XXIV, 1950, pp. 190-6.
7. C.S. Coon, "Cave Exploration in Iran," *University of Pennsylvania Museum Monographs*, pp. 1–63, (Philadephia, 1951).
8. J. Hawkes, op. cit., pp. 223–24.
9. J. Mellaart, Catal Hayuk, *Archaeologia*, No. 17, p. 56. Chronological table, (July–August 1967, Paris).
10. S. Lloyd and F. Safar, *journal of Near Eastern Studies*, IV, pp. 257–80 (Chicago, 1945).
11. R.J. Braidwood, *Journal of Near Eastern Studies*, III, pp. 48–68 (Chicago, 1944).
12. H. Frankfort, "Studies in the Early Pottery of Near East," *Royal Anthropological Institute*, Occasional Papers 6 and 8 (London 1925–27).
13. Ghirshman, Iran, p. 30 (pelican, 1954).
14. Ibid., pp. 29–30; J. Mellaart, op. cit. Chronological Table.
15. S. Piggott, op. cit., p. 55, (1961).
16. M.E.L. Mallowan, Civilized life begins: Mesopotamia and Iran, *The Dawn of civilization*, p. 68.
17. D.H. Gordon, "Sialk, Giyan, Hissar and its Indian connections," *Man in India*, Vol. XXVIII, No.3, pp. 215, 230.
18. D. McCown, *The Comparative Stratigraphy of Early Iran*, University of Chicago, Oriental Institute, Studies in Ancient Oriental Civilization, p. 23, (1942).
19. J.M. Casal, "Fouilles de Moundigak," *Memoirs de la Delegation Archaeologique Fran-caise en*

Afghanistan, p. 17, (Paris, 1961).
20. D.H. Gordon, op. cit., pp. 215–30.
21. Op. cit., p. 40 (1950).
22. W. Frazer, cf. V.D. Krishna Swamy, op. cit., p; 38.
23. M.H. Krishna, Prehistoric *Deccan, Presidential Address*, 29th Science Congress, Baroda, 1942.
24. H.H. De Terra and T.T. Paterson, Studies on the Ice Age in India and associated with Human culture, *Pub.* No. 493, Carnegie Institution of Washington, 1939.
25. V.D. Krishna Swami, op. cit., pp. 37–38.
26. T.N. Khajanchi, Dwelling Pits of Burzahom, *Paper Read at the International Conference on Asian Archaeology*, New Delhi, 1961.
27. TE–K'UN Cheng, *Archaeology in China*, Vol. I (Cambridge, 1960), pp. 11–60.
28. T.N. Khajanchi, op. cit,; Bridget and Raymond Allchin, op, cit., p. 160; A.P. Okladniko, "*Silka Cave*," Translated in H.N. Michael's Archaeology and Geomorphology of Northern Asia, (Toronto, 1964).
29. F.R. Allchin, "The Neolitic Stone Industry of Santhal Parganas" Bullatin, Scinece Orient and African Studies, XXV, Vol. 2, pp. 2, 306–30; A.H. Dani Prehistory and Protohistory of Eastern India, (Calcutta, 1960), pp. 222–26.
30. Bridget and Raymond Allchin, op. cit., p. l60.
31. H.D. Sankalia, *Prehistory and Protohistory in India and Pakistan*, p. 269
32. A.H. Dani, *Prehistory and Protohistory of Eastern India*, pp. 47–74 (Calcutta, 1960).
33. Indian Archaeology A Review, 1959–60, p.14, fig. 6, 1960–61, p. 4.
34. A.H. Dani, op.cit., p. 266.
35. Ibid.
36. "The Neolithic Stone Industry of Santhal Parganas" *Bull. Science Orient and African Studies*, XXV, 2, pp. 306–30.
37. G.W. Anderson "Note on Prehistoric stone implements found in Singhbhum district" *Journal Bihar and Orissa Research Society*, Vol. III, pp. 349–62.
38. E.C. Worman, "The 'Neolithic' Problem in the Prehistory of India," *Journal, Washington Academy Science*, Vol. 39 No. 6, pp.191–200, (1949).
39. H.D. Sankalia, op. cit., p. 245.
40. Ibid., p. 242.
41. F.R Allchin, op. cit. p. 325.
42. H.D. Sankalia and B. Deo, *Report on Excavations at Nasik and jorwe*, pl. XXXIII, No. 4 and 6.
43. *Indian Archaeology* : A Review 1957–88, pl. XXVI and XXV.
44. Ancient India No. 4, 1947, fig. No.7, 1950, fig. 51.
45. "The Chalcolithic Blade Industry of Maheswar and a Note on the History of the Technique," *Bulletin of the Deccan College Research Institute*, Vol. XVII, No. 2, p. 34, pl. XX, 10, 13.
46. H.D. Sankalia, op. cit., p. 244.
47. R. Hiene Geldem, "The coming of the Aryans and the End of Harappan Civilisation," *Man*, 56 (l956), pp. 136–39.
48. H.D. Sankalia, op. cit. p. 281.
49. J. Mellaart, op. cit., p. 48.
50. F.R Allchin, op. cit., pp. 320–30.
51. H.D. Sankalia, op. cit., p. 157.
52. E.C. Worman, 'The Neolithic' Problem in the Prehistory of India, *Journal Washington Academy Sciences*, XXXIX, (1949), pp. 181–201.
53. V.D. Krishna Swami, "The Neolithic pattern of India," Ancient India, No. 16, (Delhi, 1960), p. 25.
54. Ibid., pp. 48–49.
55. H.D. Sankalia, op. cit., pp. 267–74.
56. J.R. Braidwood and B. Howe, *Prehistoric Investigation in Iraqi Kurdistan*, pp. 73 ff.

57. C. Yon Furer. Haimendorf, "The Problem of Megalithic Cultures in Middle India; Man In India, XXV, (1945) pp. 73–86.
58. E.C. Worman, op. cit., pp. 190–200.
59. M. Wheeler, *Early India and Pakistan,* (London, 1950), p. 89.
60. F.R. Allchin, *Piklihal Exacavations,* pp. 100 ff, (Hyderabad, 1960).
61. Ibid.
62. Ibid., p. 113.
63. J. Hawkes, op. cit., p. 82.
64. R.J. Braidwood, 'Reflection on the Stone and Bronze Age of Asia:' Presidential Address, delivered at the *International Conference on Asian Archaeology,* New Delhi, 1962.
65. J. Mellaart, op. cit., p. 61.
66. H.H. Coghlan, Man, 1939, p. 92; *Antiquaries Journal,* XXII (1942), pp. 22–39; M.E.L. Mallowan, op. cit., p.84.
67. J. Mellaart, op. cit., p. 14.
68. V.G. Childe, *What Happened in the History,* p. 59, (London, 1960); R Ghirshman, op. cit., pp. 30–31,
69. V.G. Childe, *New Light on the most Ancient East,* pp. 195–96.
70. V.G. Childe, *What Happened in the History,* pp. 58–96.
71. S. Piggot, op. cit., pp. 195–200.
72. V.G. Childe, op. cit., p. 239.
73. M.E.L. Mallown, op. cit., pp. 84–85.
74. V.G. Childe, *New Light on the Most Ancient East.* pp. 93, 195.
75. J. Mellaart, op. cit., pp. 48–49.
76. V.G. Childe, op. cit., p. 196.
77. R Ghirshman, Iran, p. 32.
78. J. Mellaart, op. cit., p. 48.
79. V.G. Childe, p. 195.
80. Ibid.
81. Ibid.
82. R. Ghirshman, *Iran,* p. 40.
83. Ibid.
84. A.W.A. Fairservis; *Harappan Culture,* p. 10. (New Yark, 1963).
85. Ibid.
86. M. Wheeler, "India and Iran in Pre-Islamic Times," *Ancient India,* No.4, p. 89, (1947–48).
87. S. Piggot, op. cit., p. 68.
88. Ibid., p. 126 (1951).
89. S. Piggot, "Chronology of Prehistoric North West India," *Ancient India,* No. I, p. 18.
90. McCown, *The Comparative Stratigraphy of Iran,* University of Chicago, Oriental Institute Studies in Ancient Oriental Civilization, 23, (London, 1942).
91. S. Piggot, op. cit., p. 56.
92. Ibid.
93. Ibid., p. 72.
94. D.H. Gordon, *Man in India,* "Silak, Giyan, Hissar and its Indian connection," Vol. XXVII, No.3, p. 230.
95. Ibid., p. 227.
96. Ibid., pp. 217–18.
97. D.H. Gordon, *"The Prehistoric Background of Indian Culture,"* p. 225 (Bombay, 1958).
98. D.H. Gordon, *Man in India,* Vol. XXVIII, No.3, "Sialk, Giyan, Hissar and its Indian connection," p. 216.
99. S. Piggot, *Prehistoric India,* p. 126 (1950).
100. Ibid., p.129.

101. D.H. Gordon, op. cit., p. 215.
102. S. Piggot, *Antiquity*, XVII, 1943, pp. 172–73.
103. *Journal of Near Eastern Studies.* Chicago, Vol. V, 1946, pp. 284–96.
104. H.P. Frankfort, *Studies in the Early Pottery of the Near East*, occasional papers 6 and 8.
105. D.H. Gordon, op. cit., p. 225.
106. S. Piggot, Dating the Hissar Sequence–the Indian evidence, *Antiquity*, December fig. 1, 2, 7. (XVII, 1943).
107. D.H. Gordon, op. cit., p. 225.
108. S. Piggot, Prehistoric India, (1951), p. 75.
109. A. Stein. Innermost Asia, CXIII and CXIV; Andrews, Neolithic Pottery in Sistan, Burlington Magizine, 1955.
110. D.E. Mac Cown, op. cit., fig. 13, 134.
111. D.H. Gordon op. cit., p. 220.
112. S. Piggot, op. cit., p. 95
113. P.A. Khan, Preliminary Report on Kot Diji Excavation, (1957–48), p. 16.
114. D.H. Gordon, op. cit., p. 215.
115. A. Stein, *Archaeological Reconnaissances in North West India and South Iran*, (London, 1937), pl. 25, Nur 37.
116. Ibid., pl. II, 48 and A88.
117. D.H. Gordon, op. cit., p. 218.
118. Ibid., p. 220.
119. S. Piggot, op. cit., pp. 116–117.
120. H. Frankfort, op. cit.
121. A. Stein, op. cit., p. 24, 91 and 25 Nur 31.
122. D.H. Gordon, op. cit., p. 219.
123. V.G. Childe, op. cit., p. 201.
124. H. Frankfort, *Archaeology and Sumerian Problem*, (London, 1932), pp. 68–70.
125. V.G. Childe, op. cit., p. 202.
126. S. Piggot, op. cit., p. 116.
127. V.G. Childe, op. cit., p. 201.
128. S. Piggot, op. cit., pp. 117–118.
129. Ibid.
130. Ibid., p. 118.
131. Ibid., p. 116.
132. Ibid., p. 104.
133. Ibid., p. 105.
134. Ibid.
135. V.G. Childe, *New Light on the Most Ancient East*, pp. 201–2.
136. Ibid., p. 201.
137. Ibid.
138. D.H. Gordon, op. cit., p. 219.
139. Ibid.
140. A. Stein, op. cit., pl. 16.
141. Ibid., pl. 29.
142. D.H. Gordon, op. cit., p. 220.
143. A. Stein, op. cit., pls. 9, 11, 13.
144. D.H. Gordon, op. cit., p. 219.
145. S. Piggot, *Prehistoric India*, op. cit., p. 116.
146. F.R. Allchin, A Neolithic pot from Andhra Pradesh, *Antiquity*, Vol. XXXVI, No. 144, 1962, pp. 302 ff.
147. H.D. Sankalia, "New Links between Western Asia and India of 4000 years ago: Excavation in

the Huge 'Dust Heap' of Ahar, near Udaipur, *Illustrated London news,* September, 1962, pp. 322-26.

148. Ibid.
149. F.R. Allchin, op. cit., pp. 302–3.
150. E.F. Schmidt, Excavation at Tepe–Hissar, Damghan, publication Iranian Section, University Museum Philladelphia, 1937, pl. xxiii, H. 2889 and pl. xxvi, H. 4161.
151. *Exploration in Turkistan,* Edited by R. Pumpally, Vol. I, p. 163. fig. 350.
152. H.D. Sankalia, "Navdatoli Dancer" *Antiquity,* xxix, 1955, pp. 28–31.
153. H.D. Sankalia, Prehistory and Protohistory of Indian and Pakistan, p. 273.
154. H.D. Sankalia, Four thousand years old Links Between Iran and Central India, *Illustrated London News;*
155. H.D. Sankalia, "Spouted Vessels from Navdatoli (M. Bharat) and Iran," *Antiquity,* xxix, pp. 114, 112–14, (1955).
156. H.D. Sankalia, *Pre-history and Protohistory in India and Pakistan,* p. 25
157. V. G. Childe, "Notes on some Indian and East Iranian Pottery," *Ancient Egypt and the East.*
158. R. Ghirshmn, "Fouilles de Sialk," Vol. I., Frontispiece, 1938, of H.D. Sankalia, op. cit., p. 19.
159. H.D. Sankalia, op. cit., p. 200.
160. H.D. Sankalia, op. cit., p. 273.
161. H.D. Sankalia, "Spouted Vessels from Navdatoli and Iran," *Antiquity,* xxix, 1956, pp. 112–5.
162. H.D. Sankalia, *Prehistory and Protohistory in India and Pakistan.,* p. 189.
163. F.A. Schaffer, *Stratigraphie et Chronologie,* (London, 1948), fig. 245, 255.
164. *Bulletins Deccan Research Institute,* Vol. XI, (1950–1), pl. II- VI.
165. H.D. Sankalia, op. cit., p. 25 and fn. 29.
166. E.F. Schmidt, *Excavations at Hissar Damghan,* (philadelphia, 1937), p. XLVIII, H. 3500.
167. A. Stein, "An Archaeological tour in the Ancient Persia," published in *'Iraq"* vol. ill, p. 152, (British School of Archaeology in Iraq, 1936).
168. H.D. Sankalia, op. cit. p. 209.
169. R. Heine Geldern, loc. cit., p. 136 ff.
170. R. Ghirshman, *Fouilles des Sialk,* Vol. I (Raris, 1938), pl. LXII, 8, 448.
171. *Indian Archaeology,* A Review, 1958–59, p. 33.
172. R. Heine Goldern, *Man.,* No. 151, Vol. LVI, 1956, p. 136.
173. B.K. Thaper, "The West Asian background to the Prehistoric pottery of India, in the Second and First Millennia B.C.," Paper read at the *International Conference on Asian Archaeology,* New Delhi, 1962 .
174. H.D. Sankalia, op. cit., p. 255.
175. G. Contenau and R. Ghirshrnan, *Excavation at Tepe Giyan,* pl. XII and pl. 23.
176. F.R. Allchin, Piklihal Excavations, *Andhra Pradesh Government Archaeological Series,* No. I (Hyderabad 1960), pl. 24, 26, 28, 31, F. Rand B. Allchin, A Neolithic Pot from Andhra Pradesh, *Antiquity,* Vol. XXXVI, No. 144, 1962, pp. 302–3.
177. F.R. Allchin, op. cit., pp. XVII–154.
178. B.K. Thapar, op. cit.

3

The Indus Valley Civilization

The Indian culture was largely believed, before the discovery of the Indus Valley civilization to be the work of the Aryans, although the Rigveda which is their earliest document did not provide the necessary clue or meaning or many unintelligible ingredients of the Vedic culture. More often it was asserted by the western scholars followed by some in India that the non-Aryan elements in the later Vedic culture were either borrowed from somewhere or were brought by some people who entered the country at a time unrecorded now. It was once held that civilization of any sizeable antiquity could not have grown indigenously in India and we conceivably looked for it towards the Ancient East (ancient Iran and the Mesopotamian region) where a full fledged urban civilization of higher order was already recognized to have been born in the remote past (c. 5000 BC). But the discovery of the Indus civilization in 1924 brought to light a phase of India's Past which was by then believed to be non-existing. The exploration opened new chapter in the history of India. The vestiges showed some common features of urban civilization similar to those of Iran and Sumer.

The discovery of the Indus civilization put India on the map of the old world and at the same time it opened new vistas for investigation. The foremost was the problem, if the Indus civilization was an indigenous growth or was it transplanted from outside. The answer warrants a comparative study of the contemporary cultures.

Whereas the Indus Valley culture, in general, is adequately comparable to its contemporaries in Mesopotamia and Iran, it differs in detail from them in many respects. Thus like the cultures in Western Asia, the Indus civilization too is literate and urban, using copper and bronze but not iron for implements. But there is nothing in contemporary Persia or Mesopotamia to compare with the well-planned baths and spacious houses of the Indus Valley. The elaborate drainage of the Indus culture is unique and conspicuous. It thus appears to be akin to them on the face of it but it had become essentially different when it reached maturity. One thing which even a cursory scrutiny yields is certain that Indus civilization hitherto revealed is not an incipient civilization but one already age old and stereotyped on the Indian soil. The point whether the local developments proved to be decisive factor in shaping the character and composition of this civilization or outweighed the original inspiration, if any has yet to be examined.

The scholars scrutinized the issue in detail and, controversial as it is, different view-points were authoritatively expressed. On a critical examination of the urban civilizations in the Western Asia and the Indus Valley, a fantastically strange characteristic was noticed that while they show a general homogeniety, still each differing widely maintains its own local and individual traits which differed from the other equally developed and in some respect superior to the civilization of western Asia. Piggot thinks that the origin of the Indus civilization outside India is inherently improbable; but the point where and in what form it originated could not be explained. Wheeler firmly believed in the dictum 'ideas have wings.' He is inclined to believe in a contribution or at least an inspiration from earlier civilization of Mesopotamia to the Indus Valley. Marshall maintained that the birth of civilization can not be ascribed to a particular country alone, and honour should be shared by Egypt, Mesopotamia, Iran and India, which are certainly most important areas where early signs of the growth of civilized society were initiated.

(a) Origin

The thrilling discovery of the Indus Valley civilization makes an event of importance and significance in the history of India in particular and the world at large. It widened the horizon of our knowledge and suggested immense possibilities of the inter-relationship with other ancient civilizations of the west Asia. Though the scholars have been persistently engaged on the subject, its origin which gave rise to fully evolved urban civilization in this part of the world, is shrouded in mystery.

With regard to the Harappan culture (the Indus Valley civilization is so called after the site of Harappa) there are divergent views about its origin. Some of them may be discussed briefly. Marshall defined it as "not an. incipient civilization but one already age-old and stereotyped on Indian soil."[1] Wheeler described it as an "explosive phenomenon"[2] whereas Heine Geldern perceived, "a sudden emergence without any trace of prior development."[3] Piggot believed it to be "enigmatic to a degree surpassing its contemporaries in western Asia."[4]

(i) *Nucleous Area of Urban Civilization*—As it has been pointed out in the preceding chapter that the civilization germinated and flourished in western Asia, whence it migrated to the rest of the world. West Asia's claim of priority in evolving farming, pottery-making, potter's wheel, metallurgy, script and other essentialities of the urban life, has been universally acknowledged and it has aptly been designated as the nucleolus area by Braidwood. It is in no way without reasoning that the scholars relate other farming communities or urban cultures of the old world to this nucleolus area, either by direct migration or diffusion or both.[5]

The Indus civilization presents the Chalcolithic phase of urban culture of a very high order, which in general features offers strong resemblance to those of the west Asia. Hence it is not unwise to think that the Indus culture could not have evolved independently of the cultures of Sumer, Elam and Ancient Iran.[6] But we have yet to examine precisely whether the Indus civilization is either the result of Sumerian colonization or Sumerian inspiration or of indigenous growth. The various views expressed on this controversial question need further elucidation.

(ii) *Sumerian Colonization or Inspiration*—The divergent theories about the source of this civilization are being summarised below:—

It was once a general view that it grew as a result of Sumerian colonization or at least was largely inspired by the Sumerian culture. The theory of Sumerian colonization gained great support from D.H. Gordon[7] Arnold Toynbee went a step further and propounded the theory of migration by sea. "In transmarine migration the social apparatus of the migrants has to be packed on board ship before they can leave the shores of the old country and then unpacked again at the end of the voyage before they can make themselves at home on the new ground. All kinds of apparatus-persons and property, techniques and institutions and ideas are equally subject to this law. Anything that cannot stand the sea voyage at all has simply to be left behind; and many things, and these not only material objects, which the migrants do manage to take with can only be shipped after they have been taken to pieces-never, perhaps to be reassembled in their original form."[8]

This hypothesis of Toynbee seems to be based on a mere surmise. He does not explain why the Sumerian deserted their fertile country to colonize the 'inhospitable' and 'menacing' land of the Indus Valley.[9] The archaeological evidence shows connections between the two regions dated back to 2200 BC when the Indus culture was fully developed.[10] These connections were mostly related to trade and nothing else. The unsoundness of the theory is evident from the fact that a physical transfer of certain materials of the nature Toynbee imagined never helps the growth of a culture evidently goes against this theory. It is the ideas and the knowledge which are the roots of a culture and its subsequent growth. Mere transfer of a pot or a chair without the idea or the knowledge of its construction or use would be of no avail. Hence Toynbee's theory does not solve the problem. The strong individualistic character of the Indus culture rules out such wild speculation.

Instead of colonization some scholars preferred to trace its origin from the Sumerian inspiration. Particularly Wheeler believed that the urban life of the Indus culture was inspired from the western Asia.[11] Kramer also believed it to be the result of Ubaidian inspiration.[12] Similarly Mackay gave all credit to the diffusionary impulses from Sumer to shape this marvellous culture.[13]

No doubt this new approach to the vexing problem provided a possible alternative of the earlier theory, but it, too, has pitfalls in as much as it fails to explain the local character of this culture. The diagnostic traits of the Sumerian culture hardly fit in the individualistic character of the Indus civilization. The ziggurats are hallmak of Sumer while religious building are conspicuously absent in the latter.[14] The use of carts in Indus in place of the ass-drawn vehicles of Summer is another point to rule out the Sumerian influence. The Indus script bears hardly a point of resemblance to the cuneiform of Sumer. The Harappan flat spear head without mid-rib is reasonably decisive to negative such influence. The Sumerians used well developed mid-rib-spearhead. Finally contrasting to urbanized agricultural civilization of Sumer, the Harappan culture presents agriculture-based urban civilization. Fairservis observed" . . . in contrast to a multiplicity of sites we have majority of village sites and only two, perhaps four settlements large enough to be labelled cities."[15] The basic concepts of life thus inherently differ and it is not conceivable if Sumer inspired Indus, how the latter could have escaped from borrowing these vital features of the former.

(iii) *Were the Authors of Indus culture, Dravidians?* As it has been shown, the Indus culture is comparable to that of Sumer in general but strikingly differing in detail. This tantalising relationship baffles the scholars and tempts them in the last recourse to believe in indirect influence from Sumer. They surmise that Sumerians and Dravidians are off-shoots of the same stock and the latter, viz., the Dravidians, were the authors of the Indus culture. H.R. Hall believed that the Sumerians and Dravidians branched off from their original home which was located somewhere in the east of Mesopotamia.[16] The theory received support from the existence of Brahui, a pocket dialect of Tamil in Baluchistan. H. Heras concurred with the theory and claimed to have deciphered the script of the Indus seals as old as Tamil.[17] This theory also rests on unsound basis. According to Marshall the ethnic relation between the Dravidian and the Sumerian is very doubtful.[18] The Brahui-speaking people are now Iranians.[19] Heras's reading has also been challenged from all quarters. S.K. Chaterji noted, '1t is highly improbable that in epigraphs from a culture-age going back to say, 2500 B.C., there should be found a language, which is not much older than 500 AD."[20] Likewise A.L. Basham observed, "Historians have regarded the civilization of Mohenjodaro and Harappa as Dravidian, but ritual bathing, phallic worship, the Mother Goddess and the scared bull are not essentially South Indian."[21] It is not probable therefore, that, the Sumerian culture could have inspired the Indus civilization even indirectly through the Dravidians with whom it was not possibly related.

(iv) *Were the Authors of Indus culture, the Vedic Aryans?* Some scholars believe that the Indus culture was the work of the early Aryans. But this too is not admissible. Archaeologically the Indus culture is the oldest civilization of India. The scholars, who believe that India is the original home of the Aryans, identify the Harappans with the Aryans along with their respective cultures. Some scholars claim to decipher the script on the Indus seals and read the names of Aryans deities in Sanskrit language.[22] Such fantastic theories do not rest on the sound footing. Sometimes they are self-contradictory and do not deserve serious consideration. Indisputably the two cultures are unrelated and widely apart. The Rigveda portrays the village culture with the knowledge of iron and horse in contrast to the urban Harappan culture in which iron and horse were unknown.[23] In the Indus religion inconism, the bull cult, phallic worship and that of Mother Goddess are prominent. The Aryan religion is normally aniconic. They were fire-worshippers par excellence. The phallic worship was entirely abhorent[24] and cult of Mother Goddess was unknown to them. Contrary to the Harappans, the Aryans venerated cow and had a general aversion to fish.[25] The total absence of any ethnic relation between the two is the weakest point in the theory.[26] Besides we have yet to fix the physical character of the Aryans.

(v) *Indigenous Origin*—The strong individualistic character of the culture, which has ever since been enigmatic, always suggested the scholars to look for the origin of the culture within itself. Piggot impressively believed that its origin outside India is inherently improbable.[27]

The recent archaeological discoveries in the sub-continent have brought to light various pre-Harappan settlements in the area and pre-Harappan vestiges at Mohenjodaro and Harappa. The citadel at Harappa was built on earlier settlement, the pottery of which is alien to the typical Indus pottery. It finds its analogies at Periano Ghunai in the Zhob valley.[28] In Sind Majumdar excavated early Amri ware which is super-imposed by Harappan ware.[29] Ghazi Shah and Pandi Wahi exhibit an overlap of the two.[30] The similar overlap is seen at Pai-jo-kotiro in the Gaj valley[31] This pottery shows strong Kulli influence.[32] These were certainly earlier stratas which in a more or less degree mark the various stages of its early growth and development. The recent excavations at Kalibangan also shed some new light on obscure phases of the origin of the Indus culture. The pottery unearthed there bears semblance to that found at Kot Diji.[33]

These discoveries provide ample evidence to revise the commonly held view that there was a cultural vacuum in the sub-continent before the emergence of the Indus culture. The village cultures such as Zhob, Kulli, Quetta, Amri-Nal and Sothi existed long before the emergence of the Indus culture. These settlements of the peasant-potter communities are earlier to the Harappan culture. But whether they made any contribution in the making of the Indus culture is still to be decided. A comparative survey of these cultures with the Indus culture may help us to establish antecedents of the latter.

(vi) *Near Home Harappan Analogies*, Piggot, Gordon, Fairservis, Childe and F.A. Khan have very ably dealt with the relations of the Indus culture with these pre-Harappan village cultures. Certain analogies between them merit serious consideration. (Fig. 23; Fig. 19-XXII-XXVII-XXXII-XXXIII-XXXIX).

(A) QUETTA CULTURE

(1) The early Harappan pottery discovered at Ghazi Shah, Pandi-Wahi and Damb Buthi has strong resemblance with the Togau ware with designs of animals, human, ibex head and of hook pattern.[34]

(2) The Amri ware is quite identical to the Kachi Beg pottery.[35]

(B) ZHOB CULTURE

(Fig. 35, PI. XV, PI. XXIII; Fig. 31-IlI; Fig. 19-XI-XLI)

(l) The Indus terracotta figurine of Mother Goddess has its analogies at Dabar Kot, Mughal Ghundai, Periano Ghundai and Surjangal.[36]

(2) The fertility symbol from Indus culture bears a point of resemblance with phallus carved in stone at Mughal Ghundai and with another probable example of enormously exaggerated female vulva and thigh from Periano Ghundai,[37]

(3) The scale patterns at Sur-Jungal are very close to that of Harappan ware.[38]

(4) The red ware beakers from Periano Ghundai correspond exactly with those at Chan-hu-daro.[39]

(5) The hook-fringe patterns from Awaran, Mushkai and Nundara are convincing link with hook fringe of the Indus.[40]

(6) A fine buff pottery with register of painted humped bull or spiral horned black buck in this culture offers a positive link with Indus culture.[41]

(7) A lively connection is evidenced between the Indus and Periano Ghundai where the stone implements of microlithic type show close resemblance with stone blades which are later on found replaced by copper or iron but were in constant use everywhere in India.[42]

(C) AMRI-NAL CULTURE

(Fig.27-II; Fig.28; Fig.29)

(1) The burial features in the cemetery at Amri disclose close link with the first phase of cemetery 'H' of Harappa.[43]

(2) The papal leaf motif and intersecting circle pattern of the Amri culture

offer an interesting point of comparison to the Indus culture.[44]

(3) The Nal copper tools such as spear-head, saw and long bar chisel are identical with the Harappan series.[45]

(4) The Nal affinities are noticeable in the early black-on-red Harappan ware.[46]

(5) The use of faience at Nal for making beads is very common in the Indus culture.[47]

(6) A perforated stone weight from Nal and of similar two from Nichara are identical in shape with those from Mohenjodaro.[48]

(7) The shell bracelets and pottery unearthed at Damb Buthi cemetery have striking link with Harappa.[49]

(8) The blades at Harappa corresponds with chert blade and core at Amri.[50]

(D) KULLI CULTURE

(Fig. 19-XXI-XXII-XXIII-XXIV; Fig. 32-III; Fig. 30-I-V)

(1) The Maltese square and Swastika patterns akin to the Harappa culture are very common in Kulli.[51]

(2) The carving of the incised pots at Dast river is comparable to that of a typical fragment from the lower level at Mohenjodaro.[52]

(3) The bird whistles commonly found in the Indus culture point their origin in the Kulli culture where at Mehi the hollow bird model has a hole at the tail.[53]

(4) A fragment of circular vessel of Kulli style has been found in the earliest settlement of Mohenjodaro.[54]

(5) It is quite reasonable that the Harappans imitated the bull and tree design of Kulli.[55]

(6) The animal friezes from Chan-hu-daro, Karchat and Shah-jo-kotiro must have been derived from Kulli culture.[56]

(7) A naturalistic pipal design on pots from Lohum-jo-daro, Ghazi-Shah and Pandi Wahi surprisingly corresponds with pipal tree design of Kulli and Mehi.[57]

(8) The zones of small figures at Thale Damb and Surjangal in Kulli and Mehi have their analogies at Karchat and Shah-jo-Katiro.[58]

(9) The ibex zone painting bears a close resemblance to those from Karchat, Shahhjo-kutiro and Chan-hu-daro.[59]

(10) The arrow head on the tree top at Kulli and Mehi offers strong resemblance to the peculiarity of Ghazi-Shah in the Indus culture.[60]

(11) A sherd from Mohenjodaro, having the decoration of an animal with peculiar fringed feet corresponds exactly with a Kulli sherd from Bazdad Kalat.[61]

(E) SOTHI CULTURE

(Fig. 32-II-III)

(1) A terracotta cake of Sothi culture unearthed at the lower level of Kot Diji serves a link to the typical Harappan artifact.[62]
(2) The pottery with external ribbing at Harappa and Mohenjodaro points its origin in the Sothi culture.[63]
(3) The short stemmed dish-on-stand of the Sothi finds its analogies to Harappa.[64]
(4) The Harappan level at Rupar yielded basins with deep incision or shallow combings in the interior which is without doubt a Sothi features.[65]
(5) Wheeler[66] found the ring stand below the citadel at Harappa, which corresponds exactly in its details of obliquely cut rim and recurved base with a similar form at Mohenjodaro.[67]
(6) The pipal leaf and fish scale patterns serve to link the two cultures.[68]
(7) The external cord impressions which are striking feature of the Sothi culture show strong similarity with the finds at Mohenjodaro.[69]

It is worthwhile to note that the mutual influence and inter-relationship among the village cultures of Baluch and Sind which Piggot and Gordon have worked out have come to stay. The Sothi culture more or less has the same relation with them. The Sothi[70] pottery is comparable to the Periano Ghundai pottery found below citadel at Harappa and to pre-Harappan pottery at Kot Diji[71] and Kalibangan. The same technique seems to have been applied for the rustication of the lower parts of the Sothi vessels and surface treatment of the Quetta ware.[72] The decoration of the Sothi pottery affords strong similarity to those of the Kili-Gul-Mohammad black-on-red slip ware, Jangal course and painted ware of Surjangal III and Mehi Nundara ware.[73]

The comparative study pf the aforesaid cultures shows that the earlier phases of the Indus culture are strongly linked with the prehistoric Baluch-village culures and later on the former largely imbibed the considerbale elements from the latter. In other words the survey makes one fully convinced that the Harappan culture was merely the last and probably the most elaborate of a long series of cultural evolution. It cannot be denied that the subsequent phases of these village cultures show apparent Indianization which took place probably because of the rise of equivalent culture of the Indus Valley.[74] Here the term "urban" used for the Indus culture creates wide gulf between two distinct cultures. But new evidences brought by the recent researches make us certain that the pre-Harappan village cultures were achieving urbanity before the Harappan culture had emerged.

(vii) Transition of Urban Life Among Pre-Harappan Village Cultures in Baluchistan and Sind—At Kot Diji Majumdar had unearthed a small fortification.[75] The defensive wall with bastions at regular intervals, shows that the foundation was laid with the stones and the upper part of wall was built of mudbricks. A small settlement on a hill at Kohtras Buthi exhibits double defence wall and similar fortification is reported on Tharro hill.[76] Sind presents another settlement at Dhillan-jo-Kot with rampart,[77] Structure at Kohtras Buthi had four exterior bastions and a bathroom occupied the corner of one room by entrance of the house showed the remains of stairs implying access to the upper storey.[78] Fairservis wrote, "A number of typically Harappan features including figurines, bangles and decorative elements have been found in pre-Harappan context at Kot Diji."[79] It is now certain that fortification found below Harappan level at Kot Diji indicates that culture was approaching if not achieving urbanity.[80]

Some structures at Kargushki Damb in Nundara and at Rod-Khan in Baluchistan show walls of houses built of stone slabs set in mud mortar upto the window height.[81] Excavations at Damb Sadaat in Quetta valley brought into light the stone drains associated with mudbrick structure and a large platform which most likely had the buildings.[82] Edith Sahr.[83] in Las Bela district yielded a settlement of Late Kulli affiliation, the complex 'A' of which exposed large structures of ascending stages in ziggurat fashion and crowned at the top with platform supporting brick buildings. The structural complex has intervening lanes or streets, stone paved floors and drains or cisterns built on these floors.[84] Fairservis is inclined to believe that the culture discovered here had approached urbanity.[85] The typology shows that the late Kulli culture, Damb Sadaat III and the pertinent level of Loralai-Zhob are all almost contemporaneous and rather slightly earlier than the Harappan culture of Sind.[86] In the Quetta valley, at Zhob, Kalat and Las Bela, Fairservis observes the traces of phases of development beginning with villages with the limited farming and "expanding to an elaborated ceremonial complex, complete with monumental building "fertility" figure and probable use of ablution and sacrifice as a part of ritual."[87] He further says that a large number of sites so closely adjacent to one another in Las Bela appear to be approaching urbanization.[88]

It can, now, obviously be claimed that these pre-Harappan village cultures gradually developed the Indus culture. It is rather misleading to describe the Indus culture as an "explosive phenomenon" or "a sudden emergence without any trace of prior development" or "being known in India in its mature form with no known beginning." The foregoing survey discloses that many prototypes of Harappan traits occur in Baluch-pre-Harappan culture. It further more indicates the pre-Harappan evidence in Sind and increasing culture complex in pre-Harappan Baluchistan. These factors suggest that the Indus civilization is the culminating phase of the above cultural evolution.[89]

(viii) Roots of the Harappan culture are Iranian—The dictum "natural birth is un-natural phenomenon" rules in archaeology. There seems to be no reason to challenge the exclusive claim of the western Asia for diffusing its culture to the contemporaneous urban civilizations. These two potent factors always force the scholars to look for direction from which the transmission of idea or diffusionery impulses were received by the pre-Harappan village cultures in Sind and Baluchistan. Iran affords the key. It has been shown in the last chapter that during 3000 BC the farming communities in Baluchistan, Sind, Punjab, and Rajasthan reflected an unambiguous influence from Iran. Fairservis who did extensive study of these cultures notes, "The cultural influences discernible in this sequence indicate that its earlier phases are Iranian. Later, however, an apparent 'Indianization" took place formalizing the specific character of the later Baluch cultures and setting them off from those of the remainder of the Iranian Plateau."[90]

This makes out that Iran afforded impetus to these pre-Harappan culture which ultimately gave rise to the Indus valley culture, there is every reason to believe that though Harappan culture was Indianized yet its essential roots are undoubtedly Iranian.[91]

(b) Indus Religion

Religion is certainly one of the most important elements of a culture. The Indus religion is very interesting and its some influence is discernible in present day Hinduism. Further we find its link with the old cult of the western Asia. None the less certain elements of the Indus religion are still obscure. The Indus script could not be deciphered so far inspite of various efforts. The seals are the sealed books. No building of definitely religious character has been discovered in the Indus Valley.[92] Whatever materials we have at our disposal to form an idea of the religion are notably scanty. Neverthless it gives some valuable information. The seals, sealings, copper tablets, statuary and terracotta figurines unearthed during excavations throw a considerable light on the religious beliefs of the people.

(i) Mother Goddess—A large number of terracotta female figurines have been recovered from various Harappan sites. Some of them may be mere toys,[93] but most of them have religious sifnificance. They are identified to be Mother goddesses. Sir John Marshall believed them to represent a goddess with attributes very similar to those of great Mother Goddess.[94] The west Asian examples support the identification.[95] (Pl.XV, Fig. 38).

Fairservis believes that Mother Goddess worship and cult of bull and water ablution are the characteristic features of the Indus religion.[96] But ubiquitous and preponderant quantity of the female figurines over the male and bull conclusively confirm that Mother Goddess was the supreme deity of the people. Further researches reveal that the Indus religion centres round the cult of Mother Goddess.

(ii) Origin of Mother Goddess Cult—Archaeology asserts that in the Chalcolithic age the region between Indus to the Mediterranean and Nile was culturally homogeneous.[97] The range of kindred examples of the female figurines discovered in the Indus valley extends throughout in this region.[98] There is ample evidence from the old World to show that the cult of Mother Goddess must have originated somewhere in the fertile crescent. Anatolia and Persia singularly or jointly may be place of origin. The cult may be taken for granted to have entered Indian frontier from Persia alone.

It appears that the cult had widely diffused from Persia. But Marshall holds that the western Asia received the diffusionary impulses of the cult from Anatolia.[99] Even if this view is accepted, it does not deprive the claim of Persia being its original home but on the other hand it gives further support to our view. We know that Persia and Anatolia equally shared the origin of painted pottery and metallurgy.[100] It is most likely that they equally spread the origin of the cult of Mother Goddess. In all respects the cult appears to have speared from the highland of Anatolia and Persia.

Whatever had been its cradle it is to be admitted that it spread over Baluchistan and Indus Valley from Persia. E.G. James remarks, "The Iranian plateau by virtue of its geographical position was destined to become the connecting link between the west and the east in the development of a composite myth and ritual, as well as in other respect of a complex culture in which many streams met . . . lay . . . and to the east the plain of the Indus Valley with hill villages of Afghanistan and Baluchistan, Markan and Sind, to the west of the Punjab forming another line of communication with India. So placed in the very heart of the cradle land of the agricultural civilization of the western Asia the Iranian plateau hardly could fail to make its contribution to the development and diffusion of the Goddess cult which was firmly established in the peripheral regions of ancient Persia.[101]

(iii) Other Cults of the Indus People—The terracotta figurines, statues and some seals show that the fertility cult or tree, phallic, bull, and snake worships and the subordinate male god are also important religious beliefs of the Indus people.[102] The Mother Goddess figurines discovered from the south-west Persia, northern Iraq, Crete and Aegean show that the bull cult, snake worship, and the objects such as the double-axe and the dove are closely associated with the Mother Goddess.[103] This tends to show that the cult of Mother goddess pervades the religious beliefs of the Indus people.

(iv) Male God—The seals, pottery, sculptures and terracotta figurines recovered from the Harappan sites show the prevalence of a male god. He appears frequently horned.[104] and usually nude; only in a few cases wearing on the arms and neck bangles and necklaces,[105] with the generic organ prominently depicted.[106] He is recognized a prototype of the historic Siva.[107] One carved seal from Mohenjoaro shows a three-faced male deity sitting in Yoga posture on a low stool, wearing a number of bracelets on the arm, with horned-dress and penis exectus.[108] He is surrounded by animals, and identified as Pasupati.[109] The male god is three-faced showing the philosophical idea of triad or trinity in Hinduism (as Brahma, Vishnu and Siva). This is as old as the Harappan culture.[110] and bears close resemblaces to the triads of Sin, Shamash and Ishtar or of Anu, Enlil and Ea in the western Asia. In Minoan Crete the nameless god and goddess seldom accompany with lions or leopards and are known as the master or mistress of animals.[111] (pl. XXIX).

(v) Legend of Gilgamesh and Enkidu—Certain Sumerian seals show the fight between a nude demon-man and lions, which is recognised as a well-known legend describing deeds of a hero called Gilgamesh and his friend Enkidu.[112] This scene has parallel in some of Indus seals showing a half human fighting with tigers.[113] Marshall observes an unambiguous Sumerian influence in this scene.[114] Dr. Heinz[115] Mode has contradicted it. Piggot suspects a faint strain of common tradition.[116] In fact although animals chosen are different in the Sumerian and the Indian scenes, the two legends certainly have remote connection. The Sumerian legend most probably suffered certain variation in Persia. Frankfort tells that in Persia the old Mesopotamian theme of a hero between beasts has quite different form.[117] It stands to reason that India received the legend indirectly through Persia where the theme once filtered and filtered again when it reached India and during this the change might have occurred. (pl. XXX).

(vi) Animal Worship—Animal worship has a very remote history.[118] The totemism was once current throughout the world. (pl. XVII, XVIII, XIX, XX, XXI) Every ancient religion retained a trace of old conception of totemism in one form or the other.[119] That is why the animal worship occupied an important place among the religious beliefs of the ancient people.[120] The seals, sealings and terracotta figurines prove that several animals were worshipped in the Harappan culture and they range from natural species to that of mythical character.[121] The bull cult and the unicorn worship are the two noted features.

(vii) Bull Cult—The bull cult was once widely spread is borne out by the finds in Mesopotamia.[122] Persia,[123] Baluchistan[124] and the Indus Valley. Abundant quantity of bull figurines found in the Indus Valley leads Fairservis[125] to hold that the bull cult stands equally important as the Mother Goddess workship. The short horned and humped bulls were revered in the Indus religion.[126] The latter is now taken as a distinctive symbol of the Indus culture. It has been derived from Persia as may be observed on certain sherds found at Susa [127] and is also on some of the asphalt vases of Susa II.[128] Another unique feature of the animal worship in the Indus culture is that animals worshipped are invariably accompanied by a "manger."[129] A bone cylinder seal of the ''bull and manger" found at Susa II[130] displays close striking link between India and Iran. (Pl. XXI).

(viii) Unicorn Worship—The unicorn is believed to be a mythical animal.

With the exception of one from Harappa, the animal is shown with one horn.[131] A curious object an "incense burner" is usually connected with this animal, and a series of necklaces similar to those of Mother Goddess[132] and the ring bracelet[133] quite identical with those of three-faced god adorn the neck of the animal. (Pl. XXXVII) The worship of this mythical animal has a marked individuality which sets Indus culture apart from the ancient civilizations of the Ancient East. But O. Schrader traces the origin of this mythical animal from the sculptures at Persepolis[134] in Persia. It appears that it may have been borrowed from early Iran.

(ix) Snake Workship— There is enough evidence to prove that the snake was worshipped in Crete,[135] Persia, Mesopotamia[136] and in the Indus Valley.[137]

A faience sealing showing a snake deity has been discovered at Mohenjodaro[138] and snakes appear on some sherds found at Lothal.[139] One seal from Mohenjodaro shows a snake recoiling on a low dais of a tree,[140] and in another seal two snakes are seen following the persons in kneeling posture flanking the central deity.[141] Dr. Heinz Mode tells that snake is closely connected with Mother Goddess worship.[142]

(x) Cult of Fertility—The tree and phallic worship are the most important phases of the Mother Goddess cult. The association of tree worship with Mother Goddess is noticed in all ancient civilizations.[143] The finds from the Indus Valley display the same relationship. One of the seals shows a nude female standing between two branches of pipal tree, with a human headed goat and seven female ministrants.[144] Another seal shows a tree coming out from the vulva of the Goddess.[145] The pipal tree in India is recognised as a tree of knowledge under which Buddha got enlightenment.[146] The scholars believe that just like the concept of "tree of life" was the belief among the Sumerians and the Chaldians in Persia, the Harappans had a belief of a "tree of knowledge."[147]

(xi) Phallic Worship—The phallic worship which was once widely spread takes its origin from the Ancient East.[148] India affords clear evidence that the phallic worship which is connected with the Siva cult owes its origin to the Indus culture.[149] This is confirmed by the finds of stone phallies[150] in the Indus Valley. In Persia and Babylone[151] phallic amulets were very popular. (Pl. XXXI, XXXIII).

(xii) Dove—One very interesting figurine of Mother Goddess has been unearthed at Mohenjodaro, which is surrounded by doves.[152] This figurine bears close point of resemblance to the statues from Create and Tepe Hissar in Persia.[153]

(xiii) Disposal of The Dead—There is little common between the funerary practices prevalent in the Indus culture and the rest of the ancient world. The Persian practices initiated at Sialk[154] are traceable in the Indus Valley also where the deads were buried under the floor of house.[155] Marshall tells that Harappans disposed of their dead either by the method of complete burials or fractional burial or by cremation.[156] The complete or fractional burials of Mohenjodaro correspond exactly to those discovered at Nal. Piggot[157] tells that cemetery at Nal bears a close point of resemblance with the grave of R. 37 of Mohenjodaro regarding number of vessels as grave furniture and there was one brick-lined grave comparable with those at Nal.[158] The practice of complete or fractional burial discovered at Nal is quite identical with that of Musyan in western Persia.[159] These facts led the scholars[160] to arrive at the conclusion that the complete and fractional burials have been introduced to the Indus Valley by the people migrating from Baluchistan and Persia.[161]

The practice of cremation was not in vogue in the western Asia.[162] Still a link is traceable between funerary custom of Persia and the post cremation burials in the Indus Valley. Marshall identifies the Harappan practice of cremation with that at Mehi.[163] The cemetery at Mehi exhibits certain painted red ware vessels like flower-pot and shallow-footed cups which show Harappan affinities on the one hand and on the other hand to similar vessels in the Khurab cemetery in Persian Makran.[164]

(c) *Town Planning and Architecture* (Pl. -II)

The architecture and town planning of the Indus culture has a marked individuality which sets it quite apart from its contemporaries in the western Asia. In contrast to the lack of town planning,[165] irregular[166] streets and incipient system of drainage[167] in Ancient Asia, Harappan cities show a puzzling novelty in the elaborate and systematic scheme of town planning.[168] The streets[169] were planned on a fixed and regular system with highly advanced system of drainage.[170] On the other hand the Indus architecture was of a starting- utilitarian character without any architectural ornamentation.[171]

In spite of this individuality certain architectural similarities are traceable between the Harappan culture and Mesopotamia and Persia. It is known that mud-bricks had been invented in Persia.[172] Unlike the Sumerian plano-convex[173] the Harappan bricks[174] are comparable to the plain rectangular bricks of Iran.[175] 'L' shaped bricks used commonly in the bathrooms at Mohenjodaro[176] are similar in shape to those discovered from a wall at Susa in Persia.[177] Just like in Persia.[178] no Ziggurat or building of its type has been discovered in the Harappan settlements.[179] The corbelled arch is a common feature at Mohenjodaro and in the south-western Persia.[180] Mackay[181] traces the origin of the Harappan walls from the pise houses of the Sialk I and II phase. He recognizes.[182] the long and too high niches in the Harappan houses as ventilators and observes that similar ventilators were commonly used in houses in the Persian Gulf. The collegiate building of Mohenjodaro corresponds in general feature with the pillared halls at Susa.[183]

(d) Indus Ceramic

The most valuable contribution which the ancient Iran made to the urban civilization of the Ancient East is in the field of wheel-turned and painted pottery. Dr. Hall[184] says that the potter's hand-wheel originated in south-west Persia and "the epoch making invention of-the cart-wheel was also probably made there." The painted pottery takes its origin from Iran[185] and it spread widely to other far flung regions. (Pl. IV; Fig. 32-I-II-III-IV).

The pottery forms in the Harappan culture show little semblance with the pottery discovered in Persia or in Mesopotamia.[186] But it does not negative the influence from either countries. Archaeology reveals that ware of same origin underwent suitable modifications in shape in different countries. We know "the wares of even adjacent countries are seldom much alike in form."[187]

(i) Potter's Wheel—With the exception of a few examples of hand made pottery, the Harappan pottery is wheel turned.[188] It is fairly certain that foot-wheel was introduced in India during historic times by foreign invaders.[189] Certainly Harappans used the hand-wheel which is commonly now used nearly all over India.[190] It was most likely introduced into the Indus Valley from Persia where it was invented.[191]

(ii) Kiln—The Indus pottery is well baked. The kilns[192] found in the Harappan culture resemble those prevalent in ancient Persia. They were circular with a hole and furnance beneath the floor which was perforated and originally covered by a domed-roof.[193] They were evolved[194] from those found in Sialk III. They are notably comparable with those discovered at Susa in Persia.[195]

(iii) Method of Pottery—Making Generally pots were made in one piece, but certain jars made in two pieces. The rim was united to neck to complete it.[196] This typical making of jars in two or more parts is notably comparable to those found in Mesopotamia and at Susa and Musyan in Persia.[197]

(iv) Slip—The unpainted pottery usually shows slip of cream colour, occasionally of yellowish tinge or almost white.[198] The chocolate colour or pinkish slips[199] are met with but very rarely. Exceptionally the vessels had two coloured slips,[200] the brilliant red slip on the painted or unpainted Indus potteries was the rule[201] which corresponds exactly with the Mesopotamian wares and vessels from Musyan and Susa II in Persia.[202]

(v) Shape of Pottery—The pottery presents in various forms and shapes; The Indus pottery reveals remarkable similarities to the pottery found in Persia, for example: (Pl. XIV-XVI-XXV-XXVII; Fig. 31-III, 2, 3, 4; Fig, 32-I-II-III-IV; Fig. 13).

(1) The squat type of offering stand has wide diffusion in the Ancient East,[203] but its earliest example is traceable in the south Persia during the first period of Susa.[204]

(2) Spouted jars were popular in south-west Persia.[205] Mohenjodaro also presents two examples of similar spouted vessels.[206]

(3) The suspensary jars although rarely found at Mohenjodaro recall the similar design of the vases of Musyan in Persia.[207]

(4) A jar from Mohenjodaro, with squateness and the sharp angle between its shoulders and the body with its painting is similar with the corresponding ware of south-west Persia.[208]

(5) Mackay holds that jars termed as "scored pottery" most frequently found at Mohenjodaro ware meant for attachment to an appliance for raising water and they resemble exactly that is used in Persia. He further adds that water wheel in India is known as "Persian wheel" which suggests that it was introduced from that country.[209]

(6) The Iranian pottery shows the decoration by cutting, the decoration discerns from a Indus sherd[210] which is conceived to have once formed a part of a square stand similar to that discovered at Susa in Presia.[211]

(7) Although rarely, certain Indus vases[212] show the angular projection carination at the junction of shoulder and body.[213] This is the popular method of making ware in Musyan and Susa.[214]

(8) The high straight necks of a few Indus vessels recall the height of straight neck seen among the wares of Musyan and Susa II in Iran.[215]

(9) Mackay pointed out that handles were very rare among the wares of both countries.[216]

(10) The curious mode of ornamenting jars with knobs which is rarely found at Mohenjodaro[217] has a very wide geographical and long chronological range.[218] The earliest example of stuck-on knob is found to have been used for decorating certain wares in Susa I in Persia.[219]

(11) A theriomorphic vase in the form of a ram is only one of its finds discovered at Mohenjodaro[220] Such vessels are well-known in Persia, Anatolia and Mesopotamia.[221]

(12) The cups carved to immitate basketry are common at Susa in Persia and at Mohenjodaro.[222]

(13) A red slipped pedestalled bowl of distinctly Harappan shape and a dish of Harappan style have been unearthed from a grave in the neighbourhood of Bakun in Persia.[223]

(14) A fragment of an engraved greenish grey steatite vessel which had two compartments had been discovered at Mohenjodaro. The design on it is exactly the same as found on one part of the complete double steatite vessel discovered at Susa.[224] (Fig. 14).

(vi) Painted Pottery—The. above comparison is referred to the early phase of the Indus culture. It is interesting to note that painted Indus pottery bears the Iranian influence to a far greater degree as enumerated below: (Pl.XV, Pl.

XXV; Pl. XXVII; Pl.XXVI; Pl.XVI; Fig. 32-III-3, 4-IV-6,8,9)

(A) Paste—The paste, of which the painted pottery at Mohenjodaro was made, was tempered with either lime or sand. The former was very common.[225] The same was used in Susa. II.[226]

(B) Arrangement of Motifs—Not only certain motifs but the device of the decoration on the painted pottery at Mohenjodaro bears a close point of resemblance to that of Iranian pottery. Mackay says that there is a tendency in the Indus pottery to arrange the motifs in horizontal registers rather than in the vertical panels, which is a common feature in the south-west Persian pottery.[227]

(c) Motifs—The designs on a large number of the Indus painted pottery are almost conventionalized[228] like the Iranian pottery. (Fig. 20-VI-XVI; Fig. 19-XXXVI-XXXII-XXXIII-XXV-XXVI).

(1) Animal Motifs—The zones of ibex or other animals are one of the most characteristic features of the Iranian sites, i.e., Giyan, V, Sialk III and Hisar 1.[229] There is every reason to attribute animal file motifs to the Iranian influence. The ibex was a popular decorative motif on the Indus wares. The ibex zones appear on the ware at Karchat, Shah-jo-Kotiro and Chanhu-daro in the Indus Valley.[230] The painted pottery of Bampur in Persia was persistingly ornamented with zones of ibex figures.[231] One sherd found at Mohenjodaro shows the representation of ibex with long curling horns, whose tips touch the back quite similarly as in the representation of animal on the wares of Susa I.[232] The ibex horns as repititive pattern appear on the pottery at Lohri, Ghazi Shah and Pandiwahi in the Indus Valley.[233] The similar horn motifs are found on the pottery at Tal-i-Bakun, Talli-Par, Haraj[234] and Shahi Tump at Khurab[235] in Persia. Majumdar[236] tells us that ibex whose male has "scimitar shaped horns curved backwards" does not belong at all to the Indus plain nor to the region east of the Indus.[237] its habitat is in the rocky hills of Persia and Baluchistan. He further says.[238] In this chain of evidence leading us from Persia to the valley of Indus we should probably recognize a proof of migration of an ibex knowing people from beyond western land of Sind." The cross hatching of bodies of animals was customary at Mohenjodaro. It also appears on the pottery of Jemdet-Nasr, Musyan and Susa I in Iran.[239]

(2) Bird Motif—The bird motifs are commonly used on the pottery from south-west Persia.[240] The frequent use of the 'V' motif at' Mohenjodaro is believed to be a degraded form of bird motif.[241]

(3) Fish Motif—The fish representation commonly appears on ivory model or on seals, and only once on the pottery at Mohenjodaro. It is a common device on the pottery from south-west Persia.[242]

(4) Plant or Tree Motif— The plant or tree in one form or other was a most favourite motif in the Harappan culture. Mohenjodaro pottery exhibits the plant mostly in a naturalistic form.[243] But the conventionalized.[244] plant motif is

not unknown there. The conventional form of plant with angularity is the common representation of tree on the Susain pottery.[245] One of the most characteristic features of pottery at Bampur in Persia is the tree with fringed branches.[246] The wares at Ghazi Shah in the Indus Valley show the palm trees in stylized form with the head arrow top to the tree, a marked peculiarity of this pottery recalls upturned fringes of Iranian motif.[247] V.G. Childe tells that pipal tree supplements palm tree in the Harppan culture.[248] Still the Iranian influence is manifest from both types of pipal with heap of earth at the foot of trees, which is the characteristic feature of early Harappan pottery at Chanhu-daro, Loham-jo-daro and other sites in Sind.[249] (Fig. 19-XXI-XXII; Fig. 32-III-X).

(5) Triangles—The triangle was not a common form of decoration at Mohenjodaro. The hatching of the interior of the triangle is somewhat identical with the Iranian device.[250] The double triangles are also one of the decorative motifs of the Harappan pottery, which is very commonly used at Jemdet Nasr, Musyan and Giyan.[251] Especially in borders, this double triangles decoration is usually put at regular intervals around a jar between vertical lines.[252] The same arrangement appears on the pottery at Susa in Iran.[253] (Fig. 19-XXI-XXII; Fig. 19-XXIV) Fig. 17; Fig. 11)

(6) Intersecting Circles—The intersecting circles are very popular on the Harappan pottery.[254] Mackay described it as made of a numerous linked four petalled device.[255] A notably identical geometric design appears on every seal of Susa.[256] An archaic seal from Susa exhibits a single four-petalled rosette which in Mohenjodaro always occurs in the continuous design.[257]

(7) Chequers—Chequer pattern is likely a derivative from basket works. It was as commonly used at Mohenjodaro as at Jemdet Nasr and Musyan in Persia.[258] (Fig. 7).

(8) Comb Motif—The motif which shows unambiguous Iranian influence on the Harappan pottery is the comb design. It is very common on the pottery of Mohenjodaro. Its earliest example with frequent use is found on the pottrey of Susa I,[259] Its representations at Mohenjodaro and Susian pottery are exactly sirnilar.[260] (Fig. 19-XXIX-XXXV; Fig. 30-XXXVI).

(9) Solar Motif—The solar motif is occasionally used on the Harappan pottery.[261] A remarkably identical design is found on a sherd from Susa II[262] and on a sherd from Musyan.[263]

(10) Swastika and Maltese Squares—Swastika and Maltese squares patterns are common features in Harappan culture and Susa I in Persia.[264]

(11) Lozenges and Sigmas Patterns—The 'lozenges; and 'sigmas' patterns found on the Harappan painted pottery at Ghazi Shah are identical with the design on the pottery of Persia and Mesopotamia.[265]

(D) Borders—The pottery of Mohenjodaro exhibits that a border separating various designs is formed by the zigzag pattern being placed between vertical or horzontal lines.[266] (Fig. 11) This pattern appears only on the pottery of Susa and Musyan.[267] The Susain pottery presents this motif in a much bolder form.[268] The zigzag pattern on the pottery of Mohenjodaro[269] is composed of groups of parallel lines. It is exactly similar to those on Sistan pottery in Persia.[270]

(l) Loops—The loop motif used commonly on the Mohenjodaro pottery is usually attached to an upper line.[271] This motif is found at Musyan and Susa in Iran where double loops occur.[272] A sherd from Mohenjodaro presents double wavy lines hatched in the middle.[273] A similar design is frequently used on Musyan vessels and occasionally on Susa pottery.[274]

(2) Hemispherical Borders—These motifs have been elaborated from the loop line border. This is a common motif at Mohenjodaro and its variations appear on the Sistan[275] pottery. The origin of this pattern is traced from well known Susian motifs of a file of birds lying on ground or water.[276]

(3) Bead Borders—The bead border is well represented at Mohenjodaro. A jar from Musyan in Persia.[277] exhibits a similar border and a slight modification of it is found in Sistan.[278] The Mohenjodaro pottery shows another type of this motif with lozenge shapped beads which is commonly used at Susa II in Persia.[279]

(4) Hemisphere and Triangle Borders—This border is a common featur at Mohenjodaro and with a slight modification is found at Sistan[280] only.

(5) Borders of Triangles with Inverted side—This motif is always accmpanied with leaves in the Harappan culture. The similar motif without leaves occurs on the pottery at Sistan and Musyan in Persia.[281]

(6) Miscellaneous Borders—Mohenjodaro presents a curious border of plain lines interspacing other lines set at right angles.[282] A sherd from Sistan presents the same idea.[283] Mohenjodaro renders another type of this border with vertical lines interspaced with straight or small curved markings.[284] Exactly similar markings occur on the Persian pottery of Susa and Musyan.[285]

(e) Harappan Seals

The Harappan seals are square and undoubtedly come into the class of stamp seals.[286] (Pl. XVIII, XIX, N, XVII, III, XX, XXI).

The earliest examples of the stamp seals are seen in Syria and Iran,[287] Surely, the stamp seals were popular in Iran. Besides the painted pottery, the Harappan seals also reveal the Iranian inspiration. They resemble the Iranian seals in shape and technique. The use of the identical seals in the two countries so much impressed Piggot that he, for origin of the Indus culture, looked to Iran. He wrote, "The fact that the Harappan culture is characterised by stamp seals should indicate that its eventual antecedents are likely to be found in Persia.[288]

His view gets an additional support from the pattern of Harappan seals which are remarkably identical with those of Iranian seals. The Swastika design is notably, common on the Harappan button seals. Its origin, though undoubtedly tantalizing, can be traced in Persia where its earliest example either in its simple form or in its derivatives[289] appears on the pottery of Susa and Musyan.[290] The arms of Swastika further strengthen this view. Mohenjodaro agrees with Iran in the direction of arms of the Swastika. For in both countries arms of the Swastika are found drawn clockwise or anti-clockwise indifferently.[291] The other patterns on Harappan button seals find their corresponding examples in Persia. One such seal[292] has a pattern–consisting of a number of squares set inside the other, which is common at Susa.[293] A cylinderical seal from Susa bears the identical stepped triangle motif as appears on two Harappan button seals.[294] Another button seal bears a design consisting of two parallel lines enclosed in a square and linked up in the middle by rough scratches.[295] This motif exactly corresponds with that on a jar at Susa.[296]

The cubical seals at Mohenjodaro usually bear the motif consisting of a series of parallel lines crossing one another at various angles.[297] This motif is exceedingly common in Persia where it is traceable on the clay sealing at Susa.[298] The comb motif which is characteristic feature of Persia appears amongst Harappan characters on the Harappan seals.[299] The short horned bull is a very favourite motif on Harappan seals and is usually accompanied by a manger, the use of which is a characteristic of the art of the Harappan cluture.[300] A bone cylinderical seal from Susa II bears exactly similar motif of the 'bull and manger.[301] Langdon[302] believes it to be of Persian origin alone. Some seals show humped bull marvellously carved. It also appears carved on archaic bitumen vessels from Susa.[303]

A file of animals, which is a very favourite motif on seals of Persia appears on clay sealings at Mohenjodaro.[304] Some copper tablets exhibit antelope in a typical attitude with his head turned to look back.[305] This design is a characteristic feature of the Elamite art in Persia.[306] Some seals also bear the representation of composite animals. Mackay believes that they had been invented in the south west Persia.[307] Some well-known interesting seals show a hero usually almost nude gripping a tiger on either side of him. The seals from Persia and Mesopotamia represent exactly similar scene where the tiger is replaced with lion. It is commonly agreed that these seals show unimpeachable Iranian influence.[308] A Harappan seal exhibiting a design consisting of an animal intimately connected with the sun-disc, bears a close point of resemblance to the similar seal in Susa.[309] A cylinderical seal bears a representation of scorpion which is akin to that of an early sherd from the west Persia.[310]

One seal bears Greek cross, which is found in the south-west Persia.[311] The former seal[312] has the design consisting of intersecting lines in the centre of the cross. The exactly similar motif is seen on seals at Susa.[313] Mackay takes this motif on the seal as a simple modification of the double Greek crosses which is very common in very early times in Persia.[314] He tells further that. "At Mohenjodaro at Harappa ... the device was borrowed probably from Elam where it was more frequently used than any where else throughout a very long period."[315]

One seal[316] exhibits a boat in which the human figure with a steering car on the poop of the boat is represented as the high off the seat. Exactly the same arrangement is noticeable on the archaic seals of Susa.[317] On the back of the boat, the seal shows a number of irregular rectangles or squares formed by scoring with lines. This motif is well known on the early seals in Sumer and Persia.[318] Another seal[319] shows the curious skirl device which is closely allied to the similar device on the pottery of Susa I.[320] One clay amulet from Mohenjodaro shows similar angular twist as appears on a proto-Elamite tablet at Susa.[321] (Mackay pl. XC, 23, 24) One seal bears the inverted position of animals, which is a very favourite motif in the art of the archaic period in south-west Persia.[322] The engraving of animal on this seal with the aid of a drill recalls the well-known technique on the early seals in Sumer and Persia.[323]

A copper tabloid from Mohenjodaro exhibits a very interesting hunting scene in which the hunters face an animal with bows and arrows; the animal has already been struck by arrows sticking in its body. This scene corresponds exactly with that on a seal from Susa.[324] A seal from Chanhu-daro bears a motif consisting of a bull over a portrait of a human body. This motif is exactly found in an Iranian stamp seal.[325] One cylinderical seal found at Hissar bears the design of Indian humped bull.[326]

(f) Terracotta objects

The various terracotta objects including human figurines and model animals have, in abundance, been discovered in the Harappan sites. The human figurines possess their own peculiarity but certain features betray their relationship with other countries. (Pl. XV, XXIV, XIII).

(i) Human Figurines—The male figure is notably rare. The well-known terracotta figurines of Mother Goddess are found at all levels. Not only in the Harappan culture but almost in all ancient civilizations, the terracotta figurines were coloured red. [327] (Pl.XXIV-XXIII).

(1) Hair—The Indus figurines show various ways of hair styles, for example, in a pigtail hanging down the back a twisted lock is carried down from the forehead to the side of the head. A figurine from Mohenjodaro shows the beard coiled inward at the end, which is exactly identical with that of a male figurine from Susa I in Persia.[328]

(2) Horned Mask—Horned masks as discovered in the Indus Valley appear to have had great popularity and wide diffusion. These horned masks are convincingly comparable with metal masks discovered at Susa in Persia.[329]

(3) Kilt—The Indus female figurines are seen usually wearing a short kilt which is either plain or occasionally decorated with medallions. The proto-Elamites in Persia used the same type of garment.[330]

(4) Jewellery—The Indus terracotta figurines are seen loaded with jewellery. The bracelets and necklaces of two or more strings of beads with pendant are

very common. The female figuriness found in Persia wear similar bracelets and necklaces of strings of beads with rosetted pendant in the middle.[331] (PI. V; Fig. 33; Fig. 34). (PI. XXXIII).

(5) Steatopygia— Certain female figurines from Mohenjodaro and Harappa show heavy buttocks which are parallel to those unearthed in Persia.[332]

(ii) Terracotta Figurines of Animals and Birds— Among animal models the short horned bull was exceedingly common. Humped bull that is one of the characteristic features of the Harappan culture comes next in popularity. The Indus culture is very closely related to Persia is, borne out by the fact that it is Persia where early examples of terracotta figurines of humped bulls are found at Susa.[333] Certain models of dogs found at the lower levels in the Indus Valley have long faces, upright tails and prick ears.[334] These figurines appear to be true copy of archaic Elamite sealings.[335] Turtle is believed sacred[336] in the Indus Valley and its terracotta models were discovered there. At Susa it is shown in relief on the rim of a pottery jar holding two snakes by the neck with its front flippers.[337] This reflects further link between India and Iran where the turtle was venerated.

The clay models of monkey have been unearthed in the Indus Valley in large numbers. This animal model shows a very close relationship between India and Persia. The earliest example of the model of monkey in stone is found in Persia at Susa.[338]

Ram is another scared animal that is represented both in the pottery and faience in the Indus Valley but it appears on early seals of Babylonia and Persia.[339] The model of dove was very common in the Indus Valley. It is represented with outstretched wings sitting on a pedestal with a flared base. This model shows very close Iranian affinities.[340]

The bird whistles are very common in the Indus Valley. The hollow bird models have holes at the tail. Persia, too, presents similar birds whistles. This common resemblance confirms the strong Persian influence.[341]

(g) Ornaments

The jewellery unearthed in the Indus Valley is not found in abundance but exceedingly interesting as it displays relationship with other countries. (Fig. 33; Fig. 34) (Pl. XXXIII).

(i) Beads— The Indus culture presents the beads of various materials. The beads of vitreous paste, a material allied to faience had been ever common through the occupation of Mohenjodaro.[342] Exactly similar beads have been unearthed at Susa in Persia.[343]

The etched carnelian beads of similar shape as found at Mohenjodaro appear at Shah Tepe and Hissar III in Persia.[344] Certain etched carnelian beads discovered at Mohenjodaro bear the design consisting of three joined amulets in the motif. both with and without the inner circles are exceedingly common in the early art of the south-east Persia.[345]

Segmented beads discovered at Harappa bear a close point of resemblance to those at Shah Tepe in Persia.[346] The design of black line on white ground appearing on a very unusual type of bead discovered at Mohenjodaro is paralleled to similar motif on beads at Bampur in Persia.[347] The coiled wire beads are rarely found at Mohenjodaro. These coiled wire beads either cylinderical or barrel shaped were very favourite at Tchila-Khane in Persia.[348] The terracotta beads imitating wire beads are fairly frequent finds at Mohenjodaro. The popularity of this bead here displays unambiguous Persian influence. For in early Persia at Susa I, the paste spiral cylinder bead derived from coiled wire bead was equally common.[349] Certain most interesting inlaid beads with trefoil design from Mohenjodaro recall the motif represented on a painted sherd at Tchechme-Ali in Persia.[350]

(ii) Terminals—The terminals of necklaces used at Mohenjodaro are generally made of metal. The triangular terminal is. the favourite form, but the flattened, hemispherical terminals are most interesting and important. No evidence of such terminals is traceable in Sumer,[351] but Persia renders the example of these terminals where depiction of these terminals is discernible on some painted sherds from Tepe Douecya near Susa.[352]

(iii) Pendent—A steatite pendent discovered at Harappa reveals a striking link between India and the Ancient East. The figure of an eagle with widespread wings and extended legs is carved on this pendent. This pattern is well known in India, Sumer and Persia. The pattern, though appears on a few seals[353] is comparatively rare in the Indus Valley. This pattern was a favourite motif on the painted pottery of Susa 1.[354] The pattern was known in Persia during 5000 to 4000 BC. This is borne out by its earliest example occurring on a sherd found in Iran belonging to an earlier period than Susa.L[355] This fact led Mackay to arrive at the conclusion that this eagle motif originated in the Highlands of Persia and both India and Sumer borrowed it from there.[356]

(iv) Fillets—Fillets have been discovered at Mohenjodaro. The gold fillets with perforated ends are commonly found at Mohenjodaro. The surprisingly exact resemblance of these fillets to their counterparts from Persia displays a very close striking link between the two countries.[357]

(v) Finger-rings—Finger-rings are rare at Mohenjodaro. One important finger-ring deserves to be mentioned, which is made of four continuous coils of fine copper wire and its ends are not meeting nor coming opposite each other. Similar rings made of silver and copper are found in ancient Persia and Mesopotamia.[358]

(vi) Studs for Nose or Ears—Various types of studs which are believed to be nose or ear ornament have been found at Mohenjodaro. A peculiar form of the stud, usually made of faience-is very common in the Indus Valley; it consists of a disc with knob at the back bearing the divided circle design.[359] This motif is well known on the Indus pottery but unknown elsewhere [360] except Persia where it appears on the pottery of Susa I.[361]

(vii) Bracelets—The bracelets made of different materials have been found at the Harappan sites. One type of bracelet is the most interesting and bears a striking link-between India and Persia and Mesopotamia. The Curious kink occurs in certain bracelets of this type found at Mohenjodaro. Exactly similar gold bracelets have been found at Susa[362] in Persia.

(viii) Hair-pins—Hair-pins of various materials were used by the Harappans. Certain hair-pins of distinctive design deserve to be described. They were flattened and coiled round four times to make the head. The hair-pins quite identical to this type are exceedingly common in Sumer, at the Caucasus[363] in the northern Persia in Egypt[364] and at Mohenjodaro.

(h) Miscellaneous Objects

Besides this unambiguous Iranian influence traced hitherto, there are various objects of common resemblance in the Indus Valley and ancient Persia, which strengthen the idea that antecedents of the Harappa culture should be looked for in Persia. A large number of appliances, tools and other objects of the Harappan culture, used in domestic life, show the diffusionary impulses which were introduced from Iran. The following examples may be cited: (Fig. 21XXI-XXII-XXIII-XXVl; Pl. VI; Fig. 8-II; Fig. 18-c; Pl. XIII).

(i) Shaft hole Axe—The shaft hole axe undoubtedly originated in Sumer, but such axes made of metal are totally absent in the Indus Valley. Certainly Mohenjodaro presents a similar terracotta model which seems to represent a form of the shaft hole axe.[365] This axe made its appearance besides in Sumer but also found in Al-Ubaid, Jemdet Nasr, and Persia.[366]

(ii) Flat Axes—Unlike the Sumerian example, the axes found at Harappa are the simplest flat type. Flat axes have remote history in Persia, which appeared during 5000 to 4000 BC throughout the country nearly in all the ancient sites such as Sialk III, Hissar I c. Giyan V c and Susa.[367] The Harappan axes are the true copy of precise forms of Persian flat axes, Piggot said, "It appears, therefore, that Harappan civilization was based on some culture which had inherited the early Iranian tradition of primitive flat copper or bronze axes."[368]

(iii) Axe-adze—One socketed axe-adze appears at Mohenjodaro. The socketed weapons are quite common in Sumer but Mohenjodaro. example displays Persian rather than Sumerian influence because precisely similar type of axe-adze with exactly long collared shaft has been unearthed at Tepe-Hissar.[369]

(iv) Blade axes—The blade axes of long and narrow type but slightly splayed edges and straight sides and butts unearthed at Harappa and Mohenjodaro show strong Persian influence, The early: examples of exactly similar weapons came from Susa 1.[370] The slightly tapered and parallel sided form of the broad form of Susa has been found at Mohenjodaro.[371]

(v) Spear-head—A copper spear head of precisely Harappan style has been discovered in a grave in midway between Bakun and Shahi Tump in Persia.[372]

(vi) Mace-head—Two mace-heads, one plain and the other with incised decoration found at Chanhu-daro, correspond exactly with those from Susa.[373] The lentoid type of mace-head is very common at Mohenjodaro. Similar mace-head made in lime-stone has been found at Susa,[374] but no example occurs in ancient sites of Mesopotamia.[375] Bioconical holes in certain mace-heads found at Mohenjodaro are similar to those known in the mace-heads of Mesopotamia, Persia and Egypt.[376]

(vii) Sling pellets—The ovoid and round sling pellets were commonly used by the Harappans. Similar sling-balls have been found in ancient Sumer,[377] Turkestan,[378] and at Susa in Persia.[379] Herzfeld discovered precisely similar ovoid sling balls on the Iranian plateau belonging to 5000 to 4000 BC.[380]

(viii) Chisels—Chisels of the several forms usually made of copper and occasionally of bronze apear in the Harappa culture. But no true[381] chisel or a simple sloped chisel as used in the early Egypt has been found at Mohenjodaro.[382] They have double slopes. Similar chisels appear at Susa in the early Persia and Mesopotamia.[383]

(ix) Pins or rods with the representation of Animals—Bronze pins or rods have been found at Harappa, Mohenjodaro and Chanhu-daro with ornamentation in a distinctive manner.[384] (Fig. 8-I), They had been ornamented with either spiral tops or representations of animals. These peculiar objects are well known finds in the ancient civilizations and belong to the great province of barbarian metal work extending from the Caucasus to Turkestan.[385] Where this metal work originated baffles the scholars to great extent; nevertheless Piggot very ingeniously traced it from the Highlands of Iran.[386]

(x) Querns—Saddle querns with base roughly trimmed are very common at Harappa and Mohenjodaro. Similar querns appear at Susa in Persia, at Ur in Mesopotamia and at Anau in Turkestan.[387]

(xi) Measure—Barrel-shaped weights usually made of hard black stones have been found though rarely but at both Harappa and Mohenjodaro. Similar weights made of lime stone are exceedingly common in early times in Persia and Mesopotamia and also found in Egypt.[388]

The scholars are inclined to believe unanimously that the system employed for weights and linear measures in the Indus civilization was either binary or decimal.[389] A purely decimal system appears to have been in use in Persia where it is found on Proto-Elamite tablets.[390] There is every reason to believe that the decimal system came to Indus culture from Persia; the latter is the immediate neighbour country of India. It is hardly likely that it was other way about.[391] Frankfort claims that if this assumption turns out to be correct, it becomes an unimpeachable truth that culture that shaped Indus civilization originated in the Highlands of Persia.[392]

(xii) Spindle Whorls—Spindle-whorls usually made of terracotta with one or two or three perforations in the middle have been found at Mohenjodaro in abundance. The spindle-whorls with single hole in the middle occur at Jemdet Nasr in Mesopotamia[393] and at Susa in Persia;[394] The hole type appears in Mesopotamia[395] Turkestan[396] and in south-west Persia.[397] Certain two or three holes whorls found at Mohenjodaro bear a deep groove, the purpose of which is unknown. An exactly similar shallow groove is visible around the edge of a whorl found at Susa in Iran.[398]

(xiii) Writing Tablets—Two terracotta tablets have been unearthed at Mohenjodaro, the use of which is as yet uncertain. Mackay suspects that they are writing tablets.[399] An archaic Persian cylinder seal from Susa bears the representation of two similar objects.[400]

(xiv) Ivory Plaque—An ivory plaque found at Mohenjodaro bears the representation of a male figure facing to the left with hands on hip.[401] Here Iranian influence is manifest clearly. The archaic seals from Susa exhibit the human figures in the same forrn.[402]

(xv) Shell Inlay—The stepped design appears in the certain pieces of Indus shell inlay work. This design does not occur either on painted pottery of Mohenjodaro or Mesopotamia.[403] This design again links up India and Iran. During 4000 BC. it is found on the painted pottery of Susa 1.[404]

Cross design is another motif of Indus shell inlay works. In Persia this motif with arms of equal length is known on the seals[405] and painted pottery of Susa.[406] This design with one cross inside another from Mohenjodaro bears closer points of resemblance to its counterpart in Persia.[407] Herzfeld tells that this motif survived on the Persian pottery up to 2000 BC[408] The rossette motif of the Indus shell inlay works is found at Mohenjodaro, Mesopotamia Egypt and Assyria and its prototype in the early Persia.[409] The Indus shell inlay work presents a design of fretted. roundals which is unknown in Mesopotamia.[410] But Mackay thinks that this motif came from Persia and derived from the cross enclosed in a circle that appears on the pottery of Susa I.[411]

Some pieces of shell inlay showing eye design found at Mohenjodaro are precisely similar to the pieces of ivory that were unearthed beneath the foundation of a temple at Susa.[412] A variety of the Indus shell inlay work shows another close relationship with Iran and India.[413] Pieces of shell segments have been found at Mohenjodaro. Mackay remarks, "These pieces of shell seem to have once decorated handles in a similar manner to the pieces of shell which were strung on stout copper wire alternately with similar shaped pieces of some other material to form certain wand like objects found in early Sumer and Elam.[414]

In the foregoing survey a close relationship between the Indus culture and those of early Iran and Mesopotamia has been traced. The study of Indus religion, seals, ceramics and other aspects of culture shows that Sumer is not the author of the Indus culture. The painted pottery, terracotta bird whistle, seals, flat type of axe hand-wheal, animal file motifs, 'comb' and 'step' patterns, the Mother Goddess cult, unicorn worship and the mode of disposal of the dead and absence of the ziggurat type of buildings, shaft-hole axe and ass-drawn vehicle are positive evidences to prove that essential roots of the Indus culture are Iranian and not Mesopotamian. It has already been shown that the archaeological evidence ruled out any direct intercourse between Sumer and India at such a remote period when the Indus culture had already developed into a full-fledged civilization.

We know that in Iran, the cultures found at Sialk, Susa, Hissar and Giyan expose the traits or their prototypes that generally help in making a civilization, the seeds of which were planted all over Iranian Plateau. However, the unfavourable condition of the plateau was a retarding factor and operated to hinder its full flowering.[415] The recent excavations in the border-land of India and Iran makes it clear that these prototypes of civilization travelled from Persia to India where it fully developed and was completely Indianized. In the light of this fact the unique and puzzling nature of the Indus culture which shows close affinity to the cultures of Iran and Sumer in general but is equally different in detail, can satisfactorily be accounted for.

That the Indus culture developed on Indian soil can hardly be doubted. Its roots evolved at Kot-Diji in Sind, in the village cultures of Baluchistan and at Nadi-i-Ali and Mundigak in Afghanistan.[416] It therefore, suggests as has already been shown that the earlier phases of Baluch prehistoric cultures, which largely shaped the Harappan culture, are Iranian and later on, however, Indianizaion took place. Afghanistan passed through the same stages. Mundigak in south Afghanistan reveals three phases of the culture, the earliest and succeeding phase display Iranian influence whereas the third phase shows the influence of the Indus culture.

That the Indus civilization is the latest in a long development of the prototypes of Harappan traits in the Baluch prehistoric cultures seems to be fairly certain.[417] It is most significant that bulk of the Baluch prehistoric cultures vanished when Indus culture was flourishing.[418] The Indus civilization is the most Indianized though its essential roots are Iranian.[419] This Indianization diffused to Anau, Baluchistan and Afghanistan with the later phases of their cultures.[420]

In contrast to the Sumerian urban agricultural civilization, the Harappan agriculture supported-urban civilization presents the village culture differing in no way essential features from those of Iranian Plateau.[421] These facts constrain us to believe what Piggot says, "It must be noted that all evidence is consistent with the ultimate derivation of the prehistoric culture of north-west India from Iran."[422]

References

1. *Mohenjodaro and the Indus Civilization,* Preface, VIII, Vol. I, (London, 1931).
2. *Early India and Pakistan,* pp. 3 and 10, (London, 1959).
3. The *Origin of Ancient Civilization and Toynbee's Theories,* "Diogenes," No. 13, p. 88, (1956).
4. *Prehistoric India,* p. 141, (1950).
5. W.A. *Fairseris, The Harappan Civilization,* "New Evidence and More Theory", American Museum Novitates, No. 2055, pp. 7–8 (New Yark 1961).
6. D.H. Gordon, *Prehistoric Background of Indian Culture,* p. 58.
7. *Prehistoric Background of Indian culture,* p. 58.
8. *A Study of History,* Vol. II, p. 88.
9. M. Wheeler, op, cit.
10. A. Ghosh, "The Indus Civilization–Its Origin, Authors, Extent and Chronology," Indian Prehistory, 1964, *Deccan College Building Centenary and Silver Jublee Series* No. 32, p. 113.
11. The Indus Civilization, Cambridge History of India, Supplementary Volume, p. 17 (Cambridge 1922).
12. S.N. Kramer, *Expedition,* Vol. III, p. 51.
13. E.J.H. Mackay, *Further Excavation at Mohenjodaro,* Vol. I, pp. 639-41, (Delhi, 1938).
14. Sir John Marshal, op. cit., p. 48.
15. W.A. Fairservis, op. cit., p. 15.
16. H.R. Hall, *The Ancient History of the Near East,* 5th ed. 1922.
17. *Studies in Proto–Indo Mediterranean Culture,* (Bombay 1953)
18. *Mohenjodaro and the Indus Civilization,* pp. 109–110.
19. Cf. *Cambridge History of India,* p. 42 (1922).
20. "Race Movement and Prehistoric Culture," *The Vedic age,* p. 156; *The Cultural Heritage of India,* New Series, Vol. I, pp. 80–81.
21. "Some Reflections on Dravidians and Aryans," *Bulletin of the Institute of Historical Research Madras,* II (1963), pp. 225–34.
22. T.N. Ramchandran, *Presidential Address to Section I of the Indian History Congress 19th Session,* Agra, 1956, p. 7.
23. Marshall, op. cit., pp. 110–111.
24. *Rigveda,* X.99.3; VII, 21.5
25. Marshall, op. cit., p. III.
26. *Mohenjodaro and the Indus Civilization,* pp. 638–644.
27. S. Piggot, op. cit., p. 140.
28. R.E.M. Wheeler, "Harappa, 1946," *Ancient India,* No.3, pp. 91–95.
29. N.G. Majumdar, Exploration in Sind, *Memoir Archaeological Survey of India,* No. 48, pp. 26–27 (1924).
30. Ibid., pp. 85–95.
31. Mac Cown Donald E and Krishna Deva, Ancient India, No. 5.
32. D.H. Gordon, "Sialk, Giyan, Hissar and its Indian Connections," *Man in India,* Vol XXVII, No. 3, pp. 209–17.
33. Dr. Y.D. Sharma, Prehistoric Remains, Archaeological Remains, "*Monuments and Museums,*" Part I, pp. 4–5 (Delhi, 1964).
34. N.G. Majumdar, op. cit., Pls. XXII. 11, XXXVII, 15 and 24 XXXVIII, 32 and 37, D.H. Gorddon, *Prehistoric Background of Indian Culture,* p. 38.
35. V.G. Childe, op. cit, p. 201.
36. Piggot, op. cit., p.128.
37. Ibid.
38. D.H. Gordon. "Silak, Giyan, Hissar and its Indian Connections." *Man in India,* Vol. XXVII, No. 3, p. 215.

39. E.J.H. Mackay, *Chan-hu-daro Excavation*, pl. 44, 2, pl. 45 and 81, (Connecticut, 1943).
40. D.H. Gordon, op. cit., p. 230.
41. D.H. Gordon, *Prehistoric background of the Indian Culture*, p. 42.
42. Ibid., p. 46.
43. Piggot, op. cit., p. 93.
44. Ibid., p. 94.
45. Ibid., p. 95.
46. D.H. Gordon, Sialk, Giyan, Bissar and Its Indian Connections, *Man in India*, Vol. XXVII, No.3, p. 229.
47. Piggot, op. cit., p. 92.
48. Ibid.
49. Ibid.
50. Ibid.
51. V.G. Childe, op. cit., p. 201.
52. D.H. Gordon, *Prehistoric Background of Indian Culture*, p. 48.
53. S. Piggot, op, cit., pp. 106–7.
54. Ibid., p. 111.
55. D.H. Gordon, Sialk, Giyan, Bissar and its Indian Connections, *Man in India*, Vol. XXVII, No.3, p. 229.
56. Ibid., p. 227.
57. Ibid., p. 229.
58. Ibid., p. 230.
59. Ibid., p. 219.
60. N.G. Majumdar, op.cit., pp. 27–38 (1934).
61. D.H. Gorodon, *Prehistoric Background of the Indian, Culture*, p. 47.
62. F.A. Khan, "Preliminary Report on Kot Diji Excavation, 1957–48, p. 17 (fllustrated London News, 1958).
63. M. Wheeler, "Barappa 1946" Ancient India, No. 3, p. 118, fig. 24, 10; M. Vats, Excavation at Harappa, II, pl. LXXIV, 14 (New Delhi, 1940).
64. J. Marshall, Mohenjodaro and the Indus Civilization, III, p. 58, pl. LXXIXI (London, 1931).
65. M. Wheeler, op. cit, and M. Vats, op. cit.
66. M. Wheeler, op. cit, p. 92, fig. 8, 9.
67. Marshall, op. cit., p. 58, pl. LXXIXI.
68. A. Ghosh, op. cit, p. 116.
69. Mackay, Further Excavation at Mohenjodaro, I, pl. LVIII,5, 8, 9 and 13; pl. LIX, 31 and LXXIV, 14.
70. A. Ghosh, op. cit, p. 115.
71. F.A. Khan, op. cit.
72. W.A. Fairservis, *Archaeological Survey in Zhob and Loralai Distt. West Pakistan*, p. 269, fig. 59 (New Yark 1959).
73. A. Ghosh, op. cit., p. 115.
74. W.A. Fairservis, op. cit., p. 7.
75. N.G. Majumdar, op. cit., pp. 20–30.
76. S. Piggot, op. cit., p. 77.
77. Ibid., p. 88.
78. Ibid., p. 79.
79. W.A. Fairservis, loc. cit., p. 11.
80. Ibid.
81. S. Piggot, loc. cit., p. 78.
82. W.A. Fairservis, Excavation in Quetta Valley, West Pakistan, *Anthropological Papers*, Natural History, Vol.45, pt. 2, pp. 214–15, American Museum Novitates, (New Yark, 1961).

83. W.A. Fairservis, "*The Harappa Civilization,*" New Evidence and More Theory American Museum Novitates, No. 2055, (New Yark, 1961), p. 23.
84. Ibid.
85. Ibid., pp. 23–24.
86. Fairservis, The Chronology of the Harappan Civilization and the Aryan Invasion, *Man*, Vol. 56. art. 176, pp. 153–156.
87. Fairservis, The Ancient East, *Natural History*, Vol. 67, No.9, p. 508.
88. Fairservis, "*The Harappan Civilization,*" p. 7.
89. V. Gordon Childe, op. cit., pp. 183 ff.
90. W.A. Fairservis, *The Harappan Culture*, p. 7.
91. Fairservis, op. cit., p. 11.
92. Sir John Marshall, op. cit., p. 48.
93. Ibid., p. 49.
94. Ibid., p. 339.
95. O.E. James, *The Cult of Mother Goddess*, p. 13 (London, 1959), E.I.H. Mackay, *Further Exacavation at Mohenjodaro*, Pls. LXXI, 7; LXXII, 1,5; LXXV, 10, 14, 17.
96. Fairservis, *The Harappan Culture*, p. 18.
97. Marshall, op. cit., p.50.
98. Myres, *Cambridge Ancient Indian History*, Vol. I, p. 91.
99. Marshall, op. cit., p. 50.
100. J. Mellaart, *The Dawn of Civilization*, pp. 61 239.
101. E.O. James, *The Cult of the Mother Goddess*, p. 93.
102. J. Marshall, op. cit., pp. 52–72.
103. M.E.L. Mallowan and J.E. Rose, Iraq, Vol. II, Pt. I, 1935, p. 95.
104. J. Marshall, op. cit., Vol. III, pl. XCIV, II; Mackay, op. cit., Vol. III, pl. XCIV, II.
105. J. Marshall, op. cit., Vol. III, pl. XCIV, II.
106. E.O. James, op. cit., p. 34.
107. J. Marshall, op. cit., Vol. I, p. 52.
108. Ibid.
109. Ibid., p. 54.
110. Ibid., p. 53.
111. Ibid., p. 41.
112. J. Marshall, op. cit., p. 76.
113. J. Marshall, op. cit., Vol. I, p. 76, pl. XIII 17; Dr. H. Mode, op. cit., p. 8.
114. Marshall, op. cit., p. 76.
115. Dr. H. Mode, op. cit., p. 8.
116. *Prehistoric India*, p. 203.
117. Frankfort, *The Arts and Architecture of the Ancient Orient* p. 210, pls. 176 B and C.
118. J. De Morgan, *Prehistoric Man*, p. 249.
119. W. Durant, *The Story of Civilization*, pp. 60–61.
120. Marshall, op. cit., pp. 66–73.
121. Ibid.
122. Ibid., p. 72.
123. A Stein, *An Archaeological Tour in Waziristan and in Northern Baluchistan.*
124. Ibid.
125. *The Harappa Culture*, op. cit., p. 18.
126. Marshall, op. cit., p. 72.
127. N.G. Majumdar, *Exploration in Sind. Memoir Archaeological Survey of India*, No. 49, (1934), p. 37.
128. *Mem. Del. en Perse*, T XIII, p. XXXIV, fig. 5, 6.
129. J. Marshall, op. cit., p. 70.
130. Ibid., p. 50.

131. J. Marshall, op. cit., p. 68.
132. Ibid., pl XII, 8 and 9.
133. Ibid., p. 69 seals No.4, 36, 41–42.
134. *Encyclopaedia of Brittanica,* Vol. XXVIII, p. 501.
135. E.O. James, The Cult of Mother Goddess, p. 129.
136. J. Marshall, op. cit, p. 58.
137. Ibid., p. 63.
138. Ibid., p. 68.
139. Dr. Heinz Mode, op. cit., p. 8.
140. Machay, op. cit., Vol. I, p. 360; Vol. II, pl. XC, 24.
141. Ibid., Vol. I, p. 362.
142. Op. cit., p. 8.
143. Dr. Heinz Mode, op. cit., p. 8.
144. J. Marshall, op. cit., p. 63, pl, XII, fig. 18.
145. Ibid., pp. 63-66.
146. Ibid., p. 64.
147. Ibid., p. 64.
148. W. Durant, op. cit., p. 61.
149. Ibid., pp. 59, 61.
150. Marshall, op. cit., p. 61, pl. XIV, 2 and 4.
151. Ibid., fn. 2.
152. H. Mode, *The Harappa Culture and the West,* p. 8.
153. Ibid.
154. Ghirshrnan, *Iran,* op. cit.
155. Marshall, op. cit., p. 81.
156. Ibid., p. 79.
157. Ibid.
158. S. Piggot, *Prehistoric India,* p. 207.
159. *Mem.* Del. en perse, T. VITI, p. 76; of. N.G. Majumdar, Exploration in Sind, Memoir *Archaeologicizl Survey of India,* No. 48, p. 116.
160. Marshall, op. cit., p. 20.
161. K.N. Dikshit, *The Pre-historic Civilization of Indus Valley,* p. 38.
162. Marashall, op. cit.
163. Ibid., p. 89.
164. S. Piggot, op. cit., p. 207.
165. C.F.A. Schaeffer, *Ugaritica,* 1939, I, figs. 14 and 15.
166. L. Wooly, *Antiquaries Journal,* VII, No.4.
167. *Oriental Institute of Chicago, Communication,* No. 16, 1933, p. 48 f.
168. Mackay, Mohenjodaro and the Indus Civl1ization, p. 282.
169. Ibid., p. 283.
170. Mackay, *Further Excavation at Mohenjodaro* pp. 169–70.
171. Mackay, ibid., p. 262.
172. H. Frankfort, *The Art and Architecture of the Ancient Orient,* p. 2.
173. Mackay, *Mohenjodaro and the Indus Civilization,* p. 266.
174. Ibid.
175. H. Frankfort, op. cit., p. 2.
176. Mackay, op. cit., p. 268.
177. Mem. Del. en Perse, T. 1, p. 94, fig. 130 (A).
178. Dr. Ghirshman, mustrated London News, 8th August, 1953, pp. 226–7.
179. Mackay, *Mohenjodaro and the Indus Civilization,* pp. 22, 265.
180. Mackay, op. cit., p. 265.

181. Mackay, *Further Excavation at Mohenjodaro*, p. 164.
182. Mackay, op. cit., p. 276.
183. Dr. Frankfort, op. cit., p. 265, fn. 53.
184. *Cambridge Ancient History*, Vol. I, p. 579.
185. J. Mellaart, *The Dawn of Civilization*, p. 239.
186. Mackay, op. cit., p. 287.
187. Ibid.
188. Ibid.
189. Ibid., p. 288.
190. Ibid., p. 287.
191. Dr. Hall, op. cit.
192. Mackay, *Further Excavation at Mohenjodaro*, Pls. XXIII, 2, 1, b, d and pl. XX.
193. Piggot, op. cit., p. 191; Mackay, op. cit., p. 102.
194. Piggott, op. cit.
195. Ibid.
196. Mackay, *Mohenjodaro and the Indus Civilization*, p. 290.
197. Ibid.
198. Mackay, *Further Excavation at Mohenjadaro*, p. 179.
199. Ibid.
200. Mackay, *Mohenjodaro and the Indus Civilization*, p. 290.
201. Mackay, *Further Excavation at Mohenjodaro*, p. 179.
202. Ibid., p. 189.
203. Ibid., p. 295.
204. Mem. Del. en Persa, Vol. XIII, pl. XI, fig. 4; pl. XII, fig.l.
205. Mackay, op. cit., p. 293.
206. Ibid., fn. 7.
207. Ibid, p. 293.
208. Mackay, Mohanjodaro and the Indus Civiligation, Pl. XXXIXj. Mem. Bel. en Perse, XIII, pl. XIX, fig. 1.
209. Mackayy, loc. cit., pl. L. XXX, pl. 8.
210. Ibid, p. 318.
211. Mackay, *Further Excavaion at Mohenjodaro*, p. 182, pl. LXII.
212. Mem. Del. en Perse, t. VIII, p. 80, fig. 108.
213. Mackay, op. cit., pls. LVI, 10; LVII, 1819, 25; LX. 53, 63, 62.
214. Mackay, op. cit., p. 189.
215. Mackay, ibid., p. LV; LVII.
216. Ibid., p. 190.
217. Mackay, *Mehenjodaro and the Indus Civilization*, p. 315.
218. Mackay, *Further Excavation at Mohenjodaro*, pp. 651–52.
219. Mem. Del. *en Perse*, t. XIII, pl. XXIX, fig. 1.
220. Mackay, op .cit., p. 640.
221. Ibid., p. 640.
222. S. Piggot, *Prehistoric India*, p. 117.
223. V.G. Childe, New Light on the Most Ancient East, pp. 201–2.
224. Mackay, *Further Excavation at Mohenjodaro*, pp. 321, 639, pl. CXLII, 43a.
225. Mackay, *Mohenjodaro and the Indus Civilization*, p. 318.
226. Ibid., pp. 318–19.
227. Ibid., p. 322.
228. Ibid.
229. D.R. Gordon, *Man in India*, Vol. XXVII, No.3 "Sialk, Giyan, Hissar and its Indian Connection." p. 219.

230. Ibid.
231. Aurel Stein, op. cit., 1937, pl. 7, 8, 9 and 13.
232. Mackay, *Further Excavation at Mohenjodaro*, p. 217, pl. LXVIII.
233. D.R. Gordon, op. cit., p. 220.
234. A. Stein, op. cit., pl. 29.
235. Ibid., pl. 16.
236. Majumdar, Exploration in Sind, *Memoir, Archaeological Survey of India*, No. 48, 1934, p. 153.
237. Blanford, Fauna of British India, *Mammalia*, p. 503.
238. Majumdar, op. cit., p. 503.
239. Mackay, *Mohenjodaro and the Indus Civilization*, p. 324.
240. Mackay, *Further Excavation at Mohenjodaro*, p. 219.
241. Mackay, *Mohenjoodaro and the Indus Civilization*, p. 328, pl. XCII, 8, 17.
242. Mackay, *Mohenjodaro and the Indus Civilization*, p. 219.
243. Ibid., pl. LXXXVIII, 6, 12; LXXXIX, 3, 13.
244. D.R. Gordon, op. cit., p. 324.
245. Ibid., p. 219; A. Stien, op. cit, pl. 9, 11, 13.
246. D.R. Gordon, op. cit., p. 219.
247. Majumdar, op. cit., pl. 27, 36, 37 and 38.
248. D.R. Gordon, op. cit., p. 219.
249. Ibid.
250. Mackay, *Mohenjodaro and the Indus Civilization*, p. 326.
251. *Mem.* Del. en. Perse, t. XIII, pl. 5 fig. 1, 2 and 5; H. Frankfort, *Studies in Early Pottery of Near East*, pl. I, pl. V, 5 No. 1.
252. Mackay, op. cit., p. 326.
253. *Mem.* Del. en. Perse, t. XIII, pl.VI, pl. VIII, pl. VII.
254. Mackay, op. cit., p. 221.
255. Ibid.
256. Delporate, *Catalouge des Cylindre Orrientau*, X, t, pl. 18, fig. 17.
257. Mackay, op. cit., p. 221.
258. Ibid., p. 327.
259. *Mem. Dal. en Perse*, t. XIII, pls. XV and XVII.
260. Mackay, op. cit., p. 328.
261. *Mem. Del. en, Perse*, t. 13, pl. XXVIII, fig. 8.
262. Ibid., p. 112, fig. pt. VIII, p. 112, fig. 185.
263. Op. cit, p. 329.
264. V.G. Childe, op. cit., p. 201.
265. Majumdar, op. cit., p. 32.
266. *Mem. Del. en Perse*, t. XIII, pls. IV and V.
267. Ibid., t. VIII, p. 125.
268. Mackay, *Mohenjodaro and the Indus Civilization*, p. 330.
269. Ibid., pl. XCI, 17.
270. Andrews, *Borlington Magazine*, 1925, pl. 11 No. 40 and 84.
271. Mackay, op. cit., p. 330.
272. Mem. Del. en Perse, t. VIII. pls. XXVIII, XXXI.
273. Ibid.
274. Ibid., pt. III, p. 120 and 121.
275. Ibid.
276. Mackay, op. cit., p. 230; *Mem. Del. en Perse*, t. 13, pl. XXXI.
277. *Mem. Del. en Perse*, pt. VIII, p. 107.
278. Andrews, op. cit., Dec. 1925, pl. I, Nos. 23, 26.
279. Mackay, op. cit., p. 331, pl. XCI, p. 2l.

280. Andrews, op. cit., pl. II, No. 52.
281. Andrews, ibid., pl. I, Fig. 44; Mem. Del, en. Perse, t VIII, p. 102.
282. Mackay, op. cit., p. 332, pl. XCI, 23.
283. Andrews, op. cit., pl. I, No. l.
284. Mackay, op. cit., pl. CX, XCI, 24; pl. XC, 19; pl. XCII, 8,17, pl. LXXXIX, 10 and 14.
285. Ibid., p. 332.
286. Mackay, op. cit., Vol. II, p. 37l.
287. Ibid.
288. Ibid., p. 185.
289. *Mem. Del, en Perse,* t. XIII, p. 71, fig. 193.
290. Ibid., pt. VIII, p. 110, fig. 17; pt. XIII, pl XLI, fig. 3.
291. De Morgan, *Is Prehistorie Orientale,* t. II, p. 266, fig. 293.
292. Mackay, op. cit., No. 576.
293. Mem. Del. en Perse, pt. XVI. pl. I, fig. 8.
294. Catalogue des cylindres orient, *Musee du Louvre,* t. i, pl. XVI, fig. 10; Marshall, No. 520 and 521.
295. Mackay, op. cit., p. 374.
296. Mem. Del. en Perse, pt. XII, pl. XXI, Fig. 4.
297. Mackay, op.cit., p. 375.
298. *Mem. Del. en Perse,* t. XVI, pl. I, fig.1.
299. Macky, op. cit. p. 377.
300. Ibid., p. 385.
301. J. de Morgan, *Prehistoric Man,* p. 261, fig. 171; *Mem. Del. en Perse,* t.II, p. 129.
302. D. Mackay, op. cit., Vol. I, p. 104.
303. *Mem. Del. en Perse,* t.XIII, pI. XXXIV.
304. Mackay, op. cit., p. 398.
305. Ibid., p. 400.
306. *Mem. Del. en Persia,* t. XIII, p. 43 fit. 143, 144.
307. Mackay, *Further Excavation at Mohenjodaro,* p. 333.
308. Ibid., p. 337.
309. Mackay, op. cit., p. 44.
310. *Mem. Dal, en Persia,* p. XIII, p. 58.
311. Mackay, *Further Excavation at Mohenjodaro,* p. 655.
312. Ibid., p. 656.
313. *Mem. Del. en Perse,* t. XVI, pl. XXI, fig. 314.
314. Mackay, op.cit., p. 656.
315. Ibid.
316. Ibid., pls. LXXXIII, 30; LXXXIX.
317. Mem. Del. en Perse, t. VIII, p. 23, fig.4.
318. Mackay, op.cit., p. 657, pl. LXXXIII, 36.
319. Mackay, ibid., pls. XCVIII, 641; c.
320. V.G. Childe, *Ancient Egypt and the East,* 1933, p. 24.
321. *Mem. Del. en Perse,* t. XVII, p. 67, fig. 428.
322. Macky, op. cit. p. 639, pl. e. figs. band c.
323. Ibid.
324. Dr. Heinz Mode, The Herappan Culture and the West,' p. 11 (Calcutta, 1961).
325. Ibid.
326. M.E.L. Mallowan, "Civilized Life Begins from Mesopotamia and Iran." Dawn of civilization, p. 96.
327. Mackay, op. cit., p. 341, f.n. 1.
328. Contenau Manueld Arcaolo 'e Orientale, 360, fig.

329. Mackay, Further Execavation at Mohenjodaro, p. 267.
330. *Mem. Del. en Perse*, t. XIII, pl. 33.
331. De Morgan, *Collection Ashmolean Museum*, No. 276.
332. *Mem. Del. en Perse*, Vol. I, pl. VII, Pl. VII, figs, 6 and 8.
333. S. Piggot, op.cit., (1950), Harmondsworth, Middlesex, p. 117.
334. Mackay, *Further Excavation at Mohenjodaro*, p. 286.
335. *Mem. Del. en. Perse*, p. XVI, pl. XVI, fig. 245.
336. Mackay, op.cit., p. 287.
337. *Contenau Manueld Archaecologic Orientale*, p. 349. Fig. 258
338. Mem. Del. en Prese, t. XIII, Pl XXXIX, fig. 5,7.
339. Mackay, *Mohenjodaro and the Indus Civilization*, pp. 347, 48.
340. Mackay, *Further Excavation at Mohenjodaro*, p. 295.
341. F.A. Khan, op. cit., p. 368f.
342. Mackay, *Further Excavation at Mohenjodaro*, p. 496.
343. V.G. Childe, *New Light on the Most Ancient East*, p. 139.
344. S. Piggot, op. cit., p. 209.
345. Mackay, *Further Excavation at Mohenjodaro*, p. 506.
346. S. Piggot, op. cit., p. 209.
347. H. Beck, *Antiquaries Journal*, Vol XIII, p. 389, pl. LXVI, fig. 5, 8, 9, pp. 391–97, pl. LXVIII, Fig. I 348. Mem. Del en Perse, pt. VIII, p. 278.
349. *Mem. Del. en Perse*, pt. XIII, p. 10 fig. 23.
350. Mackay, *Further Excavation at Mohenjodaro*, p. 521.
352. De Mecquenem, *Antiquity*, Dec. 1931, pp. 462-3; *Mem. Del* en Perse, t. XX, p. 113, f. 19 (6–9).
353. Mackay, Seal No. 228, 422.
354. Mackay, op. cit., p. 664.
355. Herzfeld, *illustrated London News*, May 25, 1929.
356. Mackay, op cit., p. 664.
357. F.A. Khan, An Archaeological Study of the Indus Valley Civilizations and their Relationship to the Early Cultures of Iran, Ph.D. Thesis, *London University*, 1954, p. 368 f.
358. Mackay, op. cit., p. 505, fn. 1.
359. Mackay, *Further Excavation at Mohenjodaro*, p. 532.
360. Ibid.
361. Mem. Del. en Perse, pt. XIII, pl XI, fig.3.
362. Ibid., t. VIII, pl. V.
363. Frankfort, *Archaeology and the Sumerian Problem, Oriental Institute, Chicngo*, fig.7.
364. Petrie and Quibeli, *Nagada and Ballas*, pI LXV, 15.
365. S. Piggot, Prehistoric India, p. 198.
366. Ibid.
367. Ibid.
368. Ibid.
369. Dr. E.F. Schmidt, Tepe Hissar Excavation, 1931, *Museum Journal Philadelphia*, 1933, pl. CXVII fig. 11. 168.
370. Marshall, op. cit., I p. 105, pls. CXXXVIII,XXXIX; Mem. en Perse, Vol. XIII, pl. I, fig. 11 and 12.
371. Mem. Del. en Perse, t. XIII, pl. XXIII.
372. V.G. Childe, op. cit., pp. 201–202.
373. N.G. Majumdar, op. cit., pl. XIX, 27, 36, p. 34, De Morgan, *Prehistoric Orientals*, t. III, p. 101, fig. 3, 4.
374. *Mem. Del. en Perse*, t, 1, p; 194, fig. 420, De Morgan, Ia *Prehistoric Orientale*, t. III, p. 101, fig. la.
375. Mackay, *Mohenjodaro and the Indus Civilization*, p. 460.
376. Ibid., p. 461.

377. Mackav. A Cemetery Palace, Pt. II, pI. XLIV, fig. 3; Hall and Wooly, *Ur Excavation*, Vol. 1, p. 53.
378. Pumpelly, *Exploration in Turkestan*, Vol. 1, p. 164 fig. 364.
379. *Mem. Del. en Perse*, t. XX, p. 108, fig. 11.
380. *Illustrated London News*, 25th May, 1929.
381. Mackay, op. cit., t. 502.
382. Petrie, *Tools and Weapons*, p. 19.
383. Mackay, op. cit.
384. S. Piggot, op. cit., p. 210.
385. Ibid.
386. S. Piggot, "Notes on Certain Metal Pins and a Macehead in the Harappan Culture." *Ancient India*, No.4, 1947-48.
387. Mackay, *Further Excavation at Mohenjodaro*, p. 393.
388. Mackay, *Mohenjodaro and the Indus Civilization*, pp. 463–64.
389. A.S. Hemmey, *Mohenjodaro and the Indus Civilization*, p. 591.
390. Langdon, op. cit.
391. Mackay, op. cit., p. 405, fn. 5.
392. *Archaeology and the Sumarian Problem Oriental Institute, University of Chicago.*
393. Mackay, Mohenjodaro and the Indus Civilization, p. 468.
394. *Mem. Del. en Perse*, p; VIII, p.111, fig. 368.
395. *Archaeologia*, Vol. LXX, pl. X, b.
396. Pumpelly, op. cit., Vol. I, pl. XLI, fig. 21.
397. *Mem. Del. en Perse*, pt.1, p. 118, fig. 20, Lblcl.
398. Ibid VII, p.111, fig. 368.
399. Mackay, *Further Excavation at Mohenjodaro*, p. 430.
400. *Mem. Del. en Perse*, t. VIII, p. 18, fig. 40.
401. Mackay, op. cit., p. 562, pl. CXXIII, 10.
402. *Mem. Del. en Perse*, pt. VIII, p. 11.
403. Mackay, *Mohenjodaro and the Indus Civilization*, p. 566, pl. CVL 31–3.
404. *Mem. Del. en Perse*, pt. XIII, pl. V, Fig. 9; pl. VI, fig. 5 and pl. VIII, fig. 6.
405. *Mem. Del en Perse*, pt. XVI, pl. VI, fig. 101; pl. XXI, fig. 314; pt. VIII, pt. fig. 99, p. 10, fig. 20.
406. Ibid., pt. XIII, pl. VII, fig. 1, pl. xv, fig. 4 pl. XXI.
407. Ibid., p. 94, fig. 65; p. 91, fig. 42,
408. *Illustrated London News*, Ist June, 1929, fig. 11.
409. Mackay, op. cit., p. 567, pl. LCV, fig. 36–37.
410. Ibid., p. 568.
411. Ibid., *Mem. Del. en Perse*, pt. XIII, pl. VII, fig. 1, pl. SVIT, fig. 6 pl. XVIII, fig. 3,4; pl. XXI, fig. 4.
412. Mackay, op. cit., p. 568; *Mem. Del. en Perse*, p. 120, fig. 422.
413. Ibid., pt. I, p. 121, fig. 253; pt. VII, p. 102, figs. 330, 331.
414. Mackay, op. cit., p. 569.
415. Fairservis "New Evidences and More Theory" The Harappa Civilization. 12–3
416. Ibid., pp. 7–8; J. M. asa, Feuilles des Moundigak, *Memoirs de la Delegation Francaise on Afghanistan*, Vol. XVII, Pairs, 1961.
417. Childe, op. cit., p. 183 ff.
418. Fairservis, "Chronology of Harappa Civilization and Aryan Invasions," *Man*, Vol. 56, Art. 173.
419. Fairservis, "New Evidence and More Theory," *The Harappan Civilization*, p. 13.
420. S. Piggot, op. cit., pp.100–116
421. Fairservis op. cit., p. 17.
422. S. Piggot, "The Chronology of Prehistoric North-West India," *Ancient India*, No. I, p. 18.

4

Aryans

The Harappan culture disappeared from Sind and Punjab about the middle of the second millennium BC without leaving any trace. Several reasons are assigned to the eventual destruction of this marvelous culture. The invasion from the west is often mentioned as the most important factor. The huddled skeletons found at Mohenjodaro lying in the streets, lanes and pits or on the staircases without formal burial show the possibility of a struggle between the Harappans and invaders from the outside.[1] It gets its confirmation from certain other finds at the upper stratum of Mohenjodaro.[2] Wheeler[3] claims that the cemetery 'H' affords unquestionable evidence of the arrival of new commers who destroyed the Harappan culture. The pottery found from the cemetery 'H' is entirely dissimilar to the style of the Harappan culture.[4] B.B. Lal[5] also holds that invaders from the west exterminated the Harappan culture who used horse and painted red ware. He observes the wide distribution of this pottery in the north India and traces its link with the painted red ware of the Shahi Tump cemetery and of Sistan in Persia.[6] Fairservis[7] thinks that the folk movement from the west with the new pottery, the so-called 'Ghul-ware' destroyed this culture during 1200 BC. He discovers Ghul-ware at Dabar Kot, Moghul Kala, Kaudian, Periano Ghundai and Rana Ghundai in Baluchistan and at Jhukar in the Indus Valley.[8]

Hiene Geldern argues that new people came to India from the south-western Iran during 1200-1000 BC.[9] He based his argument on the copper objects found in the Gangetic basin. He compares the trunnion axe from Shalozan with those found in Transcaucasia and Iran.[10] Heine Geldern refers the marked similarity of the antennai swords of India to those discovered in the Koban region of Persia.[11] He further identified the axe-adze from Mohenjodaro with similar forms at Tepe Hissar III C and Turang Tepe.[12] He tells that a copper rod topped by an antelope and a dog from Harappa shows a close resemblance to copper rods from Hissar III C and bronze pins from Koban and Luristan in Persia.[13]

Similarly a pin topped by two deer heads found at Mohenjodaro is paralleled with copper rods with horse heads at Hissar c and identical pins from Koban.[14] (Fig. 21-XXIII-XXII-XXV.) (Fig. 8)

Of course, the Shahi Tump cemetery in south Baluchistan explicitly shows the arrival of new people. The pottery of this cemetery is definitely different to Harappan style[15] but corresponds remarkably with those from Khurab cemetery, Susa I and Fars in Persia.[16] The copper spear-shaft hole, battle axe, and copper stamp seals from Shahi Tump offer contrast with Harappan culture[17] but recall the shaft hole weapons from Hissar III and the last finds bear a close point of resemblance to those found at Hissar II b and III b and Susa in Persia.[18] Similarly certain copper objects found at Moghul Ghundai and the pottery from the cemeteries of Jiwanri and Ziangian in south Baluchistan recall B cemetery at Sialk.[19] It indicates these invaders coming from Persia to India during second millennium. In north Baluchistan pockets of ashes unearthed at Rana Ghundai III C, IV and V phases, Sohr Damb and Dabar Kot show that the settlements were sacked and burned.[20]

It appears that these incoming invaders settled at Jhukar, Chanhu-daro and Lohumjo-daro. The pottery, weapon and other objects of these cultures offer strong contrast with the Harappan series,[21] but show several points of resemblance with the cultures at Sialk and Hissar in Persia and Shahi Tump cemetery in Baluchistan.[22] Commenting on these cultures Piggot observes, If . . . the smaller portable objects such as seals, beads, metal implements and weapons and habit of dress implied by the use of pins all suggest the arrival of new blood in the region."[23]

Persia likewise underwent similar cultural change during the second millennium BC. The archaeological evidence of folk movement is detectable in north Persia where Hissar II, Turang Tepe and Shah Tepe explicitly show appearance of implements, weapons and ornaments of novel types[24] constrasting strongly with their primitive tradition. Sialk and Giyan present a semi-barbarian culture with innovation of chariotry and the use of horse.[25] The eastward movement of the people is traceable in Afghanistan at Nad-i-Ali [26] where bronze arrow heads and typical pottery-are positive evidence.[27]

Who were these invaders who destroyed the Harappan culture? They are commonly recognized as the Aryans. It is the discovery of Sir William Jones that Sanskrit, Old Persian and the European languages came out of the same common source which no longer existed. This common source is named as Indo-European. Hence its speakers are termed as the Indo-Europeans and in the instance of the Rigveda and the Avesta they are popularly known as Aryans. The Aryans are believed to be living once somewhere in Eurasia. They subsequently dispersed into various branches and migrated to different parts of Eurasia. Indo-Iranian is most important branch which bifurcated into Iranian Aryans and Indian Aryans, the former settled in Iran and the latter came to India.

(a) Original Home of Aryans

Where Aryans originally lived as a united stock is a subject of great controversy. Ever since the discovery of Sir William many eminent scholars have been working on this point. Many theories had been established but later on discarded. In the light of new researches again new theories came up and ultimately they also lost the ground in turn. The controversy has not yet died down on the problem of the original home of Aryans which has been tossed over a vast tract of Eurasia extending from Arctic ocean to India and from Scandinavia to Altai mountain.

The Asiatic origin of Aryan people was once the most popular theory. European philologists and archaeologists have ever since been trying their best to prove Europe as the cradle of the Aryans. Their arguments centre round three main points:—

(1) The multiplicity of the Aryan languages in Europe.
(2) The most archaic character of the Lithuanian.
(3) The linguistic palaeontology.

Evidences in favour of the Asiatic origin of the Aryans are more convincing and powerful which are as follows:—

(1) The high antiquity of Sanskrit and its linguistic purity.
(2) The European Aryans are described as descendants of Asiatic brachycephalic stock.
(3) The references to the Airyanam Vaejanh, an Aryan homeland in the Avesta.
(4) The silence of the Rigveda regarding the original homeland of the Aryans outside of India.
(5) The discovery of Tocharian, a centum language in the heart of Asia.
(6) The migration of Vase Painters from Asia to Europe.
(7) An Aryan migration from central Asia ushered in Iron Age in Europe.
(8) The discovery of both satem and centum languages on the fringe of the Anatolian plateau.

Now the south Russian theory is also largely acceptable to the scholars. The main force of the argument is that the climate and physiographical features of the south Russia are remarkably identical with the characters of the original home of Aryans, as deduced by linguistic palaeontology.

Thus the problem has been dealt with from different angles both inductively and deductively with the result that numerous theories have cropped up. It is to be noted that both the continents Asia and Europe present equally strong evidences for the possible home of Aryans and the matter warrants an extremely careful study and sifting of the historical data.

(i) The Discovery of Tocharian—In contrast to Aryan languages in Asia being in minority surrounded by Semitic, Asianic, Mongolian, Chinese and, Dravidian languages the multiplicity of long established Aryan languages in Europe is a very strong evidence in favour of European home.[28] But the discovery of Tocharian in Chinese Turkestan gave a rude shock to this theory and invalidated this line of argumentation. It has now been unimpeachably established that Tocharian represents most archaic character of the Indo-European.[29] The partisans of the European theory have made attempts to prove Tocharian being the late arrival in Chinese Turkestan and a band of Celts carried it thither.[30] We know that the tide of migration of the Huns and the Turks in the eighth century BC or even before was flowing westward.[31] The efforts to connect Tocharian with Celtic have been crowned with no success.[32] The Celtic peculiarity that is assimilation of p to q, is altogether missing in Tocharian.[33] Hence it can hardly be denied that Tocharian is the last survival of the original Asiatic Aryan stock in the central Asia.

(ii) Migrations from Asia to Europe During Neolithic Period—It is a well-known fact that the Aryan culture belonged to the Neolithic age. It is admitted that Europe was entirely depopulated at the end of the Ice Age and the New Stone Age in Europe was ushered in by the advent of the Neolithic brachycephals that came from Asia.[34] The brachycephals commonly known as the 'bell beaker folk or the Prospector' had played an important role for the foundation of the Bronze Age in Europe.[35] Sergi and Morgan recognize them as the Aryans.[36]

The migrations from Asia are further attested by the cultural links between Asia and Europe. As the last glaciers retreated, an unique vase painting culture emerged on the scene from the Yellow Sea to the Adriatic. The scholars are of the opinion that diffusion of this magnificent art over the far-flung regions denotes a migration of culture if not of a people.[37] The painted ware have been discovered at Kansu, Chih-li and Honan in China,[38] Anau,[39] the Punjab,[40] Baluchistan,[41] Khorasan, Helmond in Persia,[42] Mesopotamia, Cppadocia, Syria, Palestine,[43] and the sites in Europe [44] from Dnieper to Transylvania, Bulgaria, Thessaly and the south Italy. Dr. Christian[45] and Peake [46] claim these vase painters as Eurasiatic, but this mysterious civilization is one of the most notable links between the Aryan lands of Asia and Europe. Childe says, "The Asiatic sites where painted pottery has turned up do indeed coincide rather closely with the earliest centres where Aryans appear."[47] Fiest[48] informs that in 300 AD. an Aryan dialect was spoken in Kansu which is not far away from the domain of Tocharian. The 'Airyanam Vaejanh' might be located in Helmund. We know that other remaining sites come under the jurisdiction of the Aryan culture.

It is worthwhile to note that these vase painters possessed the culture quite identical with that of the Aryans as deduced by the linguistic palaeontology. Childe admits that this ceramic art was introduced into Europe from Asia.[49] We have forceful evidence that the culture radiated from Anau where first settlement exposes mud-brick huts and the tradition for disposal of children in jars under the houses.[50] The similar tradition persisted among the Indians, Persians, Thessalians, early Aegeans, primitive Palestinians and the Europeans villagers.[51]

(iii) The Rite of Cremation—One of the most fundamental customs of a people is the mode of disposal of the dead that is most tenaciously preserved. In the present state of knowledge none can claim that Aryans had any particular association with the cremation or all Aryans practiced this rite. The rite is detectable in Italy,[52] Greece, France, Spain, Scandinavia, Hungry,[53] Britain,[54] the Neckar Valley,[55] Rhineland,[56] North Germany,[57] Moravia,[58] Palestine,[59] Babylonia,[60] India,[61] Turkestan [62] and Siberia.[63] The find spots make it manifestly clear that a distribution of this rite harmonizes exceptionally well with the distribution of Aryan languages. The new researches lend further support to this view. Dr. Michelis[64] claims that the rite was introduced into Italy by the Terramarieoli who were Aryans and similarly it crept into north Europe through Aryans. Ridgeway also holds the Aryan responsible for spreading the rite in Greece, Spain, France and north Germany, Christian [65] and Myres claim that the brachycephalic race both in Europe and Asia regularly practiced cremation. It is significantly important to recall that brachycephals originally lived in Asia. De Mortillet[66] unambiguously admits that the brachycephals, bringing with them the rite of cremation, introduced Aryan, speech to Europe. Mackenzie says, "The bulk of the Archeological evidence seems to point to the invaders, who are usually referred to as 'Aryans' having introduced cremation ceremony in 'Europe."[67]

If it is so where and how the Aryans adopted the rite of cremation is an important point to study. The Indo-Iranians who are believed to have lived at the Aryanam Vaejanh disposed of their deads by both the methods of cremation and burial. It is plausible to surmise that Indo-Iranians came in contact with any fire-worshipping tribe and borrowed the rite of cremation. Archaeology affords the earliest evidence of cremation at Anau I in Turkestan.[68] Turkestan affords the key where a fire-worshipping tribe, Buriat living near lake Baikal practiced the cremation since remote past.[69] This view gets an additional support from the fact that the Ashvamegha of the Indian Aryans and the horse sacrifice of the Mongol Buriats are remarkably identical.[70]

(iv) Ugro-Finns—Philology reveals that Ugro-Finns language took many words from Indo-Europeans. Kossinna and Taylor hold that both languages came out from a common stock. J. de Morgan negatives the Indo-European borrowings from the Finnish. But, however, it is certain that the Aryans came in contact with Finns somewhere in Eurasia. Penka, Kossinna, Schrader and others based their Scandinavian or German and South Russian theories on the present location of Ugro-Finns. The Finish assimilated a large number of the words of satem group par excellence the Indo-Iranian vocables.[71] The partisans of the European theory surmise that the Indo-Iranians, first of all branched off from the parent stock and remained in touch with the Ugro-Finns for some time. These assumptions are not tenable. The Indo-Iranians borrowed not even a single word of the Finnish,[72] which rules out any direct contact between the Indo-Iranians and the Finnic people but refers to the fact that any branch of the Indo-Iranians enriched the Finnish with the Indo-Iranian words.

(v) Lithuanian—The supposed most archaic character of Lithuanian is the backbone of the European theory.

Indeed, Lithuanian represents its archaic character but it does not supersede Sanskrit. Lithuanian and Indo-Iranian both belong to the satem group and are closely related to each other in vocabulary and grammar.[73] But the Indo-Iranian possesses wider sphere. Greek belongs to centum group but it is strikingly connected to Indo-Iranian.[74] Moreover, it is only Indo-Iranian that has retained the original meanings of the primitive Indo-European words.[75] Oldenberg admits that Sanskrit is "the chiefest witness as to what was the first form and first meanings of words."[76]

(vi) Relation of the Indo—Europeans with the Sumero-Akkadians and the Sino—Tibetans-It has been, now, established that Indo-European words cow, star, axe, roudhos were derived from Sumero-Akkadian 'gu(d),' 'ishtar,' 'pilakhu,' 'urud(u).'[77] This implies that the early Aryans must have lived in the neighbourhood of Mesopotamia. It supports the South Russian theory to some extent. But recently some scholars, like Roberet[78] Shafer who arrived at the conclusion on the basis of study of sixty four words, hold that Indo-European and Sino-Tibetan sprang from a common speech, the so-called 'Eurasial.' Kopper[79] already pointed out that Uralo-Altaic and Caucasian are two components of the culture and language of the Indo-European. It stands to reason to postulate that the primitive Indo-Europeans were living originally somewhere in the region between these two groups.

(vii) Linguistic Paleontology—The linguistic paleontology provides us with the data that reflects at least the vague image of the Aryan cradle. The fauna corresponds to cow, sheep, horse, dog, goat, swin, wolf, bear, otter, mouse, hare, bower, quail, snake, duck, goose and some birds of prey. Hot summer and knowledge of snow and rain show that the climate of cradle was continental. The comparative paleontology exposes the physiographical features that refer to mountaneous country with rivers and streams common.

No region other than the central Asia can better corresponds with the fauna, flora, climate and physiographical features as deduced by the linguistic palaeontology. It is well-known fact that the Aryan animals such as the Asiatic urns and the turbary sheep of Neolithic Europe had been tamed at the mountainous country in the central Asia.[80] The most powerful argument of all is the cradle of swift horse which is the peculiar symbol of the Aryans. The horse is certainly the Aryan animal.[81] Durest [82] informs that the people of Anau (the eastern Iran) first of all domesticated the swift desert horse. The absence of name of ocean in the primitive Indo-European lends an additional support to this view and rules out all probability of European or South Russian theory.

Childe remarks, that the pure pastoralism on which Schrader mainly bases his advocacy of the South Russian steppes appears to be exaggerated."[83] On the basis of certain trees the region extending from south Russia to Scandinavia is claimed to be the cradle of Aryans. Bender invokes birch to pinpoint Aryan origin in the region between Vistula and the Nieman.[84] Schrader[85] uses the tortoise to prove the South Russian theory. But we should keep it in mind that only the European languages agree in terms for tortoise and these trees. Schrader's[86] advocacy that Aryans had no knowledge of mountain reckons with no support. The absence of terms for gum and fish in the Indo-European poses real difficulty to the champions of the South Russian and the European hypothesis.

Childe has raised a strong objection against the central Asian home. He argues[87] that camel was known in Turkestan from the earliest times but there is no word for camel in Indo-European. It may frankly be admitted that it cannot easily be explained away. Nevertheless this heretical view against so many strong evidences in favour of the central Asia, has but very little weight. There are other several words the absence of which is equally strange. A.B. Kieth[88] remarks that the Indo-Europeans knew honey but not bee; and butter, feet, and snow but not milk, hands and rains.

(viii) Horse—The horse is essentially associated with the Aryans. We are informed[89] that the horse was, first of all, domesticated at Anau. The advocates of the European theory also claim the early presence of horse in Germany. But the Aryan words for horse, asva; equus, asu, acer mean 'swift'. Hence it infers[90] that it was definitely not the stout German forest horse but steppe horse or desert swift horse of Anau.

We have another more forceful argument against the Aryan home in Europe or in the south Russia. The Babylonian name for horse is "the ass of the east."[91] It is well-known that an Aryan branch introduced horse into the Ancient East during 2000 BC. The Babylonians had trade and cultural relations with the distant parts of Europe and Asia. They must have known the native place of the animal. But they named the animal the ass of the east" It indicates that the native place of horse lay in the east and the Aryans entered the Ancient East from east.

(ix) Cuneiform Inscriptions—The Boghaz-Keui inscription mentions the names of the Vedic gods-Indra, Varuna, Mitra and Nasatya. The clay tablets discovered at Boghaz keui mention certain Aryan numerals such as aika, tera, panza, satta and nav.[92] The Tell-el-Amarna tablets describe the Mitannian princes as Sutama, Dusratta and Artatama.[93] These tablets also tell the names of the contemporaneous ruling dynasties of Syria and Palestine as Yasdata, Suwardata, Biridaswa and Artamanya.[94] The names of Mitannian kings show Indo-Iranian elements such as Surias, Murattas, Bugas and Indas.[95]

It is certain that these personal and divine names are distinctly Indo-Iranian. Mironov holds the view that the Indian character of the numerals is obvious.[96] The gods mentioned above are reasonably Vedic.[97] So far personal names are concerned, the principal elements in these names are Indian, along with Iranian names side by side.[98] It is also certain that the language of these cuneiform inscriptions approximates more closely to that of the Rigveda.[99] This implies three possibilities -the Aryans either went to Punjab from Mesopotamia, or the Mitannian Aryans separated from the parent stock while the latter were moving towards India, or they came from the Punjab and colonized Mesopotamia.

The view that the Aryans came to India from Mesopotamia is wholly unsound. The Mitannian Aryans were a small minority of adventurers, who themselves adopted the local language and culture.[100] Moreover it does not stand to reason that the great civilizations of Aryan, Iran and Vedic India could be the achievement of a handful of people. The orthodox views that the Mitannian Aryans branched off from the main body near the Caucasus while the latter moved towards India. In support of this theory it is contended[101] that the several Mandalas of the Rigveda had already been composed in the Caucasus. But it can hardly be denied that the scene of the Rigveda is laid in the Punjab or Afghanistan.[102] Moreover it is a matter of surprise why the parent stock preferred the bleak table land of Iran to the attractive fertile plain of Mesopotamia. Certain other scholars[103] assert that the personal and divine names and numerals are definitely Indian forms and they were introduced by a body of Sanskrit speaking people from India. This view is supported by other facts also. The gods mentioned in Boghaz-Keui inscription appear side by side and in the same order as in the Rigveda.[104]

In the light of the above facts it is quite reasonable to conclude that one branch of the Aryans who came from the side of India colonized Mesopotamia during 1700 BC. The presence of the Iranian elements here and there and preservation.[105] of the 's' sound in certain divine and personal names confirm that they were unseparated Indo-Iranians; but they certainly belonged to the branch having preponderance of the Vedic traits.

(x) Avestic Airyanam Vaejanh—The Avesta contains certain very important passages having direct bearing upon the question of the Aryan cradle-land and their migrations therefrom to different regions. The first Fargard of the Vendidad mentions that Ahura Mazda created the first best region, Airyanam Vaejanh.[106] The Airyanam vaejo signifies that it was the birth land of the Aryans. The Avestic baejo corresponds with the Sanskrit bijo, meaning seed or source. The same Fargard enumerates fifteen more best regions created by Ahura Mazda later on. The fifteenth is Hapta[107] Hendu which is unmistakably identified with Sapta Sindhu or the Punjab.

One school[108] is reluctant to attach any historical value to these passages. On the other hand the other school[109] recognizes in these passages a half historical and half mythical memory of the original home of the Aryans. In the light of the inscriptions of the Achaemenian kings and the records of the Greek writers, ten out of the sixteen regions have been identified[110] with certainty. This implies that the account of these passages is real and not mythical. It is pertinent to point out that from the designation of Airya the name Iran for the whole country is derived. These facts forcefully convince the prominent scholars to take the Avestic Airyanam Vaejo, the original birth place of the Aryans.[111] No doubt the location of Airyanam Vaejo is much disputed, nevertheless the consensus of the opinions is veering round the eastern Iran.[112]

(xi) Rigveda—It is a fact that the Rigveda is the oldest surviving literature of the Aryans and it certainly preserved their primitive ideas. But it preserved no memory of the Aryan homeland away from the Sapta Sindhu.[113] It contradicts the orthodox view that the Aryans came to India from outside. But the geographical background of the Rigveda shows the Aryans coming from outside to the inner parts of India. Of course, the Rigvedic river named Rasa has its Iranian equivalent in Ranha and Sarasvati in Harahahuiti.[114] Both the rivers are believed to have been located in Iran. If we admit that the Indo-Aryans colonized Iran and Mesopotamia; it does not explain as to why they had not Aryanized the whole of India. Still the Rigvedic evidence cannot easily be dispensed with. It is the best possible view that the Aryan cradle lay near to India and in between, the region was culturally homogeneous. This is why migrating to India the Aryans never felt that they were entering a new country.

It transpired from the evidences discussed above that the original home of the Aryans lay somewhere in the region extending from Pamir to the Hindu-Kush.

References

1. M. Wheeler, *The Indus Civilization*, p. 98, 1960.
2. S. Piggot, op. cit., p. 228, 1961; Archaeological Traces of the Vedic Aryans, *Journal of Indian Society of Oriental Art*, IV, pp. 87–113, 1936.
3. M. Wheeler, *The Dawn of the Civilization*, p. 249.
4. M. Wheeler, *Ancient India* No.3 pp. 84–86.
5. B.B. Lal, Prehistoric Investigation, *Ancient India, Silver Jubilee Number*, 1953, p. 88.
6. B.B. Lal, The Painted Grey Ware of the Upper Gengetic Basin, *Journal of Royal Asiatic Society of Bengal*, Vol. XVI, 1950, No.1, pp. 89–102; M.S. Vats, *Excavation at Harappa*, Vol. I, p. 203f.
7. W. Fairservis, 'The Chronology of Harappan Civilization and the Aryan Invasion," "A Recent Archaeological Research," *Man*, LVI, (1956), pp. 153–56.
8. Ibid., pp. 153–54.
9. R. Heine Geldern, 'The Coming of the Aryans and the End of the Harappan Civilization, *Man*, 56, (1956), pp. 136–39.
10 Archaeological Traces of Vedic Aryans, *Journal of Indian Society of Oriental Arts*, Vol. IV. 1936, pp. 87–113.

11. Ibid.
12. R. Heine Geldern, op. cit., pp. 137–38.
13. Ibid .
14. Heine Geldern, *Art and Archaeology*, V, June, 1937, "New Light on the Aryan Migration to India, pp. 7–16.
15 A. Stein, An Archaeological Tour in Gedrosia, Memoir, *Archaeological Survey of India* No. 43, pp. 88–105.
16. Ibid., pp. 106–10; S. Piggot, op. cit., p. 218.
17. Ibid., p.219; S. Piggot, *Antiquity*, Vol. SVII, pp. 178–81 (1943).
18. E.P. Schimidt, *Excavations at Tepe Hissar Damghan* I. XXVII, Philedelphia 1937.
19. D.H. Gordon, *Man in India*, Vol. XXVII No. 3, 1947, p. 234; S. Piggot, *Prehistoric India*, 1961, p. 240.
20. A. Stein, *Archaeological Tour in Waziristan and North Baluchistan*, p. 57; Hergreaves, *Excavation in Baluchistan* 1925, p. 57; *Journal Near Eastern Studies*, Vol. V, pp. 284–316, (1946).
21. N.G. Majumdar, *Exploration in Sind*, Memoir, *Archaeological Survey of India*, No. 48 (1934), pp. 51–58.
22. A.S. Piggot, op. cit., p. 223; Mackay, *Chanhu-daro Excavation* 1943, p. 103, fn. l; N.G. Majumdar, op. cit., pp. 51–58.
23. S. Piggot, p. 226.
24. S. Piggot, *Prehistoric India*, 1961, pp. 239–40.
25. Ibid., p. 240.
26. Ibid.
27. R. Ghirshman links up the pottery and bronze arrow heads with an Iranian Complex: "*Reserches prehistoriques dans a partie Afghana du Seistan.*"
28. V.G. Childe, *The Aryans*, p. 95.
29. Benveniste, *Tokharian et Indo European, Festschript of H. Hirt* (Herdenberg, 1936), p. 227.
30. Giles, "The Aryan," *Cambridge History of India.*
31. Childe, op. cit., p. 96.
32. Ibid., p. 8.
33. Pokorny, *Indogermanisches johrbuch*, p. 43.
34. J. de Morgan, E.G. *Syria*, IV, p. 28 f; G. Sergi, *Gli Ari in Asia in Europe.*
35. Childe, The Dawn of European Civilization, pp. 121 f, 135, 185.
36. Sergi, op. cit.; Morgan, E.G. Syria, IV, p. 28.
37. Childe, The Aryans, p. 104.
38. T.J. Arne, *Palaeontologia, Sinica Series* D, 1, 2; *Survey of China*, 1925.
39. R. Pumpelly's *Explorations in Turkestan.*
40. *Illustrated London News*, September 20, 1942, pl. VI.
41. *Archaeological Survey of India*, Annual Report 1904–5, pp. 105 ff, pl. XXXIII.
42. E. Pottier, *Memoires de la Delegation en Perse* XIII.
43. H. Frankfort, *Studies in Early Pottery of the Near East*, 1924.
44. Childe, *Dawn of European Civilization*, pp. 71, 87 and 318.
45. Christian, *Mitheilungern der Anthropoligischen Geselchaft in Wien*, LIV.
46. H. Peake, *The Bronze Age and the Celtic World*, (London, 1922).
47. Childe, op. cit. p. 109.
48. S. Fiest, *Kultur, Ausbreitung and Herkunft der Indogermanan*, p. 425. (Berlin, 1913).
49. V.G. Childe, op. cit., p. 113.
50. R. Pumpelly, op. cit.
51. Childe, op. cit. p. III.
52. E.de. Michelis, *L.Origin degli Indo-Europei*, pp. 131 ff, (1871).
53. W. Ridgeway, *The Early Age of Greece*, (Cambridge, 1901).
54. Childe, op. cit., pp. 288–96.

55. K.F. Wolff, "Neolithische Brandgraberder umyebung Von Hanau," *Prahistorische Zeitschrift, I.*
56. Childe, op. cit., p. 257.
57. Mannus, XI–XII, pp. 312 ff.
58. *Wiener Prahistoische Zeitschrift*, VI, p. 41 f.
59. Mac Alister, *Excavations at Gazer.*
60. *Orientalische Literaturzeitung*, XXI Berline.
61. Marshall, op. cit.
62. R. Pumpelly, op. cit.
63. J. Curtin, *A Journey in Southern Siberia*, p. 101.
64. Op.cit., p. 13l.
65. Op. cit.
66. De Mortillet, *Formation de la nation francaise*, (Paris, 1897).
67. A. Mackenzie, *Indian Myth and Legend*, pp.XXXVII.
68. R. Pumpelly, op. cit.
69. J. Curtin, op. cit.
70. Ibid.
71. T. Burrow, *The Sanskrit Language* (London), p. 18.
72. Ibid.
73. T. Burrow, op. cit., pp. 19–23.
74. Ibid., p. 22.
75. S.K. Chatterji, *Indo-Aryan and Hindi*, p. 11 (Ahmedabad, 1942).
76. H. Oldenberg, *Ancient India. Its Language and Religion*, p. 90, (Trans. Calcutta, 1962).
77. Ipsen, *Indogermanische Farschungen*, XLI, p. 417.
78. R. Shafer, 'Eurasial,' *Orbis*, XII, pp. 19–444 (1963).
79. W.C. Kopper, *Anthropos*, (1935). p. 90.
80. V.G. Childe, op. cit. p. 109 (London, 1926).
81. Ibid., p. 83.
82. Durest in Pumpelly, op. cit., Vol. II.
83. Op. cit., p. 90.
84. J. Bender, *The Home of the Indo-European*, p. 33, 1922.
85. O. Schrader, *Reallexicon der indogermanische Sparache*, pp. 10 f.
86. Ibid.
87. Ibid., p. 88.
88. Cf. Childe, *The Aryans*, pp. 88.
89. Durest in Pumpelly, *Exploration in Turkestan*, II, p. 431, Pub. No. 73.
90. V.G. Childe, *The Aryans*, p. 88.
91. A. Mackenzie, *Indian Myth and Legend*, p. XXIX.
92. N.D. Mironov, *Aryan Vestiges in the Near East of the second Millenary*, BC, *Analeda Orientalia*, Vol. XI, 1935, pp. 1440–217.
93. Cambridge *Ancient History*, II, p. 331.
94. ibid.
95. Yale *Oriental Series*, I.
96. N.D. Mironov, op. cit., p. 24.
97. F. Spiegel, *Die Arische Periode*, 1887.
98. N.D. Mironov, op. cit.
99. V.G. Childe, op.cit., p. 30.
100. A. Goetze, *Kulturgeschichts desalten Orients*; Kleinasien, p. 63; J. Friedrick, "Aryan en Syrien un Mesopotamia" *Reallexikon der Assyridogie in Zeitschrift fur Indologies und lranistik*, 1927, p.147.
101. W. Wuest, Ueber das Alter des Rigveda, X.Z.K.M. XXXIV, 1927, p. 164–214.
102. H. Brunnhofer, Arische Urzeit, 1910.
103. Konow, The Aryan Gods of Mitanni People, 1921, pp. 4–5.

104. Rv. X–125–1; VIII -26–8; Cf. S. Konow, *Aryan Gods of Mitanni People*, pp. 44-5, 1921; P. Thieme, The Aryan Gods of Mitanni Treaties, *JAOS*, LXXX, p. 303, 1960.
105. E. Meyer in the *Reallexikon der Assyriologue*, I, Berlin, 1928, p. 146.
106. Venedidad, I, II, 1–4.
107. Ibid., I, II, 19–72–73.
108. J. Darrnesteter, "The Zend Avesta," *SBE*, Vol. I, Introduction.
109. E. Herzfeld, *Iran in the Ancient East*, pp. 191–192.
110. A. Stein, The Indo–Iranian Border lands, their prehistory in the light of Geography and of recent Explorations, JRAI, 1934, pp. 179–202.
111. Herzfeld, loc, cit., p. 192.
112. E. Herzfeld, *Zoroaster and his Word*, Vol. II, p. 699.
113. A.C. Das, *Rigvedic India*, p. 71 (2nd edition).
114. D.C. Sircar, *Select Inscriptions*, 1942, pp. 3–14.

5

Linguistic Affinity

Relation between Sanskrit and Avesta

Men must have taken several thousands of years to become civilized and this stage of the civilized life is the result of his zealous efforts, hard patience, tough perseverence and his constant endeavour. Ever since the beginning of his existence man had a prime desire to control his environment, so he took to fashion tools and thus accelerated the whole course of technical and scientific advancement. The process of progress centred round not only technique of tool making, but man gave his attention simultaneously to the intellectual pursuits. We see even during the dawn of culture, the appreciable development in art, religion, ethics and philosophy, going hand in hand with advancement in tool making techniques. For proper basis of history, archaeology is entirely dependent on material remains, over-emphasizing the technical and scientific advancement and dispensing with the other aspects of culture. Thus certain elements of culture remain obscure. To understand the abstract ideas or intellectual development of a primitive race, language rather than archaeology brings us much nearer to reality. In fact language which is the main organ of expression of man's feeling very faithfully represents the nature of the culture of its speakers. The words inevitably connected with culture conceal its certain important aspects. V. Gordon Childe observed, "Philology may, therefore, claim a place among the historical disciplines, the functions of which are to reanimate and interpret the process whereby man has raised himself from animalism to savagery, from savagery to barbarism, from barbarism to civilization."[1] Language which is a purely mental manifestation is the easiest way for expression of man's spiritual pursuits. No doubt we are highly indebted to religion that revolutionized the primitive life during the dawn of culture and made the greatest contribution to our present civilization. To begin with, religion of the primitive man was nothing but embodiment of rituals and incantation of magic formulas. Hence language that is very closely connected with the primitive religious beliefs can only explain the original conception of religion. Harneck remarks, "The history of religion is reflected in the history of language, and that only he who knows the latter is in a position to seek to decipher the former."[2]

In case of the Aryan history language occupies even more important place. Their material culture was not very high. They were nomadic people. They were nature worshippers par excellence and built no temples at all. Idolatory was unknown to them. Their houses were built of perishable material. We have, therefore, at our disposal, comparatively very few remains of copper implements or pot sherds associated with them. Under such circumstances an adequate knowledge of the Aryan language is essentially required to reconstruct their cultural history.

The cultural history of India and Iran during second millennium is largely associated with Aryans. In both countries Aryans came from outside, subdued the original inhabitants and stabilished their hegemony. These new comers of both countries were ethonologically one people. they belonged to an important branch of Endo-European, which is commonly known as Indo-Iranian. The Indo-Iranian ultimately branched off into two distinct groups, viz., Indo-Aryans and Iranian Aryans, resulting in bifurcation of the common language Indo-Iranian into Sanskrit and Avesta.

In order to study the cultural developments of India and Iran during the half second millennium BC a comprehensive knowledge of the original state of Sanskrit and Avesta and new developments in these languages during this period is indispensable. Hence it is also essential to study the parent language, i.e., Indo-European as well as Indo-Iranian, the mother of Sanskrit and Avesta.

(a) Indo-European Languages:

The Indo-European language is defunct today. But it certainly once existed and spoken by a united people of this stock. Reasons are unknown, the Indo-European people deserted their original home and they split into several branches. Indo-Iranian, the mother of Sanskrit and Avesta, is one of its branches.

Even before the separation of its different branches, Indo-European presents two distinct dialectal divisions within itself. These divisions are based on phonetic changes known as centum and satem groups and they are so named from the treatment of Indo-European k in the Indo-European word khtom for 'hundred'. The centum languages preserved k as such whereas satem languages change this k to some kind of sibilant. Thus k and s sounds form a remarkable dividing line between the two groups. Indo-Iranian, Balto-Slavonic, Armenian, Thracian, Phrygian and Albanian are satem languages and centum group comprises of Greek, Latin, celtic Germanic, Tocharian and Hittite. Velars or so Palatals' alatals' k, g, gh are preseved in the centum languages while the satem language changed them to the sibilants s, z, zh. *w w w* Another characteristic feature which distinguishes the two groups is that labiovelars, k^w, g^w, gh^w of Indo-European remain as such in centum and are palatalized such as k, g, gh into satem.

(b) Reconstruction of Indo-European:

(i) Indo-European Phonology—The Indo-European died out soon after it had split into a number of dialects. These dialects are found to have been prevalent even during the prehistoric time over the vast region in Eurasia extending from Atlantic ocean to the basin of Tarim and the Ganges. Its construction has become possible only because of the comparative study of its various branches now spoken all over the world. It is rightly believed that the original Indo-European sounds have been badly affected. Hence an original phoneme can be deduced from the comparison of forms derived from it that occurs in various Indo-European languages. But the method is complicated and creates many difficulties. The easiest way is to postulate the original Indo-European phoneme that occurs in a number of the existing languages with constantly unchanged form.

(A) Consonants: The phonemes, d, s, t, w, v, y are widely preserved in various Indo-European languages. They may reasonably be claimed to be attributed to the parents stock. Sanskrit possesses sonant aspirates, bh, dh, gh as a class. The corresponding surd aspirates in Greek and fricatives in Latin and other Italic languages took the place of Sanskrit sonant aspirates. Whereas Iranian, Lithuanian and O. Slavonic have lost the aspiration altogether. It is only sonant aspirates series which very simply and satisfactorily accounts for the various changes that appeared in other languages. There is therefore, little doubt that the sonant aspirates are primary phonetics of the parent language.

The surd aspirates ph, th, kh appear in two or three languages. The comparison also establishes that the surd aspirates are the later development of the Indo-European phonetic system. Their origin is believed to be result of a combination of Indo-European h with a preceding unspriated surd.

Hittite presents 'h' in basic Indo-European words whereas it has disappeared in the corresponding words in all other languages. Since Hittite has preserved so many other archaic characters of the primitive Indo-European, the sound 'h' is certainly attributed to the original phonetic system.

(B) Vowels: Just like consonants the primitive Indo-European vowels may also be reconstructed. The vowels a, a, ai, ai, au, au, e, e, ei, ei, eu, eu, eu, i, i, o, o, oi, oi, ou, ou, u, u and sonant liquid r and 1 and nasals M and M as Avowel are preserved in majority of the languages.

Sonant nasals n m are preserved nowhere and, sonant liquids r e are found only in Indo-Iranian. Nevertheless the assumptions of original sonant nasals and sonant liquids for Indo-European are essential to account for the variation in the associated vowels in several languages.

(ii) Formation of Noun—The ancient Indo-European nouns were either root or words formed by adding suffix to a root or a word already ending in a suffix.

The primary suffixes were generally all the available phonemes, but r, n, s, t, y I i, v lu, m, h and k were most commonly used. Some where they appeared in their weak form just as -r, -n, -s, -t, -m they might appear also with guna, i.e., preceded by the thematic vowel e.g., er, ar, en, in, es. The primitive neuter action nouns, as a rule, were formed commonly by the compound Indo-European suffixes, i.e., -sar, -tar, -mar, -var, with variant of n stem, but as a matter of fact in noun derivation during early Indo-European the most important distinction was not between different suffixes simple or compound but in a difference of accentuation, according to which a word formed with the same suffix functioned as an action noun, adjective or agent noun. The neuter action nouns were accented on root whereas if suffix was accented, it was either adjective or agent noun which was originally common gender.

(iii) Compound Words—In old Indo-European the independent words combined together and formed a new word. The considerable traces of the compound words of such formation are found in various languages. The compound words thus formed may function as nouns or adjectives.

(iv) Gender—It is noticed in connection with the formation of nouns that all Indo-European languages except Hittite possess three fold system of gender, i.e., masculine, feminine and neuter. Feminine gender is absent in Hittite which has only dual system of gender. We know that Hittite has preserved archaic features of Indo-European. It appears that three-fold system of gender is a later development in Indo-European. Originally there were only common and neuter genders as Hittite had preserved and later on masculine and feminine came out from common gender.

(v) Noun Cases—In Indo-European, cases are found in three numbers, i.e., in singular, plural and dual. Generally gender is also shown. It appears from the comparative study of various Indo-Eureopean languages that originally cases in singular number were also used in plural. The plural is a later development which always declines in s.

(vi) Pronouns—Unlike the other primitive languages such as Semitic, Indo-European shows no difference of gender in pronouns. Pronouns present three numbers, e.g., singular, dual and plural. The use of different stems having different radical elements expresses the distinction of number. The inflection of the plural is partly identical with that of the singular. Pronouns do not agree with nouns in many respects, so far case endings are concerned. Particularly the inflections of personal pronouns differ widely from that of nouns.

In the early Indo-European, the pronouns had no case endings and a full system of inflection for pronouns is a later development. It is borne out by the fact that many pronouns have no exact correspondences in other Indo-European languages. Moreover certain Indo-European languages have preserved the enclitic forms which are forms of stem and have no case ending. Later on use of inflections for the accented personal pronouns abolished the older system which is preserved in certain Indo-European languages in the forms of enclitics.

(vii) Prepositions—Prepositions during the early Indo-European period were used with freer order and looser connection of nouns which were governed by them. Only Vedic Sanskrit preserved this system. It appears that later on Indo-European developed a system in which the preposition was placed before noun which was governed by the former.

(viii) Verbal prefix—This is the unique feature of Indo-European that it compounded the common prepositions as the prepositional prefixes with verbs. The system is well-developed nearly in all Indo-European languages.

(ix) Verb—In the early Indo-European language, just like noun, verb could be either a root itself or a root already having suffix. These suffixes are identical with the corresponding nominal suffixes and similarly may be simple or compound. But enlargements of the verbal root appear to be of early stage of Indo-European stem formation. For the suffixes n and r, which play a very important part in nominal stem formation are rarely used as Averbal enlargement. On the other hand the suffixes s and h are of great importance in the verbal stem formation. It is noticable that though all the Indo-European consonants and-semi-vowels can be used as a suffix for formation of verbal stem, their number is comparatively smaller. The common suffixes -as/ s, -am, i, -t, -th, -d, -p were commonly used for formation of the verbs.

(A) Denominative Verbs : Denominative verbs are made on the basis of a noun stem. For formation of denominative verbs a specific suffix–ya is added to the nouns existing in the language. Many Indo-European languages have prepared denominative verbs.

(B) Prefixes, Reduplication and Augment : In addition to suffixation, Indo-European had a system of prefixes to make reduplication, augment and tense stems. A particle 'e' is prefixed to the imperfect, pluperfect, aorist and conditional preterites to show past time.

The perfect, the desiderative, the intensive the reduplicated aorist and one class of present show a system of reduplication in which the initial consonant of a root with Avowel is normally repeated. The vowel may or may not be the same as the radical vowel.

(x) Voice—Indo European had two voices-Active and Middle. When the subject is mainly implicated in the result of the action in some way, the middle voice is used whereas active is used if it is not so.

When the direct object of the verb is a member of one's own body, middle is also used. Indo-European languages preserved this distinction between active and middle.

(xi) Tenses—The comparative study of the Indo-Eurpean languages reveals that the primitive Indo-European had only two tenses-present and perfect. The Indo-European perfect is a special type of present tense in origin. Later on the perfect developed into a preterite.

The present tense indicates present time whereas past time is expressed by a preterite which is formed in the later stage on the basis of the present stem and is the so-called imperfect. Future and aorist also came out from the present. The future is a specialised kind of present stem with the denominative formation in -ya. Just like the present stems the future also forms a preterite which functions as a conditional. In origin aorist is also special kind of modification of the present formation. Certain type of the present stems and some of the aorist stems are quite identical in form which shows the close relation between two formations.

Later on double set of preterites developed. One became imperfect (past indefinite of English) and the other developed into the aorist which has a special sense quite different to the present tense. In contradiction to the imperfect the aorist expresses a special kind of past time. It describes an action which has just recently been completed.

(xii) Personal Terminations—For the active and the middle voices Indo-European has two different type of personal terminations. These personal terminations are again sub-divided, which appear in different tenses. The present and the future tenses have the personal endings -mi, -si, -ti, in the 1st, 2nd and 3rd persons respectively which is known as primary endings, in Indo-Iranian and Hittite. The secondary ending is -m, -s, -t which is found in the aorist imperfect and optative. No other languages except Hittite and Indo-Iranian made distinction between primary and secondary endings. As a matter of fact in Indo-European the secondary is primary endings and vice versa and i was later added to -m etc., to show present time. Subjunctive has option to take either. The perfect has quite different endings from primary and secondary endings. The imperative also possesses a special endings.

(c) Indo-Iranian

Indo-Iranian which is the mother of Sanskrit and Avesta is Avery important branch of Indo-European.

Indo-Iranian occupies Avery significant and a distinct position among the Indo-European languages. Not only it received the largest heirloom from its parent stock but it preserved many primitive features of the Indo-European. In respect of vocabulary, roots, conjugation and syntax, Indo-Iranian is the key to the Indo-European study. It is only the branch that has link in one way or other nearly with all the other Indo-European branches. The Balto-Slavonic group is closely related to Indo-Iranian. In case of vocabulary there are a large number of words of the Balto-Slavonic group which have identical counter-parts in Indo-Iranian and these words are not found in other Indo-European languages. For example-Skt. aja, Lith. oz ya, 'goat,' (same suffix). Skt, phena Av. spoayno, Lith spaine 'foam', Skt. daksina, O.S.I. desinu, 'hand', Skt. misra, Lith. misr, 'mixed'. In the field of grammer as we have already noticed that a considerable number of special features are common to both these group. The western languages, i.e., Germanic, Cetlic and Italian have no special feature common to Indo-Iranian but they still have close link to the latter. There are a large number of common words in both groups which have been totally eliminated from the rest of the Indo-European languages, as–Skt. s radha , Lat. credo, Ir. cretim, 'believe,' Skt. y bs, Av. Yos , Lat. issue, 'justice' Greek is a centum language but has no trace of a close relation with any of other centum language. The compartive study of grammar has confirmed it well that there are a considerable number of correspondences between Indo-Iranian and Greek in the sphere of conjugation. Indo-Iranian and Greek agree on another point that both eliminate the renderings of medio-passive.

It is the most important feature of the Indo-Iranian that it preserved the original Indo-European words and roots with their original meanings. Indo-Iranian[3] preserved the Indo-European words, gwer 'stone,' melg 'to rub,' mel'to make weak,' sei 'to throw a missible,' perkom 'rift in the ground,' as gravan, mrs, mal, sayaka, parsa with same original meanings; but in non-Indo-Iranian languages they appear as quem, milk, mal, semen, or sow, furrow with the newer meanings. H.Oldenberg tells, "the daughter should be thygater in Greek and tochter in German, neither the Greek nor the German language could explain it. But Sanskrit did seem able to explain it. the history of the Sanskrit word for daughter seemed written on its very front. Since this word fell under the root duh (to milk), it seemed obvious that she was originally the milker–a domestic idyl from domestic antiquity."[4]

(d) Reconstruction of Indo-Iranian

No doubt, centuries had elapsed since Indo-Iranian separated from its parent language. But during this period it came into contact with various foreign elements. So it lost many features of its ancestral heritage and made a considerable innovations under the different environments.

(i) Phonology—

(A) Consonant: The Indo-European phonetic system is more or less preserved by Indo-Iranian. Certain sound of course, underwent a new change:

(1) Though aspiration is lost in Iranian, it is convincing that sonant aspirates (bh, dh, gh) are preserved by Indo-Iranian.
(2) The surd aspirates (ph: th, kh) are preserved only by Indo-Iranian and here they are found with any frequency.
(3) The palatal series (k, g, gh) after the first palatallzation results in s.j. h in Sanskrit and s, z, i in Persian, such as Skt. svan, Av. span (dog), Skt. j anu, Av. zap-u, (knee); Skt. hima Av. zima, (snow). The comparison between Sanskrit series' s, j, h and with the Persian series s, z, z gives out

the fact that Indo-Iranian had the intermediate forms s, z, z" which explain most of the Indo-Iranian development.[5]

(4) While series s, z zh remained unaltered till the end of the Indo-Iranian period, the series k, g, gh took second palatalization in Indo-Iranian itself into c," j, jh," for example–Lat. sequitur, Skt. sacate, Av. Hacciti; Lat. Vivus Av. Javiti, Skt. jiva, 'alive;' Ir. geguin, Av. jainu, Skt. hanti, 'slays.' These illustrations show that as a result of second palatalization which effected before vowel e,' i" and y, Sanskrit has series c, j, h whereas Iranian possessed c,' j, jh. These Sanskrit and Iranian series certainly developed from Indo-Iranian series c,' j, jh.

(5) In Sanskrit after k, r, r, i and u the dental sibilant is changed into the celebral but under the same condition Iranian changes s to s It reflects that this tradition belongs to Indo-Iranian and ultimate change form had s. Illustrations Skt. vaksyami, Av. vaxsya; Skt. aksa, Av. a s a, 'axle;' Skt. dhrsnoti, Av. adarsnaus, 'he heard;' Skt. visa, Av. visa, 'poison;' Skt. jus. Av. zaos, 'enjoyment.'

(6) It is a characteristic feature of Indo-Iranian that it changes Indo-European 1 indiscriminately into r, such as–Lith. alga, Skt. argha, Av. arejaiti; Skt. gur, Av. gar; Lat. clunis, Av. sraoni, Skt. srosi, 'buttock;' O.Sl. slovo, Av. sravah, Skt. sravas, 'fame.'

(7) In Indo—Iranian the whole group is voiced when sonant aspirate combines with surd and the aspiration is shifted to the second consonant, as-Skt.dagh + ta = dagdha, labh + ta = labdha similarly, Av. augdha, aoxta, druxta, dapta; Skt. daddhe, Av. dazde.

(8) In the early Indo-Iranian when s,' z' and z' h, combine with dental occlusive they are changed to s" and z" e.g., Av. vasti, Skt. vasti, 'he wishes;' Skt. uzdha, they Av. uzdha. Thus rule also holds good in connection with other consonants as, Skt. vizbhyas, Av. vizibyo. Av frasna.

(9) Indo-European z, which came out from the combination of s with sonant/occlusive, changed into z in Indo-Iranian under the same condition in which s became s," as–Av. Miz"da, Skt. hizd, pizd. Moreover z" came out in early Indo-Iranian from the combination of sonant aspirate+s, as-Av. augh+sa=aogz" a, Skt. gh+s=gz" h, bh+s=bz"h, dh + s' adz" h."

(10) In Indo-Iranian combination gh+s produces ks in the final position and intervocally it became g z h.

(11) In Indo-European many consonants might stand in the final position but Indo-Iranian has not more than one consonant in the final position. In Indo-Iranian as in final position became –o e.

(B) Vowels:

(1) A special development of Indo-Iranian is of its possession of 'a'

coresponding to three vowels a, e, o, in the other languages. Similarly a in Indo-Iranian is corresponding to a, e, o. elsewhere Hittite, Slavonic and Germanic also show the confusion of a and o which may have been inherited from Indo-European but only Indo-Iranian changes e to a which is one of the most characteristic features that distinguishes it from the other languages. Illustrations–Skt. sana, Lat. sensex, Skt. raj, Lat. rex, Skt. asthl, Gh.' osteon, Av. vaxs, Lat. os.

(2) The sonant nasals developed in Indo-Iranian into a. This development is found in Greek also and nowhere it is found as such. It is one of the so many features that links the two groups. The vocalic r is preserved only in Indo-Iranian as–Skt. krp, Av. kehrp, 'body.'

(ii) Formation of Nouns—In the sphere of noun formation Indo-iranian made considerable innovations.

(1) Indo-Iranian, besides original system, made action nouns with vriddhi of root having the accent of the suffix - a, as - Skt. dAva, tara, sAva.
(2) The locative infinitives are formed in Indo-Iranian with neuter suffix - tar-, for example - Skt. Dhartari, 'to hold;' vidhartari, 'to bestow,' Av. barethri, 'to support;' vidoithri, 'to look at.'
(3) In Indo-Iranian the compound sufffix-ant which is made from Indo-European neuter suffix with extension -t forms the adjectives, e.g., Skt. ru sant, 'bright;' mahant, 'great;' rhant, 'small;' Av. mazant, 'big;' berezant, 'high.'
(4) The adjectives are also formed in Indo-Iranian with compound siffix - vant. For example–Skt. vivasvant, 'brilliant; arvant, 'swift;' satvant, Av. dragvant, 'wicked;' erezvant, 'straight.'
(5) Indo-Irania,n uses the compound suffix -ina also to make adjectives - Skt. harina, 'yellowish;' asina, 'old,' Av. dravana, 'wooden,' izaena, 'made of leather.'
(6) The adjectives in Indo-Iranian are also fanned with the is- and us,. stems, e.g., Skt. mahisa, 'great' parusa, Av. pourusa, 'grey.'
(7) Adverbs are formed in Indo-Iranian with suffix -ut and its variations, as– Skt. sanat, 'of old;' cikitvit, 'carefully,' Av. paityaoget, 'backwards.'
(8) The abstract nouns are formed besides old system with the neuter suffix tva, e.g., Skt. devatva, 'divinity,' satrutva; 'enemity;' sucitva, 'purity,' Av. ratuthwa, 'office of ratu;' vathva, 'herd;' staothwa, 'prayer.'
(9) Indo-Iranian forms the gerundives with the suffix tva, e.g., Skt. hantva, to be slain;' Av. gathwa, 'id;' Skt. kartva, 'to be done' vaktva.
(10) The suffix -tat produces several abstract nouns in Indo-Iranian as -Av. haurvatat, 'wholeness;' Skt. sarvatat, 'completeness,' devatat.
(11) The passive aorists of the third person singular are made with i-stem,

such as–Av. sravi, 'is heard;' Skt. darsi, kari, sadi, padi.

(12) The suffixes in is and -us make the genitive singular, as–Av. Pitars," Skt. agnes, suno's.

(13) In Indo-Iranian suffix-ka is added to a noun, simply as an extension which changes nothing in meaning but sometimes produces diminutive meaning as-Skt. Suska, Av. huska, 'dry;' Skt. atka, Av. adka, 'garment;' Skt. putraka, 'little son.'

(14) Certain thematic formations are made with the suffix -j, e.g, Av. bisaz, Skt. bhisaj, 'physician;' Skt. usij, Av. usiz, 'a priest.'

(15) The thematic formations are also made with suffix -d, e.g., Skt. sard, Av. sared, 'autumn;' Skt. darad, Av. (dard), darada, 'cliff.'

(16) Indo-Iranian has developed a new system of derivation with vriddhi. The system was introduced in the later Indo-Iranian period. The vriddhi is used with a number of suffixes which in earlier languages function without being associated with vrddhi. The suffixes -a,-i, -ya, ma yana form adjectives with vrddhi on the basis of the old neuter suffixes, as–Skt. maruta, 'relating to the Maruts;' angirasa, 'descended from Angiras;' Skt. Agnivesi, 'a descendant of Agnovesa;' saumya 'relating to Soma;' daiveya, 'divine;' vayavya; 'belonging to the wind;' Av. ahuiri, 'belonging to Ahura;' margava, 'inhabitant of Margiana;' mazdayasni, 'belonging to the Mazdayasnian religion;' xstavaenya, 'descendant of Xstavi.

(17) Indo-Iranian inherited nominal composition system from Indo-European but it also innovated certain new systems.

(I) Certain compound words are formed, which possess a participle first member, governing the second member, as -Skt. bharadvaja, 'carrying of prize;' taraddvesa, 'overcoming hostality;' viddavasu, 'winning wealth;' Av. vanat pasana, 'winning battles.'

(II) Indo—Iranian developed another type which is called Dvandva compounds in which the compound word has dual, each retaining its own accent, e.g., Skt. dyava–prthivi, 'heaven and earth;' Mitra–Varunau, 'Mitra and Varuna;' usasa-nakta, 'dawn and night;' Av. 'pasuvira,' a paurvaire, 'water and crop.'

(III) Case Termination-Indo-Iranian inherited the older system of the case termination but it made certain innovation here and there.

(1) While in other languages in accusative singular masculine and feminine -a or -n appear in the final position after consonantal stem. Indo-Iranian innovated -am, as - Skt. pa dam, pitaram (Gk.poda).

(2) Indo-Iranian developed a new case, i.e., Instrumental singular in which a regular ending -a appears. Skt. pada, vrka; Av. vehrka but in the case of feminine i-stem is found. Skt. citti, Av. cisti.

(3) From the Indo-European ending -ei, Indo-Iranian developed -ai in dative singular, for example–Av. pithre, berezaite, Skt. Pitre pade.

(4) In the declension of thematic stem, ablative singular presents -at in place of Indo-European -a d, e.g., Skt. vrkat, sanat, Av. adrat, garoit.

(5) Outside of thematic class in genitive ablative singular Indo-Iranian replaced old termination -as -es; -os by -s in -i and -u and in some re-stems. For example—Av. pitars, Skt. agnes, sunos.

(6) In connection with the accusative plural of feminine, Indo-Iranian presents no trace of Indo-European n(ns) but -a or -as, e.g., Av. urvara, Skt. kanyas.

(7) In place of ending in -bhos of other languages Indo-Iranian has an element-bhyas in plurals of dative-ablative.

(8) The plural normally takes s in all cases but genitive plural shows the absence of this 's.' In Indo-Iranian the termination of this case is -am but in vocalic stem an - n - is inserted before the termination.

(9) Opposed to -si of Greek and other languages Indo-Iranian has the ending in -su of locative plural, as patsu.

(10) The termination of nominative, vocative and accusative of dual in Indo-Iranian is -au, as - Skt. padau, devyau!'

(11) Indo-Iranian developed a secondary -m and thus uses -bhyam in making instrumental, ablative and dative of dual, as–Av. brat byam, Skt. vrka bhyam.

(12) The termination -os appears in genitive and locative of dual as - Skt. pados, pitros, Av. zastayo.

(iv) Pronouns—In case of the pronouns Indo-Iranian developed so many new systems.

(1) Quite different from other languages Indo-Iranian innovated a suffix -am, in nominative singular of the first person, e.g., Skt. aham, Av. azem. Similarly second person also has this suffix -am which is absent outside of Indo-Iranian, e.g. Skt. tvea m, Av. tvem. The same innovation appears in accusative singular of the first and second persons. These cases have the final -m, as Skt. mam, tvam; Av. mam, twam.

(2) Contrary to Indo-Eropean instrumental singulars of both first and second persons Indo-Iranian presents new form–Skt. ma ya, tva; Av. thwa. The forms of ablative singular in both persons also differ slightly, from those of other languages. As opposed to Latin forms med, ted Sanskrit has mat, tvat and Av. mat, thwat. The new origin of Indo-Iranian in dative singular is the final element a which is absent elsewhere. As opposed to Latin mihi, tibi, Avesta or Umbrian mehe, tefe, Sanskrit presents mahya, tubhya and maibya, taibya.

(3) As elsewhere the same additional-am appears in the nominative of plural in first and second persons, which is absent in Indo-Iranian as–Skt. vayam yuyam, Av. Vaem, yuzem.

(4) Excluding nominative all cases in plural of first and second persons are formed from the cases ahma asma and yusma as opposed to IE. amme and umme. The forms of the genitive plural Skt. asmakam yusmakam; Av. ahmakem, yusmakem present Indo-Iranian innovation -kam.

(5) In nominative and accusative dual, the element -m is a secondary addition of Indo-Iranian. Indo-Iranian made another innovation in nominative and in other cases of dual. Stem a is prefixed to the bases, e.g., Skt. Avom, Avam, dvat, Av. eeava.

DEMONSTRATIVE, INTERROGATIVE AND RELATIVE PRONOUNS

(1) Demonstrative, interrogative and relative in neuter nominative and accusative of singular take ending in -t as opposed to Indo-European -d, as - Skt. tat, Av., tat; Skt. yat, Av. yat, Skt. hat, Av. ha.t.

(2) Different to the Indo-European -s-, an element -sy-is found before the termination in the dative, ablative, genitive and locative of the feminine singular, e.g., Skt. tasyai, tasyas, Av. ahyai, ainhai, ainhra.

(3) The stems esa-/eta 'this' alternate like sa/ta. They are combination of e + sa/ta. These compound stems are of Indo-Iranian origin. Example– Skt. esa, eta; Av. aisa, aiso, aetat.

(4) Indo-Iranian developed certain new pronouns, e.g., Skt. ena- Av. en, 'him, her, it;' Skt. tva-, 'a certain one,' 'many a one,' Av. thwat; Skt. sva, Av. hvo, 'he;' Av. amata (adv), Skt. avia, 'this one;' Av. naoma, Skt. nema, 'a certain one,' Av. hama, Skt. sama, 'any, every;' Skt. asau, Av. hau.

(v) Adverbs :

(1) The formation of adverbs from suffix tra is the Indo-Iranian development, e.g., Skt. atra, Av. ithra, 'here;' Skt. tatra, Av. athra, 'there;' Skt. kutra, Av. kuthra, 'where;' Skt. daksinatra, 'in the right hand,' Av. vanathra, 'at the place of dwelling.'

(2) The adverbs of manner are formed in Indo-Iranian with the suffix - tha as Skt. -tatha, 'so;' anyatha, 'otherwise;' katha, Av. kutha, 'how;' Skt. ittha, Av. avatha, 'thus.'

(3) Apart from IE, suffix -da that makes adverbs, Indo-Iranian forms certain adverbs from suffix -di also, as - Skt. yadi, Av. yeidi, 'if.'

(4) Certain adverbs in -aya as well as with stems in -u are found in Indo-Iranian, as Skt. naktaya, by night;' rtaya, 'in the right way;' svapnaya, 'in a dream;' Av. angraya, 'evilly;' asaya, 'rightly;' Skt. raghuya, 'quickly.'

(vi) Conjunction—Indo-Iranian developed a new conjunction (Skt. uta, Av. uta, 'and).' Particle - Skt. hi, Av. zi, 'for' is found in Indo-Iranian.

(vii) Verbal Prefixes—Indo-Iranian inherited many verbal prefixes from Indo-European and it developed certain new ones, as–Skt. adhi Av. aidi, 'on, above, on to;' a, 'at, to, upto;' Skt. ni, Av. ni, nay, 'down;' Skt. nis, Av. nis, 'forth, out;' Skt. para, Av. para, 'away, forth;' etc.

(viii) Verb—Indo-Iranian preserved a large majority of old verbs and suffixes for formation of verbs, nevertheless it innovated a few verbs and certain suffixes to make the verbs, e.g., suffix -dh forms Skt. edh-, Av. azdya, 'to prosper;' suffix -c, Skt. yac, Av. yas, 'to ask,' etc.

(ix) Voices—Indo-European had only two voices-active and middle. Indo-Iranian developed the passive which is its own innovation. Indo-European used to express a passive sense by different other means but the future and the perfect had no other means of expressing a passive sense, so the middle was used to express this sense in these tenses. In Indo-Iranian such uses of middle became the passive. Moreover the fourth present class of Sanskrit possesses a large majority of the intransitive verbs with middle inflection, as–tapyate, 'becomes hot;' pacyate, 'becomes ripe.' Because a large number of verbs of the fourth class had differently formed transitive presents beside them. Such differentiation in two formations developed the passive system. Thus the formation of the passive is based on the fourth present class. Only the position of the accent makes the difference between the passive and the middle of the fourth present class. The root is accented in the middle of fourth class whereas the accent is put on the suffix ya in the passive such as–(middle) - nranyate, 'thinks;' (passive) pacyate, 'is cooked.' Iranian has also such form of the passive, as kriyante. In the present system the passive is accented whereas in the perfect and future the middle very often functions as passive, such as karisyate, 'will be done.'

(x) Reduplication

(1) In place of IE e the reduplication with the vowel a appears in Indo-Iranian as—tata na, similarly a is found in place of IE e as ja garti.

(2) Indo-Iranian developed a new system of reduplicated formations with intensive reduplication with gunAvowel and with similar reduplication with repeated final r, n, etc., such as—Skt. nenikte, Av.naenizaiti; Skt. dediste, Av. daedoist; Skt. varvrtati.

(xi) Personal Terminationn

(A) Active Endings:

(1) Singular first person terminates in primary ending -o in the Indo-European thematic classes but Indo-Iranian in such case innovated -mi as Skt. bhara mi Av. bara mi. Similarly as opposed to Indo-European,

Indo-Iranian in non-thematic verbs has full ending am in secondary ending, as–Skt. asem aham, 'I am.' Indo-Iranian made another innovation in the subjunctive in the ending by ani, as–bharani, '1 will bear.'

(2) In the first person plural Indo-Iranian has a new primary ending -masi, e.g., Skt. masi, Av. amahi, 'we are.'

(3) One form corresponding to the secondary ending of Indo-Iranian was used for both primary and secondary ending in Indo-European in second person plural. But Indo-Iranian made distinction in both and developed a new ending-tha in the primary as–Skt. bharata, Av. Xsayatha. No ending is found in the perfect which is also Indo-Iranian origin, as vida.

(4) Third plural formations in Indo-Iranian present the secondary ending r with enlargement of additional s instead of the Indo-European alternative secondary ending -vr- e.g. Av. akoiteres.

(5) The perfect in second and third persons of dual terminates in suffix -ur which is Indo-Iranian creation, e.g., Skt. cakratur, Av. yaetatare.

(B) Middle Endings:

(1) As opposed to the other languages the Indo-Iranian formations of first person singular possess the ending in -e in the primary as–Av. yaze, Skt. yaje, 'I worship' and -i- in the secondary, e.g., Skt. abri, 'I have done,' Av. aoji, 'I have said.' The suffix in -e- in the perfect -ai in the subjunctive and -ya in the optative are Indo-Iranian creation, e.g. (Pf.) Skt. susruve, Av. susruye (Sbj)/Skt. yajai, Av. yazai(Opt), Skt. tanviya, Av. tanuya.

(2) The primary ending of second person singular in -se is Indo-Iranian creation, as–Skt. bharase, Av. peresahe, 'you ask.'

(3) The imperative ending -am in the third person singular is also Indo-Iranian innovation, e.g., Skt. dhattam, Av. verezyatam.

(4) Different to the IE endings, the primary ending in -madhai and secondary ending in -madhi in first person plural is Indo-Iranian creation, as–(Primary) Skt. yaja mahe, Av. yazamaide, (secondary) Skt. abharamahi, Av. Varemaidi. Similarly in second person Indo-Iranian developed the suffixes -dhve and -dhuam, as (primary) Skt. by aradhva, Av. merengeduye; (secondary) Skt. abharadhvam, darayaduem.

(5) Third person plural in perfect takes r- endings, as Skt. cakrave Av. caxrave which is Indo-Iranian origin. The secondary endings in -ra, -ran and -ram are also Indo-Iranian innovation, e.g., Skt. aduhra, aduhran, aduhram, Av. vaozirem.

(6) In first person dual Indo-Iranian created the suffix -vadhi in the primary and vaidi in the secondary which are absent outside of Indo-Iranian, e.g. (primary) cakrahe (secondary) Skt. abharavahi, Av. duaidi.

(7) Indo-Iranian created innovation in both primary and secondary endings

of second and third persons dual. The second person has -athe and -atham and third person -ate and -atam, e.g., (second person primary) Skt. carethe, Av. caroithe; (secondary) Skt. abharetam, Av. j'asaetem (third primary) Skt. bharete, Av. visaete (secondary) Skt. asruvatam, Av. asrvatem.

(xii) Tenses—

(A)Future: The future ending in Indo-Iranian is slightly different from the older one. Here the future is formed with the suffix -sya- as Skt. dasyati, 'he will give;' Av. vaxsya, 'I will say.'

(B) Aorist:

(1) In Indo-Iranian the reduplicated aorists are formed from all roots which have causative besides their normal aorists, as opposed to the IE system they have endings in -at Skt. ajijanat Av. azizenet.
(2) Just like the l,E s- aorist, Indo-Iranian developed the is- aorists as Skt. apavis, arocista, Av. Xtenevisa, cevist.
(3) In the latter Indo-Iranian period the sa- aorists came into existence. It is formed from the roots which have a medial vowel i, u and r and a final consonant that is compounded with the s of the suffix to create -hs- as Skt. adiksat, Av. niyapisam.
(4) The passive aorist in -i is also an Indo-Iranian origin. It is found in third person singular and unaugmented forms. It appears in the indicative and the injunctive which have the accent on the root syllable. But these roots are found in guna grade, which contain medial vowel i, u and r, as Skt. adarsi, sravi, asarji, Av. sravi, adariy.

(C) Perfect:

(1) In formation of the perfect, Indo-Iranian also has certain innovations. The IE system is that the strong form of the root is found in three singular persons of the active and elsewhere the weak form exists. The strong form is normally guna but in Indo-Iranian wherever medial a appears before a single consonant in the strong stem, in the singular third person vrdhi is substituted, eg, cakara, bibhaya, tatapa.
(2) As opposed to Indo-European, Indo-Iranian made reduplication an essential part of the perfect formation.

(D) Imperative:

(1) Contrary to the other languages, Indo-Iranian preserved the original ending (-dhi) of the second person singular in the non-thematic verbs as–Skt. gadhi, 'go'; vrdhi, 'to cover'; Av. idi, 'to go.'
(2) Indo-Iranian; innovated the suffix-sva in the middle of the second person

signular, e.g., Skt. hrsva, bharasva Av. barantiha. The addition of -am appears in the third person singular and plural which is also of Indo-Iranian creation. Skt. asatham, Av. verezyatam, Xroasentam.

(3) In the later Indo-Iranian period the ending tat appears without any discrimination in the active and the middle both, e.g., brutat, 'say;' dhattat, 'put.'

(E) Injunctive: The unaugment form of injunctive is the Indo-European system. But in Indo-Iranian augmentation is used for formation of injunctive. Another Indo-Iranian innovation is the use of ma with unaugmented aorist form in the sense of probhibition, as ma gah, 'do not go.'

(F) Subjunctive: As oppose to the IE ending in -a the suffix -ani developed in the active of first person singular in Indo-Iranian. Another Indo-Iranian creation is the addition of the thematic suffix to a root already provided with such as –bhava.

(G) Optative: The non-thematic ending of the optative is the Indo-Iranian creation. Extension of the strong forms appears in the case of roots in -a as -adha ma, we placed yamas, 'we go.'

(H) Intensive: Although no evidence is available outside of Indo-Iranian, the origin of the intensive is believed to go baek to Indo-Iranian. As a matter of fact intensive developed in Indo-Iranian only.

(1) The intensive is formed with roots preceded by strong reduplication but if the roots possess i or u this reduplication contains the corresponding gun Avowel, e.g., Skt. johaviti, Av. Zaozaomi, Skt. dediste, Av.daedoist.

(2) If roots contain the vowel a the corresponding long vowel is found in the duplication, as Skt. nanadati, Av. naeni-zaiti.

(3) In case roots terminate in r, it is repeated in reduplication. Skt. careketemahi, Av. careketemahi.

(4) A type of intensive inflects exclusive!y in the middle which forms its stem by the addition of suffix -ya- as marmarjyate, Av. dardairyat.

(5) The intensive forms optative commonly in Indo-Iranian,-as Av. veviya t, dardairyat.

(I) Causative: Indo-Iranian made the distinction between causatives with strengthened root and non-eausatives with weak root, as rucaya, 'shine'; rocaya, 'illumine.'

(J) Desiderative:

(1) Certain desideratives present an abbreviated stem in which the

reduplication and the root are contracted into one syllable. Desiderative Skt. dipsati, Av. diwzaidyai is formed from dabh and the comparison of Sanskrit and Iranian forms give Indo-Iranian dibzha. There are several such formations, as -siksa, lipsa, dhiksa.

(2) Reduplication with the suffix -sa is, as a rule, the desiderative stem in which i is normally the vowel of the reduplicating syllable but if the root contains u, in place of i, u appears in the desiderative, as bibhitsati, yuyutsati.

(K) Infinitive: Indo-Iranian forms the locative infinitives from the root stems in -tar-, as, Skt. dhartari, 'to hold;' vidhartari, 'to bestow;' Av. barethre, 'to support' vidoithre, 'to look at.'

(L) Participles: Middle participles are formed with the suffix in ana which is Indo-Iranian innovation, as, duhana, 'milking;' adana, 'eating.'

(e) Differentiation of Sanskrit and Persian:

What were the causes are not known exactly, but the Indo-Iranian peoplebifurcated into two branches. One branch entered India from north-west frontier and settled in Sapta Sindhu, which is known as Indo-Aryan branch, the other that got the nomenclature of Iranian Aryan remained behind and settled in Persia. Both the branches being placed in different environments and all connections between them being cut off, they developed their own distinct cultures and assumed their own characters in the sphere of the language also. The language of the Iranian Aryans is Avesta which developed different dialects such as, Gatha, Ancient Bactrian, old Persian, Pehlvi, Soghdhi, Zabuli, Siksi, Hirvi, Deri or Dardic, Kafri, Khotanese and Pashto. Sanskrit is the language of the Indo-Aryan branch, the off shoots of which are Sindhi, Punjabi, Hindi, Oriya, Bengali, Asamese and Gujrati dialects.

(i) Phonology—In the field of phonology Sanskrit and Avesta present a considerable changes.

(1) Avesta has without exception h in place of initial s in Sanskrit, e.g., Skt. sa, Av. ha, 'he;' Skt. sama, Av. hama, 'same;' Skt. Soma, Av. Homa; such change appears in certain words themselves, e.g., Skt. asu, Av. enhu, 'life.' The Sanskrit s is normally preserved in Avesta in the last syllable, as, yazae-sa, s remains at the end in Avesta, if it is preceded by a, then -as is changed into o, e.g., Skt. kas, Av. ko, but in such case s is kept only before the enclitic particle cha, as Ahuras cha.

(2) Avesta generally changes Sanskrit h into z in case it is not original but only derived sound, e.g., Skt. hima, Av. zima, 'winter;' Skt. hve, Av. zve, 'to invoke;' Skt. he Av. zi, 'then.' Similarly in place of Sanskrit j Avesta has z, as - Skt. jihva Av. hizva. Skt. jan, Av. zan, 'to produce.'

(3) In the sonant aspirates series Avesta lost aspiration whereas Sanskrit

preserved it, e.g., (bh) Skt. bharati, Av. baraiti (dh) Skt. madhu Av. madu(gh) Skt. megha, Av. mega, Sanskrit also lost aspiration in certain cases, of dh and bh as (dh) hita for dhita, iha for idha, saha for sadha are found in the later language Sanskrit loses aspiration when another aspirate followed. Such examples are seen in case of reduplication, e.g., dadhau, babhau.

Before final s or t a sonant aspirate lost its aspiration in Sanskrit as we have adhoks, aqhokt, adhokt, dhruks from the roots dhugh, dhagh, dhrugh which contain two aspirates and in these only initial aspiration is preserved.

(4) In the first palatalization Avasta has s for Sanskrit s, z and for Skt. j and h both, e.g., (k) - Skt. vis, Av. vis, Skt. sru Av.sru, 'to hear;' (i) Skt. janu Av. zanu, Skt. ajati, Av. azaiti (gh) Skt. hima, Av. zima. Old Persian substitutes d in place of s, z in. Avesta, e.g., dasta, Av. zasta, 'hand" dard Av. sared, 'year.'

(5) In the second palatalization Sanskrit changed Indo-Iranian into c j while Avesta. changed them c, j and Indo-Iranian" jh became h in Sanskrit and j" in Avesta if series k, g and gh come before vowels e, I and y, e.g., Skt. scate, Av. Jainti.Av. hacaiti; Skt. jivati, Av. Juaiti; Skt. hanti, Av. Jainti.

(6) There are few istances in which Sanskrit changed j of the palatal series into g as–yaga from yaj and sarga from srj.

(7) The cerebral replaced the dental sibilant after k, r, r, i and u in Sanskrit but in such cases s" apears in Avesta, e.g., (k) Skt. vaksyami, Av. vazsya (r and n) Skt. jus, Av. huska. In Sanskrit celebralization of s is not found immediately before r and r, but no such restriction appears in Avesta, e.g., Skt. visra, Av. vaesa; Skt. tisras, Av. Tisro.

(8) In accordance with the Indo-Iranian system Iranian changed I into r, but Sanskrit retained I in many instances e.g., Skt. palava, 'chaff'; palita, plihan, dala, 1ohita, Av. raoidita, ratha, perethu, sraoni, gar. The classical Sanskrit reversed the Indo-Iranian system, in which I replaced r as leghu, (Vedic raghu) plu (Vedic. pru) lip (Vedic. rip) lih (Vedic.rih). (Similarly Modern Persian also presents certain exceptions, as–lab, listan, lasin, sald).

(9) In few cases peculiar sound of q in Avesta corresponds with Sanskrit s, e.g., Skt. dasyu, Av. daque, Modern Persian daku.

(10) The whole group is voiced and the aspiration attached to the second consonant in combination of dental + surd in Sanskrit, but Iranian substitutes the sibilant s or z in these positions, e.g., Skt. rugh+ta = ruddha, similarly Skt. vettha from vid+ta but Av. Vosta. In such combination Iranian changed Sanskrit d into z, as–Skt. daddhi, Av. dazdi.

(11) In Sanskrit, the combinations of Indo-European gattural+s and Indo-European palatal+s become ks, but Iranian distinguishes two type of the

combinations, having in the former xs and s in the latter, as–(a) Skt. ksap, Av.xsap; Skt. bhaks. Av. baxs; (b) Skt. maksu, Av.mosu; Skt.ksi, Av. ai; Skt. taks, Av. tas. In Sanskrit when ks follows t, in place of ks either k or s appears, e.g., (k) bhakta from bhaks(s) tasti casti from taks, caks; s disappears when ks is final, as- cak vit from vaks, vits Sanskrit s+s = ts and s+s = ks, e.g., avatsit from vas and dveksi. from dvis but in Iranian s+s = s. In Sanskrit when s follows palatal c, it is changed into s, as sascati and Skt. s + s = cch as dus+suna = ducchuna. Sanskrit uses ch in the beginning and cch in the middle of a word. Iranian has s for both ch and cch, e.g., Skt. chid, Av. sead, Skt. gacchati Av. jasaiti.

(12) Iranian preserved Indo-Iranian z and z but Sanskrit eliminated them (a) when z and z follow unlike consonants, they change into d and "-respectively, e.g., adga (Av. azg), (b) when z follows dental d,dh; it disappears and a preceding vowel a changes into e. Skt. edhi (Av. zdi), Skt. sedur (Av. sazdur) Skt. medha (Av. mazda), (c) If z derived from Indo-European s and follows d, dh, it appears celebralizing these consonants and lengthening a short vowel, e.g., Skt. nida, (Av. nizdo) Skt. midha (Av. mizda), (d) between consonants z is eliminated, as -jagdha from jagzdha, (e) Indo-Iranian combinations gh+s = gzh and dzh, bzh are preserved in Iranian as-augh + sa = augzha and dibzha and Sanskrit changed them into ks, ts, ps respectively, e.g., aduksat, dipsati.

(13) Sometimes Iranian represents g for Sanskrit k as -Skt. kesa Av. gaesa (hair).

(14) In Sanskrit occasionally pl to kl, kl to tl and tn to kn and vise versa are altered which is not found in Iranian except kl, tl.

(15) In Sanskrit if initial s is followed by s in the next syllable it is changed to s. Similar change s to s occurs in case of l,' the same change is found in reverse order also. But no such change of sibilants are found in Iranian, e.g., Skt. s'vasura Av. huasura (father-in-law) (s) suska, Av. huska 'dry' (reverse order) s as a, khot, saba, 'have.'

(16) Sanskrit allows the occlusives unvoiced series p, t, t, k to in absolutely final position but voiced series b, d, d, g are substituted before voiced consonants and vowels.

(17) Sanskrit and Iranian differ remarkably in treatment of consonant group, in the former consonant group are drastically reduced. Although Indo-Iranian presents many, in Sanskrit not more than one consonant may stand at the end of a word.

(ii) Noun Formations—Many IE suffixes which formed nouns died out in Indo-Iranian and several new suffixes came into existence. Similarly one suffix which is obsolete in Sanskrit may be produced in Iranian and in connection with another suffix may be found reverse. Hence in addition to old nouns both languages made new nominal formations.

(1) The old neuter suffix -wer / war became nearly extinct in Sanskrit whereas it is very productive in Iranian. As opposed to one adverb sasvar, Iranian has abundant formations with this suffix, e.g, vazdvar, snAvar, dasvar, thanvar, karsvar.

(2) The compound neuter suffixes in i and r, and i and n appear in Sanskrit which are not traceable in Iranian, e.g., bahir, mahina, varina.

(3) The neuter compound suffixes -mer /rnt' and -men became extinct in Sanskrit and are found in Iranian but rarely.

(4) The neuter suffix -ter/ten went out of use in both Sanskrit and Iranian/ but one solitary instance sthatar, 'stability' is found in the Rigveda.

(5) A neuter suffix -tan appears very rarely in both languages, Sanskrit makes neuter nouns with it as naktan 'night' whereas in Iranian it is used for formation of dative infinitives, e.g., cartanary, 'to do.'

(6) Both Sanskrit and Iranian have no trace of the compound neuter suffix -sar/san but in the former few adjectives are made with this suffix, as-matsara, mandasa na 'exhilarated.'

(7) A neuter suffix in -an is obsolete in Iranian, Sanskrit uses -ana to make neuter action noun from verbal roots, e.g., anjana, ointment, patana, 'fall'. sa dana, 'seat.' Similarly compound n-stems make few neuter formations, as- karuna 'dead;' vajina, 'race.'

(8) In Sanskrit and Iranian both the neuter suffix men/mn with extension -t went out of use but few formations are found in Sanskrit, as - s romate, 'fame.'

(9) Iranian preserved the old masculine suffix -tan whereas it disappeared in Sanskrit. Av. parenin, 'having wings'; Skt. svanin, 'keeping dogs.'

(10) A new accented suffix vin developed in Sanskrit which is absent in Iranian, e.g., Skt. tapasvin, 'heated'; tejasvin, 'brilliant.' Similarly another suffix -min is also used to make adjective, as - gomin, 'possessing cows;' svamin, 'owner.'

(11) In Sanskrit adjectives are formed with suffixes -vara and (vala), e.g., (vara) bhasvara, 'brilliant;' is vara, 'lord;' adhvara, 'sacrifice' (-vala) palvala, (pond), vidvala, 'clever.' In certain adjectives formed by suffix -vara, t is inserted, as -jitvara, 'victorious;' itvara 'going.' these suffixes appear also in the weak form, e.g., (-ura) bhangura, 'breaking,' vidura, 'wise;' ankura, 'bud;' ksura, 'razor' (-ula) madhula, parpsula.

(12) As opposed to simple -ra suffix Sanskrit has suffix -ira for adjectival formation, e.g., badhira, 'deaf;' rudhira, 'red;' madira, 'intoxicating' and similarly -ila suffix makes the formations, such as - salila, 'flowing' (water); sittula, 'loose.'

(13) The suffixes -mar and -mal also form adjectives, as -pamara, 'scabby;'

asmara, 'stony;' (with I) paksmala, slesmala. There are certain adjectival formations from suffix -mar with t extension as–kamatha, 'workman;' harmuta, 'tortoise;' narmutha, 'jester.'

(14) A suffix -sar also forms adjective in Sanskrit, as -matsara, 'exhilarating;' rksara, 'hurting;' dhusara, 'grey.'

(15) The themaic adjectival suffixes -vara, -ura and -avena, -ona appear in Sanskrit but in Iranian only -wara is traceable Av. mithvara, (-vana) Skt. vagvana, 'talkative;' satvana, 'warrior;' (-una) Skt. Visuna, 'various;' yatuna, 'energetic;' (-avana) Skt. sravana, 'lame;' lawana, 'salty;' (-ona), Skt. slona, 'lame;' syona, 'soft.'

(16) The adjectival suffix -ina is used in Sanskrit for certain formations whereas Iranian has -aina, e.g., Skt. harina, 'yellowish;' asina, 'old;' daksina, 'right;' Av. izaena, 'made of leather;' drvaena, 'wooden.' Suffix -enya forms gerundives only in Sanskrit, as – varenya, 'desirable;' iksemya, 'worthy to hold' on the other hand suffix -yana is extinct in Sanskrit but appears in Iranian, as - siryana, 'Aryan.'

(17) The suffix -mna forms adjectives in Sanskrit and middle participles in Iranian, e.g., Skt. nimna, 'low;' sumna, 'kindness;' Av. yazemna (participle).

(18) Sanskrit makes few thematic adjectives with suffix -san but it became extinct in Iranian, e.g., Skt. krsna, 'black;' tiksana, 'sharp;' krtsna, 'all.'

(19) The adverbs of time in Sanskrit are formed with the suffixes -tna and -tana. nutana, nutna, 'new;' pratna, 'old.'

(20) Pseudo-participles in Sanskrit are formed with,the suffix asna, e.g., mandasana, 'rejoincing;' namasa na, 'rendering homage;' s avasana, 'strong.'

(21) The new compound suffix -avana and -ayana appear in Sanskrit for adjectival formations, e.g., bhragavana, 'shining;' vasavana, 'possessing riches;' turvayana, 'victorious.' Sanskrit made middle participles with suffix -ayana, e.g., palayana, cintayana.

(22) The feminines of the thematic adjectives are regularly formed with the suffix-a. But opposed to Iranian, Sanskrit uses it as an extension of feminine n-stems. Av. kainin, Skt. kanyana, 'girl.'

(23) Nouns are formed with neuter r and n stems with an extension of -a and its compound suffixes are also used in Sanskrit. In Iranian only -ra is traceable, as Av. urvara, 'crop;' Skt. matra, 'measure;' sura, 'intoxicating liquor;' (-n) trsna, 'thirst;' sena, 'army;' dhena, 'cow;' (-ana) arhana, 'worth;' vadhana, 'slaughter;' rasana, 'rein.' Similar formations are found in Sanskrit by the addition of i and u to the r and n suffixes.

(A) (-i) an guri, 'finger;' abhri, 'hoe,' (adjectives) bhuri, 'abundant;' subhri, 'beautiful;' sahuri, 'mighty' Similarly i- is added to n- suffix to form feminine, e.g., sreni, 'row;' jurni, 'heat;' glani, 'fading.' The feminine nouns are also formed by -ani, as—arani, 'firestick;' vartani, 'track;' tarani (adj.), swift.'

(B) (the suffix u with r) asru, 'tear;' dharu, 'suckling;' bhiru, 'timid;' (-nu) sunu, 'son;' dhenu, 'cow;' grdhnu, 'greedy.' Adjectives are formed with -tnu and -snu suffixes, e.g-:—kavatnu, 'mean;' krtnu,' 'reviling.'

(24) The compound suffixes from stem as developed in Sanskrit as (-tas) r etas 'seed;' srotas, 'stream;' (-nas) reknas, 'property;' apnas, 'wealth;' (Preceded by i and i as- parinas, 'abundance;' dravinas, 'property;' (-sus) daksas, 'ability;' paksas, 'side;' (-vas) pivas, 'fat;' varivas, 'expanse;' (sas) tapus, 'heat;' tarus, 'victory;' dhanus, 'bow.'

(25) The adjectives are formed with -vas suffix, as -sahvas, 'overcoming;' dasva, 'worshipping.' Sanskrit uses this suffix to form the vocative singular of stems in -van and -vant as -vibhAvas from vibhavan and bhagavas from bhagvan. But in Iranian this suffix makes nominative singular of vant stems, e.g., amava from amavant. The suffixes -vas is also used to form perfect participles in Sanskrit, as babhuvas, 'having been;' susruvas, 'having heard.' The adjectival formations in Sanskrit are also made with -vasu and -us suffixes, as - vidhAvasu, 'brilliant;' sacivasu, 'powerful' and vapus, 'wondrous;' vanus, 'eager.'

(26) Iranian uses the old suffix -yah for formation of the comparative adjectives, on the other hand in Sanskrit in such formations i is inserted between root and suffix -yas, e.g., Skt. raghiyas, Av. ranjyah, 'swifter;' Skt. mahiyas, Av. mazyah, 'greater;' sthawiyas, staoyah, 'stouter.'

(27) Sanskrit forms both adjectives and nouns with sufix -asa which is not traceable in Iranian, e.g., vacasa, 'eloquent;' camasa, 'cup;' divasa, 'day;' rabhasa, 'wild.'

(28) The suffix -usa forms adjective both in Sanskrit and Iranian as - Skt. parusa, Av. pourusa, 'grey.' But -ise is used for such formations in Sanskrit only, e.g., mahisa, 'great;' tavisa, 'strong.'

(29) The old adjectival simple suffix -t is preserved in Sanskrit and here it formed adjective and noun both, e.g., sravat, 'stream;' vehat, 'cow which miscarries;' but it in vrddhied form appears in both Iranian and Sanskrit, e.g., Skt. napat, 'grandson;' Av. ravas, carat.

(30) Sanskrit forms the nouns by adding ti, to the roots which end in the vowels i, u and r, as -rit, 'stream;' stut, 'praise;' vrt, 'army.' Moreover this appears in gerunds and adjectival formations in the character of augment jitya, 'having conquered;' krtvan, 'active.'

(31) Nouns and adjectives both are formed in Sanskrit with suffix -it, as–sarit, 'river;' yosit, 'woman;' harit, 'green;' rohit, 'red;' but suffix -ut forms

only nouns, e.g., marut, garmut, grass.

(32) The infinitives of -ti stems are found in Sanskrit, e.g., pitye, 'to drink;' utaye, 'to help;' vitaye, 'to enjoy.'

(33) The old suffix -ti which formed agent nouns has been preserved in Sanskrit whereas it is absent in Iranian, e.g., ra ti, 'liberal;' sapti, 'stead.' Similarly old adjectival formations extended by the addition of suffixal n also appear in Sanskrit, e.g., nitin, 'liberal.' The abstract nouns are formed with suffix -ati, as -vasati, 'abode,' mithati, 'conflict'.

(34) As opposed to Iranian, Sanskrit preserved old neuter suffix -tu as-datu, 'division;' vastu, 'abode;' (adverb) jatu, 'at all, ever;' (agent nouns and adjectives) tapyatu, 'glowing;' mantu, 'councillor.'

(35) As opposed to Iranian, in Sanskrit suffix -tu- is very productive for formation of the infinitives, as - (ace.) kartum, 'to do;' gantum, 'to go;' (dat.) kartava, 'to do;' datave, 'to give;' (abl.) etos, 'from going;' (gen.) kartos, 'doing;' datos, 'giving' (others) hantawai, 'to slay;' etawai, 'to go.'

(36) The Indo-Iranian suffix -tva is found in extended form -tvana to make abstract nouns in Sanskrit, as -sakhitbana, 'friendship;' mahitvana, 'greatness.'

(37) The suffix -tva formed gerundives in both Iranian and Sanskrit but suffix -tva makes gerunds in Sanskrit, as -gatva, 'having gone;' pitva, 'having drunk.'

(38) For formation of abstract nouns Sanskrit and Iranian both used suffix -ta t, but in addition to it Sanskrit used -tati for such formations, as -vasutati, 'wealth;' devatati, 'divinity.'

(39) The old IE suffix -ya which made adjective, associated with accented root, appears in Sanskrit in formation of adjectives from verbal roots which function as gerundives, ashavya, 'to be invoked;' va cya, 'to be spoken.' In connection with adjectival formations Sanskrit confounded a monosyllabic suffix-ya and disyllabic -iya. Example - avya, 'belonging to a sheep;' rathiya, 'belonging to a charriot.'

(40) The IE suffix -vi as opposed to Iranian, is well preserved in Sanskrit, as– dhruvi, 'firm;' darvi, 'ladle;' dudvi, 'shining.'

(41) The suffix -i appears as an augment or special insertion between root and suffix which is a development in the later Indo-Iranian. Whereas Iranian has very few formations of this nature. Sanskrit uses 'i' abundantly as a connecting link between root and termination in the verbal formation, as–Av. asti, Skt. atithi, 'guest;' Skt. mrdika, Av. merezdika.

(iii) Vrddhi—Vrddhi is a new system of derivation which is not known outside of Indo-Iranian:-The system developed during the late Indo-Iranian period. The use of the Vrddhi is exceedingly rare in early Iranian whereas in Sanskrit the system, is found in well-developed form. Its use is connectd with a number of suffixes. The suffixes -a-, -i and -ya with vrddhi very frequently appear in Sanskrit and Iranian. For example (-a) Skt. manava, 'human;' Maruta, 'relating to the Maruts;' Av. margava, 'inhabitant of Margiana;' (-i) Skt. Agnivesi, 'a descendant of Agnevsa;' Av. ahuiri, 'belonging to Ahura;' (-ya) Skt. daivya, 'divine;' Av. ahuiyra, 'son of a prince.' The suffix -ayana in Sanskrit and -enya in Iranian with vrddhi forms the patronymics, e.g., Skt. kanvayana, Av. xsavaenya, 'descendant orxstavi.' In addition to these Sanskrit uses other suffixes such as-iya, -ka and -eya with vrddhi for various formations, e.g., (-iya) parvatiya, 'of the mountains;' (-ka) mamaka, 'mine;' (-eya) arseya, 'descendant of a sage.'

(iv) Grammatical Gender—During the Indo-European period the feminine gender developed and thus three classes of nouns, i.e., masculine, feminine and neuter were inherited by Sanskrit. Iranian abolished the grammatical distinction among the genders.

(1) In Sanskrit -a, i and u are specifically feminine suffixes as—(-a) bala, 'girl;' as opposed to bala, 'boy;' (-i) stan, 'barren cow,' laksmi, 'good fortune;' (-u) babhru, 'brown;' tanu, ,'thin;' as opposed to babhru, tanu (masculine).
(2) The suffix -tar forms masculines and the suffix i is added for feminine formations, as datar (mas.) datari (fem.).
(3) As opposed to neuter -sur the suffix -sar is specialized in the feminine formations, e.g., svasar, 'sister.'
(4) For masculine formations Sanskrit uses the suffix -man, as -dhaman, tokman.
(5) The suffix -as functions in both masculine and feminine, e.g., apas, 'active' (mas. and fem.).
(6) The compound suffix -yas makes the formations in comparative sense which are masculine and suffix -i is added for feminine, as - bhuyas (mas.) bhuyasi (fern.).
(7) The suffixes -i and -u appear in neuter formations but non-neuter nouns formed by these suffixes are either masculines or feminines.

(v) Nominal Composition—Certain types of the nominal compounds, the so-called by the Hindu grammarians as Karmadharaya, Tatpurusa and Bahuvrihi are inherited by Indo-Iranian and well preserved in Sanskrit. Sanskrit made certain innovations in Tatpurusa. Besides the old type of the formations, Sanskrit has a new type of compounds of Tatpurusa in which its genitive ending and very often its accent are retained by the first member, as–vanaspati, 'lord of the wood;' brahaspati, 'lord of devotion;' divodasa, 'servant of heaven;' gopada, 'cow's footprint.' In Indo-Iranian certainly in its later period a quite new type of the nominal compound known as dvandva in Sanskrit developed, which has two duals, each retaining its own accent, e.g., Skt. dyava-prthivi, 'heaven and earth;' Av. pasuvira, 'beast and man.' The dvanda compound system has fully developed in Sanskrit and we find different stages of its development.

(1) Except in case of nominative accusative the first member retains the form of nominative accusative, e.g., Mitra-Varunayah.
(2) In certain instances of the above formations the accent is lost in the first member, as—Soma rudrayoh.
(3) In the final stage the first member is found in its simple stem form, as–indrava yti.

As opposed to early Sanskrit Avesta made dvanda compounds by feminine nouns. For example -apa urvaire, 'water and crops.' Such formations appear in Sanskrit in the later Vedic period, as - ja ya patt 'wife and husband'. Sanskrit has such dvanda formations in which the first member is formed by suffix -tar, as -pitaputrau, 'father and son,' similarly plural dvandas are also found in Sanskrit, e.g., pitaputra, 'father and sons'. The neuter dvandas had also fully developed in early Sanskrit, e.g., ahora trani 'days and nights.'

Adverbial compound, a new form of the nominal compounds which is called avyayibhava originated in Sanskrit in which just like simple adjectives, compound adjectives are used adverbally. Generally these compounds consist of a preposition or other indeclinable as first member as—antima tram, 'excessively'; upanadam, 'near the river;' uparajam, 'near the king.'

(vi) Case Terminations—Sanskrit and Iranian both preserved many old systems in connection with case endings, nevertheless they made certain innovations here and there.

(l) In Sanskrit and Iranian both the case ending in the instrumental singular is normally –a, as–Skt. pada, Av. vehrka and it is also found in the zero grade, e.g., Skt. citti, Av. dsti. But this form appears in Iranian in u-stems also, e.g., xratu , mainyu.
(2) The Indo-Iranian termination in the dative singular -ai developed into -e in both Sanskrit and Iranian, as - Skt. pade, pitre, Av. vise, pittre. Here also Iranian innovated -oi such as erezej' yoi.
(3) The form -a t in Sanskrit and -at in lranian is found in the ablative singular in the declension of thematic stems as Skt. vr kat Av. vehrkat. But in Iranian this form appears in other classes also. Such as–garott, athrat.
(4) The Indo-European form '-es' or Indo-Iranian '-as' for the genitive-ablative singular is found as a reduced termination -s in Sanskrit and Iranian both but it is found in Sanskrit in -i- and u-stems, whereas in Iranian in connection with r-stems, e.g., Skt. agnes, suneos, Av. pitars.
(5) Sanskrit has locative singular without ending in n-stems as–ahan. This

oldest form of locative singular is found in Iran without ending from a root noun, as–man, 'mind'. Sanskrit made some innovations, one form consists of the particle -i e.g., adati. Another form of the locative singular with -ani or -ni in n-stems. Such as - rajant rajni.

(6) The Indo-European endings for accusative plural, masculine and feminine were -ns after consonantal stems and -ns after vocalic stems. This IE -ns after consonantal stems developed into -as in Sanskrit, as - padas. The endings of the feminine vocalic stems in Sanskrit are -as, -is, -us and rs. This absence of n is noticed in Iranian in -a stems, as - urvara. The terminations in accusative plural of masculine vocalic stems in Sanskrit are -an, -in, -un and -ru.

(7) Iranian and Sanskrit preserved all four types of Indo-European terminations of nominative–accusative plural neuter. As opposed to Sanskrit, Iranian has a new series of neuter plurals which is characterised by vrddhi of the suffix, e.g., ayare, 'days;' vaca, 'words;' naman, 'names, but Sanskit added -i in such cases as- 'namani and elided n in the case of neuter n-stems, such as–sirsa, 'heads;' bhuma, 'beings.'

(8) The ending of the instrumental plural in Sanskrit is -bhis and in Iranian -bis. Similarly dative - ablative plural terminates in -bhyas in Sanskrit and byo in Iranian.

(9) The Indo-Iranian termination of genitive plural -am is preserved in Sanskrit and Iranian but an -n- is inserted before termination in vocalic stems. Iranian shows absence of this -n-in -r stems.

(10) Iranian has the ending -bya for instrumental -dativa-ablative dual. Sanskrit added an element -m to it which is its innovation and has ending -bhyam.

(11) The genitive–locative plural terminates in -os in Sanskrit whereas Iranian has -a for the genitive and -o for the locative. Such as, Skt. pados, pitros; Av. (gen.) nairikaya (loc.) zastayo.

(vii) Pronouns—Sanskrit and Iranian inherited a considerable number of Indo-Iranian pronominal inflections. Even both the languages innovated new systems. Both the languages made some slight difference in common systems also.

First and Second Persons :

(1) Singular renders the following differences in Sanskrit and Iranian (nom.) Skt. aham, Av. azem, Skt. twam, Av. twem, tum, but Iranian preserved Indo-European tu also (ace.) Skt. mam, tvam, Av. mam, thwam. (the enclitic forms used for both genitive and dative). Skt. me, te; Av. moi, me, tai te (inst.). Skt. maya, tvaya, Av. ma thwa. Iranian preserves the original system. The second persons tua identical to Av. thwa appears in

Sanskrit but very rarely. (loc.) Skt. mayi, tvayi; evidence (abl.) Skt. mathwa; Av. mat, thwat. but Sanskrit innovated new forms, such as, matas, mattas, tvattas (dat.) Skt. mahyam, Tubhyam; Av. maibya, maibyo; taibya, taibyo. Here Sanskrit innovated additional -m whereas Avestan -b-is also not original. (gen.) Skt. mama, tava, Av. mana, tava. The Avestic mana contains n- suffix which is its innovation.

(2) Plural: (Nom.) Skt. vayam, yuyam; Av. vaem, yiizam but Iranian preserved Indo-European second form, as-Av. yus. (Acc.) Skt. asman, nas, Av. ehma, ahma. Iranian preserved primitive form and particle '-an' is a Sanskrit innovation (Inst.) Skt. asmabhis, yasmabhis. The original ending of this case is preserved in Iranian as xsma, its counterparts yusma appears in few compounds. (Gen.) Skt. asmakam, yusmakam, AV. ahmakem, yusmakem; (Dat), asmabhyam, yusmabhyam; Av. ahmaibya, yusmaibya; (Abl.) asmat, yusmat; Av. xsmat, yusmat, (locative). Sanskrit made an innovation in locative, e.g., asmasu, yusmasu, (enclitic form used for accusative dative-genitive) Skt. nas vas; Av. ne, no, ve, vo.

(3) Dual: (Nom.) Skt. avam, yuvam; vam once appear in the Rigveda Av. va, yuva; va is the Indo-European and in vam -m is Sanskrit innovation; (Acc.) avam, yuvam; Av. eava, yava; (Abl.) Av. atyuvat, Av. eavat, yavat; (gen.) Skt. yuvaku, Av. yavakem; (enclitics) Skt. nau, vam; Av. na, va, which are original.

(4) The Indo-European reflexive pronoun, the initial of which varied between -sy- and -s-, disappears in Sanskrit and is preserved in Iranian in on one form or other, hvavoya, is the form of dative singular of this pronoun in Iranian. Sanskrit uses va- 'self' in compounds, such as, svayam, 'self;' svatas, 'from oneself'. An enclitic form with initial s- is found in Iranian, as hai, he, se but it is also absent in Sanskrit. The dual and plural forms of this pronoun in Iranian are hi, his.

(5) Iranian preserved the Indo-European possessive adjectives, such as, ma, 'my;' thwa, 'thy;' which Sanskrit lost but created fresh forms, as ma maka, tavaka; madiya; tvadiya, as madiya, yusmadiya, matka, 'mine.'

(6) The singular of the second personal pronoun is used for some honorific term but normally bhavan and its irregular construction bhagavan are substituted for this purpose but it is not traceable in Iranian.

(7) In place of the old reflexive pronouns, Sanskrit uses the nouns tanu, 'body' and atman, 'soul', which is shared by Iranian also.

DEMONSTRATIVE, INTERROGATIVE AND RELATIVE PRONOUNS

Pronouns sa, esa, sya

Singular

(1) (Nom. -acc. neuter) Skt. tat, Av. tat; Skt. etat, Av. aetat; tyat Skt. Yat, Av. Yat; Skt. kat, Av. kat; Skt. tvat, enat (lnst. masc. neuter) Skt. tena. Some forms in Iranian also have this lntrusive -n-. They are not made on the diphthongal stem but on the ordinary thematic, as, Av. avkana, tyana, avana (loc.) Skt. tasmin, In this form the '-in' is a Sanskrit innovation. Iranian preserved original forms with simple 'i-,' as - Av. ahmi, kahmi, eahmi, yahmi.

(2) The interrogative pronoun 'ka' is declined in accordance with the pronominal declension, but there are some exceptions which are as follows - (nom. -acc. singular neuter) Skt. kim, Av. kat, kit is also found in the Rigveda. Iranian preserved the IE an i stem and a-stem as, Av. (Nom.) cis (acc. singular) eim (nom. singular plural) caya but Sanskrit nearly abolished this form of pronoun.

(3) The enclitic pronoun—ena, 'him, her, it' appears in Sanskrit but is absent in Iranian. On the other hand 'ava' is preserved in Iranian and became extinct in Sanskrit. Tne pronoun tva- 'a certain one, many a one,' is found in Sanskrit. Similar to it Avesta has thwat in neuter singular. The pronoun sima, 'oneself' is found only in Sanskrit.

(4) Ayam Pronoun—(Nom. sg. masc.) Skt. ayam, Av. aem (Nom. sg. fern) Skt. iyam, Av. im; (acc. sg. masc.) Skt. imam, Av. imam; (acc. sg. fem.) Skt. imam, Av. ima (nom. ace. pl. fem.) ima's, Av. ima(s).

(5) Asau Pronoun—(nom. sg.) Skt. asau, Av. hau. The Iranian form is the original. (nom. ace. sg. neuter) Skt. adas. In other than Nominative, Iranian uses the stem 'ava-' which disappeared in Sanskrit.

(viii) Adverb—Formation '-s' of the adverbs is already mentioned in connection with nominal formations. Some adverbial suffixes are given below with the formations in Sanskrit and Iranian-tas, Skt. itas, 'from here;' tatas, 'from there;' daksinatas, 'from the right;' Av. xato, 'of oneself;' aiwita, 'around;' amata, 'from there;' tit - this sufix is used in Sanskrit only. Formations - praktat, 'from in front;' udaktat, 'from above,' purastat, in the -tra:- Iranian and Sanskrit both form adverbs with this suffix with a locative sense from pronominal stems, but the latter uses noun stems also, such as–Skt. atra, 'here;' tatra, 'there;' kutra, 'where;' devatra, 'among gods;' daksinatra, 'on the right side;' Av. ittra, 'here;' athra, 'there;' kuttra, 'where;' vanhattra, 'at the place of dwelling.'

-tha - :- The Indo-Iranian suffix -tha is used in Sanskrit and Iranian both for formation of adverb of manner. Besides Sanskrit uses a new suffix '-tham' for such formations–Skt. ittham, 'thus'; katham, 'how.'

-da :- The old suffix -da was regularly used in both Sanskrit and Iranian for formation of adverb. Besides Sanskrit added to it -nim and thus suffix -ta danim, as - idanim, tadanim, visvadanim.

-dha:- This suffix is a Sanskrit innovation. The adverbs formed from it are as follows - caturdha, 'four fold;' bahudha, 'in many ways;' visvadha.

-dha :- This suffix is preserved in Sanskrit in rare cases but Iranian uses it regularly in accordance with phonology in form -da-, e.g., –Skt. sadha, Av. ida, 'here;' kuda; where.' In Sanskrit it is usually weakened to -ha, as – saha, 'with;' iha, 'here;' kuha, 'where.'

-rhi- :- Sanskrit formed a compound suffix -rhi from Indo-European adverbial -r suffix and -dhi (hi) suffix. The adverbs made with it are as follows–karhi, 'when;' tarhi, 'then;' yarhi, 'where;' amurhi, 'there;' etarhi, 'now.'

(ix) Adverbs made with case forms

(1) As in case of adjective, Sanskrit uses nominative-accusative singular neuter to form adverbs from adjectives and adjectival compounds and rarely from nouns. Followings are such formations -puru, 'abundantly;' mahi, 'greatly;' bhuyas, 'more;' nyak, 'downwards;' name, 'by name;' satyam, 'truly;' similarly for meaning 'like' the adverbs are formed with suffix - vat, as - puranavat, 'as of old;' manuvat, 'like Manu.'

(2) By the use of the accusative sinsular in case of masculine and feminine nouns Sanskrit makes certain adverbs as - kaman, 'at will;' vasam, 'freely;' naktam, 'by night.'

(3) Adverbs with the use of the instrumental–sahasa, 'suddenly;' distya, 'fortunately;' daksinena, 'to the south;' uccais, 'on high.'

(4) Generally adverbial instruments in -a give the locative sense, as-dosa , 'in the evening;' diva, 'by day.'

(5) In Sanskrit shift accent makes adverbs, such as -dasina, 'to the right;' madhya, 'in the middle.'

(6) The Indo-Iranian suffix -aya is still preserved in Sanskrit and Iranian both for formation of adverbs–Skt. naktya, 'by night;' svapnaya, 'in a dream;' Av. asaya, 'rightly;' angraya, 'evilly.'

(x)Prepositions and Post-positions—As opposed to Iranian a series of prepositions are less developed in Sanskrit. In contradiction to Iranian which preserved old system Sanskrit placed adverbial formations after related noun but not before it like Iranian. But Sanskrit shows freer order and looser connection of the words with nouns which are governed by them.

(xi) The Verb—Majority of the Indo-European and Indo-Iranian suffixes which formed verbs were in use in both Sanskrit and Iranian, and in addition to them some suffixes originated such as–ar r-Skt. dhar, 'to hold; ' svar, 'to sound.'

-am –Skt. ksam, 'endure' (Iranian-Pashto-amel) Pashto-zyamel, 'endure.'

-u :–Skt. sru, 'to flow;' Av. sru, 'to hear.'

ah h :–This suffix was in use in Sanskrit and Iranian but they innovated some new formations. In the present tense the root appears in simple form where the intervening n- suffix separates the ah h s,uffix and root. The Sanskrit and

Iranian forms differ to some extent, e.g., Skt. bhrll Ci ti, Av. bhrinati, 'cut.'

-t in simple form and in combination with i and u, as -krt, 'to cut;' mrit, 'to fall in pieces;' dyut, 'to shine.'

-th :–Skt. snath, 'to pierce;' grath, 'to tie.'

-dh :–Skt. sprdh, edh but Iranian forms differ slightly, as - Av. spred, azdya-

-bh :–Skt.:- subh, 'to be bright'; stubh, 'to praise'.

-c–Skt:- yac, 'to ask;' ruc, 'to shine.'

-j-Skt.:–ruj, 'to break;' vij, 'to tremple.'

-h- :–druh, 'to injure.'

(A) Accent of Verbal Stems: It is a unique characteristic of Sanskrit that the verb of an independent clause has no accent but at the beginning of the independent clause and under certain special conditions the verb is accented in independent clauses. If verb is accented, in connection with thematic formations the verbal stem has unchangeable accent, but accent varies between stem and personal ending in case the non-thematic formations, e.g., dvesti, 'hates'; dvisanti, dviste, yunakti, yunjanti, yunkte.

(B) Augment and Reduplication: In the early stage Sanskrit has both augmented and unaugmented preterites and later on the augment became obligatory. But the unaugmented preterites mainly prevailed in early Iranian and in the later stage the augment was in regular use.

In case of reduplication the old system of Indo-Iranian continued in use in both Sanskrit and Iranian. Still certain innovations appeared in both the languages. In Sanskrit the roots beginning with the group s+occlusive, the occlusive is repeated, such as-pasparsa, tisthati, caskanda. But in such cases Iranian has's' or 'h' in the reduplicating syllable. Moreover, Sanskrit changes certain sounds in reduplicated forms. Such as, for an aspirate, a non-aspirate appears in reduplication, e.g., dadhati, and in case of h, j is found in reduplicating syllable. Before 'a' in a reduplicating syllable Sanskrit palatalises the old velar series, e.g., jaghaha, cakara.

(C) Personal Terminations-In respect of personal ending Sanskrit and Iranian differ in certain systems which are given below.

(D) Active Termination:

(1) Besides Indo—Iranian system, Iranian preserved in the thematic classes the IE primary ending (-0) of first person singular, e.g., spasya.

(2) In the imperaive of second person singular Iranian preserved IE ending -idhi in form of -di- but-Sanskrit innovated -hi- in such cases, as - Skt. jahi, Av. j' aidi, 'slay;' Skt. ihi, Av. idi, 'go.'

(3) In addition to Indo-Europeana and Indo-Iranian ending tu in imperative of third singular Sanskrit, uses an alternative IE ending tod in form of tat as -vitiat.

(4) Whereas in first person plural both old primary endings mas and -masi

appear in Sanskrit, Iranian uses exclusively -mahi as the primary ending, e.g., Skt. imas, 'we go;' bharamasi, Av. baramahi.

(5) Besides Indo-Iranian primary and secondary endings -tha and-ta in second person plural, Sanskrit uses the alternative endings -thana and tana respectively in which the na is Sanskrit innovation, e.g., vadathana, hantana.

(6) Sanskrit retained old primary ending -anti in third plural. Iranian has a corresponding weak form of the corresponding ending -at as, dadat, jigerezat. In secondary ending Iranian and Sanskrit both continued to use the Indo-Iranian ending -an, but Iranian preserved the old form an alternative endings -are and ares and in such cases Sanskrit used -ur, e.g., Skt. (impf.) adadur, adhur (aor,), syur(opt) Av. adare hyare, jamyares, (pf.) Skt. asur, cikitur, Av. auhare, cikoiteres.

(7) In Sanskrit the Indo-European primary ending '-vas' was used in first duaL In such cases in Iranian -vahi appears, a corresponding form -masi is absent in Sanskrit. Such as Skt. bharavas, Av- usvahi.

(8) Second person dual is absent in Iranian and Sanskrit has in such cases the primary ending -thas as - bharathas and in third person -tas, e.g., bhavatas, here Iranian uses to and -tho such as barato, yuidyatho. Sanskrit has -thur and -tur in perfect but -tare appears in Iranian in such cases, e.g., Skt. cakrathur, cabratur Av. yaetatare.

(E) Middle endings

(1) Iranian preserved IE secondary ending -so in form of -ha in second singular whereas Sanskrit innovated -thas in such cases, as - Skt. adhatthas, Av. zayanha.

(2) Sanskrit and Iranian differ slightly in case of termination in first plural. The former uses mahe and -mahi as primary and secondary endings whereas in the latter maide and -maidi appear, such as - Skt. yajamahe, Av. yazamaide, Skt. abha ramahi Av. varemaidi.

(3) In case of third plural Sanskrit made many innovations, the primary endings -ante and -ate and secondary endings -anta -ata -ra and -ran are Sanskrit development, which are not found in Iranian.

(4) In Sanskrit first person dual has -vahe in primary ending and -vahi in secondary but Iranian has only -vaidi in both cases, e.g., Skt. bharavahe, abharavahi, Av. dvaidi.

(5) Second dual is absent in Iranian. The secondary ending varies between Iranian -tern and Sanskrit -tam, as -Skt. as ruvatam, Av. asrvatem.

(xii) Tenses—

(A) Present tense : In accordance with the present system the roots in

Sanskrit are classified into ten classes of which six belong to non-thematic class and the rest come in the thematic type.

(B) Non-thematic presents: Sanskrit produced a new type of present in this class, e.g., caksur, duhur, ise, cite, bruve, saye, vide, dubre, sere, duhrate, serate, aisa, adhuha, aduhra, aduhran, aseran, aṣerata, duham, vidam, sayam, duhram duhram duhratam sseratam. A typical old series of this are preserved in Sanskrit in which the stem of roots is made with suffix -i which is absent in Iranian e.g. Skt roditi svapti vamite janisva stanihi hi socim i Av. Mraoiti, mraot.

(C) Reduplicating or hu- class:

(1) Various treatment developed in Sanskrit in case of roots long -a such as-dadvas/dadmas.

(2) Another type of formation appears in Sanskrit in which vowel -i- or -i- is inserted between root and termination e.g. jahimas, jahihi, sisihi, mimite thas.

(D) nu- and u- Classes: Besides old suffix nu Sanskrit presents same formations with suffix na as – vrnati, stranati, ksimati.

(E) na or kri Class: Sanskrit innovated ni- in the weak cases besides the strong form of the suffix -na whereas Iranian lost a completely in the weak grade such as–Skt. vinite, mimite, Av. verente, skrente, Sanskrit i or Iranian e appears only before the consonantal terminations but both Sanskrit or Iranian presents the simple reduced form of the suffix before vowels, such as -Skt. janate, Av. zanaite.

(F) Nasal-infixing or rudh class: Many languages use weak forms instead of the strong forms of the nasal—infixing class and the whole type is transferred to the thematic class. Sanskrit also shares this feature but it is not traceable in Iranian. Such as - Skt. vindati, Av. vinasti.

(G) Cur Class: In addition to causative sense Sanskrit uses the suffix -aya for formation of the present, asturaya, citaya rucaya.

(H) Future:

(1) Iranian forms the future with the suffix -sya- put Sanskrit uses -sya - and -is ya - both for such formations. For example–Av. vaxsya, Skt. dasyati, karisyati.

(2) Besides the ordinary future Sanskrit produced another type or periphrastic future which is used to express some specified time and based on the agent nouns in -tar. such as–karta,- kartarau, kartaras, kartasmi, kartasi.

(I) Aorist:

(1) In formation of the root aorist Sanskrit introduced vowel-i- or -i- into the middle forms in the case of roots in a such as–adita, asthita, adimahi.

(2) Sanskrit produced a number of reduplicated forms of the a- aorist/ as - apaptat.
(3) Sanskrit developed a new type of the reduplicated aorist in which it is attached not to the simple verb but to the causative, as–ajijanat aviorahat.
(4) Sanskrit made new formations of the s- aorist taking the connecting vowels -i- as – anaists, acchaitsit.
(5) Sanskrit developed the sis- aorist from a mixture of the s- aorist and the is- aorist, which is absent in Iranian as –ayasis ayasit.

(J)Perfect : Whereas in Iranian in the perfect conjugation the use of the auxilliary vowel is almost absent. Sanskrit innovated a type in the connecting vowel -i- which is found before the terminations that begin with a consonant/ such as - bubodhitha, ninayitha, daditha, paptima, dadima.

(K) Injunctive : Sanskrit lost injunctive, but ma continued to be used in connection with unaugmented aorist forms to express prohibition as–ma gah, 'do not go;' ma bhaisih, 'do not be afraid'.

(L)Imperative:
(1) In the imperative fonnations in active of 2nd person singular in Sanskrit non-thematic verbs terminate in. the ending -, hi but dhi appears after' consonantal stems. In such cases Iranian has only -edi, for example :- Skt, ihi, 'go' vidhi, 'know,' gadhi, 'go' Av. idi, 'go.'
(2) In case of 3rd person singular and plural in the active Sanskrit preserved Indo-European system of making the forms by the addition of a particle. –u-. It is absent in Iranian, such as Skt astu, hantu, santu.
(3) The 2nd person singular in Sanskrit has the ending in the middle -sua but 'uha and–sva both appear in Iranian, such as :—Skt. bharasva, Av.
(4) In the 3rd person plural of the middile, Sanskrit in addition to Indo-hranian ending am innovated -ram as duhram.
(5) Sanskrit preserved an old termination -tat which is extinct in Iranian, e.g. vittat, 'know' brutat, 'say' dhattat 'put.'
(6) Sanskrit developed an ending -si in the 2nd person singular e.g. pa'rsi 'Cross,' dha'kisi, burn-prasi, 'fill."

(M) Desiderative
(1) Sanskrit made an innovation in roots in a by keeping the strong form in the desiderative, as :—pipass, yiyase as opposed to pipisa, ditsa.
(2) Another Sanskrit development is the augmentation of the desiderativc sa with the union vowel i and appearing as -isa, such as dedhisa pipisa jihisa.

(N) Denominative verhs

Sanskrit made great innovation in denominative formations in case of thematic stems As opposed to the principles of lndo-European stem formation Sanskrit added a further suffix to a final thematic suffix, such as :—vasnayati 'bargains,' devayati, 'cultivates the gods" amitrayati, 'act like an enemy.'

(O) Infinitive

(1) The locative infinitives are fonned in Sanskrit by suffix-tari while Iranian uses there in such cases e.g. Skt. vidhartari, Av. barethri.

(2) In case of infinitive Sanskrit developed a unique feature. The infinitive and the noun which is governed by the infinitive arc place in the same case, for example "to see the sun" is expressed as drsaye suryaya 'for seeing for sun,' and "save us from falling into a pit" is expressed as tradhvam kartad avapadah "save from a pit, from falling down."

(P) Participle

(1) The middle participles are fonned in Sanskrit with the suffix amana in classes but Iranian has amna in such cases. Skt. Yajamana, Av. Yazemna.

(2) The possessive suffix-vant makes the past participle passive in Sanksrit but it is absent in Iranian, as krtavant.

(3) The suffix tva in Sankrit and thawa in Iranian makes future passive participle. such as;—Skt, Jatva, Av. "Jathwa 'to be slain' Sankrit innovated new formations (i) -iya :—vacya, guhya, devya (ii) Ihe augment of -t-srutya (iii) -tavya :—anitavya (iv) aniya :—upajivaniya (v) enya :—Varenya (vi) -ayya :—panayya.

(Q) Gerund

Gerund is development of Sanskrit which uses suffixes ya, -tva, -tvi and tvaya for its formation.

Foreign Influence on Sanskrit

Sanskrit developed certain unique features which arc not traceable in other Indo-European languages even in Iranian. Such development of Sanskrit is an innovation of the cerebral series -t, th, d, dh, n, s which is entirely absent in all other Indo-European languages; only two Iranian dialects namely Khotanese and Pasto bordering on Sanskrit area share this feature of Sanskrit. It is clear that such sounds developed in an Indo-European Language only in India and the immediate vicinity, it can be safely assumed that Sanskrit borrowed these sounds from any non-Aryan language in India. The cerebrals is are found abundantly in the Dravidian and Munda languages. But Savara which is an old member of munda languages and preserved archaic character of the family, do not possess cerebral series; and cerebrals are most ancient in Dravidian. Hence the influence of Dravidian produced the emergence of the cerebrals in Sanskrit.

The influence is detectable in the following combinatory changes by which certain groups are affected; (1) when preceded by s, originally dental t, th are changed into cerebrals, as :- vrsti, 'rain; vasti, 'wishes;' astra, 'goad' (2) Similarly when z follows originally dental d, the sibilant disappeared and the latters became cerebrals d, dh, e.g. nida, ugha (3) The occlusion of the first part of the group ss produced ts, ks, t (see above) (4) when originally dental n preceded in the same word by s, r, r, it became cerebral n, as karna, cause.

When r or r preceded dentals, the dentals became cerebral e.g. nate, actor' (cf nrt'to dance'), vikata, (enormous) (cf. vikrta) bhata, 'soldier (cf. bhrts). When r followed dentals, they very often become cerebrals, such as : - anda (egg' cf. ondarak) kheta, 'village' (cf. ksetra)

Not only the cerebral series emerged in Sanskrit by Dravidian influence but this influence is visible in two Iranian dialects namely Khotanese and Pasto which border on the immediate vicinity of the Sanskrit area.

References

1. Aryans-London, New York, 1926, p.3.
2. Encyclopaedia of Religion and Ethics, Vol. II, p.13.
3. S. K. Chatterji's Indo-Aryan and Hindi, p.11, Ahmadabad, 1942.
4. H. Oldenberg Ancient India, Its Languages and Religion, p.50.
5. T. Burrow, Sanskrit Language, p.73 (London).

6

The Indo-European Culture

Undoubtedly the cultural antecedents of the undivided Aryans are still shrouded in mystery. Archaeology helps us but very little. V.G. Childe aptly remarks that the Aryan history is, of course, "a veritable labyrinth of complicated and intermingled cultures each with a long and intricate history of its own behind. There is no single thread to guide us certainly out of maze, but rather a multitude of strands intertwined and entangled and leading along the divergent paths."[1]

So far material culture is concerned, we have very few archaeological remains such as pot-sherds or copper implements, at our disposal to know something about their cultural history. In order to conjure up the image of their cultural antecedents only the science of linguistic palaeontology guides us.

THE PRIMITIVE RELIGIOUS BELIEFS OF THE INDO-EUROPEANS BEFORE THEIR DISPERSION

In the scientific sense the religion is the backbone of a civilization. The real history of man is the history of religion. M. Muller remarks, "This is the foundation that underlies all profane history; it is the light, the soul and life of history and without it all history would indeed be profane."[2] The religion occupies an important place in the Aryan history.

We know that the Rigveda is the oldest literature of the Aryans. The Rigvedic religion is full of exuberant power and light to illumine the primitive religion of the Aryans. The Rigveda which most faithfully preserved the ancient thoughts, ancient feelings and the most primitive types of the Aryan faiths; stands as sine qua non for the Aryan religion as the Quran and the Old Testament for Islam and Judism.[3] M.Muller rightly remarks, "As the language of the Veda, Sanskrit is the most ancient type ... so its thoughts and feelings contain in reality the first roots and germs of the intellectual growth which by unbroken chain connect our own generation with ancestors of the Aryan race."[4] Hence for the knowledge of the original religious beliefs of the Aryan, the Rigveda is indispensable. A religious faith reconstructed by the comparison of similar cults, conceptions and religious traditions prevalent among other Aryan branches must be in consonance with the Rigvedic faith.

(i) Notion of God—The early Aryans were the nature worshippers. The Indo-European languages have preserved the primitive word of 'god' that reveals the source from which the first conception of divine power was derived. It is Indo- European word 'deivos'. Its Sanskrit variation 'deva' conceals the history of development of notion of God among the primitive Aryans, which appears to have come by the simple process from bright beings to the heavenly immortals. Sanskrit deva, Latin deus, Lithuanian diewas, Irish dia, Old Norse tiver, all of which mean god or gods are etymologically connected with Sanskrit root 'div' that means 'to radiate' or 'to shine.' It is apparent that deva originally meant bright or light that was an expression for the quality which the sky, the sun, the moon, the stars, the dawn, the day, the lightning and the seas all shared. It is evident that the idea of God came among the Aryans from the luminous manifestations of nature and is associated with natural phenomena.

Another general term for 'god' that has been zealously retained among certain Aryan languages, shows the abstract conception of a good god. The Avestan 'bagha,' Slavic 'bogu' are essentially implied 'god' of whereas Sanskrit 'bhaga' connotes 'god of fortune.' The word means spender of goods or blessings. It infers that the Indo-Europeans believed that these heavenly powers were beneficient.[5] Certain Aryan languages have the common word that determines the spiritual concept developed in the Aryan religion since the earliest times. The Avastan word 'spenta,' Slavic, Svetu, Lithuanian, szventas used as an attribute of divine power mean 'pure' or 'holy.' It shows that these powers were worshipped with awe and reverence.

The primitive Aryans had-the essential sentiments of belief and reverence towards their gods. Sanskrit sraddha, Celtic cretum, Latin credo meaning 'believe' and the Avestan yaz, Sanskrit yaj, Greek ay, meaning 'rever' are their expression used for their gods.

(ii) Sky—That the Aryan religion had been founded on nature worship is a well-established fact. The scene of most of the natural phenomena is sky. It appears that the primitive Aryans, first of all, deified sky. Nearly all the scholars hold that sky is the principal and supreme deity of the undivided Aryans.[6] O. Schrader remarks that worship of sky and powers of nature in its train formed the real kernel of the primitive Aryan religion.[7] The Aryans personifed sky. He is Dyaus pitar among the Vedic people, Zeus-pater among the Greeks, Diespiter or Jupitar among the Romans and Tiu and Tyr in the Teutonic world. The identity of these names can, in no case, be doubted.

(iii) Another God of Sky—Another Aryan sky god is Varuna. It appears from the comparative study of the Aryan mythologies that, if not originally, later on during the Indo-European period another god of sky was formed. He is the Rigvedic Varona, Greek Ouranos and Avestic Varena. The Scholars are at variance on the identity of these deities on the basis of phonetic difficulty. This is why some scholars deny that the antiquity of Varuna goes back to the Indo-European period. On the contrary the competent authorities[8] like Mullar, Hillebrandt, Keith, Macdonell, Hopkins, Schrader and Brugrnann derive Sanskrit Varuna and Greek Ouranos from the Sanskrit root vr, which means 'to cover' or 'to encompass,' hence Varuna or Ouranos is the encompassing sky. Bloomfield9 explains that Sanskrit Varuna is the Indo-European Uoru-nos and Greek Ouranos, the Indo-European Uorunos and claims that Uoru-nos and Uoru-nos are differing very little. The Greek Ouranos and the Vedic Varuna are identical not only in name but in character also. In the Veda Varuna is a name of firmament and especially connected with the night.[10] Hesiod tells that Ouranos covers everything and when he brings the night, he is stretched out everywhere embracing the earth.[11] M. Mullar[12] tells, ouranos in the language of Hesiod, is used as a name for the sky. He is made or born that he should be a firm place for the blessed gods." Such a striking similarity both in name and character of the two deities convinces A.C. Das that "this sounds almost as if the Greek myth had still preserved a recollection of the etymological power of Uranos."[13] In respect of Persian Varena Prof. Westergard tells "The Zend word Varena corresponds also etymologically, on the one hand, to Greek Ouranos and on the other to the Indian Varuna.

These facts force us to believe that in the Indo-European period there existed another god of the sky. He was the Indo-European Uoru-nnos who most probably represented the encompossing sky.[15] Later on this god developed independently as the Vedic Varuna, the Greek Ouranos and the Iranian Varena in different environments.

(iv) Thunder God (I)—The primitive Aryans had sky as their supreme deity; after split among the majority of the Aryan branches the thunder-god assumed[15] this position at the expanse of heaven. Originally, the supreme deity, Heaven in addition to his own office, was thunder-god too. The Rigveda[16] says that Dyaus is himself thunder-god. The Greek Zeus[17] who is 'far eyed sky' has absorbed the character of the 'thunderer.' Conversely the Lithuanian Perkunas,[18] the thunder-god has taken upon himself the functions of the supreme god of heaven. Similarly Roman Jupitor[19] besides his other office, performs the work of the thunder-god. From the above facts it is gleaned that heaven withdrew into background in favour of his son, the thunder-god. How this new development had taken place, the history of Aryan religion does not offer any clue. Only the Indo-European father-slaying-myth offers a slight hint that the special god of thunder superseded heaven or usurped his power. The Rigveda tells that Indra killed his father Dyaus.[20] In the same way Greek Cronus killed his father Uranus, the Roman Heaven.[21] It is noteworthy that the names of thunder god of various Aryan branches are not identical at all; but their mythological traits are strikingly similar. Every Aryan mythology narrates that the thunder-god kills the drought dragon in order to release the pent up water to liberate the people from the miseries. As the Vedic thunder-god, Indra[22] kills dragon Vritra, the Avestic Tishtrya,[23] Apaosa; the Teutonic Donar, the wolf Fernis;[23] the Greek Appolo, the Python, and the Hittite Inaras, the dragon IIIuyunkas.[24]

Another Indo-European myth illustrates the god liberating the cows of clouds imprisoned in a mountain. Here the Rigveda tells the fight of Indra with Visvarupa.[26] The classical myths describe the fight of Greek Herakle with Geryones and of Roman Hercules with Cacus. Even the details of Indian and classical myths are surprisingly identical. Indra liberates the cows from the avaricious who imprisoned them and did not offer them as sacrifice to the gods. Similarly Hercules carries the cattle from the monster Cacus who has stolen them from the hero and hidden them in a cave.[27] Moreover Visvarupa, Geryones, Cacus and Azi Dahaka, the adversaries of Indra, Heraklo, Hercules, and Verethraghna, all are three headed or many headed.[28] Not only this but other traits in all the Aryan thunder gods also confirm our view. Indian Indra who, having war-like character, hurls the weapon, kills the demon; and is kind to men and fond of drinking, is definitely the same god as Teutonic Thor who is the hammer hurler, the hard drinking, kindly, impulsive, the constant 'friend of men' and the inveterate enemy of demons. Apart from slaying of dragon, Indra accomplishes other Herculean deeds.[29]

The absence of a common name of the thunder god in various Aryan branches but having exactly identical mythological traits warrants the view that primitive Aryans definitely had the conception of a thunder god before their separation; but subsequently each branch framed its own thunder god.

(v) Thunder-God (II)—Parjanya is probably the real thunder-god of the Vedic peoples who has, like Lithuanian Perkunas, absorbed the functions of Father Sky.[30]

Parjanya is certainly older than Indra. For Parjanya is identical in name as well as in character with Lithuanian Perkunas.[31] No doubt there is phonetic difficulty. M. Muller remarks that there is no phonetic difficulty in identification of Perkunas with Perjanya.[32] He shows that original k and j seldom weaken as k in park; it is applicable to j in root parj.[33] Schroder holds that there lies "in the Vedic Parjanya, Slavonic perun, Lithuanian Perkunas, a primitive Aryan word for thunder, with the fundamental significance of the 'beating one'."[34] The identity of Parjanya with Perkunas is based on the sound ground. The language of the hymns addressed to Parjanya comes exceedingly near to prayer offered to Perkunas.[35] The Vedic Parjanya is definitely thunder god who "roars like a lion and thuderous strikes the evil doers."[36] The old Prussian word percunos means thunder whereas Lithuanian perkunas and Lettish porkons connote both thunder and thunder-god.[37] Hence Lithuanian, Lettish and old Prussian thunder gods Perkunas, Pehrkons and Perkunos are no other than the Vedic Parjanya. We get an additional support to our view from another quarter. The names of the parents of the Norse thunder god, Thor are Fjorgynn and Fjorgyn.[38] From Perkunas we derive the word perkunyja which means 'thunder storm'.[39] Fjorgynn, Fjorgyn, Perkunyja, Parjanya are identical.[40]

(vi) Storm God—Wind has great share in thunder storm and individually causes terrible havoc. The primitive Aryans saw an agency at work in such phenomena too. The storm gods of the Vedic people are Maruts. They certainly belong to the Indo-European period. The word 'marut' is derived from the root 'mar' meaning 'to crush;' Maruts are, therefore, 'smasher.'[41] The father of the maruts, Rudra is likewise lightning god.[42] Here we see the germ of Italic war god, Mars, in name of Maruts.[43]

(vii) Wind God—The deification of wind is undoubtedly prehistoric. We have the following equation for wind, Sanskrit vata, Latin ventus, Gothic winds and Sanskrit vayu, Lithuanian wejas, Greek vilas, Old Slavic vejati and Gothic waian.[44] The Lithuanian wind-god is Wejopatis or Wejas[45] whose identification in name as well as in character with the Vedic wind-god, Vayu and that of the Greek Vilas is beyond doubt.[46] The more primitive Vedic wind-god is Vata. The Teutonic wind-god, Wotan (Odhin) is exactly identical with Vedic[47] Vata. Vate, the father of the Teutonic Valund, the tribal deity of the Vaetlings is also compared with Vata.[48] Vedic Pavana, according to some scholars, affords the germ of the Greek forest deity, pan.[49]

(viii) The Sun-God—As a matter of fact the sun occupies an important place in the Aryan religion. In India the sun-worship is still an important cult. The sun worship among the Persians is confirmed from the accounts[50] of Curtius, Herodotus and Xenophon. Wilke informs that the sun-worship was prevalent among the Germans, the Romans, the Lithuanians, the Slaves, the Celts and the Iranians.[51] The Aryan mythology is brimful of solar myths.

It seems that next to 'father sky' the Aryans deified the sun. The gods of various Aryan branches are quite identical in both name and character. He is the Vedic Surya, Greek Helios, Lettish Saule, O. Norse Sol, Gothic Saiul, Lithuanian Saule, Slavonic Solnze and Teutonic Sunna.[52]

(ix) The Moon God—The deification of the moon in the Aryan religion also goes back to the Indo-European period. Among the Indians, the Persians, the Germans, the Greeks and the Romans, the moon worship was wide-spread.[167] The similarity in names of the moon gods of the various branches supports the idea that the primitive Aryans certainly worshipped the moon. The Vedic Mas, Persian Mah, Roman Minerva, Germanic Mani, Gothic Mena, Lithuanian Menu, Greek Mena are definitely of common origin.[54] Certain Aryan branches have preserved still more ancient name of the god. The Persian Gandarewa, Greek Gandrewa, Vedic Gandharva are undoubtedly the older name of the Aryan moon god.[55] Wilke is of the view that like the mother earth, the moon god belongs to the united Indo-European period.[56]

(x) The Twin 'Horse Men'—The Vedic Asvins are the twin 'Horsemen' in the Rigveda. The Asvins are the divinities of light and represent a certain phenomenon connected with the morning.[57] It is also certain that the Asvins take their origin from the Indo-European period. In character, though not in name several Indo-European branches have the identical divinities. A well known Indo-European myth associated with these divinities is well preserved in these branches. The comparative study of this myth as current in different quarters proves that the Asvins must originally have been the personification of the morning and evening stars.

In the Rigveda the Asvins are called 'divo napata' or 'sons of Heaven.'[58] In need they are constant helper and reliable friend.[59] Their mother is Saranyu.[60] Their charming youthful beauty attracted[61] Surya or 'Daughter of the Sun,' who fell in love with them. The Asvins wed 'Sun Maiden' or Surya.[62] Another myth illustrates that another love-affair of Surya crossed this relation. This time the Asvins appear to be wooer in the heavenly marriage between the Moon and Surya.[63] In character the Greek Dioscuri coincides exactly with the Vedic Asvins. The taming and riding of the horses are noted feature [64] of the Dioscuri. This confirms the connection with horses as is apparent in the name of the Asvins. In the Greek mythology the Dioscuri are called Anaktes [65] or 'protecting lords.' It is evident that the Dioscuri shares, the important function of the Asvins, helping in need. The Dioscuri are also the 'sons of Zeus.'[66] Another potent factor strengthens this view more. In name, the Asvins' mother, Saranyu and Dioscuri's sister, Halena correspond remarkably.[67]

The above myth in a Lithuanian[68] folk-song narrates that the Moon married the 'Sun Maiden' but, later on, however, deserted her and slunk away. He indulged in love with the morning star and ran after her. This Lettish myth is significant in a sense that it agrees, on one hand, with Vedic and, on the other, with Greek myth. Here the morning and evening stars are called the 'sons of God.'[69] The beauty of Saule or 'Sun Maiden' enamoured the 'sons of God' who, riding on their horses, come to marry[70] Saule. In name and character both, the identity of the Vedic Surya and Saule is an established fact. Moreover like the Dioscuri, the Lettish 'Sons of God' are celebrated rescuer from the ocean and deliver the 'Sun Maiden or Sun himself.'[71] This character of the Lettish gods recalls the function of the Asvins.

It becomes now more convincing that the Lettish 'Sons of God' are no other than the Deioscuri. The Greek Castor and Pollux, just like the Lettish Gods, were also the personification of morning and evening stars, is confirmed by another Dioscuri myth. It tells that the reciprocal love of the Castor and Pollux pleased Zeus who had honoured them by placing them in the heaven as twin stars Gemini or as the morning and evening stars.[72] The gigantic statues of

Dioscuri opposite Quirinal palace in Rome that have stars on their heads lend[73] an additional support to this view. This comparative study of the myths relating to these divinities current in the Aryan world, gives certain common points. Such a striking resemblances, although not in nomenclature, can in no case be ascribed to as merely accidental or developmental coincidences.[74] It infers nothing but Indo-European antiquity.[75] It leaves no doubt the Indo-European origin of the twin gods. Another important conclusion which can be drawn from this exposition is that the antiquity of these gods goes back to the Indo-European period. They must have represented the morning and evening stars. During the Indo-European period these divinities had no specific name but commonly known as 'Sons of God.'

(xi) Elves or Genii of the Seasons—The Rigveda mentions minor deities Ribhus who are three in number.

In the Rigveda they are originally not full-fledged divine beings but their antiquity goes back to the Indo-European period. The Germanic word 'elf' is comparable to the Vedic word 'rbhu' meaning dexterous. Hence the name infers that they are essentially the artificers. This is why they are believed to have been originally terrestrial or aerial elves.[76] More than in name, the Ribhus are paralleled in function to the elfin artisans of the Teutonic world. It suffices to prove that the Ribhus are originally of common origin with the Teutonic Elfins. For the former are constantly associated with Indra[77] as the latter with Thor.[78] We know that Indra and Thor are identical. Certain other similarities are far more convincing. The Teutonic Elfin artisan Egil is a well-known celebrated archer as one of the Ribhus.[79] Tvaster, the 'master workman' who is the father of the Rbhus' mother, makes thunder bolt of Indra[80] as Sindre, one of the elfin artisans is fashioner of the Thor's hammer.[81] The elfin artisans and the Rbhus agree in another character too, that both make wonderful gifts for gods.[82] The Teutonic mythology tells two groups of the wonder-smiths and between these groups tough rivalry prevails.[83] It calls up the relation between Tvastri and the Ribhus who are also rivals.[84] Lastly there is an interesting comparison of an elfin artisan Loke and the Vedic Ribhus, Dadyak. In their respective mythology both act as mischief making spy and once both saved their respective wagers by cunning and lost their own heads.[85]

(xii) Dawn Goddess—There is no room to doubt the universal worship of Dawn among the primitive Aryans. Nearly all Aryan branches have the dawn goddess, who has a common name. In character as well as in name, the Vedic dawn goddess Usa, the Avestic Ushah, the Greek Eos, the Roman Aurora, the Teutonic Ostra and the Lithuanian Auszra are identical.[86]

(xiii) Fire God—The Sanskrit word 'agni' meaning fire is cognate to Latin 'ignis', O. Slavic 'ogni,' Lithuanian 'ugni,' but only the Vedic Agni is the fire-god under this name. No doubt other Aryan branches have fire-god but they are very minor divinities and altogether dissimilar in name. He is Persian Atar,

Roman Vesta, Greek Hostia and his cult is discernible from the 'Ugni szwenta' or 'szwenta ponke' in the north Europe. These are the factors that readily give the impression that the fire-worship was not an Indo-European institution but a later development in different Aryan branches after their split. But there are so many common myths, associated with the fire-cult, preserved here and there.

The Rigveda illustrates Agni as taking the offering to gods or bringing gods to the offering; hence he is regular messenger between the gods and men; in this capacity Agni is known in the Rigveda as Angira.[87] The Vedic Angira is phonetically identical with the Latin word 'angel which also means messenger. There is another interesting evidence which warrants this view more convincingly. The Rigveda[88] mentions that sacrificial fire was produced by friction of two sticks. The sticks are called the parents or two mothers of Agni.[89] Hence in one hymn Agni is called 'Dvimata'[90] having two mothers. This word is found preserved[91] in Greek as Dimetor and in Latin as Bismatris, though a strange name, 'the child of two mothers' is quite unintelligible to their people. We know that the Greek-Dimetor or Djonysos was once a god of light.[92] The Vedic Agni is also the deity of light who dispells the darkness.[93] It is clearly evident that Greek Dionysos or Latin Bismatris is no other than the Vedic Dvimata.

It is a well known Indo-European myth that the fire was born in heaven and brought to the earth by a person. This person is named differently in different mythologies. In Greek treatment he is Promotheus. The two sticks in the Rigveda, with which the Agni is produced by friction, are called Pramantha. The Greek Promotheus and the Vedic Pramantha are indentical in name and likely in character also. Can we deny here that the Vedic Pramantha and the Greek Promotheus came out from the same source ?

The view of Schrader is partly correct. He remarks "That the worship of the single hearth fire as well as of the common perennial fire, belongs to the most ancient religious ideas and the cults of the Aryans.[94] The initial conception of the fire-worship must have been faint and unstable, during Indo-European period, and personification of the fire, must have been shadowy.[95] The dissimilarity of fire-gods, in name in all branches, supports this view. The scholars put forth another argument that the chaste figure of Greek Hestia or the Roman Vesta contrasts with the exalted male figure of the Vedic Agni.[96]

(xiv) Cosmogony—Purusa Sukta of the Rigveda reflects very primitive Indo-European conception of the cosmogony. This myth[97] explains the creation of universe from the body of a giant Purusa. His head turned into the sky, his feet into the earth and his naval into the air. The sun came from his eyes, the moon from mind, Agni and Indra from his mouth, Vayu from his breath and the four quarters from his ears.

This myth is found faithfully preserved in the Teutonic mythology. Here the gods cut up the body of the chaos giant, Ymer. His head became the sky, his blood the sea, his bones the mountains, his teeth the hills and his hair the trees and grass.[98] This conception also calls up one of the Orphic cosmologies in the Greek mythology. This Greek myth illustrates that Night, a black winged bird came from Chaos.[99] She laid an egg from which Eros 'Love' came, the halves of the shell became Sky Uranus, and Earth 'Ge.'[100] The Hesiode informs that Air and Day sprang from Night. Similarly Iranian creation myth tells that all living animals and herbs sprang from the blood of primeval ox, Geus Uron.[101]

It is legitimate to conclude that the primitive Aryans believed in the creation of the universe from a chaos giant. It is also noticed that the Vedic and Teutonic characters are not only identical in names but main ideas of the two myths resemble surprisingly. It forces us to conceive that the conception was already present in its crude form before the dispersion of the Aryans.

(a) Mythological First Man

The mythology nearly in all Aryan branches mentions a legendary personage who is par excellence the progenitor of the human race. He is Yama or Manu in the Rigveda.

The other Aryan branches also appear to be familiar with Yama and Manu. The Iranian twin, Yima and Yimak are the carbon copy of the Vedic Yama and Yami. Yima is also the first man and the hero of the flood legend.

In the Teutonic mythology Mannus is the name of a partiarch.[102] The Teutonic creation myth tells that before human race came into existence, Ymir, had been created similar to man.[103] In this sense he was the first man. There is a good reason to believe that Yama and Ymir are identical in name as well as in character.

The evidence of the Germanic mythology is unchallengeable. Here Mannus is shown clearly as the progenitor of the human race. Tacitus informs, "They (the Germans) honour Tuisto, a god who has sprung from the earth, and his son Mannus, as the originator and founder of the race."[104]

If not in name, in character Roman Janus, the creator of the world is definitely identical with Manu or Yama. We know that Janus is the personification of the sun[105] or its light. Vivasvant, the father of Manu and Yama, is identified with the sun.[106] Yama is himself the personification of the sun.[107]

In the Greek mythology there are so many fragmentary evidences that recall the Vedic myth. Here king Minos is identical with Manu in name and character. Minos gives[108] laws to the deads as Manu made laws for human beings. Minos [109] is the third judge who has deciding vote in Hades. Similarly Yama judges men as Dharmaraja and rules the shining paradise.[110]

From the above account we come to the conclusion that the antiquity of Yama or Manu goes back to the Indo-European period. The primitive Aryan conceived Manu a legendary progenitor of human race. Yama and Manu stood in the Indo-European world as Adam and Noah to the Semitics.

It is more than probable that Manu or Yama or the progenitor of the human race was the personification of the sun.

(e) Eschatology

(i) Immortality of Soul—The belief in the immortality of soul is very old. The primitive man believed that on the advent of death soul separated from the body and attained a new life in the next world. The Rigveda shows very clearly a belief in immortality of soul.[111]

The belief in immortality of soul is, of course, very ancient in Greece.[112] Throughout its mythology the conception pervades. In case of the Romans the obscurity prevails. The Teutonic mythology presents a clear evidence of the belief. It is the Avesta that presents a distinct and the most clear idea of the continuance of life after[113] death. The conception is, of course, of Indo-European origin. The primitive Aryans, during Indo-European period, had the belief that soul separated from the body, went to the other world where according to desert either it was rewarded paradise or condemned to hell. A well-known Indo-European myth very clearly refers to the belief in immortality of soul. This myth is found prevalent in the mythology nearly in all Aryan branches. This myth illustrates that after death on its journey to the other world; soul passes over a bridge or a stream reaches a dog or two who sort out pious or wicked souls. The pious soul are allowed to enter paradise while wicked ones are forced to go to hell. It is noteworthy that dog is an indispensable element in each mythology whether it is Indian or Iranian or Greek or Scandinavian. The Iranian version describes two four eyed dogs who guard Chinvat Bridge leading to heaven.[114] In Scandinavian mythology the heaven Asgard is reached by bridge Bifrost.[115] The dog, Garm guards the gate of hell.[116] The Greek mythology mentions three headed dog called Cerberus, who is the guardian of the portals of Hades.[117] Similarly Yama has two four eyed[118] dogs who guard or sit on the path leading to heaven.[119]

The Greek version resembles the Vedic myth closely. The Yama's dogs are the sons of the goddess Sarama and called Syama and Sabala.[120] Sarama is etymologically agrees with Greek Hennes who is also the guide of souls.[121] Moreover Yama's dog Sabala is exactly identical with Cerberus in name as well as in character.[122]

It is transpired from the above account that the conception appears to be an Aryan origin.

(ii) Heaven—Closely connected with the belief in immortality of soul is the idea of heaven and hell. The mythology in certain Aryan branches shows that one is to be born again after death and to receive reward or punishment according to one's works. Jackson[123] claims that this conception is of Iranian origin. The conception pervades the, Gathas and the whole later Zind literature. The Satapatha[124] Brahmana also mentions an identical conception. The Ragnarok, the final battle in the Teutonic mythology reflects the same idea.[125]

The name of the abode for wicked or pious as such found in different Aryan branches is not identical at all. Just like the Vedic conception, in the Greek mythology, Elysium is paradise where judge Rhadamanthus rules.[126] The Roman Elysium Field and the Celtic Land of Women are parallel to the Greek Elysium.[127]

It is beyond the range of doubt that the primitive Aryans during the Indo-European period had an idea of heaven. The idea was in its crude form and not fully developed and no specific name was assigned to heaven.

(iii) Hell—The belief in reward after life is essentially connected with the notion of retribution after death. It implies that the conceptions of heaven and hell must have simultaneously been born during the Indo-European period. The Avesta distinctly and very clearly mentions the abode for wicked.[128] In the Teutonic world we come across a common expression for the world of the dead.[129] It is Gothic 'halja;' Old Norse 'hel;' O.H. G.'hella,' Ancient Slavonic 'hell.' Old Norse[130] 'hel' is the goddess of hell who rules over the realms of Niflheim with her dark red bird and her rake. Teutonic 'hel' agrees more with Greek Hades, though originally it was only a home of the dead.[131] The Greek mythology tells that Tartarus, the abode of wicked lies deep down beneath Hades.[132]

Ambiguity prevails so far the Rigveda is concerned. Hence, the view that the conception of hell goes back to the Indo-European period is highly controversial.

There is a forceful evidence that confirms the fact that belief in hell is of Indo-European origin. The Satapatha Brahmana tells a story of Rishi Bhrigu who was so wise that he was consulted in several matters even by the gods. It led him to become so arrogant that he thought himself more wise than his own father Varuna. In order to teach a lesson Varuna sent Bhrigu to see the tortures in Talatala. This story calls up a well-known legend in the Greek mythology. The kings, Tantalus, Sisyphus and Tityus are called Phlegyas. They were the cleverest of men and the friends of the gods, but wicked and cunning traitors.[133] They were condemned to the rigorous punishments in Tartarus.[134] The Vedic Talatala etymologically agrees with Greek hell, Tartarus. Bhrigu and Phlegyas are identical not only in name but in character also.[135] Bhrigu was sent by his father for his arrogance just as a looker on to see the tortures of hell while the Greek kings for their arrogance were condemned to the harsh tortures in the hell. The similarity of the two myths can in no case, be claimed to be a mere coincidence. It reflects the Indo-European idea. Hence it reinforces the belief that the Aryan had an idea of hell during Indo-European period.

(c) Ancestor Worship

The worship of the dead formed an essential part of religion in each Aryan branch. The Rigveda affords a very clear evidence. The Persians had the cult of the dead. The whole Fravardin Yasht is devoted to a full description of the worship of the Fravashi. The Roman worshipped the Divi Manes and the Lares

Familiares more zealously than any other god.[136] The ancestor worship was equally important among the Greeks who worshipped their Theoi Patrooi and Daimones.[137] In the north European tribes the cult along with the worship of the dzjady[138] and Roditeli is an indispensable element of religion. Certain conceptions associated with the Fathers certainly belong to the Indo-European period. The Indians, Persians, Greeks and Romans all believed the stars to have been the souls of the pious men.[139]

(d) Social Conditiod of the Primitive Aryans

The comparative philology reveals the fact that the primitive Aryans had completely emerged from the old Stone Age and appear to be entering the Neolithic phase of life. Without exception all the Indo-European branches have common words for cattle, horse, cow, goat, sheep and duck whereas the Indo-European terminology for the chase is totally absent. It is beyond the range of doubt that the primitive Aryans positively had the domestic animals. Not only this but cattle was back-bone of their economy. For cattle was the principal source of wealth in every Aryan branch. Roman pecunia and Anglo-Saxon fech approve the use of cattle as standard of value.[140] Persian 'kushti,' Sanskrit gavisti that is the term for battle litearally means struggle for kine. The final phase of the Indo-European period appears to be passing through a stage of transition from the use of stone to that of metal. Sanskrit 'asman' means stone, bolt whereas Lithuanian 'asman' blade and Greek 'akmon' anvil it betrays the fact that the same Indo-European word connotes a stone and metal weapon. It is certain that there is no Indo-European terminology for metallurgy, nevertheless copper was definitely known to the undivided Aryans. Sanskrit 'ayas', Latin 'aes,' Teutonic 'ais' is common word for copper. The primitive Aryans were semi-nomadic pastoralist is well attested by the fact that all Indo-European branches possess common words for developed pastoral terminology but terminology for agriculture is lacking similarity in the European and Asiatic branches.[141]

(i) Social Structure—Unlike the other primitive races, the Aryans society was patriarchal. The scholars hold the view that everywhere the primitive races reckon descent through the female.[142] But it is not tenable in case of the Aryan family. The Indo-European languages are rich for common words for kindred with uniform meanings; these words plainly show the system of reckoning descent through the male. Such common 'terminology sheds sufficient light to prove agnatic relationship. It is indisputably confirmed that the Aryan family was patri-linear and patriarchal. The 'house father', Sanskrit 'dampati', Greek 'deopates' was the head of family.

(ii) Disposal of the Dead—The primitive people disposed of their dead by varied manners. But forms of disposal-burial and cremation, received a general recognition by a larger majority over the world since the earliest times.

The Aryans practised these two customs of disposal. The cremation is the rule among the Indo-Aryans. But burial is not unknown to the Rigveda.[143] The Persians also practised burial and by implication the existence of cremation is also attested.[144] The Greeks entombed their dead in partly mummified state.[145] But burial and cremation both are met with side by side.[146] The simultaneous existence of customs is found prevailing[147] among the Teutons and the Celts who seem to have gradually adopted cremation. The prevalence of both methods of disposal appear among the Lithuanians side by side.[148] Only the Slavs practised cremation exclusively.[149] It appears that the Aryans disposed of their dead by burial and cremation both.

(iii) Funeral Ceremonies—Having the dead consigned to the grave or fire, the person remained to be connected to his relatives by means of rigidly appointed service of the dead. The Aryans believed that man immediately after his death does not attend the rank of holy ancestors but wander to and fro as a ghost until and unless fixed ceremonies which are necessary to elavate him to the rank of honoured ancestors were performed. Such ceremonies are met with in the White Russia[150] to raise the soul to the rank of the ancestor or upto heaven. A similar ceremony is traceable among the Persians and the Indians. The European Aryans too perform similar ceremonies in honour of their dead.

This survey discloses certain important facts. The funeral terminology is lacking similarity among Aryan nations. On the strength of some sporadic agreement either in name or in purpose or in character of certain institutions or customs or the cult, it is reasonably claimed that the ancestor worship was the ancient cult of the primitive Aryan religion. During the Indo-European period it was in its crude form, but after split it developed independently in its various branches.

(e) Idea of State

Some sort of state positively existed during the Indo-European period. Sanskrit 'rajan,' Celtic 'ri,' Latin 'rex' means king. Philology does not ascertain whether the king was hereditary or elected by the people. It is also not certain what was the exact form of the state. Sanskrit 'vis,' O. Slavic 'vise,' Teuton 'veih,' Latin 'vicus,' Greek 'fik,' Celtic 'frich' was definitely an unit of the state, but what was the Indo-European 'vis' is very uncertain. Its meanings,[151] in Aryan languages fluctuate from clan to village and district.

(f) Exorcism and the Witch-craft

Similar to other primitive races, the primitive Aryans used witch-craft and sorcery to cure diseases, for love-affair, for prosperity and for personal jealousy and friendship. Such magic formulas are met with in the tenth Mandala of the Rigveda and the Atharva-veda is full of them. It is interesting to note that certain Atharvavedic spells surprisingly agree ad verbatum with the magic formulas current in the Scottish Highlands and elsewhere throughout Europe.[152] A Gaelic custom of nailing horse shoes upon doors for protection against evil calls up an

Atharva-vedic spell which similarly refers to charming of a house against evil spirit.[153] A Scottish Highlands charm and the hymn VI-115-1-2-2 are remarkably compared, in which "King of the Elements" is invoked.[154] A Merseburg magic incantation prevalent among the Germans is exactly identical in language and purpose with the hymn IV-12 in the Atharvaveda. In both cases the spell is against the breaking of a leg.[155] A striking coincidence is noticeable between the Atharvaveda VI-25-1-3 and a German magic incantation meant for diseases; both mention 77 and 99 diseases.[156] Certain German magic formulas for toothache caused by worms strikingly agree with a spell against toothache caused by worms[157] mentioned in the Atharva-veda V-23. Similar beliefs are prevalent in France and England.[158] A. Kuhn claims that the Atharva-veda IV-37-3-4; 7-11-12 and certain German magic incantations are indisputably identical even in their details, purpose and language; in which the demons are expelled by mantras with Ajasrngi perfume.[159]

On the basis of this it is not unreasonable to claim that the primitive Aryans, for the remedy of diseases, once believed in efficacy of witch-craft and sorcery. And it is also found that several identical magic formulas prevalent among several Aryan nations are common heirloom of the undivided Aryans.

(g) Morality

The Aryans possessed high standard of morality. The Rigveda tells a high ethical conception of rta. It is Asha of the Avesta. The basis of moral conduct of man rta or Asha is truth and right doing. The Avesta and the Slavonic mythology present much more high morality. Every Aryan branch lays a great stress on right doings and has prescribed rigorous imprisonment for the wicked. The Vedic people, the Persians and the Teutons equally share in the belief that the wicked are doomed to live in Niflheim or in dreary region of mist and darkness.[160]

In those days the murder was compensated. This custom was common among the Vedic people, the Persians and the Teutons.[161] The primitive Aryans were hospitable by nature. The hospitality among the ancient Persians and the Vedic people was considered a great virtue. Since remote past the Lithuanians, the Teutons and the Slavs are noted for their hospitality.[162]

The parents were well respected. The "house father" who was the head of the family was obeyed by all family members. The authority of the father was equally recognized in other Aryan branches.

Concubinage most probably existed during the Indo-European period. It was in practice among the Greeks[163] to a considerable extent. The custom was well known to the Persians and the Teutons and in the Post-Vedic period in India. Besides his wife, the husband was allowed to unlimited intercourses with concubines and slaves whereas the wife was bound to conjugal faithfulness on the pain of death.[164] The sexual chastity of wife had very little value. The husband could hand his wife over to a helper in generation or she could be put at the disposal of a honoured guest.[165]

(h) Socio-Religious Customs

The Indo-European period is marked with a considerable socio-religious customs and ceremonies prescribed for a man to perform in his life time. These were observed on the auspicious occasions occuring from the child-birth to the death of a man. They were associated specially to the child-birth, first cutting of hair, tonsure, initiation, puberty, marriage and death. It is more than strange that such a long time, various surroundings and the constant pressure of remodelling of ideas could not obliterate the chief features of the old customs of the primitive Aryans. It is interesting to observe that the socio-religious customs connected with the naming of the child, the first cutting of his hair, and the feast at puberty are found in every Aryan ration and with entirely identical characteristics.[166]

Tonsure is also very ancient rite of the Aryans. In India it is known as chuda or chudakarma and performed on boys occasionally on girls also; and it derives its name from tuft of hair left on the top of the boy's head. The ancient Persians[167] also performed this rite in the same way. The custom was prevalent with identical features among the Slavic nations,[168] the Bohemians and Spartians who regularly and strictly followed it.

The obligatory performance of the rite of initiation is the noticeable feature in every primitive race. It is equally important among the undivided Aryans. The European Aryans used to observe this Aryan rite in one form or the other.

The marriage was an indispensable custom among the primitive Aryans. They looked upon the marriage as a sacred and irrevokable bond. Monogamy was the rule[169] but among the men of ranks the polygamy was prevalent. The evidences in favour of polygamy can be adduced from the Teutonic mythology, the Avesta, the Illiad, the Rigveda X-85-37 and from Atharvaveda I-14-44; II-61-14-17. The primitive Aryans knew no poly-yandry. There is one fragmentary evidence of poly-yandry in the post-Vedic period in India. The primitive Aryans re-married widows. It is well attested by the Sanskrit word devar which is cognate to Latin 'levir,' Greek 'daer,' Lithuanian 'deweries,' Armenian 'taigr,' Teutonic 'tacor.' The Sanskrit word devar which is the term for husband's brother means second husband; and in the light of the Rigveda X-18-7, the re-marriage of widow is undoubtedly proved even among the Vedic people.

It is very interesting and at the same time strange to notice that ancient marriage customs of the Aryans are not affected at all by the passage of the time and various surroundings. They are found in all Aryan nations with similar forms and characteristics. The comparative study of marriage customs observed by different Aryan branches substantiates their close relationship. M. Winternitz says, "In particular, the comparison of the Greek, Roman, Teutonic and Slavonic marriage customs with the rules contained in the Grhyasutra, has shown that the relationship of the Indo-European peoples is not limited to language, have also preserved common features from prehistoric times in their manners and customs."[170]

Taking fire as a witness, the primitive people generally used to make their contract before it. Similarly the conjugal bond between bride and bridegroom was effected among the Aryans during the Indo-European period in the presence of fire and water. The Vedic Sapta padigamana (going seven steps during marriage ceremony) is undisputably an Indo-European institution.[171] The Grhyasutra informs that bridegroom, taking the bride by the hand takes round the fire on which roasted corn is offered.[172] It is noteworthy that when the bridal pair take round the fire, a new jug filled with water remains on the floor on the right side of them,[173] In certain attendant customs of the Indian marriage ceremony, the water is brought from a spring, with which the bridal pair are sprinkled or the bride takes baths in it.[174] The Romans also observed the marriage ceremony before fire altar in the presence of water.[175] This is why the Roman marriage is designated as union "eque et igni." Quite similar to the Indian custom the Roman marriage procession took round the fire altar from left to right, at which a boy carried the marriage torch and marriage water drawn from a spring, then a far-loaf was offered on the fire in the house of bride's father.[175] Hirt[177] holds that the Slavic marriage ceremony is similar to the Indo-European or the Vedic custom. The Slavic bridal pair took three round of the table or the hearth.[178] The Slavic baths and dancing through or over fire was indispensable custom of the fixed marriage rites of the Slavs.[179] The ancient German marriage ceremony calls up the Indian custom. Here, in the house of bridegroom, the bride, having stepped over a vessel of water, took three rounds of the hearth.[180] The marriage ceremony to be observed before the fire alter was also the custom with the Greeks[181] and the Lithuanians.[182]

Another ancient custom of the Indo-European marriage ceremony is found prevalent among the Indian and the Romans. In India the custom is known as Panigrahana in which under the guidance of the bride's mother, the officiating priest puts the right hand of the bride in the right hand of the bridegroom as a symbol of a union.[183] This Indian custom is quite identical with Roman dextrarum junctis.[184] The dextrarum junctis is also a symbolic act of union in which the bride under the guidance of a matron who must be only once married, placed her right hand in the right hand of the bridegroom.[185] In India, this ceremony takes place before Sapta padigamana in the house of bride whereas the Romans observed the custom either in the bride's house before the hearth or in front of some temple.[186]

There is another popular custom of the Indo-European marriage ceremony which is well known among all Aryan nations. The Indians call it Iajabarsana. During the Indian marriage proceedings at one occasion the bride's brother comes to the bridal pair with a basket full of fried rice; the bridal pair shower rice over each other until they are tired.[187] It is also one of the customs of the Persian marriage ceremony. J.J. Modi tells that during Persian marriage ceremony the officiating priest sprinkles rice over the bridal pair and bridal pair also shower rice over each other.[188] The custom of sprinkling of fried rice over the bridal pair is still prevalent among the European Aryans.[189] The primitive Aryans used to preserve continence for some time after marriage. Such demand is found to be occurring among the Indian and the Teutons.[190]

It has been noticed that the Harappan culture disappeared totally from India during the second half of the second millennium. The archaeological finds of the late Harappan settlements tend to show that Aryans who invaded the country during 1500 BC annihilated this unique culture. Aryans came from outside but where was their original home is highly controversial point in the Aryan history. There are convincing evidences which show that the original home of Aryans lay somewhere in the region between the Pamir and the Hindu-kush. Most probably the over-population forced them to migrate from their original home to other parts of the world.

The comparative study of the socio-religious beliefs and customs prevalent in various Aryan branches show that many of the original religious beliefs and social customs of the primitive Aryans are found preserved in the various branches. The sky god is found nearly in all Aryan branches with original name and function. Many legends especially those associated with the Thunder and Fire gods, the twin 'Horse men' and with the mythological first man are found preserved in the various Aryan branches with the original spirit and colour. A considerable number of social customs such as marriage and funeral ceremonies and initiation rite as observed by the different Aryan branches show many points of resemblances. It indicates that the pressure of new ideas and the passage of time could not obliterate the primitive belief.

The comparative study of the religious conceptions and the social customs also shows that the Rigveda contains original beliefs and conceptions. As a matter of fact the Rigveda is the real representative of the Aryan culture. It stands in the Aryan world as the Quran in Islam.

References

1. V.G. Childe, *The Aryans*, p. 68.
2. M. Muller, *The Vedas*, p. 23, 1st ed. (Calcutta, 1956).
3. M. Muller, op. cit., p. 52.
4. Ibid., p. 13.
5. M. Bloomfield, *Religion of the Veda*, p. 109.
6. M. Muller, *Science of Language*, Vol. II, p. 537.
7. O. Schrader, *ERE*, Vol. II, pp. 11-31.
8. M. Mullae, *Chips from a Germarz Workshop*, p. XIII f, Vol. IV, (London, 1898).

9. M. Bloomfield; *Religion of the Veda* p. 136, (New York and London, 1908).
10. M. Muller, Ibid., II, p. 65.
11. Hesiod, V–127.
12. Op. cit.
13. A.C. Das, *Rigvedic Culture*, p. 91, (Calcutta, Madras, 1925).
14. M. Bloomfield, op. cit., p. 137.
15. M. Bloomfield, *Religion of the Veda*, pp. 112–15.
16. Rv. V–58–5, V–36–5, 1–160–3.
17. M.Bloomfield, *The Religion of Veda*, pp. 111–12.
18. Ibid., pp. 112–116.
19. A. *Mackenzie Teutonic Myths and Legends*, p. 3.
20. Rv. V–18–H.H. Wilson, *Select Sanskrit Works*, Vol. III, p. 163.
21. A. Mackenzie, op. cit., p. 13.
22. Rv. IV–17–7.
23. Yasna, XLIV–16.
24. A. Mackenzie, *Teutonic Myths and Legends*, p. 14.
25. T.A. Gaster, *Thespis* p. 317 f, 1950.
26. Rv. X–99–6.
27. G.W. Cox, *The Mythology of the Aryan Nations*, p. 544, 1882; M Bloomfield, op. cit., p. 180; H.Oldenberg, *Die Religion des Veda*, p. 143 ff.
28. Rv. X–8–8; M. Bloomfield, op. cit., p. 180; *Bahram Yasht*, XIV, p. 40.
29. A. Mackenzie, op. cit., pp. 15–16; Oldenberg, *Ancient India. Its Language and Religion*, p. 60.
30. Ibid., p. 178; M. Bloomfield, op. cit., pp. 111–12; Schrader, *Arische Religion* p. 34.
31. L.J. Grimm, *Teutonic Mythology*, (Eng. Trans. London), pp. 170–72.
32. The Vedas, pp. 112–13.
33. Ibid.
34. L. Von. Schrader, op. cit., p. 33.
35. Ibid., pp. 114–15.
36. Rv. V–83.
37. Voolkel, *Die Lettischen Sprachrest*, p. 23, 1879; Cf. M.Muller, *The Vedas*, p. 113, n. 29.
38. M. Bloomfield, op.cit., p. 111.
39. Ibid.
40. Ibid.
41. A.A. Machdonell, *Vedic Mythology*, p. 81.
42. M. Muller, op.cit., p. 107.
43. Ibid., p. 108.
44. O. Schrader, *Arische Religion*, p. 35 a.
45. A. Mackenzie, *Teutonic Myths and Legends*.
46. "The Aryans" *ERE*, Vol. II.
47. A.A. Macdonell, JRAS, XXV, p. 488.
48. A. Mackenzie, *Indian Myth and Legends*, p. 24.
49. M. Muller, *The Vedas*, p. 108; Will Durant, *The Story of Civilization*, p. 58.
50. Curtius, 3. 3. 7; Herodotus I, 131; Xenophon, Kyrop, 8, 3,12.
51. Wilke, Die *Religon der Indogermanen*, pp. 130–4 (Leipzig, 1903).
52. O. Schrader, *Arische Religion*, p. 34a.
53. P.S. Deshmukh op, cit., p. 106.
54. *ERE*, Vol. XXX II, "The Aryans;" A. Mackenzie, *Indian Myths and Legends*, p. 36.
55. A. Ludwig, *Rigveda, Translation*, p. 4,157; Hopkins, op. cit., p.157
56. G. Wilke, *Die Religion der Indogermanen*, p. 145, (Leipzig, 1903); E.B. Taylor, *Primitive Cultur 57* Vol. I, pp. 354–5, 6th edition, (London, 1873) 58.
57. Rv. III–39–3, Muir, *Original Sanskrit Text*, V. pp. 239–9, Hopkins, Ibid, pp. 8, Oldenberg, op.

cit., p. 208.
58. Rv. 1–182–1; 1–184–1; X–61–4.
59. Rv. 1–112–2; 1–118–3.
60. Rv. X–17–1; X—7–2; Broomfield, JAOS, Vol. XV, p. 173 ff.
61. Rv. 1–69–4; V–73–5; VVVI–8–10.
62. Rv. IV–43-6; I–119–5.
63. Rv. I–116–7; VIII–74–7.
64. M. Bloomfield, *The Religion of the Veda,* p. 114.
65. Ibid.
66. Ibid., p. 113.
67. Prof. E.W. Fay , Cf. Bloomfield op. cit. p.172
68. Daina, Prof. Chase, *Transaction of the American Philological Association.* Vol. XXXI, p. 191.
69. M. Bloomfield, op.cit., p. 114.
70. Oldenberg, *Die Religion des Veda,* p. 232, n. 3.
71. O.S. Schrader, *Vienna Oriental Journal,* I, p. 130–1, Cf. A. Macdonall, op, cit, p. 53.
72. Hopkins, op. cit, p. 80.
73. Ibid.
74. A.A. Mecdonell, op. cit, p. 256.
75. M. Bloomfield, op. cit., p. 54.
76. Macdonell, A History of Sanskrit Literature, pp. 106–7.
77. Rv. III-60–44; IV–33–3; IV–34–6; IV–35–7.
78. A. Mackenzie, *Indian Myths and Legends,* p. 11.
79. Ibid., p. 12.
80. Rv. X–53–9; 1–85–9; III–54–12.
81. A. Mackenzie, *Teutonic Myths and Legends* pp. 35–9.
82. A. Mackenzie, Indian Myths and Legends, pp. 11–12.
83. Ibid., p. II.
84. Rv. I–166–4, 5.
85. A. Mackenzie, op.cit., p. 12.
86. M. Muller, op. cit., p. 60.
87. Rv. I–131–1.
88. Rv. III–29–2; III–3–2; II–23–3; VII–1–1; X–7–9.
89. Ibid., I–31–2; Bergaigne, *Ia Religion Vedique* II, p. 52.
90. Ibid.
91. M. Muller, op. cit., p. 74.
92. Ibid.
93. Rv. VIII–43–132.
94. O. Schrader, *Arische Religion,* p. 35–1.
95. M. Bloomfield, op. cit., p. 158; M. Muller, *Physical Religion,* p. 117.
96. M. Bloomfield, op. cit., p. 158.
97. Rv. X, 90.
98. A. Mackenzie, *Teutonic Myths and Legends,* pp. 110.
99. *IlIiad* XlV, 2444, *Hesiode* V, Cf. *The Standard Dictionary of Folklore, Mythology and Legend "Night,"* Vol. II, p. 791, (New York 1960).
100. Ibid., Romer.
101. Cf. Ibid "Ox," p. 839.
102. Ibid., p. 23.
103. Snorri, *Sturlason's Gylfaginning and Volusta;* Cf. ERE Vol. IV, p. 178.
104. Germania, Chapter 2, cf. M. Bloomfield, *The Religion of the Veda,* p. 140, n. 2, (New York and London, 1908)
105. ERE, Vol. IV, p. 175.

106. Hillebrandt, Vedische Mythologie, Vol. I, p.488 fi cf. Bloomfield, op. cit., p. 139.
107. A. Bergaigne, La, Religion Vedique, 1–89, cf A.A. Macedonell, Vedic Mythology, p. 173.
108. Odessey, XI 567; cf. ERE, Vol.V, p. 374.
109. The Standard dictionary of Folkiore, Mythology and Legend, Vol. II, p. 936, "Rhadamanthuss."
110. Rv. X, 113–8.
111. Rv. X–58; Rv. X.–15–4; X–16–2, Rotins, Religions of India, p. 153; Rv. X–14–3.
112. E. Rhode, op.cit., Vol. 1, 53 ff.
113. Yasna, XLVI–10–11; Yas. XXX–6-7.
114. Yas XLVI–10–11
115. The Standard Dictionary of Folklore, Mythology and Legend, Vol. "Asgard," p. 80.
116. Ibid, "Hel," p. 488.
117. Hesoid, cf. ibid, "Cerberus," p. 108.
118. Rv. X–14–10.
119. Ibid.
120. Rv. X–14–10.
121. The Standard Dictionary of Folklore, Mythology and Legend, Vol. I, "Hermes," p. 493.
122. M. Muller, Science on the Language Vol. II, p. 575.
123. Transaction of the 10th Oriental Congress II, p. 67–73.
124. SB. III–1–7.
125. The Standard Dictionary of Folklore, Mythology and Legend, Vol. II, "Ragnarok," p. 919.
126. Ibid., Vol. I, "Elysium," p. 343.
127. Ibid., Vol. II, "Otherworld," p. 836.
128. Yas, XLVI–11.
129. ERE, Vol. II, p. 38.
130. The Standard Dictionary of Folklore, Mythology and Legend, Vol. I, "Hel" p.488.
131. Ibid.
132. IIlied, VII, 13, Odessey, XI, 576.
133. The Standard Dictionary of Folklore, Mythology and Legend, "Sisyphus," Vol. II 1014–15, "Tantalus," 1103.
134. Oddessey, XI, 576f, cf. ERE, Vol. V, p. 374.
135. A Weber, Zeitschrift der Deutschan Morgeplandischem Gesellschaft, op. cit., p. 169.
136. Ciero, De, Leg. II, 9, 11.
137. Hesiodi Opera et Dies, V. 110–16.
138. Schrader, ERE, Vol. II, p. 13.
140. M. Muller, The Vedas, p. 133.
141. V.G. Childe, The Aryans, p. 83 (London, 1916).
142. Ibid.
143. Ibid, p. 81.
144. Rv. VIII–89–IJ X–18–10.
145. Herodotus IV–71F; 1–140.
146. Tsountas Mana, The Mycenian Age, Ch. V. VI.
147. O. Schrader, op. cit., p. 14.
148. Cf. A.A. Montelius, XVII, 151 ff.
149. O. Schrader, op. cit., p. 17.
150. Jaffe, Monusnenta Moguntina, p. 171.
151. O. Schrader, op. cit., p. 14.
152. V.G. Childe, op. cit., p. 81.
153. A. Machenzie, op. cit., p. 85.
154. Ibid, p. 86, fn. 1.
155. Ibid., p. 87.
156. M. Winterintz.

157. Ibid., p. 131.
158. Ibid., p. 133.
159. Ibid., fn. 1.
160. A. Kuhn, Zeitschriftur Vergleichende Sprachwise enschaft, Vol. XIII, p. 49 ff.
161. E.W. Hopkins, op. cit., p. 161.
162. Ibid.
163. O. Sehrader, op. cit., p. 15.
164. W.J. Woodhouse, ERE, Vol. VIII, p. 445.
165. O. Schrader, op. cit., p. 97.
166. Ibid.
167. Ibid. p. 49.
168. J. Joly, ERE, Vol. XII, p. 388.
169. Ibid.
170. Herodotus, II, 91 (Greek).
171. M. Winterintz, op. cit., p. 174
172. J.Jolly, "Recht and Sitte," pp. 13-54.
173. O. Sehrader, op. cit., p. 49.
174. Ibid.
175. Ibid.
176. Ibid.
177. Ibid
178. H. Hirt, Indogerrnaner, pp. 436–47.
179. J. Macha! ERE, Vol. VIII, p. 471.
180. O. Schrader, op. cit., p. 49.
181. Reallexicon art Heirat, p. 356 ff.
182. O. Schrader, op. cit., p. 49.
183. Ibid, Menecious.
184. Duboios and Beauchamp, Hindu Manners Customs and Ceremonies, p. 115 (3rd ed., Oxford).
185. J. Jolly, op. cit.
186. W. Fowler, ERE, Vol. VII, p. 465.
187. Ibid.
188. J. Jolly, op. cit.
189. J.J. Modi, cf. ERE, Vol. VIII, p. 456.
190. Dr. B.N. Datta, Dialects of Hindu Ritualism, p. 175.
191. Ibid.

7

The Indo-Iranian Culture

It has already been discussed that Indo-Europeans dispersed from their original home to different parts of Eurasia. This dispersion did not occur altogether but different branches left the parent stock at different times. The Indo-Iranian is the most important branch of them, which came to Persia and made it its seçond home[1] or settled somewhere near Persia or in the central Asia. This branch played a very important role in the political as well as in the cultural history of Aryans. The Indo-Iranians not only carved out two regions of the world in Iran and India but they produced two invaluable religious documents, the Avesta and the Rigveda which preserved largely the common heirloom of the Aryan culture. The great religions–Zoroastrianism and Hinduism are illuminating creations of this branch, which is an invaluable contribution to our civilization.

The Indo-Iranian people certainly lived together in their second home for a long time and developed a distinct culture. Centuries after, they, too, bifurcated into different branches. One branch that pronounced sharp sibilant as 'h' remained in or went to Persia; evolved therein the Zoroastrian religion and composed the Avesta; the other branch that pronounced sharp sibilant as's' entered India and adopted Sapta Sindhu its homeland, developed the Vedic religion and Sanskrit language and produced the oldest religious scripture of Aryans, the Rigveda. The theory that the Iranian Aryans and the Indian Aryans were, during the Indo-Iranian period, one and the same people speaking the same language, worshipping the same gods and following the same social customs and traditions, is quite convincing and is reasonably based on the affinity of Sanskrit and Avesta and striking similarity in their gods, mythology, religious beliefs, social customs and traditions. A.A. Macdonell observes that the striking similarity which subsists between Avesta and Sanskrit is so great in syntax, vocabulary, diction and general poetic style that by mere application of phonetic laws whole Avestan stanzas may be translated word for word into Vedic mantras so as to produce verses correct not in form but in poetic spirit.[2] Bloomfieed says, "No student of either religion questions that they drew largely from a common source, and therefore mutually illumine each other."[3] Hopkins observes, "For in fact two religions here and there touch each other so nearly that to deny a relation between them is impossibble."[4] M. Muller asserts, "Still more striking is the similarity between Persia and India in religion and mythology, gods unknown to any Indo-European nation are worshipped under the same name in Sanskrit and Zend, and the change of some of the most sacred expressions in Sanskrit into name of evil spirits in Zend only serves to strengthen the conviction that we have here the usual traces of a schism which separated a community that had once been united."[5] The close linguistic affinity and striking similarity in religious beliefs, cults and social customs prove conclusively that the Iranian and the Indian Aryans were ethnologically one people and once lived as one nation. They probably lived a common life in the Avestic Aeranvaejo.'[6] Aeranvaejo signifies the birth place of Aryans. If Aeranvaejo is not the original home: of Indo-Europeans it must have been the second home of Indo-Iranians where the Indo-Iranian culture developed. The location of Aeranveajo, according to the first Fargard of Vendidad, is traced somewhere on the eastern side of Persia or in the central Asia. The Fargard alludes to the Indo-Aryans migrating to the Sapta Sindhu.

The Indo-Iranian people inherited the largest share of the common heritage of the Indo-European culture. They retained it and preserved it zealously but in association with a different people in a' different country and in a different environment they attained a distinct culture of their own. Dr. Taylor tells, "It is plain from the character of the culture words common to Zend and Sanskrit that the Indians and the Iranians had before their separation advanced further in the path of civilization than any of other Aryan nations."[7]

The Iranians designated themselves as Airya while the Indians as Arya. The term "Arya" means noble or of good birth. It indicates that in order to distinguish themselves from other people the Indo-Iranians had a common name which they proudly used for themselves to show their superiority of blood and their highly advanced culture.

(a) Indo-Iranian Religion

Like the Indo-European religion, the Indo-Iranian religion too went into oblivion and became entirely extinct, as soon as the Indo-Iranians split into two distinct branches. Hence as in the case of the Indo-European religion, the study of the comparative mythology is equally helpful for reconstructing the Indo-Iranian religion. In order to have a knowledge of the Indo-Iranian religion we are left with only alternative and that is to search out and sort out beliefs, cults and conceptions from the Rigveda and the Avesta. The authenticity of the Avestic literature is not beyond doubt and this creates a great problem. The Avestic literature is not found to be preserved in an unchanged form. The unique features of the Rigvedic and Zoroastrian religion create another difficulty. The two religions are undoubtedly off-shoots of one common source, i.e., the Indo-Iranian religion but as they had attained the distinct separate entities they became diametrically opposite to each other. M.N. Dalla remarks, "The parallels in the religious thoughts which the Avestan documents offer to the Vedic concepts are many but equally so are the contrasts. The resemblance is great, but the difference is still greater."[8] Hopkins holds similar view. He observes, "For in fact two religions here and there touch each other so nearly that to deny a relation between them is impossible, while in detail they diverge so widely that it is always questionable whether a coincidence of ritual or belief is accidental or imply historical connection."[9]

The Avestic religion deviated considerably from the older religious beliefs. Some older gods were degraded to demons, whereas several others had disappeared entirely leaving no trace of their existence. When Zoroastrianism assumed the monotheistic form, all other older gods except Ahura Mazda became arch-angels. Moreover the older gods and original cults and faiths are invariably met with in ethical garb, which is the characteristic feature of the Zoroastrianism. Besides the foreign influence overwhelmed the original religious beliefs so much that the later Iranian religion became altogether different. An additional factor that changed the old Iranian religion totally is the personality of Zoroaster who institute new cults and new religious customs and instilled new religious spirit. It is quite obvious that in regard to the older faith we get from the Avesta only fragmentary informations. Hence to get an idea of the Indo-Iranian religion we have to compare the beliefs and conceptions of the Rigveda with those found in the older parts of the Avesta, we should utilize the Avestic material with great caution and always bear in mind the aforesaid factors.

(i) Conception of God—The Indo-European term 'deva' continued to be used for deity throughout the Rigveda although the same word 'daiwa' met with different treatment in the Avesta. The testimony of the Rigveda is more authentic. It proves that the idea of god even during the Indo-Iranian period was still associated with the luminous manifestations of nature and of the natural phenomena.

The older use of the term 'bhaga' was not retained in the Rigveda where 'bhaga' became an independent deity and lost its former sense of god in general. On the other hand in the Avesta the term is invariably used for god in general.[10]

In addition to the terms 'deva' and 'bhaga' for god, the Indo-Iranians had another term 'asura' for the designation of their deities, which shows a great ethical advancement in the conception. Moulton[11] derives the word 'asura' from 'asu' meaning elves or spirit. Sayana also derives it from 'asu' but interprets it as wise or powerful. The word 'asura' which means 'wise,' powerful, or full of life is used for the Indo-Iranian gods.

Asura, in form of Ahura is the name of the supreme god in the Zoroastrianism. In the earliest portions of the Rigveda the word 'asura' is used as the designation of the highest gods. The term 'asura' which signifies the devine or the spiritual is, of course, a highly honorific epithet which is given to Dyaus, Parjanya, Varuna, Indra, Agni, Savitr and Rudra.[12] In its plural form 'asura' is used now and then in the Rigveda as the common designation of all gods.[13]

But later on for reason unknown, the word had assumed the meaning quite opposite to its original one. This change in meaning is noticeable occasionally in the later parts of the Rigveda. Asura is invariably used in bad sense throughout the Yajurveda, the Atharvaveda and in all the subsequent literature as the common designation of the adversaries of the gods. On the contrary, the term 'deva' met with altogether different treatment in the Avesta. Strangely it became permanently the designation of the evil spiritual hosts in the Zoroastrianism. Mills says, "It is a strange historical fact that a glorious name should have been dethroned within a vast territory alone, while it has remained undisturbed over all India, Europe and the European west as deva, daus, zio, dia, dews."[14] Its cognate, the Avestic daiwa, modern Persian 'div' is used throughout the Avestic literature as the regular designation of devils and the Zoroastrian religion is explicitly called 'Vi-daeva' meaning "against the Devas.[15]"

The above facts show that the two terms 'asura' and 'deva' which had always been the highly sacred designations of gods in the Indo-Iranian period met with altogether different treatments in the two closely related braches of Indo-Iranian people. Among Indians 'deva' remained the common designation of a god and 'asuras' became demons while among the Iranians 'Ahura' is the name of their highest god and 'daiwas' became demons. This state of affair baffles scholars and they are unable to explain how this remarkable change in meaning took place in the course of the development of the Zoroastrianism and the Rigvedic religion. The problem is dealt with from different angles and various conflicting theories have cropped up.

Haug[16] holds the view that change in meaning of two terms 'deva' and 'asura' that resulted in degrading Indian gods into demons in Iran and Iranian gods into demons in India took place because of the religious schism in the Indo-Iranian community; in consequence of which it caused the separation of the Indian and Iranian Aryans and divided them into hostile camps–Asura worshippers and Deva worshippers. Some prominent scholars support this theory. This theory once received common acceptance but is now criticized[17] on several grounds and totally discarded.

Darmesteter[18] puts forward a new theory. He observes that in the Rigveda the epithet Asura is the monopoly of Varuna who is indispensably associated with 'maya' meaning wile or occult power.[19] The term 'maya' which is closely connected with the bad sense of Asura[20] is essentially applied to hostile beings in the sense of craft.[21] Thus Asura is looked down upon to be 'possessor of occult power,'[22] which is the main characteristic of the hostile beings. He further asserts that change in meaning of the term 'deva' in the Avesta was brought about by the misunderstanding of the old phrases such as 'wrath of gods and men' and 'trouble made by gods or men.'

L.H. Mills argues that this remarkable change in meanings of two words took place on account of "some series of calamities following upon the special use of the name in hymns, and on account of the name abounding in the battle hymns of their enemies in tribal wars."[23] Moulton[24] gives another explanation for the change in the meaning of 'deva' in Iran. He remarks that 'deva' became demon in the Zoroastrianism in which the older nature gods are denounced and degraded as hostile beings. Another explanation of this difficult problem is also put forth, which is based on the Ashur-Asura theory. It is conceived that Assyrians attacked Indo-Iranians and made the Iranian Aryans their subjects and expelled the Indo-Aryans from their homeland, who migrated to India. The Indo-Aryans revolted against 'Asur' in India because of their strong hatred towards the Iranian Aryans who became the subjects to Assyrians, the worshippers of Ashur. Hillebrandt[25] presents an ingenious theory. He explained that the difference of views is inevitably caused because of religious relations which subsisted between the Iranian Aryans and the Indian Aryans before the reform of Zoroaster but certainly after the Rigvedic period. He tried his best to show the possibility of close intercourse between the early Iranians and the Vedic people during the late Rigvedic period. But this does not stand to reason. Schroeder[26] also deals with the problem. His arguments are mainly based on the Bradke's[27] theory. He remarks that originally two distinct words asura 'spirit' and asura 'lord' existed; in order to avoid confusion, the Indians retained the former use and gave up the word 'lord'. On the other hand in Iran the use of the term asura as 'lord; prevailed.

It has been seen that the vexing problem of the change in meanings of the two terms 'asura' and 'deva' in India and Iran has been dealt with by various scholars from different angles but we have not come to any satisfactory conclusion. We know that the term 'deva' is constantly used in bad sense in the Avestic literature. It is a well-known fact that old nature gods are denounced in the Zoroastrianism and, of course, some of them such as Indra, Nasatya, etc., are degaded to demon and certain deity as Dyaus who is in true sense a nature god disappeared totally leaving no trace behind at all. We know the term 'deva' to shine used for god among undivided Aryans is essentially associated with luminous manifestation of nature. It is natural and quite in consistent with new spirit of the Zoroastrian religion that the term 'deva' became the designation of evil beings. On the contrary the Vedic people remained as nature worshippers like their forefathers. Quite indifferent to the development of the new spirit in the Avestic religion, the Vedic people did nothing in retalliation. Varuna, the counterpart of the Iranian supreme deity, Ahura Mazda, retained the supermacy among gods for a longer period and no Iranian god figured in the list of demons in the Rigveda. The term 'asura' did not lose at all the original sanctity in the earlier parts of the Rigveda where it retained high position among gods as in Iran. It is used in a bad sense only on a few instances in the later portions of the Rigveda. Only in 15 out of 105 instances the term is found used in the bad sense. It is most likely that the Vedic people forgot the old etymology of the term and recognizing 'a' negative in the first letter of 'asura' They coined a new term 'sura,' god. Thus Asura came to be used for non-divine.

(ii) Classification of Gods and their number—The Indo-Iranians worshipped thirty three gods in all. The Rigveda and the Avesta both confirm it. Vedas, particularly the Atharvaveda and Brahmans clearly mention the number of gods as thirty three.[28] The Avesta describes thrity three ratus, the heads instituted by Ahura Mazda and promulgated by Zoroaster in order to keep and prevail the best truth.[29] Haug remarks, 'A very remarkable coincidence, as the number of the divine beings worshipped, is to be found between the statements of the Vedas and the Zend Avesta."[30]

(iii) Departmental Gods—Several Indo-European branches have special deities commonly known as departmental gods. Hence some scholars hold the view that this characteristic goes back to the Indo-European period and it is reasonably conceivable that it persisted in the Indo-Iranian pantheon. This view gets support from the Avesta which definitely mentions the existence of the departmental gods. The Avestic Mithra, Homa, Apam Napat, Vayu and Tishtriya are righly regarded as sondergott or departmental gods.[31] Mithra is taken "he of the compact," Homa 'he of the plants," and Tishriya "he of the stars." But such evidences are entirely absent in the Rigveda. Dr. Grieswold[32] claims existence of the departmental gods in the Indo-Iranian pantheon. He puts arguments that the Rigvedic gods, Soma, Dyaus, Indra, Agni and goddesses Sarasvati and Sindhu are the departmental gods.

This view is not plausible at all.[33] The Rigveda confirms that Dyaus is not "he of the sky" but sky itself and Indra is not "he of the storm" but strom itself. Similarly Agni is fire itself and Usa is dawn itself.[34] In case of Soma, Sindhu and Sarasvati, the Rigvedic evidences are undoubtedly in favour of sondergott or the departmental gods. After extensive studies of these Vedic gods we find that Soma is god of Soma plant or juice and not the god supervising the plant world. Similarly Sarasvati and Sindhu are personifications of particular rivers and not the goddesses of rivers in general. The Rigveda definitely has no departmental gods.

The Avestic departmental gods tempt scholars to postulate that it is the Indo-Iranian characteristic. If this assumption be correct, it is strange how the Rigveda could have remained so immune from it. There is every possibility that departmental deities found in the Avesta are purely Iranian creation.

(iv) Sky God—Heaven was the principal and supreme deity of the undivided

Aryans. Dyaus, the sky god, who is the father of all gods and men and enjoyed the supermacy of gods during the Indo-European period, acquired and accumulated the highest power in the Latin and Hellenic world. Whether Indo-Iranians worshipped Dyaus with the same prominence and to the same extent is doubtful. Dyaus plays but very insignificant role in the Rigveda. He is invoked in few hymns but there he does not appear in marked prominence.[35] The Iranian Aryans forgot even the name of Dyaus totally. Hence there is no positive evidence to prove persistence of the Dyaus worship among the Indo-Iranians. Herodotus certainly provides invaluable information on this point. He reports, "It is the custom of the Persians, to ascend to high peaks of the mountains, and offer sacrifice to Zeus, calling the whole vault of the sky Zeus.[36] Moulton recognizes this Zeus of Herodotus as the Indo-Iranian Dyaus.[37] Whether the ancient Iranians called the sky god, Dyaus or not but there is no reason to deny that the Indo-Iranian worshipped a god of shining sky and it is probable that they conferred on this god a new name other than Dyaus confining him only with the duty of fatherhood.

The well-known Indo-European father-killing-myth lends a support to strengthen this view. The Greek mythology tells that Cronus slew his father Uranus[38] 'heaven'. Similarly the Rigveda[39] informs that Indra holding his father Dyaus by foot crushed him. This hymn reflects that Indra usurped the power and functions of his father Dyaus and pushed him in background.[40] Of course in several hymns Indra appears as a Dyaus or sky god.[41] In regard to the decadence of Dyaus, some verses in the Rigveda and the Atharvavda shed more light on this point. These verses indicate that Parjanya stands for Dyaus or steps in his place.[42] Dyaus is superseded by another deity who is the god of the encompassing sky.

It is evident that more than one deity appear in the Indo-Iranian pantheon usurping and sharing more or less certain functions stripped off from the power of Dyaus; consequently Dyaus remained merely a symbolic father. Originally the exalted designation Asura was the exclusive epithet of Dyaus. The ancient Iranians made from this Asura an abstract deity Ahura Mazda and clothed him with ethical garb.

Dr. Grieswold observes that the Iranian notion of a supreme deity Ahura Mazda was taken from the Indo-Iranian Dyaus who was already on wane.[43] Prof.

Gray also claims that Ahura Mazda was originally a god of material sky. In his opinion Ahura Mazda is the sky pure and simple and equivalent to the Indo-Iranian Dyaus but not of the Vedic Varuna.[44] The explanation of Prof. Gray as to how the true name of the deity had been supplanted by Ahura Mazda is that it had most probably become so sacrosanct as to be practically taboo.[45]

Scholars seek to prove that Ahura Mazda and his prototype Varuna are personifications of the moon.[46] Oldenberg finds in Varuna an aboriginal deity.[47] It is the mystic personality of Ahura Mazda that eludes the scholars very much.

Ahura Mazda was originally a god of sky proper. He is as a matter of fact, not the successor of Dyaus, he is the Iranian Varuna. He although does not correspond to Varuna in name but agrees exactly in character.

The first and the foremost point which convinces the identity of two deities is the name of the Iranian god itself. Just as the Iranian supreme god is called Ahura (lord), so is the Vedic Varuna, Asura. The words undoubtedly mean the same thing. Just as the association of Ahura Mazda with Mithra is found in the Avesta, so is the partnership of Varuna and Mitra in the Rigveda.[48] In the Rigveda, Varuna and Mitra are very often invoked together. Dealing with this controversy Bloomfield remarks, "It seems to me an almost unimaginable feat of skepticism to doubt the original identity of the two pairs."[49] Moral law is an essential and peculiar characteristic of these two deities. The Rigveda speaks it rta or righteousness;"[50] so Ahura is described as the "Guardian of the Asha or righteous order."[51] The Avesta describes Ahura Mazda as "Ashahe Khao"[52] whereas Varuna is called "Khatasya."[53] It is a most interesting parallel that subsists between the two deities. Bloomfield observes, "The words are sound for sound the same."[54] Moreover the figure of Ahura Mazda in the Avesta is the same as the description of Varuna in the Rigveda. Ahura Mazda is described as the absolute ruler and sovereignty belongs to him.[55] Similarly Varuna is the self independent ruler, the king of the world and attributed to sovereign power.[56] The attributes and the functions of Ahura Mazda and Varuna are very closely similar.[57] As Varuna is far-seeing,[58] so is Ahura Mazda who with his shining eyes witnesses all thing.[59] Just as Varuna is omniscient and all the secret things that have been or shall be done are known and truth and falsehood are witnessed by Varuna.[60] So is Ahura Mazda who does not sleep but observes all human deeds, overt and covert.[61] The spies of Varuna are very wise who can not be deceived.[62] Similarly Ahura Mazda has a large number of spies and can not be deceived.[63]

Such a remarkable resemblance in character of the two deities is a strong evidence to convince us the close identity of these two deities. Moulton asserts that Ahura Mazda is the Iranian counterpart of the Vedic Varuna. Mazda is merely his cults epithet and he was in existence long before Zoroaster in an earlier form as the chief deity of the pantheon.[64] Bloomfield remarks, "In common with most scholars I believe that the god Varuna is to be connected, if not identified, with the chief and wise god of the Zoroastrian faith, namely Ahura Mazdah or Ormazd, that is Wise Lord.'"[65]

The above discussion shows that Varuna was the Indo-Iranian god and his counterpart Ahura Mazda travelled to Iran with his devoted worshippers. The existence of the sky god in the Indo-Iranian pantheon is more than probable. Varuna was originally a sky god both in name and character.

It leaves little doubt that Varuna was the sky god of the undivided Indo-Iranians. Iranians made Ahura Mazda from this old deity. The later developments in India and Iran obscured the original nature of both Varuna and Ahura Mazda.

(v) Adityas/Amesha Spents—The group of seven gods-Varuna, Mitra, Indra, Aryaman, Bhaga, Daksa and Ansa, is known as Adityas. Rta, the moral law which is the special attribute of Varuna is associated with all the deities of this group. Among the Adityas the first five mentioned above are undoubtedly of Indo-Iranian origin and the last four are abstract deities.

In the Avesta Ahura Mazda and his six arch-angles are designated as the Amesha Spents, "Immortal Holy Ones." Asha, the ethical law is essentially associated with this group of seven deities. Apart from Ahura Mazda other six Amesha Spents purely abstraction.

Roth believes in the identity of the Iranian Amesha Spents and the Vedic Adityas. He asserts that the gods of this group are the Indo-Iranian creation and they are worshipped constantly as a group throughout the Indo-Iranian period.[66] Some scholars refute this theory.

It is noticeable that two groups are comparable in many respects. But it is contended[67] that six Iranian Amesha Spents correspond to the Indian Adityas neither in name nor in function.

The identity of the Amesha Spents and the Adityas, is most convincing. The objections have no force and carry little weight. Kieth asserts that number seven is evidently becoming normal number in India as early as Rigveda as number seven in absolutely fixed in case of Ahura Mazda and the six Amesha Spents.[68] It is admitted that Varuna, the chief Aditya and Ahura Mazda, the head of the Amesha Spents are identical in all respects. Certain Adityas such as Aryaman, Bhaga, Daksa and Ansa are abstract figures. The whole group of the Avestic Amesha Spents points to abstraction and is "non-naturalistic to the bone". Of course, the members of the two groups differ in name and in function. But it is not an insuperable difficulty. It may easily be explained that during the Indo-Iranian period these deities had no close connection with any sphere of nature and the later developments are responsible for such discrepancy. Keith remarks, "To presume an independent development of the ideas in both countries is realy to assume something much more improbable than a common origin."[69]

Muir remarks that in the post Vedic literature the Adityas are regularly twelve sun gods and evidently associated with the twelve months.[70] It is pertinent to point out that the names of the Amesha Spents are given to the Persian months. It refers to a certain type of relationship between the two groups directly or indirectly. It is reasonably claimed that tile Adityas are connected, if not identified, with the Amesha Spents. It is quite certain tllat the Indo-Iranian pantheon consisted of a group of seven abstract deities. It also appears that deification of abstraction owes its origin to the Indo-Iranian period, and it started from this period.

(vi) Moral Law Asha/Rta—Morality is essentially associated with the Avestic Ahura Mazda and the Vedic Varuna; and it is considered as the characteristic attribute of them. It is the Rigvedic Rta which is known in the Avesta as Asha.

The Rigveda presents three-fold aspects of Rta which may be described as cosmic order, correct cult of gods, and moral conduct of man.[71] The Avesta gives the description of the same three-fold characters of Asha. The Vedic Rta and the Avestic Asha are undoubtedly identical in name as well as in other respects.

This ethical conception is really a sublime Indo-Iranian creation. The conception is undoubtedly the best of its kind that the Indo-Iranian elaborated. It is superior to any such earlier conception of Aryans.

(vii) Sun God—The worship of the-sun goes back to the Indo-European period. But it occupies nowhere in the Aryan world such an important position as it acquired in the Indo-Iranian religion. The solar myth pervades throughout the Indo-Iranian mythology. The Indo-Iranians deified and worshipped the different aspects of the sun.

(a) Surya/Hvarkhshaeta: The Vedic Surya and the Avestic Hvarkhshaeta are the sun gods. The Sanskrit word 'svitr; or 'surya' and the Avestic term 'hvar' came out from the same Indo-Iranian word 'svar.'[72] The Avestic 'hvar' is combined with the word 'khshaeta' meaning 'king, and Hvarkhshaeta is now corrupted into Khorshed.

The Rigveda as well as the Avesta both show that this deity is regarded as the sun god and as the genius presiding over the sun.[73] The identity between the Vedic Surya and the Avestic Hvarkhaeta is indisputable. The Rigveda presents the same character of Surya as that of Hvarkhsaeta mentioned in the Avesta[74] Surya is regarded as eye of the gods.[75] The Avestic Hvarkhshaeta is also conceived as the eye of Ahura Mazda.[76] The Rigveda tells that Surya traverses his daily course through sky in a car drwan by the swift horses.[78] The Iranian Hvarkhshaeta also possesses a car which is drawn by the swift and powerful four white steeds.[78]

Indo-Iranians attach a great value to the worship of the sun. It is considered as highly efficacious and hence indispensable. Gayatri Mantra is the most sacred formula to the Vedic people, which is used for offering prayer to Surya. Similarly Iranians regard Ahunawar manthra as highly sacred in which Hvarkhshaeta is offered prayer.

(b) Bhaga/Bagha: It has been seen that Bagha or Bhaga was a common designation of divine beings in general during the Indo-European period and it persisted in the Zoroastrian pantheon but in the Rigveda Bhaga is listed among the Adityas. So in the light of the available evidences it is difficult to draw any definite conclusion about the existence of god Bhaga among the Indo-Iranians. Haug remarks, "that the Vedic god Bhaga (compare the adjective bagobhakhta, ordained by fate, which is to be found in both Veda and Zend Avesta) was believed a deity presiding over destiny and fortune of men may clearly be seen from passages in the Rigveda."[79] Wallis remakrs that in the light of the Rigveda Bhaga seems to be a survival from an ancient sun worship.[80]

(c) Mitra/Mithra: Indo-Iranians worshipped another sun god who is the Vedic Mitra or the Avestic Mithra. The Avestic Mithra is essentially the "guardian of faithfulness."[81] He is invariably and intimately connected with the sun from the earliest times. The Avestic Mithra was a solar deity originally and he is still so in the Avesta; receives a general acceptance. But the original character of the Vedic Mitra is very obscure. Scholars differ widely on his original character.

The evidence of the Avesta appears to be sound. it shows that Mithra who is closely connected to the sun is purely a solar deity. Some scholars are of the view that the Avestic Mithra was originally a god proper. But it is not tenable at all. Moulton[82] proves successfully that Mithra is the sun god. Edward[83] claims that Mithra represents nothing else than the sun. So far the nature of the Vedic Mitra is concerned, the obscurity certainly prevails. Only one single hymn is assigned to him in the Rigveda. But Mitra is one of the Adityas. It is certain that he is originallya solar deity. Kieth[84] holds the view that in the light of the later Vedic literature and rituals, Mitra is evidently a solar diety of course, in the Rigveda in the hymns V-82-9 and V-81-1, Mitra is identified with the sun god. Macdonell[85] discovers in the VII-36-2 tolerably a clear reference to the solar character of Mitra. According to Eggers[86] the solar character of Mitra in the hymn V-3-1, is irrefutable. Above all the identity of the Vedic Mitra with the Avestic Mithra leaves no doubt that he is the popular sun god of the Indo-Iranians. The Vedic Mitra is the friend of the mankind[87] whereas the Avesta describes Mithra as the guardian of oath and promise.[88] The Vedic Mitra watches the tillers with unswerving eyes.[89] The Avestic Mithra is the herald of dawn, surveys all that is between the heaven and the earth[90] and possesses piercing rays and ten thousand eyes.[91] The Indo-Iranians regard this deity as a genius of heavently light and foe of darkness, so he is considered as a friend of mankind. A god who supervises human friendship and sees that the friendship should be true, became a special guardian of faithfulness.

(d) Aryaman Airyaman: Indo-Iranians possess another sun god who is mentioned by the name of Airyaman in the Avesta and Aryaman in the Rigveda. He seems to be most probably an apotheosis of the comradeship. The Rigvedic Aryaman and the Avestic Airyaman both have double meanings. Both terms represent the proper name of the deity and the term aryaman is found in the Rigveda in an appellative sense of 'comrade' or groomsman' whereas the airyaman in the Gathas means 'client.'[92] Macdonell takes the term aryman occurring in the Rigvedic hymn V-85-7, as a parallel to mitrya, means "relating to a friend."[93] Moulton discovers the meaning of the Avestic term airyman as a "friend."[94] We can easily arrive at the conclusion that the Indo-Iranians conceive this deity as a special "guardian of friendship" and as such conception is slightly deviated from the conception of the greater Aditya, Mitra, the Friend.[95] The Vedic Aryaman is represented as the typical groomsman at wedding rites[96] whereas Airyaman figures in the Gathas as the desired friend and peersman.[97]

This deity particularly presides over Indo-Iranian marriages.[98] It is proved by the fact that the Brahmans and the Parsees both invoke him on such occasion.

But he was originally and undoubtedly a solar deity, and as in the Rigveda, Aryaman is listed among the Adityas. In connection with his original nature Haug says, "He seems to be either another name of the sun, like Mitra, Savitr, Pushan, etc., or his constant associate and representative."[99]

(viii) Fire God—The fire worship and the Soma cult are two unique and characteristic features of the Indo-Iranian pantheon that distinguish this branch from the other Indo-European nations. Although the fire worship and the conception of the heavenly mead go back to the Indo-European period. They are found there in a vague form. The Indo-Europeans when conveyed offerings to their gods used to offer libation to the fire but it indicates no more than some kind of fire worship and with it a rudimentary personification is likely to have been existed at that time. Bloomfield remarks, "The chaste figure of Hestia of the Greeks or Vesta of the Romans, contrasted with boistrous male Agni, shows that the initial conception must have been faint and unstable to enable it to produce shape so thoroughly diverse."[100]

The Indo-Iranians are fire worshippers par excellence. The fire god certainly occupies the central position in the Indo-Iranian pantheon. All the Avestic rituals centre round the fire adoration. As a matter of fact the fire worship is the main theme of the Zoroastrain religion.[101] It is so much so that the followers of the Zoroastrianism are commonly called the fire worshippers. Similarly in all Vedic rituals the presence of Agni is essentially obligatory; no religious ceremony is complete in absence of Agni; no god receives offering without Agni.

The absence of the name of the fire gad among the Mitannian gods inscribed on the Bogaz Keui inscription speaks in favour of the view that it is a later development of the Indo-Iranians. The Vedic Agni and the Avestic Atar correspond remarkably in character as well as in function but not in name. The Avestic fire priests, Atharvans are undoubtedly the same in origin as the Vedic Atharvans. This fact indicates convincingly that the fire-cult is a specific religious development of the undivided Indo-Iranians. In function and nature the two gods agree to such an extent that it emphasises strongly the unimpeachable identity. Atar is described in the Avesta as "the house-lord of all houses."[102] while Agni in the Rigveda is called grhapati "the lord of the house."[103] The Rigveda tells that Agni brings the gods[104] to the sacrifice and sometimes conveys offering to gods,[105] so he is called a duta or messenger of gods[106] and sometimes a messenger of men also.[107] Atar in the Avesta figures as a messenger who calls gods to the place where sacrificial food is offered.[108] Just as the Rigveda mentions Agni as a great benefactor,[109] most intelligent,[110] a frind[111] and Vrtrahan[112] and who also dispells darkness and drives away evil spirils;[113] so Atar is in the Avesta, who is also wise, helper in need, and repels darkness and foes and fights with the dragon. The positive evidence to confirm the identity of the two gods is that as Agni is the son of Dyaus[114] so Atar is called the son of Ahura Mazda.[115]

The elaborate system of the fire rituals is arranged by the Indo-Iranian fire priests, Atharvans who are known by this name in both the Rigveda and the Avesta. It infers that the Indo-Iranian fire cult was fully elaborate and highly advanced during this period.

(a) Narasansa/Nairyosangha: Narasansa or Nairyosangha is an Indo-Iranian god who seems, in the capacity of messenger, to be personification of the flames of fire. Narasansa is the performer of sacrifice[116] and figures in the Rigveda as the head of the gods and he makes the sacrifice pleasant to gods.[117] While Nairyosangha is mentioned in the Avesta as the messenger of Ahura Mazda.[118]

The name of the both gods means, "the praise of men" which Carnoy and Macdonell take[119] in the sense of "he who is the object of mens' worship." Haug[120] is of the view that it means "one praised by men, i.e., renowned." Bergaign[121] thinks that the Vedic Narasansa is the personification of one aspect of Agni parallel to that of the god of human prayer, like Brhaspati. Yaska tells that Narasansa the epithet of several Vedic gods such as Brahmanaspati, Pushan, Agni but it, is chiefly associated with Agni.[122] Haug observes that the Avestic Nairyosangha who corresponds to the Narasansa not merely in name but in function also, serves Ahura Mazda as a messenger, in this capacity Agni and Pushan figure in the Rigveda.[123] Harlez holds the opinion that the Avestic Nairyosangha is the "personification of the flames rising from Atar and carrying to heaven the prayer of faithful."[124] Dhalla remarks that Nairyosangha, the messenger of the Ahura Mazda is closely associated with Atar.[125] The comparison of the two gods speaks in favour of the view that Narasansa or Nairyosangha is nothing but apotheosis of the rising flames of fire.

(b) Apam Napat: The Indo-Iranian god Apam Napat is also probably a personification of one of the aspects of fire. This Indo-Iranian god retains the same name in the Rigveda and the Avesta. Apam Napat means "son of the waters." The Rigveda describes Apam Napat as golden[126] and who is clothed in the lightning,[127] surrounded by waters[128] and he dwells in the highest place.[129] and comes from heaven to the earth.[130] On the other hand Apam Napat figures in the Avesta as a spirit presiding over waters who lives in their depth and is surrounded by females. He drives with swift horses and he is said to have regained glory when in the fight between Atar and dragon, he fell in the ocean Vaurokasa.[131]

Scholars differ widely in regard to the original character of the deity. The Vedic Apam Napat presents the aqueous and the igneous characters both.[132]

On the other hand Speigal[133] is of view that Apam Napat as he figures in the Avesta renders nothing but igneous nature. Darmesteter regards the Avestic Apam Napat[134] as the fire god born from the cloud in lightning. The aqueous character of the deity is very clear everywhere in the Avesta.

The comparison of the descriptions available in the Rigveda and Avesta speaks in favour of the traditional view that the Indo-Iranian Apam Napat is the fire god born from cloud in lightning.

(ix) Soma/Homa—The Soma cult may be rightly claimed to be a specific and a new Indo-Iranian contribution to the older pantheon. The conception of the heavenly mead which is said to have been brought by an eagle from the heaven is certainly very primitive but has least relation to the well elaborate and the most sublime Soma cult of the Indo-Iranians. Keith rightly remarks, "Soma is derived from the root 'su' and means merely the pressed drink, and there is no parallel word in the other Indo-European languages, so that it must be recognized that Soma cult was special Indo-Iranian innovation presumably produced a juice pleasant to drink or at least intoxicating."[135]

It is worthwhile to note that both the branches of the Indo-Iranians preserved the name, functions and character of the god Soma and all essentials of the cult with great circumspection. The form of worship, the allied conceptions, the attendant rites and rituals and even the legends relating to the Soma cult are remarkably identical in both branches.

We get confirmation from both the Rigveda and the Avesta that drinking of Soma or Homa jusice was a common practice among the Indo-Iranians. They regard it as panacea for all disease, most efficacious for health and most sacred food to the gods. They regularly offered the sacred juice to their gods. They deified juice and plant both. The juice is medicine in the both the scriptures. As the Vedic god Soma bestows immortality to insure health and long life,[136] so the Avestic god Homa does.[137] The Rigvedic Soma grows on certain mountain or on a particular mountain as well as in the water; and Varuna placed it on a rock.[138] The Avesta tells that Homa grows on certain mountain as well as in the waters;[139] and a skilful god, Ardvi Sura placed it on the mountain Haraiti.[140] Soma and Homa both are called great kings, the mighty gods and lords of plants.[141] The mythical homes of the both are referred to in the heaven. As Soma is light-winning, and conferred with the titles of Svarsa and Sukratu by virtue of his being powerful and wise.[142] So Homa in the Avesta is known as Hraves and Hukratu. The Rigveda tells that the eagle brought Soma to Indra from heaven[143] The Avestic Homa is said to have been carried by the auspicious bird from the heaven to the peaks-above-eagles to mountain.[144] Soma insures long life in this world and heals whosoever is sick.[145] Similarly Homa is also prayed for long vitality of life and called the best healer.[146] Soma slays the wicked and receives the honorific epithet Vritrahan. Homa is also Verethraghna and he gets victory over demons.[147] Soma and Homa both bestow good horses and excellent children.[148] The Rigveda mentions Soma as a great victor and the most heroic of the heroes who is born for battle.[149] Similarly Homa is prayed to destroy the wicked who torment mankind and he bestows victory on earth as well as in battle.[150] Just as Homa is the most nutricious, the conquerer of life and the great assault of death;[151] so, "the Soma draught is even said to dispell sin from the heart, to destroy falsehood and to promote truth."[152]

The Indo-Iranians prepare the Soma juice with great care and observe the correctness in minute details regarding its preparation for rituals. The detail of preparation is the same in both scriptures, the term 'su' in the Rigveda and 'hu' in the Avesta are used for pressing. First of all they wash and then press stalks of Soma which are known in the Rigveda as 'amsu' and in the Avesta as Jasu'. The yellow juice was filtered through a sieve and then purified substance was mixed with milk. It is very interesting to see that the Indo-Iranians well remembered the names of the ancient personages who first of all prepared the Soma juice. They are Vivasvant or Vivanhavant, Trita or Thrita and Aptya or Athwya. Here the Rigveda disagrees with the Avesta as Trita Aptya is one person in the former whereas Thrita and Athwya are two different heroes in the latter.

(x) Vivasvant Vivanhvant—The Indo-Iranians conceive a god who is held responsible for the origin of the human race. The name of the deity is Vivasvant in the Rigveda and Vivanhvant in the Avesta. The two gods correspond not merely in name but in character also. As the Vedic Vivasvant is the father of twin Yama and Yami;[153] so the Avesta describes Vivanhvant as the father of the twin Yima and Yimak.[154] Just as the Avesta mentions a special connection of Vivasvant to Homa and describes him as the first man to prepare the Homa jusice; so the Rigveda also speaks of Vivasvant the first preparer of Soma and shows a very close association between Vivasvant and Soma.[155] This perfect parallelism impresses Oldenberg to see in this deity nothing more or less than a deification of the sacrificer, the ancestor of human race.[156]

It is to be admitted that the deity bears the appearance of having lost much of his original colour and life. Agni is very often mentioned in the Rigveda as the progenitor of man.[157] The sun is also illustrated as the father of men in the Vedic literature.[158] It shows clearly that the Indo-Iranian Vivasvant was originally the sun.

(xi) Yama/Yima—The father sky was not only the father of gods but father of men also in the Indo-European times. The Indo-Iranians were not satisfied with this vague and primitive conception of their forefather. They evolved the highly sublime conception of twins Yama and Yami parallel to the Semitic myth of human progeny (Adam and Eve). The Avestic counterparts of this twins are Yima and Yimak. The twins were provided with a father named Vivasvant or Vivanhvant, the conception is definitely a later affiliation. The Iranian version of this myth exactly, corresponds, even in detail, to the Vedic version. Bloomfield observes, "This myth is the clearest and best preserved common piece of property of the two religions."[159]

The Iranian and the Indian versions of the Yama's myth expose a considerable points of coincidence.

The Avestic Yima Khshaeta and the Rigvedic Yama raja agree in names and epithet. Khshaeta means the same as raja 'king'. The family names of both gods are identical. Vivanhao,[160] i.e., son of Vivanhvant in the Avesta and Vaivasvata[161], i.e., son of Vivasvant in the Rigveda.

Yima is the hero of the Avestic flood legend. But the Vedic Yama is the first mortal man who died first. He showed the way to men to heaven and receives them in his dwelling. Yima is the wordly king of the golden age,[162] so Yama who is a god also, by implication is a king or ruler of the dead, dwelling in the highest heaven.[163] The two stories present an intimately close relation in case of the twin sisters Yami and Yimak. As in the Avesta Yima is the first of the mortals, so the Vedic literature describes Yama as the first of the mortals who died.[164] The owls and pigeons[165] are envoys of the Vedic Yama whereas a bird[166] brings messages in the vara of the Iranian Yima. While the residence of Yama is in the remote part of the sky,[167] the vara of Yima is concealed either on a mountain or in some recess where the sun and the moon are not visible which appears to have been underground.[168] By virtue of having died first and discovered "a way for many."[169] Yama has a path for a dead to lead them to their abode, so following a road towards the sun Yima got new countries.[170] Just as Yima gathers round him men and asks them to assemble in his vara.[171] Similarly Yama collects the people and bestows the dead the resting place.[172] Yama is 'Lord of the settlement" and father[173] while Yima opened the earth for human race.[174]

(xii) Trita/Thrita and Traitana/Thraetona—Trita is met with in the Rigveda with epithet of Apthya[175] and Traitana is of very rare occurrence. On the other hand the Avesta shows that Thrita belongs to the Sama family and Thraetona is the son of Athwya.[176] It seems that the Indo-Iranians originally had two distinct deities and the two gods subsequently have been confounded. The Avestic Thraetona slays the three headed, three mouthed and six eyed serpent demon Azi Dahaka.[177] Haug[178] identifies the Avestic Thraetona with the Vedic Traitana who as the Rigveda[179] states, severes the head of the giant of his shoulders. In accordance with the later Vedic literature Trita is a Rishi[180] but from a scrutiny of his traits found in the Rigveda he appears a god rather than a mortal man.[181] The Avestic Thrita is the first physician who cures the disease created by the Ahriman.[182] The Rigvedic Trita is also mentioned in the Atharvaveda that he extinguishes the illness in men as the god extinguished it in him.[183] In the Brahmanas he grants long life[184] The Rigveda states that any evil thing sent to him is appeased by him.[185] Haug[186] remarks that Soma, the surname of the Avestic Thrita, which means "appeaser" undoubtedly reminds the healing character of the Vedic Trita.

The main and realistic connection of this deity is really to Soma. The Avestic Thrita is the first priest who prepared Homa.[187] Soma is noted for its healing quality so Thrita is the first healer.[188] The similar connection is found in the Rigveda between Trita and Soma. The Vedic Trita is also the first preparer[189] of Soma as well as he purifies it.[190]

Trita's regular epithet Aptya reminds us the kinship of the Avestic Thraetona who is the son of Athwya and he is known as inventor of medicine and magic.[191] The Vedic Aptya and the Avestic Athwya are identical terms derived from 'ap' meaning 'water.' Macdonell holds that the Vedic Aptya is practically equivalent to Apam Napat.[192] Thrita is mentioned in the Avesta to have dwelt in Apam Napat[193] which may be interpreted to be a locality on the earth.[194] The valorous deeds of Trita tend to identify him with the Avestic Thraetona who slew the three headed and six-eyed serpent-demon. The Vedic Trita is also Vritrahan.[195]

Trita or Thrita means 'three' but what is the actual significance of this number in the name of this deity is not easy to decide. The Avesta informs that Thrita is the third man[196] who first prepared Homa for the carporeal world. In one passage of the Rigveda the term Trita in the plural means 'third'.[197] In the Brahmanas we come across with a legend[198] of three brothers—Ekata, Dvita and Trita. Trita is thrown in a well by his two brothers. We get confirmation from the Rigveda in which Dvita actually occurs.[199] This event is hinted in the Avesta in connection with the valiant adventure of Thraetona who killed Azi Dahaka, in his expedition for this purpose his two brothers accompanied him who like the brothers of the Vedic Trita seek to kill Thraetona.

(xiii) Vrtrahan Verethragna—Verethraghna is the name of an angel in the Avesta who slays the demon and is regarded as the genius of victory. On the other hand Vrtrahan in the Rigveda is the distinctive epithet of Indra. The Vedic Vritrahan is 'slayer of dragon, 'Vritra' and is essentially connected to the well-known Indra and Vritra myth. The Avesta denounces Indra as "devil of the devils." The Avestic Verethraghna, identical with the Vedic Vritrahan which is, of course, another name of Indra in the Rigveda, is not denounced in the Avesta at all. But it is significantly noticeable that Verethraghna is unconnected with Indra or thunder storm myth designating merely a god of victory.[200]

Dealing with this point scholars express conflicting suggestions, Lehmann[201] assumes that the word Vrtrahan meaning "slayer of Vrtra" was more primitive and its primitive sense was lost in Iran. Moulton[202] does not agree to this view and suggests that the word Verethraghna "victory" to be derived from an adjective meaning, "assault, repelling, victorious" was more primitive, and its use as an epithet applied to Indra and meaning the "slayer of Vrtra" was a piece of "imaginative etymology." Harlez[203] also discusses the matter in detail and arrives at the same conclusion that Verethraghna means "victorious." Arnold remarks, 'Indra appears to have stolen his title Vrtrahan from some earlier god or gods."[204]

Of course, we come across several gods in the Rigveda who possess this epithet and share least in killing Vritra in sublime sense. Trita who slays demons but not Vritra, is also known as Vritrahan as Thrita is Verethraghna in the Avesta. Macdonell remarks, "Trita was a god of lightning ... By process of natural selection Indra seems to have ousted, this god originally almost identical in character with himself with the result that Trita occupies but an obscure position."[205] It is quite natural that Indra usurped and monopolized that epithet which lost its original meaning, which speaks in favour of the view that the Indo-Iranians possessed a deity approaching to the Vedic form of the Vritra slaying Indra.

(xiv) Indra—Now question arises whether the Indo-Iranians worshipped Indra or not. The Zoroastrianism is distinctly said to be 'vi-daevo religion,' i.e., the religion "against the devas." Indra in the Avesta is "deva of the devas." But Indra figures in the Boghaz-kew[206] inscription among other Indo-Iranian gods. This fact supports the view that Indra was worshipped as a great god among the Indo-Iranians.[207] What was the original nature of Indra during this period is not easy to decide in absence of the Avestic evidence.

(xv) Nasatyal Naonhaithya—It also holds good in case of Nasatya who also appears in this inscription and meets the same fate as Indra in the Zoroastrianism pantheon. The Avestic Naonhaithya corresponds with the Vedic Nasatya in name only, but is arch-demon next to Indra in the Avesta.

(xvi) Moon God—The deification of the moon goes back to the Indo-Iranian period. The Semitics, the immediate neighbours of the Indo-Iranians attach a great importance to the moon worship. But in the Indo-Iranian pantheon the moon appears to be a very minor deity. Herodotus informs that the Iranians worshipped the moon. The Vedic moon god, 'Mas' is comparable to the Iranian 'Mah'. Both, in their respective mythology play but very insignificant role. The Vedic Gandharva[208] and Avestic Gandarewa[209] are identified and believed to be the genius of the moon.[210] It is also suggested that he is the older moon god than Chandramas or Mah among the Indo-Iranians.

(xvii) Goddesses—In the patriachal form of the community, goddesses find no place of worship. We come across with two or three goddesses in the Indo-Iranian mythology but they occupy a very subordinate position in the Indo-Iranian pantheon.

(a) Goddess Dawn—The Indo-Iranian goddess dawn owes her origin to the Indo-European religion. The Indian goddess dawn is called Usa. The Rigveda gives her calouring of poetical form which is definitely an Indian creation. The name of the Avestic goddess dawn is Ushah who is the daughter of Ahura Mazda. The Vedic Usa is also constantly called the daughter of Dyaus.[211] Excluding only the extravagant Indian splendour of Usa, the Avestic Ushah corresponds with her Indian counterpart in name as well as in character but appears to be an insignificant deity. It emphasises the view that the worship of the goddess dawn during the Indo-Iranian period was not so popular as the Rigveda portrays.

(b) Goddess Purandhi/Parendhi—Another goddess mentioned in the Avesta is Parendhi. The Avestic evidence shows her character assoicated with riches and abundance.[212] Identical in name the goddess Purandhi appears in the Rigveda. Darmesteter[213] adequately proves the identification of the Vedic Purandhi and the Avestic Parendhi. Spiegal as well as Mills support this view.[214] It is rightly believed that she is the Indo-Iranian goddess of plenty.

(c) Goddess Earth—The earth goddess is listed by Herodotus in the Iranian pantheon.[215] The earth goddess Prithvi is invoked in the Rigveda in association with Dyaus. But in the Avesta there appears no goddess of this name. Aramaiti listed as an arch-angel among the Amesha Spents is a genius of earth and of wisdom.[216] Aramaiti as the earth is invoked to restore at the happy time perpetuation of life. In the Rigveda Aramati is a personification of 'piety' or 'devotion'[217] and shows no connection with the earth.

The Vedic Aramati is the same word as the Avestic Aramaiti. Sayana explains Aramati by the word 'Bhumi'.[218] It is convincing to account for her character that she is a servant of men who, if well treated (cultivated), yields abundance in food.[219] It stands to reason that the Indo-Iranians worshipped Aramati as goddess of earth.

(xviii) Demons—The Indo-Iranians mythology excludes demonology. In contrast to Semitics, the Indo-Iranians do not propitiate evil beings to appease them in order to ward off their evil influence. The Indo-Iranian religion ascribes no invocation, no offering and no worship to demons. They are always regarded as malevolent and inveterate enemies of gods. They are met with in the Indo-Iranian mythology here and there with reference to the. victims of the gods.

The Avesta mentions the 'Druj' as the evil spirits who are always victims of Mithra. Identical to the Avestic Drujs, the Druhs figure in the Rigveda as a group of the injurious evil spirits. Macdonell[220] identifies the Vedic Druhs with the Avestic Drujs and tells that they are a group of 'injurious demons' in the Indo-Iranian mythology.

The Indo-Ianians have the conception of another group of the demons who are mentioned as Yatus both in the Rigveda and the Avesta. The Avesta mentions that Yatus inflict the mankind by their sorcery and witchcrafts.[221] The Vedic Yatus are chiefly connected with sorcery.[222] It is conceived that they disturb rituals and sacrifices and undo their effects. The Indo-Iranian Yatus eat the flesh of men and horses and drink the milk of cows.[223] They are feared and Indo-Iranians pray to the gods for their destruction.

The Rigvedic 'Danava' is an adversary of Indra.[224] He is recognized an arch-demon Vrtra whom Indra vanquished and ultimately slew. The Avesta states that the gods constantly wage wars against the Danavas.[225] Haug suggests that the Vedic Danava is the same demon as the Avestic Danava.[226]

Another category of the demons, mentioned in the Rigveda is called Gandharvas who dwell in waters with their, Apsaras. They form a distinct class in the Rigveda which illustrates them' as hostile beings to gods especially to Indra.[227] The original nature of the Gandharva is very obscure. Gandarewa occurs in the Avesta only in singular.[228] The Avestic Gandarewa is distinctly mentioned as a dragon-like-monster.[229] Threatona fought with Gandarewa and killed him. Scholars identify the Vedic Gandharva and the Avestic Gandarewa and put forth the suggestion that hostile beings as a class gradually developed from a single being.

(xix) Chinvat Bridge/Vaitarni River—The conception of the immortality of soul goes back to the Indo-European period. It is a world-wide belief[320] that the departing soul on its journey to the other world must pass over a bridge or cross a stream and reaches a dog or two who are believed in one mythology the guards of heaven or hell and in other they are to sort out the pious and wicked souls. The conception finds its place in the Indo-European religion also but it is not fully developed there. The Indo-Iranian religion presents the conception in its highly advanced form.

The Avesta mentions a bridge similar to the Semitic bridge Al-Sirat which is conceived to be finer than a hair and sharper than the edge of a sword as well as it has other awful impediments. The Avestic bridge is named as Chinvat Peretu which is believed to be spanned between heaven and hell. Chinvat Peretu means "the bridge of the Judge" or "the bridge of the gatherers" the Avesta tells that only the pious souls pass over the Chinvat Bridge while the wicked fall from it down to hell.[231]

The conception of bridge or stream is not met with in the Rigveda but it appears in the later Vedic litrature. In the Indian conception a stream named Vaitarni figures which is to be crossed over by souls. The Vaitarni is a "terrible river, the current of which is supposed to run with great impetuosity, hot, fetid in odour and filled with blood, hair and all the manner of foulness."[232] It is customary among the Hindus even today to present the funeral priest with a vessel full of black sesamum and a cow to whose tail the soul clings in crossing the river Vaitarni.

(xx) Vata/Vato and Vayu-The Indo—Iranians worshipped a wind god. It is only the wind god who is mentioned by its very name Vayu both in the Rigveda and in the Avesta.[233] He is not listed among demons in the Zoroastrian pantheon. According to the Avesta Vayu is wind and Vato, air. The very imperfect personification is found in the Avesta whereas Vata is mentioned to exist in no form.[234] The Vedic Vayu is chiefly the god and his personification in the Rigveda is slightly more advanced; while Vata is the element.[235]

The identity of the Indian and the Iranian wind god is definitely conclusive. We get another inference from this comparison that Vayu is the Indo-Iranian wind god and Vata is purely an element.[236]

(b) Cosmogony

The Indo-Iranian cosmographical conception points out seven divisions of the whole world and a great mountain at its central point. The Rigvedic people conceive that whole world consists of seven Dvipas and the central mountain is Meru which is sacred residence of gods. The Avesta also mentions seven divisions of the world; each division is called Keshvar. The holy mountain Haro Barezaiti is conceived to be existing at the centre point of the world, on which supernatural beings live.

(c) Indo-Iranian Worship

Our knowledge about the correct form of the Indo-European worship is inadequate. Only it may be claimed with certainty that the Indo-Europeans used to offer something to their gods and it was thrown into the fire. But the Indo-Iranians developed a highly advanced form and an elaborate system to propitiate their gods.

The offering to gods is an essential element of the Indo-Iranian worship is borne out by the Vedic term 'ahuti' Avestic 'Azuiti' which connotes the general meaning 'gift'. The Indo-Iranians offered to their gods the food and the flesh of some animals' which they liked and themselves ate. The Soma juice which stimulated and exhilerated human beings was considered as the best offering to the gods.

The very name for priest in the Avestal Atharvan and in the Rigveda Atharvan substantiates that the Indo-Iranian worship centres round the fire cult. The term 'atharvan' is derived from the Avestic word 'atar' meaning fire. The fire . is conceived as the mediator between men and gods, who takes the offering to the gods or brings the gods to the offering. Hence to feast gods the fire is an indispensable element in all rituals and ceremonial rites of the Indo-Iranians. No Indo-Iranian worship is complete without the sacred fire. The Rigvedic people must first offer some portion of the offering to the fire and then enjoy it themselves whereas the Iranians never throw anything into the fire, so they only show it to the fire and then eat it.

The Vedic yajna, the Avestic yasna which means sacrifice and is identified with 'worship' points to animal and Soma sacrifices. Herodotus who had seen the actual performance of the Persian sacrifice gives its detailed description in his account. He says, "The manner of the sacrifice of the Persians to the gods is as follows: they neither make the altars nor kindle fire when about to sacrifice; they use no libation, no flute, no garlands, no meal. But as one desires to sacrifice to each of these deities, he takes the victim to a pure place and calls upon the god . . . then when he cuts up the victim and seethed the flesh, he spreads out a carpet' of the tenderest herbage, especially clover, and sets all the flesh thereon. When he has thus disposed it, a magian man stands by and chants the theogony thereto, for such the Persians say the chants. Without a magian it is not lawful for him to offer sacrifices. And after waiting a little time the sacrificer takes away the flesh and uses it as he wills[237] Edward remarks that the description of the Persian sacrifice given by Herodotus is an-approximately correct outline of the Indo-Iranian sacrifice.[238]

Gifts and sacrifices formed an essential part of the Indo-Iranian worship but a good hymn of praise is equally essential. the term 'aziuti' or 'ahuti' is also interpreted as the invocation of a deity with the offering. The Vedic Hotr or the Avestic Zaotar is the Indo-Iranian invoking priest. It is naturally certain that the Indo-Iranian gods were priased and pleased by the invoking priest Hotr or

Zaotar, before they would descend to brahis or barezis to partake of the sacrifice. It shows the extra-ordinary stress on the composition of good hymns during the Indo-Iranian period. To begin with, when the Indo-Iranians propitiated their gods they invoked them by a formula like "a, Gracious God, give thou to me that, I offer thee this." Later on, in order to secure the favour, the gods were flattered by the praises of the beneficial aspects of them and by extolling their great deeds. Thus the good hymns of praise came into existence, which were used to invoke gods in the ceremonial rites and worship. The terms connected to the ceremonial rituals reflect the true feelings of an Indo-Iranian worshipper. The Indo-Iranian 'stu' to praise the Vedic 'stator,' the Avestic 'staotar' a singer, the Vedic 'Stoma,' the Avestic 'Staoma' a hymn of praise, and the Vedic mantra, 'the Avestic manthra' prayer, the Vedic 'sukta,' the Avestic 'hukta' well uttered word or hymn as well as the Vedic 'uktas,' the Avestie 'ukhta' hymn, the Indo-Iranian gatha, hymn, confirm convincingly that the praise of the gods is the central point of the Indo-Iranian worship. These hymns were recited by the chief priest at several points in the course of the worship in accordance with the prescribed procedure.

(d) Institution of Priests

Atharvan is the common name of the Indo-Iranian priests, which continues to be used in the Avesta in the same sense but in the Rigveda the word connotes only the Soma and the fire priests. The Indo-Iranian sacrifices are somewhat complicated, hence they need several officiating priests.

The efficacy of the Indo-Iranian sacrifice depends upon its correct proceedings and correct recitation of the mantras. A slight mistake might change the effect. This important and difficult tasks were entrusted to the chief priest who was normally intelligent and a man of learning. It is the duty of the Avestic Zaota to chant the manthras correctly as the Hotr performs the same duty in the Vedic rituals. For the assistance to the chief priest, there was a managing priest who is known as Adhvarya in the Rigveda and Rathvi in the Avesta. His main work was to prepare all for the chief priest.

It was commonly believed that sacrifices were occasionally attacked and destroyed by evil spirits if they could get chance. Hence in order to check the evil influence, the Indo-Iranians employed one priest in every sacrifice to ward off evil spirits. The Vedic Pratiprasthata holding a wooden sword in his hand has to drive away the evil spirits during the time of any sacrifice. In the Avestic rituals the Sraosha Vareza is also armed with the same weapon for the same purpose.

The comparison of the Atatevakshe who is incharge of pots in the Avestic ritual with the Agnidhra who holds the fire in the Vedic sacrifices, shows that the Indo-Iranians rituals required another officiating priest who was incharge of pots, utensils and the fire.

(e) Sacrifices and Ceremonial Rites

The Indo-Iranians observed several ceremonies and performed the various sacrifices particularly on the auspicious occasions throughout the year. These religious observances and the sacrificial rites mentioned in the Rigveda and the Avesta show considerable similarities and many striking points of resemblances. The comparison of the rituals of the two faiths certainly brings us to the approximately original outlines of them.

All the elements of the Avestic Izeshne ceremony are comparable to the different parts of the Vedic Jyotishtoma sacrifice. The Agni-stoma is the opening ceremony of the Jyotishtoma sacrifice in which four goats are killed and their flesh is offered to gods by throwing it into the fire. Similar practice is observed in the Izeshne ceremony in which no animal is sacrificed. Only hair of one ox are shown to the fire. It is undoubtedly a relic of the animal sacrifice. The gaus-hudaho and the gau-jivya of the Izeshne ceremony are correctly identified with the butter and ghee required at the time of Prajjajas of the Agnistoma and with the fresh water needed for the performance of the Upasad ceremony respectively. The consecrated water is used in the Izeshne and the Jyotishtoma ceremonies. It is the Avestic Zaothra and the Vedic Udaka Santa.

The offering of the Soma juice is obilgatory in the Jyotishtoma sacrifice as in the Izeshne ceremony. Haug holds the view that the contrivances for obtaining the juice and the vessels used in the Jyotishtoma sacrifice and in the Izeshne ceremony show some discrepancies but a closer enquiry upholds the original identity.[239]

The Rathan Taram ceremony of the Jyotishtoma sacrifice is obligatory to the Vedic people and it is believed to carry the sacrificer to heaven. In this ceremony three officiating priests chant the Samanas successively, one by one, in a very solemn manner. Every Saman is divided into five parts and used for singing. The Avestic Ahura Vairya prayer shows the similar five divisions and the solemn singing of the manthras. Similar to the Vedic ceremony the Ahura Vairya is also the most important prayer.

In the Shastrani ceremony of the Rathan taram in order to praise and extol the Saman, the singers chant the verses from the Rigveda. One of the Hotrs repeats these verses not in the usual way of repetition but in manner approaching the recital of the Yajurveda. This peculiar practice is recognized in the Ahura Vairya prayer of the Parsees who consider the practice most meritorious to this worship. The Parsees invoke the verses of the songs at the end of the different, 'Has' of the Yasna especially its Gatha portion like divine beings.

(1) Apri/Afrigan Ceremony—The Vedic Apri and the Avestic Afrigan ceremony are identical in name as well as in their detail and purpose. This ceremony is preparatory to the killing and offering of the sacrificial goats. The Vedic apri or the Avestic 'afri' means to invite hence it indicates an invitation to

the gods or divine beings in whose honour this ceremony is performed. In the Vedic ceremony the names of different gods are mentioned who are invited to come and relish the offerings. To the Parsees this solemn singing of invitation is a benediction. In the Avestic ceremony the name of angel or a deceased is mentioned.

(2) New and Full Moon Sacrifices: The sacrifices performed at the time of new and full moon are called in the Rigveda the Darsa Purnama ishti and in the Avesta the Daran ceremony. These ceremonies are very simple. The Rigvedic people offer Purodasa or solemn sacrificial cakes to different gods under certain order and recitation of two mantras to each god is essential. The Avestic ceremony is similar but sacred bread Daran is a flat kind of bread.

(3) Sacrifices for Seasons: The prevalence of sacrifice for seasons among the Indo-Iranian is certain. But how many times this sacrifice was celebrated throughout the year is not definitely known. It is commonly known in the Avesta a Gahanwar ceremony which is observed six times in a year. It is to be recognised in the Vedic Chaturmasya ishti which is celebrated to four months or two seasons.

(4) Purification Ceremony: The Purification ceremony appears to be very old. In order to remove all the impurity from the inferior body this ceremony is performed. In this ceremony the Parsees purify themselves by means of gomez or cow urine. The Vedic people use Panchagavyam. Panchagavyam consists of five things urine, dung, milk, butter and ghee of the cow which is regarded as the most sacred animal.

(f) Disposal of the Dead:

The Indo-Iranians inherited from their fore-fathers the primitive customs for disposing of the dead. They continued to dispose of their dead either by burial or by cremation. It is true that the cremation is the rule in India since the early Rigvedic period but the hymns VII-18-1 and X-IS-10 tend to confirm that burial was also a popular practice among the Rigvedic people,[240] Both practices of the disposal of the dead were in vogue among the early Iranians. Herodotus presupposes burial the only form among the Persians.[241] The Avesta prescribes severe punishments for those who cremate their dead.[242] It betrays the fact that cremation was previously in vogue but later on it was, however, discarded.

The Avesta gives sanction to expose the dead in the open air. The early Persians used to expose their dead on "Tower of silence" to be devoured by dogs, birds and beasts of prey. The custom appears to be of Indo-Iranian origin. The Rigveda also refers to this custom. In addition to cremation and burial as the Rigveda alludes to the dead were disposed of by Paroptah and Uddhitah also. Macdonell and Kieth explain Paroptah as "casting out" and Uddhitah as "exposure of the dead." It may be said that exposing the dead was equally a honourable practice among the Indo-Iranians. This custom is not traceable among the Indo-Europeans. It is certainly an Indo-Iranian creation.

(g) Funeral Purfication Rite

The Indo-Iranians considered the body of the dead and the house in which one died and all the persons who participated in the funeral procession as highly defiled. To the Persians the corpse is highly defiling. Whosoever touched it or the house in which a person died or the whole atmosphere whence the dead body is taken were unclean. It was the belief that Druj Nasu in shape of a fly taking possession of the dead bodies spread contagion. It could be expelled from the bodies only by means of glance of a dog "Sagdid." Barashnum "the purification of nine nights" was conducted especially to restore purity to those contaminated by contact with the dead on the tenth day after, death. The same notion of impurity prevails among the Rigvedic people also. The Indians bathe after the corpse is fully consumed by fire. But impurity generally lasts for three days after death or for a period from the third to the tenth day. On tenth day a prohita purifies the house as well as its inhabitants by muttering mantras and by sprinkling its all comers with holy water.[243]

(h) Social Condition

(1) Intiation Rite: The rite of initiation is considered as an obligatory duty in every primitive race. No person is taken as a member of the community until and unless the rite of initiation is performed. The rite was in vogue among the Indo-Europeans. The rite attained a considerable significance and an important place in the Indo-Iranian faith. It is enjoined as a religious duty. As long as this ceremony is not performed one is not a real member of the Indo-Iranian community. The ceremony is known in the Vedas as Upanayana Sanskara in which a sacred cord is invested to a boy. The Indians perform this ceremony between at ages of eight and sixteen. The Avesta designates this ceremony as Aiwyachanem in which a boy receives the investiture with sacred girdle and shirt. A parsee boy is generally invested in his seventh year.

(2) Fourfold Division of Society: The antiquity of the division of society is traced back to the Indo-European period but division of four professional classes is definitely an Indo-Iranian creation. In India the caste system of four Varnas is the back-bone of the society. Although during the Rigvedic period no caste system in any form is traceable. It is the last Mandala of the Rigveda in which the Purusha Sukta mentions Brahmans, Rajanya, Vaisya and Sudra who are said to have come from the different parts of the Purusha. The scholars hold the view that Purusha Sukta is a later interpolation.[244] But in the wake of similar evidence found in the Avesta it can reasonably be claimed that four-fold division of the society was an old institution and existed among the Indo-Iranians. The Persian society was also divided according to profession. The Avesta[245] describes the classes of people as the Atharvan or priests, Rathaeshtars or warriors, Vastrya or agriculturists and the Huiti or the artisans. This division of the Persian society is exactly identical with the Indian four Varnas even in names. Shah Namah

informs that this social sub-division of the people in four professional classes was done by Jamshed or Yima.[246] During the time of Ardashir Papkin the people of one profession had to secure the permission of the state to take up another profession.[247] All this supports the view that the division of the four professional classes is the Indo-Iranian creation.

(3) Hespitality and Moral Conduct: The Indo-Iranians were highly cultured people and their daily life presents a high order of the civilization. They were noted for their hospitality, generosity, faithfulness, kind heartedness and good conduct of life. Consideration for a guest is regarded as the sacred religious duty of the Rigvedic people. No wish of a guest is turned down. The Vedic Sacred Law Books attach a high meritorious value to hospitality. The Rigveda condemns niggardliness and Indra is implored to punish Panis for their niggardliness, who had accumulated good wealth and were not bountiful to the priests. Generosity is enumerated a great merit in the Rigveda, Geden[248] says, "Probably in no country in the whole world may be passing way-farer be so confident that his need will be met in whatever village he may find himself."

Hospitality is enjoined in the Avesta as the obligatory sacred duty.[249] The Pursisniha XXIX ordains that a righteous man must be given reward, thanks, contentment and paitizanti 'welcome' which is one of the three earthly things best for Ahura Mazda.[250] The Avesta mentions the obligation of friend to succour friend in his need.[251] Frarti-rati 'generosity' is highly admired in the Avestic literature,[252] and spoken of the greatest of good works.[253] In the Avesta illiteracy is considered a sin.[254] When soul of a righteous man who practiced hospitality in this world arrives in the heaven of Endless Light, it is met by the righteous men[255] who may be no else than angles of all descriptions.

Of course, the Indo-Iranian is the most important branch of the Aryans. The above comparative survey reflects highly developed culture of the Indo-Iranians. The common words of culture occurring in Sanskrit and Avesta confirm that the Indo-Iranians advanced further in the path of civilization than any of the Aryan nations. In order to distinguish themselves from the other people and to show their superiority of blood and their highly advanced cultur the Indo-Iranians designated themselves as 'Arya' meaning 'noble' or 'cultured'. They had produced two invaluable religious documents which undoubtedly preserved the original beliefs, conceptions and traditions of the undivided Aryans. Their invaluable contribution to our civilization is their illuminating creation of three great religions of the world, e.g., Hinduism, Zoroastrianism and Buddhism.

The critical and comparative study of the Rigveda and the Avesta shows very clearly the close affinity between Sanskirt and Avesta and striking similarity in their gods, mythology, religious beliefs, social customs and traditions. It seeks to establish the fact that the Iranians and the Vedic people were once one and the same people, speaking the same language, worshipping the same gods and following the same social traditions.

The Indo-Iranians in their second home developed a distinct culture. They inherited the largest share of the common heirloom and preserved it very zealously but they innovated some new cults, conceptions and social traditions. The ethical law (the Rigvedic rta or the Avestic Asha) is undoubtedly a marvelous creation of the Indo-Iranians; which is as a matter of fact, a highly sublime conception and the like of which was beyond the reach of any other people during such a remote past. The fire cult and the Soma worship are specific Indo-Iranian innovations. In regard to the primitive conception of human progeny they developed the more illustrative myth of Yama and Yami; which corresponds to the Semitic myth of the origin of the human race. The nature worship still persisted in the Indo-Iranian religion but it makes the beginning of the creation of abstract deities; and they attached ethical attributes to their older gods also. In the sphere of eschatology the highly developed conceptions appeared in the Indo-Iranian pantheon, which show a considerable points of resemblances with the Semitic beliefs. The elaborate system of the rituals and ceremonies is another great creation of the Indo-Iranians.

References

1. J.H. Moulton, observes that the very name Iran came from the adjective of Airya found in the Avesta which is used to describe the land from which the Airya folk came *ERE*, Vol. VIII, "Iranians," p. 518 a.
2. A.A. Macdoonell, *Vedic Mythology*, p. 7.
3. M. Bloomfield, *The Religion of the Veda*, p. 13 (London and New Yark, 1908).
4. E.W. Hopkins, *Religions of India*, p. 16.
5. M. Muller, *Chips from a German Workshop*, Vol. I, p. 83.
6. Aeranvaejo=Aeran (Aryans) + Vaejo (seed), Aeranvaejo is mentiooned in the Zend Avesta as the original home of the Aryans but it is surprising that it has been totally forgotton by the Rigvedic people.
7. Dr. I. Taylor, *Origins of the Aryans*, pp. 189–90.
8. M.N. Dhalla, *Zoroastrian Theology*, p. 4, (New Yark, 1914).
9. Hopkins, op. cit. p. 16.
10. Yasht, X–141; Yasna, X–10, LXX–I; M.N. Dhalla, op. cit., p. 153.
11. *Moulton, Early Religious Poetry of Persia*, p.34, (Cambridge, 1911).
12. Rv. 1–35–7; 1–24–14; 1–54–3; IV–2–5; VII–2–3; 1–35–7; V–42–11.
13. Rv.I–108–6.
14. LH. Mills, ERE, Vol. II, p. 451.
15. *Yasna*, XII; *Fargard*, CIXIV.
16. M. Haug, *Essays on the Sacred Language, Writing and Religion of the Parsees*, pp. 244, (London, 1878).
17. A.B. Kieth, The Religion of Philosophy of the Vedas and Upanishad , p. 231, (London, 1925).
18. Darmesteter, *Ormuzd et Ahriman*, pp. 266 f.
19. A. Hillebrandt, *VOJ*, Vol. XIII, p. 320.
20. *Rv.* X–124–5; X–138-3.
21. A. Bergaigne, *Ia Religion Vedique*, pp. 3–8.

22. H. Oldenberg, *Die Religion des Veda*, Vol. I, pp. 162–5.
23. L.H. Mills, *An Exposition of the Lore of the Avesta*, p. 61, (Bombay, 1916).
24. J.H. Moulton, *Early Religious Poetry of Persia*, p. 55, (Cambridge, 1911).
25. A. Hillebrandt, *Vedische Mythologie*, Vol. III, pp. 430 f.
26. Von Schroeder, *Arische Religion*, Vol. I, pp. 317 ff.
27. Von Bradke, *Dyaus Asura*, pp. 29 f.
28. *Rv.*III–6–9; Av. X–7–13.
29. *Yasna*, 1–10, III–2.
30. M. Haug, op. cit., pp. 232–33.
31. H.D. Griesworld, *The Religion of the Rigveda*, p. 116, n. 3.
32. Ibid., pp. 81 f, (London, 1923).
33. P.S. Deshmukh, *Religion in the Vedic Literature*, p. 125, n. 1.
34. Ibid.
35. H.D. Grieswold, op. cit., p. 90.
36. Herodotus, I–131.
37. J.H. Moulton, *Early Zoroastrianism*, p. 391, n. 3.
38. A. Mackenzi, *Indian Myths and Legends*, p. 13.
39. Rv. IV–18–12.
40. J. Muir, *Original Sanskrit Texts*, Vol. V, p. 33.
41. Ibid.; M. Muller, *The Vedas*, p. 165, (Calcutta, 1956).
42. A.A. Macdonell, *Vedic Mythology*, p. 84.
43. H.D. Grieswold, The Religion of the Rigveda, pp. 25, 98–108, (London, 1923).
44. L.H. Gray, *Ratanbai Kiltrak Lecture Delivered at Oxford.*
45. Ibid.
46. H. Oldenberg, *Die Religion des Veda*, Vol. II, pp. 285-98; A. Hillebrandt, *Vedische Mythologie*, Vol. III, pp. 151 f; A.J. Carnoy, *Journal of American Oriental Society*, Vol. XXXVI, pp. 307 ff; E. Hardy, *Vedische Brahmanische Period.*
47. H. Oldenberg, op. cit., pp. 187 ff.
48. H. Oldenberg, op. cit. pp. 185 f.
49. M. Bloomfield, *The Religion of the Veda*, p. 121.
50. Rv. 1–23–5.
51. Yasna, XLIII-6.
52. Yasni, X–4.
53. Rv. II–28–5.
54. M. Bloomfield, op. cit., p. 126.
55. *Yasna*, XXVII–I; XXI–3.
56. Rv. II–28–1; V–85–3.
57. *Sacred Books of the East*, Vol. IV, p. 376.
58. Rv. VIII–90–2; 1–25–5.16.
59. Yasna, XXX–5; Yast, XIII–3.
60. Rv. 1–25–9.11; VIII–49–3.
61. Yasna, XXXI–13; XIV–4; Vendidad, XIX, 20.
62. Rv. 1–24–13; VII–67–5.
63. Yasna, XLIII–6.
64. J.H. Moulton, *Early Zoroastrianism*, pp. 29 ff.
65. M. Bloomfield, The Religion of the Rigveda, p. 20.
66. Roth, ibid., Vol. VI, p. 69 f.
67. F. Spiegal, op.cit., p. 199; C. de -Harlez, *Journal Asiatique* 1878, pp. 11, 129.
68. A.B. Kieth, op. cit., p. 102.
69. A.B. Kieth, op. cit., pp. 102–3.
70. J. Muir, OST, Vol. IV, pp. 119–121.

71. M. Bloomfield, *The Religion of the Veda*, p. 126.
72. A. Kuhn, *Zeitschrift*, Vol. I, p. 358.
73. M.N. Dhalla, *Zooroastrian Theology*, p. 126 f; A.A Yasht, Vl-2-4; *Sacred Book of the East*, Vol. XXIII, p. 86.
74. Rv. VII–63–2.4; X–7–3; 1–191–8.9; VII–63–1; Yasht, VI–2–4; Sacred Book of the East, Vol. XXIII, p. 86,
75. Rv. vii–66–10; I–115–I.
76. Yasht, 1–11; F. Spiegal, Arische Period, pp. 190–1.
77. Rv. VII–63–2; 1–116–3; X–37–3; X–49–7; V–29–5; IV–13–3; 1–50–8.9.
78. *Khorshed Nyayis*, VI.
79. M. Haug, op. cit., p. 231.
80. Wallis, *Cosmology of the Rigveda*, p. 11.
81. Eggers, *Windischmann, Mitra*, pp. 42–3, (Leipzig, 1859).
82. J.H. Moulton, *ERPP*, p. 36 f.
83. D.M. Edward, *ERE* Vol. VI, p. 291.
84. A.B. Kieth, op.cit., pp. 97–98.
85. A.A. Macdonell, Vedic Mythology, p. 30.
86. Eggers, op. cit, pp. 16–19.
87. A.A. Macdonell, *Vedic Mythology*, p.30.
88. Weber, *Indische Studien*, XXVII, p. 212.
89. Rigveda, III-59–1.
90. Yasht, X-13–95.
91. Yasht, XXIII–6, XXIV–4.
92. M. Haug, op. cit., p. 231.
93. A.A. Macdonell, op. cit., p. 45.
94. J.R. Moulton, *Early Zoroastrianism*, p. 117.
95. Ibid.
96. M. Bloomfield, op. cit., p. 129.
97. Mills, *Sacred Books of the East*, Vol. XXXXI, p. 293, n. 2.
98. M. Haug, op. cit.
99. Ibid.
100. M. Bloomfield, *The Religion of the Veda*, p. 158.
101. A.B. Kieth, op.cit., (London, 1925), p. 161.
102. Yasna, XVII–11.
103. Rv. VII–15–2; III–1–5.
104. Rv. VII–14–2.
105. Rv. 1–72–7.
106. Rv. VI–1–9.
107. X–46–10.
108. M.N. Dhalla, *Zoroastrian Theology*, pp. 134–35.
109. Rv. X–79–5; VII–3–7; VII–16–10; III–20–4; V–4–9; VII–12–2.
110. Rv. IV–1l–3; III–11–17; X–21–5.
111. Rv. 1–75–4.
112. Rv. VII–13–1.
113. Rv. III–15–34.
114. Rv. X–45–8; IV–15–6.
115. Yasna, LXII.
116. Rv. V–5–2; 1–13–3.
117. Rv. X–70–3.
118. *Vendidad* XIX–3; XXII–7.
119. A.J. Cornoy, *Iranian Mythology*, p. 285; A.A. Macdonll, op. cit., p. 99.

120. M. Haug, op. cit., p. 232.
121. Bergaigns, *Ia Religion Vedique*, Vol. I, pp. 305–8.
122. Yaska, *Nirukta*, VIII–6.
123. M. Haug, op.cit., p. 232.
124. C. de Harlez, *Introduction to the Avesta*, p. 165.
125. M. N. Dhalla, *Zoroastrian Theology*, p. 137.
126. Rv. V–2.
127. Ibid., 1–95–4; 1–95–5.
128. Ibid., II–35–3; II–35–5.
129. Ibid., V–14.
130. Ibid., 1–143–1.
131. A. Hillebrandt, *Vedishe Mythologie*, Vol. I, pp. 377–8.
132. *A.A. Macdonell, Journal of Royal Asiatic Society*, Vol. XXXVII, pp. 955–956; H. Oldenberg, *Die Religion des Veda*, Vol II, pp. 177–120.
133. F. Speigal, Die Arische Period, pp. 192–3.
134. Darmesteter, *SBE*, IV, p. xiii.
135. A.B. Kieth, op. cit., pp. 171–72.
136. *Rv.* IX–113–7. 8.
137. *Yasna*, IX–2–19.
138. Rv. II–97–4; IX–46; IX–83.
139. Yasna, X–3–4.
140. Yasna, X–10.
141. *Rv.* IX–97–98; 1–99–22; M.N. Dhalla, *Zoroastrian Theology*, p. 122.
142. *Rv.* VIII–48–15.
143. *Rv.* III–43–7.
144. Yasna, XX–II.
145. *Rv.* XX–25–11; VII–68-2; 1–94–6.
146. *Yasna*, IX–19, XX–9.
147. C. de Harlez, *Introduction to the Avesta*, p. 16I.
148. A.A. Macdonell, *Vedic Mythology*, p. 114.
149. *Rv.* X–66–15; I–91–2I.
150. *Yasna*, IX–30.
151. Yasna, IX–16–20.
152. A.A. Macdonell, *loc. cit.*, p. 109.
153. *Rv.* X–144–5; X–17–I.
154. *Yasna*, IX–4.
155. *Rv.* IX–99–2; IX–14–5; IX–10–5; IX–28–4.
156. H. Oldenberg, *Die Religion des Veda* Vol. II, p. 122.
157. *Rv.* X–53–6; 1–96–2.
158. A. Hillebrandt, *Vedische Mythologie*, Vol. I., p. 488 f.
159. M. Bloomfield, op. cit.
160. M. Bloomfield, op. cit., p. 141, Vendidad, II.
161. Rv. XX–14–1.
162. A.J. Cornoy, *Iranian Mythology*, pp. 310–11.
163. Rv. X–51–1; X–64–3; X–92;11, IX–113–8; X–14; X–16–9; X–14–8.
164. *Arthavaveda* XVIII–3–13.
165. *Rv.*X–144–135; X–14–15.
166. *Vendidad* II.
167. *Rv.* IX–113–3; X–14–8.
168. *Sacred Books of the East*, Vol. N. p. 20, n.1.
169. *Rv.* X–14–2.

170. *Vendidad,* II.
171. Ibid.
172. *Rv.* X–14–1; X–14-2.
173. *Vendidad,* II.
175. *Rv.* V–41.
176. *Yasht,* V–34; *Yasna,* IX–7. 8.
177. *Yasht,* V–60.34; *Yasna,* X–8.
178. M. Haug, op. cit., p. 235.
179. *Rv.* 1–158–3.
180. *Rv.*I–105.
181. *Rv.* 1–187–1; 1–52–5; M. Haug, op. cit., p. 235.
182. *Yasna,* IX–7.
183. *Rv.* VI–113–I.
184. *Ts.* 1–8–10-2.
185. *Rv.* VIII–17–1.
186. M. Haug. op. cit., p. 235.
187. *Yasna,* IX–7 .
188. Vendidad, XX.
189. *Rv.* II–II–20.
190. *Rv.* IX–34–4.
191. Yasna, IX–8; *SBE,* Vol. W, pp. 245-46.
192. A.A. Macdonell, *JRAS,* Vol. XXV, p. 450.
193. *Yasht,* V–72, XIII–113.
194. F. Spiegal, op. cit., Vol. I, p. 193.
195. Rv. X–8–8.
196. *Yasna,* IX–I0.
197. *Rv.* VI–44–23.
198. Commenting on hymn 1–105, Sayana refers to a story of Satya Yamins.
199. *Rv.* VIII–47–1; V–18–2.
200. O. Benefy, *Orient und Occident,* Vol, I p. 49.
201. Lehmann, Cf. Moulton, ERPP, p. 39.
202. J.H. Moulton, *ERPP,* pp. 39–40.
203. C. De Harlez, loc. cit., pp. 159–63.
204 E.V. Arnold, *ERPP,* p. 40.
205. A.A. Macdonell, *Vedic Mythology,* p. 69.
206. H.D. Grieswold, *The Religion of the Rigveda,* p. 115.
207. M. Muller, *The Vedas,* pp. 165-66, (Calcutta, 1956).
208. Rv 1–63–2; X–92–13.
209. *Yasht,* V–37; XIX–41.
210. Ludwig, *Rigveda,* Trans. Vol. IV, p. 158; E.W. Hopkins, *Religions of India,* p. 157.
211. *Rv.* I–30–22.
212. Darmesteter, *Ormazd et Ahirman,* p. 25.
214. F. Spiegal, op.cit., pp. 207–9; L.H. Mills, *SBE,* p. 25.
215. Herodotus, 1–131.
216. J.H. Moulton, *Early Zoroastrianism,* p. 10, n. 2; Edward, *ERE,* Vol. VI, p. 291.
217. *Rv.* VII–1–6; VII–34–21.
218. 42–4.5; Sayana on Rigveda VII–36–8; VIII–4–3.
219. M. Haug, op.cit., p. 261.
220. A.A. Macdonell, *Vedic Mythology,* p.163.
221. F. Siegal, op. cit., pp. 212–18.
222. Rv. VII–I04–23; VII–60–20.

223. Rv. X–87–16.17.
224. *Atharvaveda,* IV–24–2.
225. *Yasht,* V–73.
226. M. Haug, op. cit., p. 238.
227. *Rv.* VIII–17–14; VIII, p. 1–28.
228. *Yasna,* XIX–41.
229. *Yasna,* V–37.
230. I. Taylor, *Primitive Culture,* Vol. II, p. 94.
231. *Yasna,* XLVII–I0–ll.
232. W. Crooke, *ERE,* Vol. II, p. 238.
233. Rv.VI–50–12; X–90–13; *Ram Yasht.*
234. C. De Harlez, *Introduction to the Avesta,* pp. 158–9.
235. A.A. Macdonell, *Vedic Mythology,* p. 81.
236. M.N. Dhalla, *Zoroastrian Theology,* pp. 132–4.
237. Herodotus, 1–132.
238. E. Edward, *ERE,* Vol. XI, 'Sacrifice' (Iranian), p. 18 A.
239. M. Haug, op. cit., p. 239.
240. Rv. X–15–14; VIII–2–34; Roth, *Journal of German Oriental Society,* VIII, p. 467.
241. Herodotus, IV–71 f.
242. A.A. Macdonell andA.B. Kieth, *Vedic Index of Names,* Vol.I, pp. 8–9 (1912).
243. Dubois and Beauchamp, *Hindu Manners, Customs and Ceremonies,* p. 485.
244. Arnold, *Vedic Meter,* p. 167; Macdonell and Kieth, *Vedic Index of Names,* Vol. II, p. 252.
245. *Yasna,* XIX–26–27.
246. Vuller's ed, Vol, I, p. 24.
247. J.J. Modi, *Anthropological Society of Bombay* XIII, No.8, pp. 1–7.
248. A.S. Gaden, "Hospitality" (Indian), *ERE,* Vol. VI, p. 812.
249. *Yasna,* LXII–8.
250. J. Darmesteter, Zind Avesta, Vol. III, p. 70 (Paris–1892–93).
251. Yasna XLIII–14, XLIV–1, XLVI–2 Vendidad IV–44–46.
252. Yasna IV–3 LVIII–4, IX–5 Vispard XXI–3, Pursisniha XXVI.
253. Din-i-Mainag-i-Xrat, IV–4, XXXVII–4.
254. Vendidad XVIII–31 Artai-i- Viraf Namar.
255. Yasht XXIV–62, 62.

8

The Indo-Aryan Culture

Ethnologically and culturally as a common people the Indo-Iranians lived unitedly in their common home probably for several hundred years. Ultimately they split into two distinct branches namely,—Iranian Aryans and Indo-Aryans, and the latter moved towards India. The Indo-Aryans at last entered India and settled in the Sapta Sindhu. The region extending from the Indo-Iranian home-land to the Sapta Sindhu was culturally homogeneous in those days. The Indo-Aryans when came into India, they, in no way, realized that they were entering a new country. While migrating to India, the Indo-Aryans met with the same aboriginal tribes, Dasa and Dasyus on their way even in the Sapta Sindhu region, who had a constant struggle and conflicts with them in the neighbourhood of the Indo-Iranian home-land. Such conflicts between the Aryans and these aborigines are recorded not only in the Rigveda but the Avesta also mentions similar frequent encounters.

The Indo-Aryans, on the way in their migration to India, must have sojourned for sometime in Afghanistan and some early portion of the Rigveda was composed here. Kabul, Kurrum, Gomal and Svat, the rivers of Afghanistan are correctly recognized in Kubha, Krumu, Gomati and Svastu the rivers mentioned in the earlier portion of the Rigveda. The other rivers mentioned in the earlier portion of Rigveda are Rasa and Sarasvati and the rivers which belong to the region of the Sapta Sindhu.

The Aryans certainly subdued the aborigines of India and made their settlements mainly in the Punjab. Later on they seem to be moving towards the Gangetic plains. The Rigveda refers to the Jamuna thrice and the Ganges once.[1] One hymn clearly mentions the occupation of Kurushetra.[2]

(a) Rigvedic Culture

It has already been referred to in the foregoing chapter that when the Aryans came to India, it was not a no man's land. It is attested by the changes in Sanskrit that population in the north India consisted of the majority of the Dravidian elements at the time when the Aryans came here. The Indus culture was flourishing, which was annihilated by these people. The Scholars hold the view that the population of the Indus culture presents its cosmopolitan character in which the Austric element is overwhelmingly represented.

The Australoids are most probably the pre-Dravidian aborigines and the primitive existing race in India.[3] The borrowed vocabulary in Sanskrit confirms that one important section of the contemporary aborigines spoke Austric languages. This new environment affected the fusion of the Aryan and primitive Indian cultures and the Rigvedic culture appeared in the shape of the Brahmanism and the Hinduism. Of course, the later portion of the Rigveda shows the synthesis of the two cultures. This is the background in which we have to study the Rigvedic and the later Vedic cultures.

For the knowledge of the Rigvedic religion, the Avesta is considered reliable source. Certain scholars lay a great stress on the comparative study of the Indo-European religions. No doubt for the knowledge of nature and conception of certain primitive Vedic deities such as Dyaus, Parjanya, the Asvins and Indra about whom the Avesta is silent or speaks little, the comparative mythology helps us to a large extent and affords some valuable information.

(b) Concept of God

The original Indo-European idea of God was closely associated with the natural phenomena. The Rigvedic Aryans adhered to their old faith unlike the Iranians. The Vedic people revived the concept of deva as general term for god. But they did not accept the abstract conception of god as represented by the term bhaga and as conceived by their fore-fathers. Gradually the term asura was also losing in India its original sense and its importance. In place of Asura, Sura came to be used as a general term for god. It shows clearly that this new development in the conception of god is the antithesis of the Indo-Iranian idea of god. In the later portion of the Rigveda the conception of one god finds its echo here and there.[4]

(c) The Rigvedic Gods

Certainly the Indo-Iranians received from the common heirloom a lion's share and whatever the Rigveda received from it, it preserved scrupulously. As such the Rigveda maintains the original spirit of the old faith. The Indo-Aryans also carried on those religious beliefs which had developed in the Indo-Iranian religion. In India the religious beliefs of the primitive aborigines had largely influenced the Rigvedic religion and as a result of this religious fusion, new divinities and new cults and conceptions appeared in the Rigveda. Thus the Rigvedic gods may be classified into three groups vis.—Indo-European, the Indo-Iranian and gods of the Indian creation.

(d) The Indo-Europeans Gods

(1) Dyaus :Undoubtly Dyaus is the oldest Indo-European god. The word dyaus is occasionally found used in the Rigveda as a common noun to mean 'sky' and 'day.' As a deity the Rigveda preserved the original conception of Dyaus. He is still the personification of the god of heaven. His paternity is the characteristic feature of his personification in the Rigveda. He is the consort of the earth and progenitor of the gods. He is devaputra "they whose sons are god.[5]" As the universal parent the Rigveda mentions him as a father in general.[6] Dyaus is occasionally called Asura.[7] The antiquity of Asura goes back to the Indo-Iranian period. The Iranian notion of a chief deity, Ahura Mazda is certainly derived from the Vedic Asura.[8] But Dyaus occupies very insignificant position in the Rigvedic pantheon. Not even a single independent hymn is addressed to him. He is mentioned in six hymns with earth as dvayaprithivi but here also he does not appear in marked prominence.[9]

The past history of this deity convinces the scholars that Dyaus held the same supreme position as Zeus among the Greeks.[10] He enjoyed this position till Indo-Iranian period.[11] In view of the position which he occupies in the Rigveda it is held that he was already on wane on the Indian soil,[12] Sayana commenting on hymn I-54, identifies Dyaus with Indra who in accordance with the scholars seems to have succeeded to the functions assigned to the former.[13] It is also well recognized that Dyaus provided the Iranian notion of the supreme god. The Rigveda certainly presents him declined in power.

(2) Parjanya: Parjanya is the most probably the Indo-European god though nothing is heard of him during the Indo-Iranian period. But he figures in the Rigveda as the storm god.

(3) Vata or Vayu: Quite distinct in character and in importance the Rigveda has two wind gods. Vata and Vayu. During the Indo-Iranian period very little is known of Vata Like other nature gods the Avestic Vata is regarded as demon.[14] But in the Rigveda he is elemental deity and 'Vayu' retains the Indo-Iranian character.

(4) Usas: No doubt Usas is the Indo-European goddess. But the Indian cult of the goddess Usas owes its origin to the Indo-Iranian period and developed on the Indian soil. 'Ushas' is the Avestic counterpart and both are identical is name and character. Her worship appears not to be prominent in the Indo-Iranian religion; but Usas figures prominently in the Rigveda, to whom twenty independent hymns are addressed. The hymns addressed to Usas are most brilliant and beautiful in the whole of the Rigveda and present highly poetic expressions. It is supposed that the hymns to Usas genetically differ from other hymns in the Rigveda and are believed to have been composed outside of India. Hillebrandt suggests that the dawn cult owes its origin to the place where the winter is so severe that the cattle are to be stalled in security from the cold.[15] He adduces the Avestic legend of Vara in support of his theory.[16] Tilak argues that

the Vedic description of Usas is in consistence with a polar dance.[17] This view is open to serious objections. Keith is of the view that the Rigvedic worship of the Usas had commenced from the Punjab where the phenomena of nature are such as to evoke the real poetry of the dawn.[18] Hopkins assigns early date to the Usas hymns which point out the natural phenomena in the region, south of Ambala.[19] A.C. Das criticises the theory of Tialk.[20] The Rigvedic cult of Usas is really Indian creation. It does not mean that the goddess is not of the Indo-European origin. It means only that the Vedic people inherited the idea of goddess Usas and the germs of her worship, but this definitely matured on the Indian soil.

(5) Varuna: That Varuna is an Indo-European god, is sometimes disputed. Varuna is identified with the Greek Ouranos. But antiquity of this god certainly goes back to the Indo-Iranian period. It has already been told that Ahura Mazda is the Avestic Varuna.

Hillebradt and Hopkins[21] derive the word from the root 'var' to mean' to cover, hence Varuna is encompasser. Sayana also connects the word to this root but in sense of enveloping or confining the wicked with his bonds like darkness.[22] Ludwig[23] holds that the word 'varuna' came out from 'var' (velle) and defines him as the lofty god who wills. Varuna is etymologically connected with 'vari' or 'vara' river; 'vari' water and with 'varas' rain hence he is water as coverer. Another suggestion is to derive the word from 'var', which means to shine.[24] Bergaingne[25] who conceives that Varuna and Vritra developed from the same idea, derives both terms 'varuna' and vrtra' from root 'var' to mean to restrain, and takes Varuna a god of waters but sees in him identity with Vritra, a restrainer of waters. He holds that luminous side of Varuna to be antique and the conception of Varuna's cord is based on the tying up of waters. It has already been discussed that the basic conception of the Varuna's nature is the personification of the encompassing sky. The Rigveda presents Varuna as a mysterious personality. The etymological meaning of Varuna is that which covers. His original nature is understood differently. He is believed to be the sky with numberless stars, which covers seas, or clouds of water of the aerial ocean which covers the sky or darkness that covers the earth at night.

The Rigveda presents the loftiness of Varuna's character. Varuna was omniscient and omnipresent. He controlled and regulated all the natural phenomena by his immutable laws and he was supreme lord of land, ocean and sky. Bergaigne mentions him "most august of the Vedic deities."[26] Hopkins remarks that in the hymn I-25 the protrait of Varuna nears to monotheism and here he is a solitary deity[27] Undoubtedly the conception of Varuna approaches more closely to Unitarianism.

Varuna appears at later stage with marked changes in his character. In contrast to the picture of fair god Shatapatha Brahmana describes Varuna as a bald yellow-eyed old man.[28] The Brahmanas associate Varuna with the nocturnal sky.[29]

The most significant change in his character is the marked tendency to deprive him of all other powers and restrict him to the realm of waters only. The Atharvaveda presents Varuna as deprived of his powers as an universal ruler having only control of the department of waters. The Brahmanas mention him as a god of rain.[30]

The protrait of Varuna presented by the later portion of the Rigveda itself speaks that, he as a sovereign deity, faded away in the later stage and the dominions of the waters only remained in his jurisdiction. He ultimately became an Indian Neptune or deity of the sea. Berth observes that in the later stage Varuna is already in a state of decadence. Scholars differ on this point. Hopkins claims that "divinity of Varuna stood still intact."[31] Bergaigne[32] Hillebrandt[33] and Hopkins hold that rainy side of Varuna is basic and indispensable of his character. Hillebrandt remarks that when Varuna is praised in elevated language, his fundamental rain side is ignored.[34] Hopkins draws the attention between decadence of greatness and decadence of popularity. He believes that in the later stage the Rigveda shows the loss of Varuna's popularity, not his greatness. Scholars may differ on the point whether it is decadence of greatness or decadence of popularity of worship that affected his personality; but it can hardly be gainsaid that in the later Vedic period, Varuna is already reduced to a very inferior position whereas Indra is deliberately raised above all gods.[35] Varuna has not even a single independent hymn in the tenth book while Indra claims forty five. Indra is commonly regarded in the early portion of the Rigveda as younger and inferior god in comparison to Varuna. One late Rigvedic hymn refers to Indra boasting that he dethroned Varuna and invites Agni to enter his own service instead. Roth is of opinion that this change results from the growth of Prajapati as a supreme deity.[36] The later portion of the Rigveda offers sufficient evidences for decline of Varuna and the growth of Indra as a supreme deity.[37] A.C. Das[38] holds that Varuna became exclusively the lord of ocean in a much later stage when the Aryan civilization in India became far advance. At that time Indra came forward and usurped many functions dethroning Varuna from the sovereign seat of the sky and aerial ocean to the terrestrial ocean below. Das further tells that this transition is extremely slow and gradual. He adduces the hymn I-17 and III-38 in which Indra and Varuna appear at par, although the people acknowledge the former to be the greatest god of the time. The hymns II-28-I and II-82-2 show that Varuna is divested of limited power and jurisdiction and his name is dropped altogether from couple Indra-Varuna and Indra alone reigns supreme. He points out that the hymn IV-42 clearly reflects the struggle between Varuna and Indra for supermacy.

Scholars surmise various causes that led to Varuna's dethronement from his supreme position in the hierarchy of the Vadic gods. The old theory that as Iranians degraded Indra as demon and exalted Ahura Mazda as the supreme, so the Indians in retaliation raised Indra to the stature of Varuna, is totally discarded. It is said, "The decrease of Varuna worship in favour of Indra results partly from the more peaceful god of rain appearing less admitable than the monsoon god, who overpowers storm and lightning as well as wets the earth."[39] The problem is dealt with from another angle. It is believed that the elevation of Indra is, of course, of philosophical conception which is much more advanced than all the monotheistic greatness attained by Varuna. Varuna was supplanted by Indra as Mitra by Savitr for the same reason because each represents the same priestly philosophy. Das is of the view that Varuna in the later stage was conceived as restrainer and encompasser in the shape of darkness and cloud. Thus Varuna and Vritra are in certain aspect identical. Vritra was first called deva and Brahman. Later on it was realized that his functions are detrimental to the performance of sacrifice and to the successful carrying on agricultural operations. He is regarded as a malevolent power and inimical to men and gods both. Vritra stripped off some of Varuna's functions who thus crippled of his power, came to occupy secondary position in the hierarchy of the Vedic gods. When Aryans passed on from pastoral to agricultural life and from non-sacrifice to sacrificial stage, Indra had been discovered and his divine services requisitioned to suit the changing needs of the time. When we look at the character of the two great gods, we arrive at the conclusion that in the later Rigvedic period the practical equality of the two gods is given place to the superiority of Indra, as the nature of Varuna could not satisfy the needs of the specifically Indian character. The orthodox view that decadence of Varuna in India is owing to incapability of the Vedic Indians of having such a deity as Varuna whom they brought with them from the Indo-Iranian home, does not seem to be correct. As a matter of fact the affect of the admixture of race in India itself was fatal to the conception of Varuna.[40]

(e) Indo-Iranian Deities

(1) Mitra: Just like Dyaus, Mitra is also a waning god. In the Rigveda he has no real independent entity. In the whole of the Rigveda 'Mitra' claims only one hymn. He is regularly invoked in combination with Varuna, he shares with Varuna practically all his functions and attributes. Because of his close and constant association with Varuna, Mitra lost real independent identity. The nature of the Vedic Mitra is problematical.

It has already been told that the Indo-Iranian Mitra was the sun god in his original character and the name of the god originally signified friend or ally and this attribute must have been ascribed to the sun god in this aspect of a beneficent power of nature. The Avesta refers Mithra to the ethical side of his character as the guardian of the faithfulness.[41] The Vedic Mitra is essentially a kindly god,[42] and the word mitra occurs in the Rigveda usually in the meaning of friend. In the later Vedic literature Mitra appears as a god of peace.[43]

It is well established fact that the Indo-Iranian Mitra is undoubtedly the sun god. The Rigveda also affords evidence, although it is very scanty. In the Rigveda Mitra is identified with Savitr[44] and Vishnu takes his three steps by the laws of Mitra. Here Mitra appears to be the regulator of the course of the sun, one of the traits ascribed to Savitr as 'bringing men together' accords with the attributes of Mitra who 'brings men together by uttering his voice.' Macdonell finds here a clear reference to Mitra's solar character. The view of Grieswold that Mitra was an abstract deity is wholly incorrect. Mitra never became consistent with abstract, representing faithfulness or friendliness. Even the Vedic Mitra is unmistakably referred to the beneficent power of the sun. Most probably the word 'mitra' had no direct and definite bearing to anything physical in the sun; his connection with the sun was constantly maintained as long as the conception of this god was new. But when physical basis was forgotton, the Indo-Iranian at that time had no idea to form an abstract deity, Mitra started to lose his individuality as the sun god. In Persia Mithra after sometime seems to have regained his original character while in India Mitra deviated from it. He is regularly mentioned in the Rigveda as a friendly and guardian god. In the later Vedic period Mitra is associated with day or conceived as the god of day. Day is said to belong to Mitra.

(2) Agni: It is stated already that the sacrificial fire is most probably an Indo-European institution. The fire-gods of other Indo-European branches differ considerably from the Indo-Iranian fire god in their character, which indicates that the personification of fire god was extremely shadowy in the Indo-European period. The fire cult holds the key position in the Indo-Iranian religion. The Vedic Agni is certainly the Indo-Iranian Atar. He inherited a considerable characteristics of his prototype. But he developed on the Indian soil in his own manner. Many old attributes of the Indo-Iranian fire god persists in the Indian cult. It is the Indo-Iranian character of the fire-god that he burns and dispells the evil spirit and hostile magic.

The origin of Agni in the water is, of course, an Indo-Iranian conception. The notion of Agni in the water is prominent throughout the Vedas.[45] The Rigveda tells that Agni is the son of waters or embryo of waters.[46]

The descent of fire from the heaven is a very old Indo-European conception. The Rigveda tells that Matarisvan brought Agni from the Heaven.[47] The threefold birth of Agni affords the idea of his triple character.[48] Sakapuni regards three-fold existence of Agni as being in heaven, earth and air.[49] The earliest Indian trinity is believed to have owed its origin to his three fold characters of Agni and it is the most significant conception in the religious history of India.

It is a very old Indo-Iranian notion that Agni is more closely connected with human life. Such an intimate association is hardly discoverable in the worship of any other god.[50] Agni is grahpati "lord of house" and damunas "domestic."[51] The Rigvedic expressions remind the time when the fire was a centre of domestic life.

(3) Soma: The Soma cult was undoubtedly a special Indo-Iranian innovation. In consistence with the new spirit of Zoroastrian religion Homa met the same fate as other nature gods in the Avestic pantheon. Whereas the Soma cult developed on the Indian soil in its own way, it acquired an exalted position in the hierarchy of the Vedic gods. Among the Rigvedic gods, Sòma comes third in order of importance. Of course, Some sacrifice forms the main feature of the Vedic ritual.[52] Bergaigne holds that the whole of Rigveda is but a collection of hymns for Soma worship.[53] The Avestic Homa and the Vedic Soma show very close similarity in nature and character. Although the Rigveda revised certain Indo-Iranian traits of the prototype of the Indo-Iranian Soma.

The Indo-Iranians conceive that Soma was brought from heaven by a bird. The Rigveda describes this legend in a very interesting manner and in detail.[54] It recalls the old Indo-European myth of mead which shows a remarkable similarity of Soma-bringing eagle of Indra with the nector bringing eagle of Zeus and with the eagles of other nations bringing mead from the heaven.[55] It is undeniable that the Indo-European mead is simply water of rain. The Indo-Iranians discovered an intoxicating and delightful drink Soma and identified with the Indo-European mead and transformed the old myth into something very important and real legend.[56]

The god Soma takes a new turn in the history of his development in the later Vedic period. The later Vedic literature identifies Soma with the moon. The Atharvaveda very often mentions Soma as the moon.[57] In the Yajurveda Soma is explicitly identified with the moon and it is stated that the former is the husband of Naksatras.[58] The Chandogya Upnishad also identifies Soma with the moon. As a matter of fact in the later portion of the Rigveda itself Soma is certainly identified with the moon.[59]

The process how Soma came to be identified with the moon in the later stage is not difficult to understand. Soma was a personification of the moon is merely a secondary mythological growth.[60] Soma is called 'indu.'[61] He is bright and yellow[62] His abode is heaven.[63]. He dispells the darkness and swells in the water.[64] These traits show a remarkable similarity with the moon. Comparison with the moon would, therefore, easily suggest itself. On the other hand, the conception developed on the poetic expressions such as, 'Soma in the bowl' appears like moon in the moon.[65] "Soma goes through the purifying sieve" may be supposed to imagine as the moon passing through sieve-like clouds. The moon may be imagined in the expression, the drop (Soma) lights up the stars at nights.[66] The belief of the Indian aborigines that tree or plant is in the moon has probably given rise to this conception.

(4) Vivasvant: Vivasvant is the Indo-Iranian deity who is most probably the deification of the first sacrificer of the ancestor of the human race. Vivasvant in his Indo-Iranian character is not likely a god of light. But Vivasvant must primarily

have been a personification of the sun or 'Agni,' which suits best the obvious etymological sense of his name. The sun or fire is universally conceived as the progenitor of the human race. It stands to reason that the conception of Vivasvant as the sun in the capacity of a progenitor of human race is much older than his worship under this name. His old relation with the sun had most probably been forgotten even in the Indo-Iranian period. It shows that the god bears the appearance of having lost much of his original colour and life.[67] While Vivasvant figures in the Rigveda as the first sacrificer or ancestor of human race. He is very often identified with the sun and Agni. Roth remarks that as a mythological figure he seems to have faded by the time of the Rigveda like Trita.[68] In the Rigveda the gods are said to be off springs of Vivasvant,[69] but in the later literature men are his offspring.

(5) Apam Napat: Apam Napat means "son of the waters." Thus Agni is characteristically Apam Napat. It has already been discussed that the Indo-Iranian Apam Napat in his original character is the lightning; one of the forms of Agni born from the clouds. Thus Apam Napat possesses both aqueous and igneous character. But his aqueous character only predominates in him in the Indo-Iranian religion and his igneous nature is forgotten and confused to certain extent. The Rigveda revives it although in confusing manners.

The association of Apam Napat with water is essential in the Rigveda which mentions this relation in different ways. In rituals his connection with waters is very clear. The hymn in which he is invoked in connection with rituals ceremonies is exclusively concerned with the waters,[70] Macdonell remarks that his aqueous nature predominates in the hymn II-35.[71]

Once Agni is clearly identified with him. ' Agni' is mentioned as son of water, who as a priest sat down on the earth.[72] Agni and Apam Napat are identical in having the same epithet as Asuhe swiftly speeding.

(6) Trita Aptya: Trita has already been mentioned as a god of lightning. The Rigveda always designates him with the epithet of Aptya which Sayana explains as 'son of water.' It is pointed out earlier that Trita is an older god than Indra who largely usurped the powers of the former as an important deity with the result that he figures in the Indo-Iranian religion even in the Rigveda in an obscure character. His original connection with Soma definitely signifies the bringing of Soma from heaven by lightning which is an obvious allusion to the legend of eagle and Soma. But owing to insufficient evidences a considerable divergent views have cropped up in regard to his nature.[73] In consistent with his original Indo-Iranian character Trita appears in the Rigveda in close association with the Soma as well as with Indra, Agni, Apam Napat and the Maruts.

Trita appears in the Rigveda in the special capacity of a preparer of Soma[74] In regard to his deeds Trita is almost identical with Indra.

The later Vedic literature presents him in a more obscure character. The

Atharvaveda mentions him as a-far-off god to whom guilt or dreams may be banished.[75] The Yajurveda tells that he bestows long life.[76] It gives a clear reference to him as a presser of Soma. The Brahmanas mention him along with his two brothers- Ekata and Dvita, and calls them the sons of Agni and who are born from the waters.[77]

(7) Aryaman: The Indo-Iranian Aryanman is definitely an apotheosis of the comradeship. In the Rigveda he is listed among the Adityas. He retains his Indo-Iranian character in the Rigveda and continues to be invoked as such regularly in the marriages. As an Aditya he is naturally regarded as either the personification of one of the aspects of the sun denoting as a friend or his constant associate. Bhagvata Gita mentions him as the head of the priests.[78]

(8) Bhaga: Bhaga as a deity appears to be the god of destiny or fortune. In the Rigveda he is also listed among the Adityas, hence he is also regarded as the sun god. Like Aryaman he is personification of one of the aspects of the sun as bestower of fortune. His close and regular association with Savitr[79] is a clear testimony that he is the sun.

(9) Narasansa: The Indo-Iranian Narasansa is admittedly the apotheosis of the rising flames of fire in the capacity of a messenger. Narasansa figures in the Rigveda in a very obscure character. But he is invariably a messenger between men and gods. He is mentioned in the Brahmanas as three-headed and six-eyed.[80] It is a clear reference to identify him with Visvarupa the son of Tvastr. Hillebrandt who identifies Visvarupa with the moon sees in him the moon character. The suggestion of Oldenberg that it possibly refers to Narasansa's partaking of three Savana daily, duplicated by the twin offices of Hotr and Udgatr, seems to be more plausible.

(10) Surya and Savitr: In fact Surya is an Indo-European god but he is the most important deity in the Indo-Iranian religion. Savitr is certainly an Indian creation.[81] Savitr is an epithet of Surya, but it becomes an independent deity. 'Savitr; is derived from 'su' meaning 'stimulate', 'vivify.' Yaska defines Savitr as the stimulator of everything.[82] Oldenberg suggests that as an abstraction of idea of stimulation he is merely assimilated with the sun.[83] The suggestion received the common acceptance. Thus Savitr is distinguished from Surya as a more abstract deity whereas Surya is a more concrete god. Outward form of the sun or its orb is the original conception of Surya.[84] In certain respects Surya and Savitr are the same deity but in many respects they differ from each other. The Rigveda shows that Savitr is the personification of the devine power of the sun and Surya is merely a concrete deity. The Taittiriya Brahmana tells that Prajapati becomes Savitr. Where he creates living being. he is Pushan in his movement and has close connection with him. Once Savitr is identified with Mitra.[85] In the later stage Savitr was invoked at the beginning of the Vedic studies.[86]

(11) Yama: During the Indo-Iranian period Yama was the king of the golden age. He is the earthly king in the Avesta while the Rigveda mentions him as the

ruler of heaven. Although he is not expressly mentioned but he figures in the Rigveda as god. The Rigveda preserves the Indo-Iranian conception that Yama produced the human race with his sister Yami.[87] 'Yama' is the first mortals died. The Rigveda states that Yama had chosen death and abondoned his body and thus showed the way to many.[88] He is styled as the gatherer of the people, which recalls the Iranian conception. Yama possesses a Pasa 'foot-fetter' with which he catches his victim.[89] The owls and pigeons are mentioned as his messengers. But his regular messengers are his two dogs who guard the path to heaven and track out among men those who are to die.[90]

The Pasa of Yama is paralleled to the bonds of Varuna.[91] This trait in addition to his dreadful dogs as his messengers made Yama an object of fear in the Rigveda itself. In the later Vedic mythology he is connected with the terror of death and becomes the god of death. The later Sanhitas identify him with Antaka 'the ender;' Nirti 'dissolution' and with 'death' and, Mrityu is also styled as his messenger.[92]

The Rigvedic notion is that death is the path of Yama; it is highly emphasized in the post-Vedic mythology.

(12) Asvins: We know that in character, the Asvins are the Indo-European deity. It is already pointed out that in their original character they are the personification of the morning and the evening stars. But nothing or little is known about their Indo-Iranian character. Their counterpart Naonhaithya is mentioned in the Avesta but as a demon. Nasatya is another name of the Asvins. Nasatya is listed among other gods in the Boghaz-keui inscription, which indicates that he is a great and an important god of the Indo-Iranians.

The original nature of the Indo-European Asvins is already discussed. The character in which they appear in the Rigveda is certainly very obscure. Hopkins remarks that the Asvins "have been variously interpreted, yet in point of fact one knows no more now what was the original conception of the twins then was known before the occidental scholars began to study them."[93] Even the Brahmans during the later Vedic period forgot their original nature. The opinion of Yaska is also very obscure. He remarks that some identify them with 'Heaven and Earth' others with 'Day and Night' and some others with 'the Sun and the Moon;' whereas the Itihaskaras understand that they are 'two kings of holy rather meritorious deed.'[94]

Such a complex figure of the Asvins in the Rigveda makes their character obscure. The theory of the sun and moon is not plausible at all. The Asvins are twin. The sun and the moon are eternally separate; when one is seen the other is absent. The theory of 'twilight' also does not give any satisfactory solution. The theory does not explain that one of the Asvins is born here and the other elsewhere. One is the son of Dyaus, and the other the son of night.

The theory of the morning and the evening stars suits best according to the Rigvedic evidences because of their luminous nature and the time of their appearance. But the Asvins are twins, while the duality of the morning and the evening stars does not stand to reason. This difficulty can easily be solved if it is accepted that the Asvins were originally the personification of that part of the day and the night which starts with the appearance of the morning star and ends with that of the evening star. The morning and the evening's stars were possibly regarded as the two representatives of this period. The two stars were supposed to be linked with this bright period. Here the twin character of the gods is manifestly obvious. It accords with the Rigvedic evidence for example the Rigveda tells that they are 'separately born' and 'born here and there'[95] Yaska comments, 'one is called the son of night, the other the son of dawn.'[96] One hymn tells that they appear in the morning and evening.[97] Another hymn[98] speaks of the Asvins traveling always from the morning till evening, on their ordained path on which Agni also travels. Here we see the trinity of the two stars and the bright period of the day and night. This trinity is noticeable in the Rigveda. The curious quality of the Asvins car having all its parts triple-may most probably be a reference to this trinity. In the mythology of the Rigveda Asva means the sun, hence Asvin may be interpreted as 'pertaining to Asva.' It is quite logical to conceive that the bright period of 24 hours is essentially connected with the sun. This theory explains all the legends associated with the Asvins quite satisfactorily. The sun is visible or powerful during this period of the day and night.

(13) Indra: Indra is the most popular, favorite, national and the greatest god of the Vedic people. One fourth of the Rigveda is devoted to him. In character he goes back to the Indo-European period. In name he is the Indo-Iranian deity. He is in the Rigveda the subject of many myths and appears in his highly anthropomorphized character. He is originally a thunder god. He conquers the darkness, demon of draught, liberates waters and wins light. Being a god of battle he helps the Aryans in their fight against the aborigines of India.

It is a matter of great controversy that what actually Indra is or what does he represent. He is identified with the sun, lightning the sky, the year as well as with fire in general and with the 'thunder and strom.'[99] In the light of the Rigvedic evidence, Hopkins is led to arrive at the conclusion that "he is too stormy to be sun; too luminous to be storm; too near to the phenomena of the monsoon to be year or sky; too rainy to be fire, too alien from every one thing to be any one thing; he is too celestial to be wholly atmospheric; too atmospheric to be celestial; too earthly to be either."[100] That he is the storm god receives a general acceptance.

In the later portion of the Rigveda Indra emerges out as the supreme god. The theory of Roth, followed by Whitney that the supremacy of Varuna was transferred to Indra during the Rigvedic period is partly correct.[101] The matter has already been dealt with in detail. Benefy[102] and Berea, hold that Indra in the Rigveda appears to have superseded the ancient Dyaus.[103] But the view is getting a general acceptance that Indra ousted the Indo-Iranian Trita and usurped his power and became supreme.

(f) Divinties of the Indian Creation

(1) Adityas: Like the Indo-Iranian, the number of the Adityas is not definite in the Rigveda. The Rigveda once gives their number as six[104] Only once it is stated as seven[105] and once as eight.[106] The priority of number seven is noticeable from the fact that Aditi, their mother at first presented only seven to the gods, and the eighth Martanda 'sprang of dead egg' came afterwards. The priority of the number seven is also confirmed from the ritual of the Yajurveda,[107] although then twelve was the established number for the Adityas. The later Vedic literature invariably enumerates them as the twelve sun gods, evidently connected with the twelve months.[108]

(2) Pushan: The god Pushan is an Indian creation. Some scholars trace his origin from the Indo-European period. It appears to be doubtful. This god is not traceable in the Indo-Iranian religion. But certain characteristics of this god are discovered in the Greek Hermes. The germs of this conception might have infiltrated in the Rigvedic religion.

(3) Vishnu: Vishnu is a very minor deity having subordinate position in the Rigveda. In the later Vedic period Vishnu emerges out as a great god. His chief characteristic is of his three strides: It is an established fact that three steps of Vishnu refer to the course of the sun.

The conception of three steps of Vishnu prominently prevails throughout the later Vedic literature. In a post Vedic ritual, the sacrificer imitates the steps[109] of Vishnu. This act brings the sacrificer in close connection with or merges him to the deity. It is note-worthy that in the Avesta the three steps of the Amesha Spents are similarly[110] imitated. Certain scholars hold that these parallels might have risen independently. But such a close similarity in the two traditions speaks itself in favour of the view that it is an Indo-Iranian custom. From this it appears that the idea of god Vishnu was already present in the Indo-Iranian religion.

(4) Rudra: Rudra, is purely Indian creation. He is the strom god but occupies a very minor and subordinate position in the Rigveda. In the later Vedic period he emerges out as the greatest god with the conspicuous personality. The term 'rudra' is occasionally used as an attribute of Agni.[111] The Yajurveda tells two new names of Rudra as 'Sarva' and 'Bhava.'[112] Arbman is of opinion that Sarva and Bhava, who were non-Aryans gods, were originally identical with Rudra and worshipped outside of the Vedic circle.[113] The Vajasaneya Samhita enumerates Agni, Asani, Pasupati, Bhava, Sarva, Mahadeva, Isana and Ugradeva with others as forms of one god.[114] The Shatapatha Brahamana tells that Rudra, Sarva, Pasupati, Ugra, Asani, Bhava, Mahadeva represent eight forms of Agni.[115] The same Brahamana explains Asani to mean 'lightning.'[116] In the later Vedic period he is described as to be easily invoked,[117] and inauspicious or Siva.[118] Siva

is the post Vedic name of this deity. Some scholars suggest connection of Siva with the Tamil Sivan meaning 'redman.' In the Brahamanas the Rudra appears to have been deviated very much from his original character. Undoubtedly the Rigvedic Rudra is quite different from the Yajurvedic Rudra who absorbed so many foreign elements in his character. The influence of the aboriginal Indians on the cult of Rudra is clearly traceable. The phallic worship became an essential part of the Siva cult. The Rigveda condemns the phallic worship but it is a most popular cult of the aborigines of India. The snake worship which was prevalent throughout India among the primitive aborigines, finds no place in the Rigveda. But the Brahmanas show much more connection of Rudra with the snakes, which is clearly marked out in the Epics. The Sutras tell that snakes are also among his servants.[119] In the later stage the snake worhsip is merged with the cult of this deity. The Shatapatha Brahmana lends an additional support to this view.[120] It informs that Sarva was a name of Agni among the eastern people and Bhava among the Balhikas. In the later Vedic period Rudra came to be known as Sarva and Bhava. It shows that Rudra absorbed local gods after gods. Commenting on the tendency of Rudra to assimilate local gods, Kieth remarks, "It is certainly possible that a forest and mountain deity or some kindred gods, such as vegetation spirit, and even a god of the dead may be united with the Vedic lightning god to form a composite figure of the Yajurveda."[121] At the later stage his greatness reaches high peak of its height.

(5) Maruts: Some scholars are of the view that the Maruts are Indo-European deities. They identify them with the Italian god Mars. But nothing is heard of them in the Indo-Iranian religion. It may safely be said, that they are the Vedic creation. The Maruts are the great gods in the Rigveda.

(6) Ahi Budhnya: Ahi Budhnya figures in the Rigveda as a deity in the form of a snake. Macdonell holds that Ahi Budhnya is, of course, a form of Ahi Vritra regarded as divine and not merely an enemy of Indra.[122]

It is, in indeed, a significant change in the religious belief of the Rigvedic people. The snake worship finds no place in the religious conception of the Rigveda. In the Rigveda Ahi or serpent is conceived to be an enemy of man; and his head, Ahi Vritra is regarded as an arch enemy of the gods and men. The propitiation of Ahi Budhnya is a quite religious concept, which is most probably a foreign inspiration. The snake worship, as we know was an important cult of the Indian aborigines.

(7) Brahaspati: Brhaspati is a most prominent deity of the Vedic pantheon. He appears in the Rigveda as a one of the forms of Agni. The later Vedic literature associates him with certain stars. In the Yajurveda he is the god of constellation of Tisya.[123] While the post Vedic literature mentions him as the regent of the planet Jupiter.

(8) Creator and the Agent Gods: The later portion of the Rigveda mentions a god by name Visvakarman who is all-seeing and has eyes, face, arms and feet on every side.[124] Thus Visvakarman is the prototype of Brahma of the later mythology, who is four-faced and four-armed. He is designated as Dhatra and Vidhatra, the disposer of sky and establisher of earth. Visvakarman is once used as an attribute of Indra and once of the sun as all-creating.[125] In the Brahmanas Visvakarman is an attribute of Prajapati.[126] In the Satapatha Brahmana Visvakarman is clearly identified with Prajapati.[127] In the post-Vedic literature he assumes a very humble position as the artificer.

Prajapati 'Lord of off-sring once occurs in the Rigveda as an attribute of Savitra who is described as the Prajapati of the world and supporter of heaven.[128] In the later portion of the Rigveda Prajapati appears as a distinct deity.[129] The Rigveda tells that he created the heaven and the earth. The Satapatha Brahmana informs that he existed alone in the beginning.[130]

In one hymn[131] Prajapati is designated as Hiranyagarbha 'the golden germ', because of this attribute Prajapati became the supreme deity in the Atharvaveda and in the subsequent literature.[132] The post-Vedic literature made him a designation of personal Brahma.

Tvastr is the most prominent amongst the agent gods. Etymologically the name of Tvastr is explained as fashioner. Hence Oldenberg insists that Tvastr is more than the personification of the creative activity.[133] He figures in the Rigveda as an artificer and as most skilfull workman well-versed in crafty contrivances[134] In the capacity of a fashioner of forms he presides over generation and off spring.[135] He creates the world and is a universal father.[136] He bestows blessing and long life and has excellent wealth.[137]

The Rigveda clearly shows that Tvastr as an artificer is definitely a later creation. Hence Tvastr was originally the personification of the creative aspect of the sun. Later on he appeared as a regular divine artificer in the pantheon.

It has already been said that the Rbhus are identical with the German "Elbs" and they appear to be terrestrial or aerial elves and have attained divine greatness.[138] These deities are not traceable in the Indo-Iranian religion.

(9) Rivers: Rivers also receive veneration in the Rigveda. The river cult takes its origin from the Indo-Iranian religion. The Indo-Iranian Rasa and Sarasvati are most sacred rivers and received the veneration. Sarasvati is equally celebrated in the Rigveda. She is regarded as the river goddess.[139] The Brahmanas tell that she is the goddess of speech.[140] In the post-Vedic mythology she became the goddess of eloquence and wisdom and is regarded as the wife of Brahma.

(10) Moon: The Moon god is a prominent deity in the Indo-European religion. But the Indo-Europeans attached the importance to the Moon as giving the means of measuring time. The Indo-Iranians retained the Indo-European conception of the Moon. In the Rigveda the Moon is a very minor and subordinate deity. In the later portion of the Rigveda the Moon figures prominently in his connection with Soma. Occasionally he appears in union with Surya as Suryamas or Suryachandramas.

(11) Goddesses: In the Rigveda, Usa and Sarasvati are certainly important goddesses. The Indo-Iranian goddess Purandhi figures in the Rigveda. In the later portion of the Rigveda Uma appears as the wife of Rudra. She is the goddess of mountains. It is note-worthy that word 'ama' is identified with the Sumerian word "umm" and the Dravidian amma meaning mother. Uma is believed to be the mother goddess of the Dravidians. There are many other goddesses who figure in the Rigveda, but as very minor deities.

(12) Gandharvas: The Indo-Iranian mythology knows Gandharva as a divine individual but the Gandharvas as a class are found in the Rigveda. The Apsaras are supposed to be the wife of the Gandharvas. In the later Vedic texts Gandharva stands in close association with Fata-Morgana.[141] It recalls the Iranian parallel and shows the Iranian influence.[142] The Rigveda refers to hostility of Indra to Gandharva.[143] It indicates the Babylonian influence. Carnoy also sees in it contamination of the storm myth and a Semitic monster of the abyss.[144]

(g) Cosmogony

The Rigveda mentions many theories of cosmogony. They are quite different to one and other. Sometime the universe is conceived to have come into existence by natural generation. Sometimes it is mentioned as the result of mechanical production. Whereas in the Avesta Ahura Mazda created the whole Universe.

The birth of gods is described in different ways. The notion of priority fixes the parentage of gods. In other words the phenomenon preceding another is its parents. The Rigveda also tells that the gods are the sons of immortality.[145] It shows that an abstract quality is figuratively mentioned as the parents of the sons who are eminently associated with that quality. It is a Semitic conception par excellence.[146] In accordance with the new spirit, the Zoroastrianism adopted this idea and it, however, crept into the Rigveda..

(h) Concept of Soul

The belief in the immortality of soul is very old. The Indo-Iranians also regarded the soul as immortal. The Shatapatha Brahmana mentions that soul attains immortality after departing from the body.[147] The Avesta presents a distinct and the most clear idea of the continuance of life after death.[148] Some Scholars[149] go to that extent that Persia was the only birth place of the conception and from that quarter it was borrowed even by the European nations.[150] But in the later Vedic period the conception of Transmigration of soul became a necessary element of the Vedic religion. The traces of the doctrine is totally absent in the Rigveda. On contrary the Rigveda shows very clearly a belief in immortality of soul.

This sudden change in the religious out-look of the Aryan people is strange. The origin of this doctrine is a difficult problem. Jacobi says "Certainly the Indian.

doctrine of Transmigration is not to be derived from one definite source alone there are undoubtedly several streams of thought, which hardly admit of being definitely traced, but which were distinct in their origin."[151] Some scholars claim that the Rigvedic people got the idea of Transmigration from the aboriginal belief of the savage people of India, who conceive that souls pass into plants and bodies of birds and animals.[152] A.C. Das remarks that germs of Transmigration are traceable in the Rigveda itself.[153] It is likely that the Rigvedic hymn X-16- contributed largely to the origin of the doctrine. It says that at death the eye of man goes to the sun, the breath to the wind, the speech to the fire, and other members are also dispersed. First of all Oldenberg[154] suggested that the doctrine of Transmigration developed in the Rigvedic conceptions that the birds are forms of the Fathers and the Fathers creep about the roots of the plants. It is more than probable that this conception maintained its hold upon the lower straturm of the Rigvedic society and in course of time with the incentive of aboriginal belief the doctrine of Transmigration developed.

The Rigveda tells that the soul goes to the heaven either by a car or by wings.[155] The Atharvaveda further informs that the soul of the dead wafted upwards by the Maruts fanned by soft breeze.[156] It recalls the Iranian notion that a wind of good odour coming from southern direction carries soul upto the other world.[157] The Rigveda states that the soul of the dead on its journey passes through two fires which destroy the wicked and the good pass by. We notice that there is clear evidence of the Iranian influence. The Avesta says that soul of the pious alone can pass over the Chinvat bridge, while the wicked fall from it into the fires of the hell.[158]

The normal conception of the Rigveda is that the soul leaves the body on death and goes to heaven which is the chief place of the dead. Scholars[159] recognize that this conception is of Iranian origin. The conception pervades the Gathas and the whole later Zind literature. Future life and some kind of abode as a reward is a common conception of the Rigvedic Aryans. Hence hell is a natural complement to heaven. But the Rigveda does not specifically mention hell. The idea of hell was not fully developed during tte Rigvedic period but it was present in a embryoic stage. First of all the Atharvaveda specifically mentioned hell. It clearly describes Naraka Loka in contrast to Svarga. The conception appears to be fully developed in the Brahmanas.[160] The Shatapatha Brahmana states that after death the souls are born again, weighed in a balance and awarded reward and punishment according to their deserts.[161] Here Iranian influence is obviously clear.[162] The final judgment is not traceable at all in the Rigveda.[163] This is purely Iranian and in the Avestic mythology it is a key point in connection with the future life of the soul. This Iranian inspiration is found prevailing throughout the post-Vedic literature. The Aitareya Aranyika[164] tells that before Yama the truthful and untruthful are sorted out. But it is not clear that Yama acts here as a judge.[165]

There is world-wide conception that the soul on its way must cross a river or a stream.[166] The Avesta mentions Chinvat Bridge "the bridge of judgment" which every soul has to pass. The pious souls pass over safely and the wicked fall down in the fires. This conception is also entirely absent in the Rigveda. This conception appears in the Shatapatha Brahmana. A terrible and dreadful river Vaitarni is to be crossed by every soul.

(i) Cult of Mother Goddess

The cult of Mother Goddess is unknown in the Rigveda. The cult appeared at the end of the Vedic period. Saktism is an important phase of the cult of Mother Goddess, in which Mother Goddess is regarded as the creator and the supreme deity and having a male partner as her subordinate. It has already been shown that this cult is very primitive and widely diffused among the Harappans and other aborigines, in India. Later on this cult was associated with the cult of Siva.

In the later Vedic period Durga is recognized as a great Mother Goddess and also the consort of Siva. Just like her consort, Siva, she also presents a terrible character.

This cult is certainly an outcome of the aboriginal influence and shows a parallel development just like the cult of Siva. In her dreadful character she is designated originally as goddess Durga. Quite similar to her consort Siva, she absorbed several deities and local goddesses of similar mythological conceptions. She has several names, the local goddesses who were amalgamated with her, gave various names to her. Her other-names are Uma, Parvati, Gauri, Devi, Chandi, Chumunda, Kali, Kapalini, Bhavani, Viyaya, etc. Thus this goddess presents very diverse aspects. This trend of combination became complete during the later Vedic period; when the goddess Durga emerges out as more powerful. But history of this development goes back to the Rigvedic period. Another name of Durga is Ambika which is mentioned in the Vedic literature. The Vajasaneya Samhita mentions Ambika as the sister of Rudra but in the Taittiriya Aranyaka she became his wife.[167] It is interesting to note that the Mother Goddess in the West Asia is always associated with a male partner, either as her son and lover or as her brother and husband.[168] In an invocation in Taittiriya Aranyaka, Durga is styled as Vairochani "daughter of the sun or fire."[169] Two more names of Durga as Kanyakumari and Katyayani are met with in a hymn addressed to Agni in the Rigveda.[170] Kena Upnishad tells that Uma is the daughter of Himavat.[171] Two of the seven tongues of Agni are called Kali and Karali. In the Munduka Upnishad Kali and Karali are two names of Durga.[172] Durga stands in close connection with Sarasvati who is styled in the Taittiriya Aranyaka[173] as Varada Mahadevi and Sandhya Vidya but at a later stage Varada Mahadevi and Sandhya Vidya are described as the consort of Siva.[174]

The above facts clearly show that at the end of the Vedic period many goddesses are elevated to the rank of wives of Rudra-Siva and have been blended in one consort of Siva, who is commonly known as Durga. These characters obviously betray the diversity of her origin.[175] It is also to be noted that certain goddesses are associated with the mountain and with fire. In her benign character, Durga is a goddess of mountain, but in terrible form she represents the fire which is devouring as well as expiating elements. It is also probable that other goddesses of female demons were worshipped by various classes of people in different parts of the country. All these were ultimately submerged into great goddess Durga. In the later portions of the Rigveda, the seed of Sakti worship is clearly traceable.[176] The Khila [177] of the Rigveda prominently mentions it. The goddess figures as a supreme deity in the Devi Sukta.[178]

(j) Magic in the Vedas

The Zoroastrianism is well-known for the magical rites. The earliest portion of the Rigveda is free from the crudest form of the magic. In few late hymns the Rigveda certainly deals with the magic. In the Atharvaveda the magic and religion are extricably blended. The Atharvaveda is undoubtedly composed of ancient material and full of the magic rites. Here the Iranian influence is quite obvious. This is why the Atharvaveda was not recognised for long time as a sacred Veda and only three Vedas were invariably enumerated but in due course the Atharvaveda received recognition when religious outlook of the Vedic people had undergone a change in accordance with the cultural environment. The magical rites are also popular among the aborigines of India, and they are regarded as a cultural link between the Vedic people and the original inhabitants of India. Oldenberg traces out many magical rites from the Vedic literature and compares them with the customs prevailing among the aborigines.[179] He tells that belief in the power of formula 'mantra,' anointing of king, and initiation and marriage ceremonies show the magical practices. In order to destroy the enemies, the figures are wounded.

It clearly refers to the practices of sympathetic or mimic magic. The Atharvaveda mentions the use of homeopathic magic for the cure of jaundice or baldness. Crooke remarks, "The fact that such beliefs were common among the Aryans and the non-Aryans naturally facilitated that contamination of the earlier and purer theology which developed first into Brahmanism and at a later date into Hinduism."[180]

(k) Monotheism in the Regveda

Since their separation from the Veclic people, the Iranians adopted the monotheistic faith unlike their forefathers. But the Vedic people adhered to the primitive belief of the polytheism. In the later portion of the Rigveda, the idea of monotheism in crude form appeared. In the early portion of the Rigveda the idea of monotheism is totally absent. There is plurality of gods and every important god is generally represented as a supreme and absolute deity. It is quite clear that the Rigvedic religion is polytheistic.

No doubt Varuna is "the august of the Vedic deities." In certain hymns he figures as a solitary deity. According to some scholars the portrait of Varuna nears to monotheism. But it is merely an exaggeration.[181] We definitely get in the later portion of the Rigveda the fragmentary references to the faint idea of monotheism. Such conception is seen in the later Vedic hymns; where the idea is expressed that various deities are different manifestations of a single divine Being.[182] One hymn mentions that he is one, the wise call it by different names, Agni, Yama and Matarisvan.[183] Here the seed of the monotheism is traceable. At the end of the Vedic period, the conception of monotheism is found fully developed. Brahmanas recognize Prajapati as the chief and the father of the gods and tell that he existed from the beginning. Later on in the Uanishad, Brahma as universal soul or the absolute took the place of Prajapati.[184]

It is more than probable that the primitive belief of the original inhabitants of India had contributed largely to the monotheism in the Rigveda. Crooke remarks that there is nothing antecedently improbable in the view that the conception of one supreme god had prevailed in India since remote past even before the rise of the Vedic polytheism.[185] Lang supports this view.[186]

But it is more plausible that the idea of the monotheism was already borrowed from the Iranians and it was latent among the Vedic people when they entered India. At the later stage it caught hold the imagination of the Vedic people and gradually it blossomed forth into a full-fledged conception.

(i) Ritual Ceremonies

The rituals ceremonies are the essential part of the Rigvedic religion. They were well-established in all respects during the Indo-Iranian period. The Indo-Iranians established an institution of priest which fully developed during the Rigvedic time. The Indo-Iranian sacrifices and rituals were very simple and needed no more than two or three priests. During the Rigvedic period the religious ceremonies and rituals developed and continuously went on expanding and grew in complexity. In this stage in the performance of certain rituals more priests were needed.[187] The Vedic priests evolved an elaborate system and the performance of some rituals which took several days or months or even a year. Meticulous accuracy was strictly observed. Even the slightest mistake in observing its minutest detail would destroy the efficacy of the whole ritual. Thus the place of the priest became very important and the office of the priesthood constituted a distinct profession and it was hereditary.[188] The constant development of the rituals made them more and more complicated, which resulted in a considerable variations in the detail of the rituals.

(m) Social Condition

(1) Division of the Society: The caste system or four varnas is the backbone of the Hindu society. In the early Rigvedic period this four-fold division of the society is not traceable. Undoubtedly the Avesta mentions that the Persian society was divided on the basis of the professions.[189] In the later portion of the Rigveda the four-fold division of the society appeared. In the Rigvedic period this professional division did not come in the way of marriage between one class and the other. But in course of time the Vedic people who took pride of their race, formulated rigid rules to avoid admixture of the aborigines of India. As a result of which the caste system became very rigid disallowing intermarriage and inter-dining.

(2) Veneration of Cow: In the later portion of the Rigveda cow is regarded as sacred animal. As a matter of fact no worship of cow is traceable in the Rigveda. It is a fact that cow is aghanya 'not to be killed' is a very new conception. The tradition, especially the beef of the cow was cooked for the guest, was prevailing throughout the Rigvedic age.[190] It is also confirmed from the term for the guest, 'gogna' "killer of cow." The name of Atithigva indicates his hospitable habit of slaying cow for guests. There is no slightest reference to it that eating of meat was forbidden in the Vedic age. The great Vedic philosopher used to eat meat if it was coming from the shoulder or firm.[191] It is the Atharvaveda that recognizes fully the worship of cow and the cow as the sacred animal.[192] The Satapatha Brahmana later on advocates the doctrines of Ahansa. It warns that he who eats beef is to be born again on earth as a man of evil fame.[193] The Kausitaka Brahmana also tells the dreadful consequences of meat-eating.[194]

(3) Marriage: It is worthwhile to note that a common word for marriage is lacking in the Indo-European languages.[195] But later on marriage came to be called by a term meaning 'lordship' or 'patitva' of the husband over wife.[196] It may be inferred that during the Indo-European stage marriage had been either by capture or purchase.[197]

In the Indo-Iranian society the marriage was an indispensable and sacred custom. In the Rigveda it is regarded as an irrevocable bond. The Indo-Iranian marriage had been considerably changed. The Indo-Iranian custom did not find favour in India. The marriage between brother and sister was a usual practice among the Avestic people.[198] But the Rigveda looks down upon this practice as a sin. The dialogue between Yama and Yami mentioned in the Rigveda in connection with incestuous intercourse between them corroborates this fact more fully. In the Indo-Iranian society monogamy was the rule.[199] But later on polygamy was practiced among the men of rank. In the later portion of the Rigveda[200] the polygamy became common. The Athrvaveda shows that the men of rank had more than one wife.[201] It appears that in the post Vedic period polyandry also existed to some extent. The Maha Bharata informs that Drupadi was married to the five Pandvas. The Indo-Iranians remarried the windows. The custom of remarriage of widow survived even in the later period of the

Rigveda.[202] But later on in the later Vedic period more stringent rules were framed to forbid such marriages.

Concubinage was in vogue among the Indo-Iranians. The custom was very common in Iran. It is not traceable in the Rigveda. But it appears in the post-Vedic period in India. The later Vedic literature shows that husband was allowed to unlimited intercourses with concubines and slaves whereas the wife was bound to conjugal faithfulness on the pain of death.[203] The sexual chastity of wife had very little value. The husband could hand his wife over to a helper for generation or she could be put at the disposal of a honoured guest.[204]

We see that Indo-Aryans split from the common stock, leaving behind their cousins, moved towards south east and ultimately settled in the Punjab. On the way to their final destination they must have come across with different races and other alien cultures. In India itself they found quite different environment and they had to deal with the primitive aborigines. It is but natural that their culture must have been influenced by foreign elements. Of course, the culture which the Rigveda presents appears to be greatly changed from the Indo-Iranian culture. The Rigvedic religion and its later phase, Brahmanism, show a large number of ingredients which are most probably contributed by the primitive aborigines of India. Undoubtedly in consequence of this religious fusion the new conception, cults and even new divinities emerged out in the Rigveda. Certain old Indo-European and Indo-Iranian gods went into oblivion and certain old great gods reduced to insignificant minor position. Whereas some minor deities superseded some of the old great gods. Vishnu, who is a very minor deity in the Rigveda emerged out as a supreme god. Rudra who is later on commonly known as Siva, absorbed local gods after gods and came forward to rival Vishnu. Varuna who was the most august of the Rigvedic gods reduced to a very minor position and only waters remained in his jurisction. The younger god Indra superseded Varuna and appeared with tall personality as a national deity of the Indians. But in turn he also lost the ground in favour of Vishnu.

Moreover several local aboriginal gods crept in the Rigvedic pantheon. Phallic worship, the cult of Mother Goddess and snake worship found the place in Brahmanism. The Vedic people accepted the local popular gods of the Indian aborigines but in the Vedic colouring. So they were merged into the akin Vedic deities. The foreign cults also appeared in the Vedic religion but under the garb of Vedic appearance. This phenomenon of religious fusion is certainly the outcome of the compromise between the old religious concepts of the Aryans and the popular religious beliefs of the Indian aborigines. The Transmigration of soul is a very important development in Brahmanism which had changed considerably the religious outlook of the Vedic Aryans.

The social condition also did not remain unaffected. In consistence with the new environment the burial and the marriage customs had undergone appreciable changes. The Vedic culture admittedly borrowed certain elements of Babylonian and the Chinese cultures. Scholars are of the view that the Indian Naksatras are the contribution of China. The flood legend, Indra and Vritra myth and conceptions of soul are borrowed from the Semitic sources. But, however, Persia continued to influence the Rigvedic culture. Sorcerism, magic and the fire cult are the great Zoroastrian contributions to the Rigveda. There are certain factors at work having made caste system rigid which later on became the back-bone of the Brahmanical society.

This comparative study proves conclusively that the Rigveda is the real representative of the Aryan culture. It certainly contains very old thoughts, original feelings and primitive ideas of the Aryan people.

References

1. *Rv.* VII–18–19; VIII–54–11, 14.
2. *Rv.* III–23–4
3. Thruston, *The Madras Presidency*, pp. 124–5
4. *Rv.* I–164–46.
5. *Rv.* VII–53–1; J. Muir, *Original Sanskrit Texts*, I, p. 93.
6. *Rv.* I–64–34; N–73–10; IV–72–3; I–90–7; H.D. Grieswold, *The Religion of the Rigveda*, p. 99.
7. *Rv.* I–122–1; 1–133–1; VIII–20–17.
8. H.D. Grieswold, *The Religion of the Rigveda*, pp. 25, 98, 100, and 114, (London 1923).
9. Ibid., p. 90; E.W. Hopkins, Religions of India, p. 58.
10. Von Schrader, *Arische Religions*, Vol. I, p. 290 ff.
11. J.H. Moulton, *Early Zoroastrianism*, pp. 391–3.
12. H.D. Grieswold, loc. cit.
13. J. Muir. *OST*, Vol. V., p. 33.
14. *Von Schrader, Arische Religion*, p. 285.
15. Hillebrandt, *Vedische Mythologie*, Vol. II, pp. 38 f.
16. *Vendidad*, II–23.
17. B.G. Tilak, Arotic, *Home of the Aryans in the Vedas*, pp. 82. f.
18. A.B. Kieth, *The Religion and Philosophy of the Vedas and Upanishad*, p. 121.
19. Hopkins, *JAOS*, XIX, p. 28 ff.
20. A.C. Das, *Rigvedic India*, Vol. I, p. 390 ff.
21. Hillebrandt, Vedische Mythooloogie, pp. 9–14.
22. Cf. Rv. 1–69–3; Geldner, *Vedische Studien*, II, 22n.
23. Ludwig, Cf. Hopkins, *Religions of India*, p. 65.
24. ZDMG, XXII, p. 693.
25. Bergaigne, *La Religion Vedique*, Vol. III, pp. 117–19.
26. Cf. Hopkins, *Religions of India*, 64.
27. Hopkins, ibid., p. 63.
28. SB.XIII–3–6–5.
29. J. Muir, *Original Sanskrit Text*, Vol. V., pp. 74–76.
30. Hillebrandt, *Varuna Und Mitra*, p. 67.
31. Hopkins, op.cit., p. 71.
32. *Ia Religion Vedique*, III, p. 119.
33. *India: What Can It Teach Us*, pp. 197–200.
34. Cf. E.W. Hopkins, op.cit., p. 67.
35. AV. XX–100; Hillebrandt, *Vedische Mythologie I*, pp. 82, 131.

36. Roth, *Journal of the German Oriental Society*, VI, p. 70 f.
37. IV–42–124.
38. A.C. Das, *Rigvedic Culture*, p. 847 ff.
39. Hopkins, op. cit., p. 68.
40. Kieth, op.cit., pp. 101–2.
41. H. Oldenberg, SBE, XIVIII, pp. 241–87.
42. Keith, op. cit., p. 98.
43. TS.II–1–8–4.
44. Rv. V–81–1.
45. A. Macdonell, *Vedic Mythology*, p. 92.
46. Rv. III–12–13.
47. Rv. III–21–1. 7; VIII–1–1.
48. A.A. Macdonnell *JRAS*, XXV, p. 468; SBE, XLVI, p. 231; Oldenberg, op.cit., p. 106; J. Muir, op. cit. p.206.
49. Av. X–88–l0, Yaska Nir. VII–28.
50. Oldenberg, op.cit., pp. 132–133.
51. Rv. VII–15–2; I–60–4.
52. H. Oldenberg, ZDMG, XLII, p. 241.
53. Cf. Hopkins, op. cit. p. 125.
54. Rv. V–27; I–80–2; VIII–71–9.
55. H. Oldenberg, op. cit., p. 176.
56. A.B. Kieth, op. cit., p. 172.
57. Av. VII–8–3–4; XI–6–7.
58. A. Weber, *Naksatras*, Vol. II, p. 274 ff.
59. Hillebrandt, *Vedische Mythologie*, p. 289 .
60. Bergaigne, *la Religion Vedique*, I, p. 160.
61. *Rv.* VI–49–1.
62. *Rv.* IX–37.
63. *Rv.* IV–20–6.
64. *Rv.* IX–85–10.
65. Rv. VIII–71–8.
66. *Rv.* VI–39–3.
67. Kieth, op. cit., p. 113.
68. Roth, *ZDMG IV*, p. 424.
69. *Rv.* X–63–l.
70. *Rv.* X–30.
71. *Macdonell, JRAS*, XXVII, p. 955–56.
72. *Rv.*I–143–l.
73. *JRAS* XXV, p. 4, 14–23.
74. *Rv.* II–II–20.
75. *Av.* I–113–131, XIX–56–4.
76. *TS.* 1–8–10–2.
77. *SB.* 1–23–1–2; TS. III–2–8–10–11.
78. *Bh*–G–X–291.
79. *Rv.* I–130–2.
80. *TB.* III–6–13; MS. IV–13–8.
81. Macdonell, *Vedic Mythology*, p. 23.
82. Nir. X–31.
83. Oldenberg; op. cit., pp. 63–64.
84. *Rv.* I–35–9; I-124.
85. TB. I–64; Weber; *Omenta and Portenta*, pp. 386, 292.

86. Whitney, *Cole Brooke's Essays,* II, p. 111.
87. Spiegal, *Eranische Altermuskunde,* I, p. 5–27.
89. *Rv.* X–97–16.
90. *Rv.* X–14–10, 12.
91. Bloomfield, AJP, XI, pp. 354–55.
92. *Av.* V–30–12; XVIII–2–27; V–24–13; VS. XXXIV–13; M S. II–5–6.
93. E.W. Hopkins, op. cit. p. 80.
94. Nir XII–I.
95. *Rv.* V–73-4; 1–181–4.
96. *Yaska,* Nir. XII–2.
97. *Rv.* X–39–1.
98. *Rv.* III–29–6.
99. Perry, *JAOS,* XI, p. 119.
100. Hopkins, op. cit., 91.
101. *JRAS,* III, p. 327.
102. Benefy, *Orient Und Occident,* I, p. 48.
103. Hercules et Cacus, p. 101.
104. Rv. II–27–I.
105. Rv. II–114–3.
106. Rv. X–72–8.
107. TB. II–3–1–5.
108. J. Muir, *Original Sanskrit Texts,* IV, pp. 119–21.
109. Kieth, *Taittiriya, Samhita,* I, p. CXXVII.
110. Darmesteter, *Avesta,* French Translation.
111. *Rv.* 1–27–10; IV–3–13; VIII–61–3.
112. *VS.* XVI–18–28.
113. Arbman, op. cit. p. 29.
114. *Vs.* XXXIX–8.
115. *SB.* VI–1–3–7.
116. *SB.* VI–1–3–10.
117. *Rv.* II–33–6.
118. Rv. II–33–6; X–92–9 .
119. AGS. IV–8–28; *Arbman, Rudra,* p. 252.
120. *SB.* 1–7–3–8.
121. Kieth, op.cit., p. 148.
122. Macdonell *Vedic Mythology,* p. 73.
123. *TS.* IV–l0–l; Weber, *Die Naksatra,* II, p. 371.
124. *Rv.* X–81; X–82; X–87–2; X–170–4.
125. *Rv.* VIII–87–2; X–170-4.
126. *Vs.* XIII–6l.
127. *SB.* VIII–2–10.
128. *Rv.* IV–53–2; *Bloomfield, AJP,* XIV, p. 493.
129. Rv. X–184–1; X–169–4.
130. SB. II–2–4–1.
131. *Rv.* X–121–1
132. AV. IV–2–8; V–5–1–2.
133. Oldenberg, op. cit., p. 237.
134. *Rv.* 1–85–9; III–54–12; X–53–9.
135. *Rv.* III–4–9.
136. *VS.* XXIX–9.
137. *RV.* X–70–9; X–92–11; –98–6.

138. Carnoy, op. cit., p. 219.
139. *Rv.* VIII–35–2.
140. *SB.* III–9–1–7; AB. III–1–10.
141. Hopkins, Epic Mythology, p. 157.
142. E.H. Meyer, *Indogermanan My then*, I, p. 99 f.
143. *RV.* VIII–27–5.
144. *JAOS*, XXXVI, p. 312.
145. J. Muir, op.cit., p. 52.
146. Macdonell, op. cit., p. 12.
147. *SB.* X–4–3–9.
148. Yasna, XLVI–10–11; Yasna, XXX–9.
149. Muir's Article on Yama in the *Journal of Royal Asiatic Society*, p. 10.
150. Ibid.
151. Jacobi, *ERE*, XII, p. 434.
152. Jacobi, op. cit.
153. A.C. Dass, op.cit., p. 424.
154. Oldenberg, op.cit., pp. 553–56.
155. *RV.* IV–34–4.
156. *AV.* X–14–8–10.
157. M. Haug, loc. cit., p. 197.
158. Yas. XLVI–10–11.
159. *Transaction of the 10th Oriental Congress*, II, pp.67–73.
160. Hopkins, op.cit., p. 175.
161. *SB.* XI–2–33; Weber, ZDMG, IX, p. 238.
162. Jackson, *Transaction of the 10th Oriental Congress*, II, pp. 67–73.
163. Schermann, *Vision-literature*, pp. 152–53.
164. AB. VI–5–13.
165. Oldenberg, op. cit., pp. 541–2.
166. Taylor, *Primitive Culture*, II, p. 94.
167. *TA* X–18.
168. E.O. James, *Cult of Mother Goddess*, p. 228.
169. *TA* X–I.
170. *RV.* X–1–7.
171. Kena Up. III–25.
172. Mun. Up. I–2–4.
173. *TA* X–26–30.
174. Weber, Cf. J. Muire, *OST*, (1858), IV, p. 428 f.
175. Jacobi, ERE, Vol. V, p. 117.
176. B.K. Chattopadhyaya, *Vishvaveshranand Indological Journal*, Vol. III, Pt.1, March, 1965.
177. Khila, X–127–12.
178. RV. X–125.
179. Oldenberg, op. cit., pp. 508–9 (Berlin, 1894).
180. W. Crooke, ERE, Vol. VI, p. 688.
181. Ibid.
182. Macdonell, op. cit., p. 16 f.
183. *Rv.* 1–164–6.
184. Hopkins, op. cit., pp. 67–172 (1896).
185. W. Crooke, op. cit., p. 690.
186. A. Lang, *The Making of Religion*, Ch. IX ff, (London, 1898).
187. Kieth, op. cit., p. 480.
188. H. Zimmer, *Altindische Leben*, p. 194 seq.

189. Yasna, XIX-26–27.
190. Oldenberg, *SBE*, XLVI, p. 282.
191. Macdonell and Kieth, *Vedic Index of Names*, II, p. 145–7.
192. *AV.* XII–4–5; ZDMG, XLII, pp. 447–9.
193. *SB.* III–1–2–21.
194. *KB.* XII–3.
195. S. Fiest, *Kultur*, pp. 108 f, (Berlin, 1913).
196. H.D., Grieswold, *The Religion of the Rigveda*, p. 9, (London, 1923).
197. Ibid., p. 10.
198. W.H.R. Rivers, ERE, Vol. VIII, p. 425.
199. Herodotus, II–92.
200. *Rv.* X–85–37.
201. *AV.* I–14–44; II–61–14–17.
202. *Rv.* X–18–7.
203. W.J. Woodhouse, *ERE*, Vol. VIII, p. 445.
204. O. Schrader, op. cit., p. 97

9

Conclusion

This brief survey of the evolution of culture which took place in the most ancient times in India and Iran in its various phases under a myriad variety of conditions and an analytical study of the cultural actions and interactions and the influences which determined the growth of a civilization unit leads to some extremely interesting and useful conclusions which have, either been missed or obscured in rendering labyrinths of mutually conflicting data. Africa might have been the cradle of man but civilization grew and developed in the region which extends from Egypt, Syria and Asia Minor in the west to Central Asia and the Indus river in the east. India is, thus, geographically situated on the eastern border and Iran in the centre of this cultural region. Iran is the immediate neighbours of India on its western frontier and any cultural inspiration which came to India naturally passed through Iran, taking with it whatever influences Iran could afford to bestow upon it. Obviously since earliest phase of civilization, Indian culture was largely influenced by its Iranian counterpart.

Thus, India's close contact with Iran can be systematically traced since the Neolithic period. The archaeological evidences tend to show that the region in between India and Iran during the Neolithic and Chalcolithic periods was culturally homogeneous. The settlement at Kili-Gul-Mohammad (c. 4000 BC) shows that peasant communities of Iran migrated to India about this time and settled at different centres. Village cultures developed in Baluchistan at various sites. The archaeological finds from the Neolithic settlements at Mundigak and Nad-i-Ali confirm the constant inflow of the farmer communities from the Iranian centres, i.e., Sialk, Hissar and Giyan, to India. The Iranian typical distribution of Red and Buff wares is detectable to be persisting upto Baluchistan with same geographical context. These peasant communities penetrated even to south India where Iranian influence has been archaeologically established. For example, the culture discovered at Piklihal appears to be of Iranian origin. The black-an-red pottery, grey ware, the pottery forms such as perforated vessels and spouted and channel-spout-pots, the use of tabular basalt, and the stone working technique are conclusive evidences to relate the Southern Neolithic Culture to Shah Tepe and Hissar in Iran.

It may be noted that the Neolithic cultures which developed in northern and eastern India were not related to the cultures which developed in other parts of the land but were largely influenced by Iran. A Neolithic culture of a high order had developed in north India at Burzahom. Certain elements of this culture such as bone tools and pottery betray that Iran also shared in making up this culture. Certain typical features of the Eastern Neolithic culture set it quite apart from the Iranian influence. But black-on-red pottery and stone tools remarkably identical to the copper weapons discovered in the Gangetic basin indicate Iranian diffusionary impulses whether directly or indirectly.

The Baluch cultures because of their proximity were most susceptible to the Iranian cultural influence. During Neolithic period these village cultures exhibit deep impact of Iranian cultures. The Iranian influence appears to be the greatest and the most intensive in the Kulli branch of the Baluch cultures. Kulli was most probably situated on the southern route from Iran to India which was most possibly the easiest inroad of inter-communication and consequently of cultural influence.

These Baluch cultures contributed largely to shape the Harappan culture, which they preceded by at least a millennium. The Iranian influence on the Harappan culture is perceptible in painted pottery, stamp seals, comb motifs, step pattern, spear-head, flate axe, jewellery, several tools and other items of domestic usage. A large number of appliances, tools and other objects also show the diffusionary impulses which were introduced from Iran. It is fairly certain that the Indus religion centres round the cult of Mother Goddess. It is also admitted that cult was already firmly established in the peripheral regions of Ancient Iran. Iran by virtue of its geographical position being placed in the very heart of the cradle land of the agricultural civilization of the Western Asia, did not fail to make its contribution to the development and diffusion of Goddess cult in the Harappan culture. The archaeological finds discovered from various cemeteries situated in between Iran and India tend to show that the Harappan funerary practices, the complete and fractional burials have been introduced to the Harappan culture by people migrating from Iran. In fact, an intensive study of the Indus religion, seals, ceramics and other distinctive aspects of culture shows that Sumer was not the author of the Indus culture and it was the Iranian influence which played a decisive role in its formation. There has been widespread confusion over this matter. The recent discoveries in the borderland in India and Iran have shown with positive affirmation that prototypes of civilization traveled from Iran to India where it further developed in its Indianised version. Thus the fact that the Indus culture developed indigenously can hardly be doubted but its essential roots were laid in the village culture of

Baluchistan which were Iranian in origin. It is this way that the Harappan culture owes to the Iranian influence. It may be noted that the Sumerian culture even at its agricultural level was urban, i.e., city based while the Iranian culture was largely village based. The same pattern of agricultural life, based on the pattern of villages not on cities is met with in the Harappan culture which thus shows that it was from Iran and not from Sumer that the Harappan life was inspired.

Cultural relation between Iran and India were renewed from time to time under new surges, stresses and impulses. New cultural relations developed between the two regions after the disappearance of the Harappan culture. It looks strange and extra-ordinary that the indigenous Harappan culture little influenced the growth and development of various succeeding cultures of India of the Chalcolithic period. On the other hand, they were again, influenced from Iran. The black-on-red pottery is a sure link between the post-Harappan Chalcolithic India and Iran. For example, the Banas culture, which flourished at Ahar and Gilund in Rajasthan, shows strong Iranian influence. The pedestalled grey-ware-bowls, the unique chandelier-like dish-on-stand, animal handled lid, a bowl-on-stand in burnished grey ware with the hollow type of stand unearthed at Ahar show remarkable points of resemblance with the pots from Hissar and Shah Tepe in Iran. Gilund is also closely linked to Iran by its typical pottery such as the dish-on-stand in the black-on-red and red were, the high necked jar, the basin with cut-spout in the red ware, the lipped basin and vase with strap handle in the burnished grey ware. Likewise, Iranian influence is abundantly noticeable at Navdatoli, Maheshwar, in the central Indian Chalcolithic culture. The finds at Navdatoli exhibit an unambiguous Iranian influence. The narrow-necked vessel with dish-like top, round bowls decorated with hallow-circle filled with dots, pedestalled champagne, channel and pinched spouted bowls, low and high footed bowls and goblets, the pedestalled-bowls and the channel-spouted bowls and the geometric patterns such as birds, animals and the dancing human figure on a white slipped pottery discovered at Navdatoli display an extremely deep impact of the culture of Sialk, Hissar and Giyan. Certain finds from Maheswar also mark the incontrovertible Iranian influence. Similarly in the Northern Deccan Chalcolithic cultures laid bare at the sites of Daimabad, Chandoli and Prakash show close association with Iran. It appears that old Iranian site Sialk largely shaped the cultures at Daimabad and Prakash. The culture discovered at Daimabad exposes extremely extensive Iranian influence. A remarkable style, depicting animals with elongated and hatched bodies on a white slipped ware as noticed on the pottery of Prakash is definitely the characteristic feature of the Sialk ware. Certain tools such as chisel, adzes, pockers, and flat axes, with slightly tapering sides and straight convex or flaring edges link the two cultures even more closely. Similar cultural phenomenon seems to have been at Prakash. The painted pottery of Prakash bearing the designs like the spotted tiger with its neck turned back and crane like-bird among reeds and bushes indicates conclusively extremely deep impact of Sialk. Cups or bowls with high multi-legged stands show similar cultural connection between Chandoli and Giyan. Particularly the pottery of the Neolithic-Chalcolithic settlements of the Deccan discovered at Brahmgiri, Maski, Piklihal and Sangan Kallu betray strong Iranian influence. Iranian diffusionary impulses are undoubtedly felt at Piklihal and Brahmgiri. The characteristic cups or bowls of Giyan having ringed or footed bases with high multi-egged stands reappear at these settlements. The legged stands; the perforated or the handled pots, the bell-shaped jars with flaring rims, potting technique and the grey ware complex of Iran show a remarkable close association between the Indian settlements at Brahmgiri, Maski, Sangan Kallu and Piklihal and with the Iranian culture of Sialk, Giyan and Tepe Hissar.

Among various reasons assigned to the disappearance of the Indus valley civilization, the invasion of the Aryan from the north-west appears to be the most convincing. They were essentially a pastoral-agricultural community with swift horses, well-built bodies and fair complexion and their own peculiar religious beliefs in the natural phenomena. The controversy as to their original home has been widely debated. National bias and prejudice have made this matter most complicated. It looks fairly certain, however, that originally they lived somewhere in the region between the Pamirs and the Hindukush. Thence they migrated gradually to Europe and Iran. They lived together in Iran for a considerable period of time which has been extended to half a millennium or even more. Thereafter a branch of this stock migrated to India where it destroyed cities, conquered aboriginal people and settled there.

A comparative study of the socio-religious beliefs and practices of the various Aryan branches made in the fore-going pages tends to show that these beliefs were mostly or in majority quite identical in form and spirit. As for example, conception of sky god, the sun god, the moon god, the legends associated with the thunder-god, the fire-god, the twin 'Horsemen' and the mythical first man are found preserved in the original form in the various Aryan branches. Undoubtedly the god of heaven was the highest creation of the Indo-Europeans. The conception of father of the heavenly ones is the oldest notion and was exclusively and closely associated with this god. The very name of this god in the various branches, viz., The Vedic Dyaus pitar, the Greek Zeus pater or the Roman Diespiter or Jupiter betrays that the conception of paternity is essentially connected with him. The position which this god possessed in hierarchy of various Aryan branches makes it fairly certain that his worship was real kernel of the primitive Aryan religion. Later on he was dethroned. A myth hints this eventual development. The Greek Cronus slew his father Uranus. Similarly the Vedic Indra holding his father Dyaus by his feet crushed him and became supreme at his expanse.

Several myths connected with the storm god are found well preserved in many Aryan nations. For example, in order to release the pent up water the Vedic thunder god, Indra slays Vritra, the Avestic Tishtriya, the Apaosa; the Greek, Appolo, the Python; the Teutonic Donar, the Wolf Fernis; and the Hittite Inaras, the dragon Illuyunkas. Another myth illustrates the fight of Indra with Visvarupa; of the Avestic Verethraghna with Azi Dhaka; of the Greek Herakle with Geryones and of the Romon Hercules with Cacus. The detail of this myth is remarkably identical in every version. Indra liberates cows from the avaricious who imprisoned them. Similarly Hercules carries the cattle from the monster who has stolen from the hero and hidden them in a cave. Moreover Visvarupa, Geryones, Cacus and Azi Dahaka, the adversaries of Indra, Herakle, Hercules and Verethraghna, all are three-headed or many headed. The myth associated with the "Twin Horsemen" is the best preserved Indo-European myth Even the elements of this myth are same in every mythology. The Vedic Asvins married Surya and the Lithuanian "Sons of God", Sun Maiden. Another love-affair of Surya crossed this relation, the Lithuanian legend narrates similar event and in both cases the moon is involved. The Greek Dioscuri also coincides exactly with these gods. In each case these gods are twins, and Sons of God, they help is need, and show connection with horses. The Vedic Manu the Teutonic Mannus, the Greek Minos and the Roman Janus as a mythological human progenitor disclose remarkable coincidences.

The social customs especially marriage ceremony and initiation rite also present several points of resemblances. The primitive Aryans used witch-craft and sorcery for prosperity, for love affair and for personal jealousy and to cure diseases. It is interesting to note that certain Atharvavedic spells surprisingly agree ad verbatom with the magic formulas current in the Scottish Highlands and elsewhere throughout Europe. It is more than strnage that several marriage ceremonies are found in every Aryan nation with entirely identical characteristics. In the Vedic Sapta padigamana, bride-groom taking the bride by hand takes round the fire, a new jug filled with water remains on the floor on the right side of them. The Romans also observed the marriage ceremony before fire altar in the presence of water. This is why the Roman marriage is designated as union "eque et igni." The Roman dextrarum junctis is remarkably parallel to the Indian Panigrahana in which right hand of bride is placed in the right hand of bridegroom. Another ceremony of the Indian marriage commonly known as Iajabarsana is prevalent in its identical form in Europe; in which the bridal pair shower the fried rice over each other.

It shows that in spite of the passage of time and pressure of remodelling of ideas, certain fundamental concepts and beliefs which were commonly shared, persisted in the mind of the Aryan people placed in different physical and cultural environments. A large number of these elements of the primitive Aryan culture were preserved by the Indo-Iranian branch. This is most particularly noticed in the Rigveda which most invariably contains such socio-religious concepts and beliefs of the common heritage. It masterly enumerates the original thoughts, feelings and aspirations of the primitive Aryans. The Rigveda, as a matter of fact, is the source book of the Aryan culture and stands to the same importance in the Aryan world as the Quran in the Islam.

A linguistic survey also brings about same extremely interesting readings. Intellectually the primitive Aryans were highly advanced. Their language, i.e., the Indo-European had the capacity to express the most abstract thoughts. With the help of inflection the crudest idea was expressed admirably. The Rigveda, the Avesta and the Illiad show that this language had already developed a beautiful meter system. With tribal migrations a linguistic branching off also took place. The Indo-Iranian became the most important off-spring of the Indo-European thoughts, it had link in one way or the other with other Indo-European languages of which the Greek is nearest to it. It is strange that Greek which has very little affinity with languages of its own group shows close relationship with Indo-Iranian. As for example, in the sphere of conjugation Greek and Indo-Iranian present a considerable number of points of coincidences. Another striking similarity is that both eliminate the rendering of medio passive.

Indo-Iranian also branched off into two distinct languages, viz., Sanskrit and Avesta a study of which shows that these two languages are closely related to each other in syntax, vocabulary, diction and general poetic style so much so that by mere change of phonetic laws the whole Rigvedic mantras may be translated word for word into the Avestic so as to produces verses correct in form and spirit.

But by virtue of being placed in different environments and in contact with alien cultures Sanskrit and Avesta both made a considerable innovations. Certain phonetic changes such as differentiation of 's and h,' l and r,' 'h and z' 'd and zd' and 'j and z' and elimination of aspiration in Avesta brought about forms of two languages quite distinct.

A comparison of Sanskrit with other Indo-European languages again shows that Sanskrit occupies a unique position among these languages. It has in its possession a granary of the primitive Indo-European words and roots with their original meanings. Sanskrit preserved the old phonetic system to a great extent. The sonant aspirates (bh, dh, gh), sonant nasal (m, n) and sonant liquids (r, l) are found preserved in Sanskrit only. Greek is very closely associated with Sanskrit in the field of conjugation. Germanic, Celtic and Italian have close link to Sanskrit. There are a large number of common words in these languages and Sanskrit. These words do not occur in any other Indo-European languages which shows that only Sanskrit is intimately related to these Indo-European languages but also confirms the fact that Sanskrit occupies the central position in this group and it might have been the source of other languages.

Later on, Sanskrit absorbed foreign elements besides, it showed its contact with the Munda and the Dravidian languages. It innovated the cerebral series, t, th, d, dh, ns which is entirely absent in all other Indo-European languages.

The Indo-Iranians inherited the largest share from the common heirloom and preserved it; they lived together in their second home for a long time and developed a distinct culture. Because of their unique advanced state of culture they designated themselves as 'Arya' (noble, cultured).

Over and above the religious beliefs they had inherited, the Indo-Iranians also created their own conceptions, e.g., rta, as is testified by the Tel-el-Amarna tablets about the 2nd millennium B.C. it was an extremely sublime conception, the like of which was beyond the reach of any other people. They also elaborated the systems of worship, ritual and ceremonies; their gods were though still associated with natural phenomena, ethical attributes were also attached to them. The Indo-Iranian religion in essence marks the beginning of the creation of abstract deities which could have been the Semitic contribution to its growth.

The Indo-Iranians developed two new cults in their religion, viz., the fire cult and the Soma cult. Both are specific Indo-Iranian innovations. Fire gradually assumed such a sacred place in the ritualistic hierarchy that no worship could be deemed to have been done without it. The Soma cult developed presumably by the discovery of Soma plant in the region which they inhibited. Both the Rigveda and the Avesta attach great importance to these two cults.

The Indo-Iranians were not satisfied with the vague and primitive conception of their forefather regarding the origin of the human race; they developed it into the more illustrative myth of Yama and Yami which could be paralleled to the Semitic myth of human progeny, (i.e., of Adam and Eve). The Semitic influence, as it seems, also filtered in other thoughts. The Indra and Vrtra myth had been formed for example, from the prevalent material of the Semitic creation myth. Similarly the idea of a bridge or stream which soul crosses is a Semitic conception. The concept of Heaven and Hell is also identical to the Semitic belief. These conceptions are not met with in the earlier portions of the Rigveda, only the later Sanhitas allude to them. This shows that the germs were already there in embryoic form and came to India from Iran.

It is noticeable that the Zoroastrianism and the Rigvedic religions are undoubtedly the off-shoots of one common source but as they attained the distinct separate entities they became diametrically opposite to each other. There are many parallels but equally are the contrasts in detail they diverge so widely that it is always questionable whether a coincidence of ritual or belief be accidental or imply historical connection. The Iranians never offered anything in the fire as the Vedic people did, but showed to it. In contrast to the Rigvedic religion they denounced the nature worship. As opposed to the Vedic polytheism Zoroastrianism is the monotheistic. As a matter of fact this wide gulf in the religious outlook of the two allied people had been brought about by the Iranian prophet, Zoroaster who bequeathed upon the primitive Iranian religion a quite new spirit.

The Indo-Aryans split from the common stock and leaving behind their cousins they moved into India and ultimately settled in the Punjab. It was a long-drawn process and they passed through several alien cultures. In India itself they found themselves given up to a different physical and cultural environment. Particularly as far as the available data affirms, the vanquished people were far more civilized and the Indo-Aryan culture which developed after their permanent settlement in India was largely influenced by the indigenous culture. The Rigvedic religion and its later phase, Brahmanism present considerable ingredients which were most probably contributed by the primitive aborigines of India. It is the result of the religious fusion that new concepts, cults and even new divinities emerged out in the Rigveda. Certain old Indo-European or Indo-Iranian gods lost their original importance and other minor deities superseded them. Vishnu, who is a very minor deity in the Rigveda emerged out as a supreme god. Varuna who was the most august of the Rigvedic gods reduced to a very minor position and only waters remained in his jurisdiction. The younger god, Indra superseded Varuna and appeared with tall personality as a national deity of the India. But in turn he also met the same fate and left the ground in favour of Vishnu. Moreover several local aboriginal gods crept in the Rigvedic pantheon.

Under the new influences, phallic worship, Mother Goddess cult and snake worship found a place in the Brahmanism. The Transmigration of soul is a very important development in Brahmanism which had considerably changed the religious outlook of the Vedic Aryans. The Rigveda which was compiled in India presents the religion advancing into Brahmanism which in turn developed into the Hindusim in the later Vedic period.

Sorcerism and magic are great Zoroastrian contributions to the Rigvedic religion. It may be noted that the Vedic people preserved the old cults and conceptions more faithfully than any other Indo-European branch. This conservative tendency of the Vedic people is the main factor to distinguish it from the Zoroastrianism. While the Iranians gave up worship of several old gods and evolved new gods and cults in keeping with the new spirit of their faith, the Vedic people adhered to their old conceptions and continued to retain their old faiths and beliefs. This conservative tendency of the Vedic people played a very important role in the development of the Rigvedic religion. Many Indo-European gods who had receded into background in the Indo-Iranian religion reappeared in the Vedic pantheon with the old dignity. At the same time, the Vedic people liberally accepted the popular gods of Indian aborigines, in their own way, each one being given a specific place in the hierarchy. The new cults and gods thus evolved were the outcome of the compromise between the old religious concepts of the Indo-Aryans and the popular religious beliefs of the people they had conquered. This is adequately borne out by the Rigvedic evidence. The Vedic people accepted the local popular gods of the Indian aborigines but in the Vedic colouring. So they were merged into the akin Vedic deities. The foreign cults also appeared in the Vedic religion but under the garb of the Vedic appearance. Rudra was more susceptible to the foreign influence. Undoubtedly the Rigvedic Rudra is extremely different from the composite figure of the Yajurvedic Rudra. No doubt he absorbed so many foreign elements in his character. The snake cult, phallic worship, vegetation spirit, mountain deity and even a god of the dead were merged with the cult of this god. His numerous names such as Sarva, Bhava, Pasupati, Siva, Ugra, Asani, Isvara and Mahadeva betray that Rudra absorbed local gods after gods and emerged out in the later Vedic period with a tall personality to rival Vishnu. This phenomenon of religion fusion is certainly the outcome of the compromise between the old religious concepts of the Aryan and the popular religious beliefs of the Indian aborigines.

Thus the two cultures of the same stock evolved into different environments. Howsoever did they differ in details they retained the fundamentals upon which rested the whole structure. More important than this is the fact that even after separation they maintained a close contact and India came even closer to Iran during the Rigvedic period. Thus the cultures of the two countries are distinct by their face value only; they are similar if not the same in spirit and in essence. During this period, the history of one country is so intractably associated with that of the other that the history of one is not intelligible without the other.

Appendix

The Original Home of the Aryans: Various Theories

The galaxy of scholars champion the cause for the original home of the Aryans in India. They have based their theories not exclusively on prejudice. Schlegal asserts the high antiquity of Sanskrit and its linguistic purity and holds that the parent language itself originated in India and spread thence westward.[1] The divine and personal name discovered from cuneiform inscription in Asia Minor which are the oldest actual specimens, are generally taken to be Indian. It leads Jacobi[2] and Konow[3] to believe in India, as the original home of the Aryan and thence a body of Sanskrit speaking people emerged in Mesopotamia. Darmesteter[4] indirectly refers to the original home localizing in India. He strongly believes that the Vedic gods and rites were borrowed from the Indians who came to Iran from the Punjab during 1500 BC. The Indologists have a strong weapon in favour of Indian home for the Aryans. H.K. Bhattacharya,[5] A.C. Das,[6] and Ganganath Jha,[7] L.D. Kalla, D.R. Bhandarkar,[8] D.S. Triveda and K.M. Munshi[9] argue that the Rigveda preserves no memory of the Aryan home outside of India and moreover presents the geographical background of north west India. On the other hand T.N. Ramchandaran,[10] A.D. Pushalkar,[11] K.N. Shastri,[12] Swami Sankara nand[13] and Dr. B. Praksh[14] plead that the authors of the Indus culture were the Aryans.

T.R. Ramchandran[15] has remarkably paralleled many pictures conjured up by certain Indus seals with the Rigvedic passages. S.D. Giyani[16] has propounded the theory of coexistence between the Harappans and the Aryans in Sapta Sindu.

Following Jacobi's interpretation of the Mitanni names, Pargitar[17] who locates the original home of the Aryans in Tibet, believes that the Aryans went to Asia Minor from India to carve out their colonies there. He does not rely too much on the Brahmanic traditions but appeals to the Kshatriya traditions that lead him to the view that the Aryans, prior to the composition of Rigveda entered

India through the central Himalayas.[18]

Meyer[19] gives all credit to the Pamirs to be the Aryan urheimat. The main force of his argument is the similarity of the Aryan mode of burial to that of Mongols[20]. The discovery of Tocharian in the Tarim basin lends further support to his view.

The Avestic evidence referring to 'Airyanam Vaejanh' an Aryan homeland, leads the scholars to pinpoint the origin of the Aryans in Iran. For the Iranian hypothesis Pott, Renan, Mommsen and Picket take this evidence as an impeachable truth.[21] Moret asserts that the Aryans migrated from Bactria to Iran.[22] Harzfeld identifies Airanvej with the valleys of the Oxus and Jaxartes.[23] Sergi holds that the new stone Age in Europe was ushered by the advent of brachycephals.

He recognizes the ancestors of the European Aryans a brachycephalic stock originally inhabiting the region to the north of the Hindu Kush.[24] Prof. Rostovtseff[25] also champions the cause of the Iranian hypothesis. He tells that Scyth and Cimmerians migrated from Iran to Europe and other parts.[26]

Harshe holds Altai mountain, 'Mount Meru' of Indian mythology and the region juxaposition the cradle land of Aryan. Schmidt[27] and Dandekar[28] are also inclined to extend the Aryan home to the Altai mountains.

J. de. Morgan[29] asserts that Siberia was habitable when Europe was under the spell of Ice Age. He is of opinion that the Aryans originally lived in Siberia and their second home was Central Asia , later on centum group moved to Europe and satem group to Iran.

The astronomical evidences that the Rigveda renders convince Tilak[30] to believe strongly that the Arctic region was the Aryan home.

With the Help of linguistic paleontology a group of the scholars reconstructs the environment of the still undivided Aryans and conjures up the image of their socio-religions culture. They are arrived at the conclusion that the Central Asia is the home land of Aryan.

Charpentier puts[31] it in the plains of Turkestan, the fauna and flora (the grasslands, the birch, willow and fir tree, the horses, sheep and cows) of which are inconsistence with the comparative paleontology, Hubert[32] holds the same views. Schmidt[33] who is convinced that Turkestan marked the Aryan home states that Indo-European adopted horse here and moved to Europe in three waves (bringing horse as (i) the animal for food (ii) the animal to drive chariot (iii) the animal of riding) Marija Gimbutas who is of the view that the Aryan home lay in the region stretching from Uzbekistan and Kazakhstan to the Altai mountains identifies the Aryans with the authors of the Kurgan culture that developed there.[34] She asserts that the primitive words of the reconstructed Indo-European offer surprising correspondence to the mode of disposal of dead, horse sacrifice sun symbolism, stock breeding the farming social structure and pattern of habitation that kurgan culture presents.[35] Impressed with the same feelings H. Peaks and M.J. Fleure extend it from South Russia to the Central Asian steppes.[36] Eickstedt thinks that it lay in Kazakhistan.[37] Brand Stein believes that the comparative semasiology of the Aryan languages reflects the Aryan home localizing in the steppe land at the foot of mountain range which can, in no way, be other than the Khirghiz steppes.[38] In the light of Tocharian which, he says, presents most archaic character of the Indo-Europeans. Benveniste locates the Aryans home in the tract from South East of Russia to the Kirghiz Steppes.[39] The same view is espoused by Dandekar[40] who accepts it second *home* whence the Iranian branched off from Mitanni and Indo-Aryans. Heine Geldern[41] conceives that the Trunnion-celt, the antennai sword, harphoon, the axe-adze with shaft-hole, copper forks, dagger and spear-heads, copper pins and double-animal-headed-protons belonged to the Aryans. On the basis of these finds he thinks that the region from the Caspian upto Anau marked the presence of the Aryans since 1500 BC.

A.H. Sayce[42] locates the Aryan cradle in Asia Minor. He has deducted the view from the presence of both Satem and Centum languages on the fringe of Anatolian plateau.[43] Dr. Christian shows the presence of the Aryans in Asia Minor in the third millennium.[44] Feist[45] is another champion of Asia Minor hypothesis. He asserts that the Germans who were originally non-Indo-European were subsequently Aryanized by the diverse influence. Certain finds in the Indo-Iranian borderland constrain A. Stein to trace Aryan migration from Anatolia.[46]

E. Forrer claims that Kanesic (Hittite) presents the most archaic character of the Indo-Europeans and is simpler in construction, hence ancestral home of Aryan lay there.[47] E. Horrowitz is of the opinion that Indo-Iranian dwelt in Balkh and Babel.[48]

The other group of the scholars put the Aryan cradle land in Europe. Their arguments center round three points: (i) the multiplicity of Aryan languages in Europe (ii) the most archaic character of Lithuanian (iii) the linguistic palaeontology.

Greenland was the Aryan ancestral home is the view of Strzygovski.[49] T.J. Endelbrecht tells that the end of the Stone age witnessed the use of horse and chariot in the Swedish Coasts. They are closely associated with the Aryans, Hence no other than Swedish Coastal region has better claim to be the home of the Aryans.[50]

The home land in North Europe was, once, a most attractive theory, C. Panka[51] followed by K.F. Wolff[52] considers the Aryan homeland in Scandinavis. In support of his theory Panka at once appeals to history, anthropology and philology. He states that no foreign conquest is traceable in Scandinavian history from the pre-Neolithic times to the retreat of glaciers. Anthropologically Penka identifies the Aryans with the blondex Dolichocephalic people of fair complexion and blue eyes who are detectable inhabiting from, earliest times in the North Europe.[53] Maintaining that the blonde race was "ever conquering and never conquered." he discovers by the blood of blonde race that dispersed from Scandinavia running in the Achaean[54] hero, the Vedic Aryans,[55] the Kurds and the Galchas[56] of Iran, the Mitannian chiefs[57] and the people of the Central Asia.[58] Linguistically Penka gallantly claims that Teutotonic preserved the original Aryan phonetic system in a purer from.[59]

A profound disciple of Penka, Pro. G. Kossinna supports N. European theory but tends to dispense with the support of linguistic paleontology which is a great pitfall in the Penka's theory. With a profound mastery of the archaeological material Kossinna.[60] locates Aryan urheimat in Scandinavia, Denmark and N. Germany. He conceives that the Aryans represent Nordic race that is a product of the brachycepals of Dobbertin and Dolichocephals of Ellerbeck and the Germans are their direct descendents.[61] H. Hirt[62] agrees with Kossinna that archaic character of the Lighuanian and the close link of Ugro-Finn language to the Indo-European are sure guide to pinpoint the Aryan origin but he extends it from Germany to E. Europe. Sprockhoff,[63] who supports the Kossinna's views that Megalithic Nordic culture reflects the image of Aryan, also extends the homeland to east and west of Germany.

Meillet[64] according to whom the Aryans do not stand for race believes that primitive Indo-European originated in N. Europe. Kreschmer[65] is of the view that the Indo-European already branched off into two groups during Neolithic period; one branch moved to the central Germany and the other to the Central Europe where they produced corded and striped potteries.

Some scholars gives credit to the Central Europe for Aryan homeland. Dr. Giles[66] brilliantly champions the claim for it in the country now called Hungary, Austria and Bohemia. He believes that the Danubian culture is the creation of the Aryans or his wiros". He states that the linguistic paleontology reflects the prominence of agriculture and swine breeding, hence the primitive Aryan culture really corresponds very satisfactorily to the Danubian manner of life.[67]

E. de Michelis [5] bases his theory on a distribution of a cultural peculiarities which harmonize exceptionally well with the distribution of the Aryan languages. He observes the change to cremation in the Danube valley and the same is detectable in Italy, France, Spain, Greece, North Europe, Asia Minor and India. De Michelis believes that the spread of new rite was due to the Aryan migration setting out from Hungry.

De Lapouge[69] holds that Aryans represent Nordic race but he puts that area of characterization of the Nordic Aryan branch in Hungary..Krahe[70] Bosch[71] Gimpera and Pittioni[72] support the Central European hypothesis.

The eastern Europe is also referred to being a claimant for the Aryan homeland .The scholars like Garasanin[73] and Whatmough[74] are of the opinion that the Aryan urheimat lay in Balkan.Antoneiwicz[75] puts it in Ukraine but Pokorny[76] extends it further east up to White Russia .

The theory that is taken to be well documented and that has attracted the minds of a large number of people is the South Russian home. The credit goes to Nehring[77] who first of all proposed the Aryan origin in the south Russia; subsequently it reckoned with strong support from the prominent scholars .Schachermeyr asserts that the Aryans are traceable in the south Russia even in Paleolithic period.[78] Among others Hawkes,[79] R..Hauschild[80], Smith ,Grierson,[13] Brjussow and Trager share the view that the Aryan cradle lay in South Russia. O. Schrader insists on the climate and physiographical, features of South Russia harmonize a remarkable degree with the Aryan cradle as deduced by linguistic palaeontology.[81] Myres[82] and Cornoy[83] entertain the same view. Myres, Haddon[84] and Peake[85] identify the Neolithic people of Kurgan culture in the South Russia with the Aryans without qualification. V.G. Childe[86] and Peake appeal to archaeology and the ochre sepulchers of the South Russia that afford invaluable material to buttress their theory. Childe believes that the people here interned are generally tall, dolichocephalic, Orthognathic and lept or Hine, in a world nordice.[87] He discovers the genesis of the perforated battle-axe, a characteristic attribute and symbol of the Aryans or the Nordic cultures in South Russia.[88] With the help of the archaeological data Childe satisfactorily accounts for contract between undivided Aryans and the Sumero-Akkadians.[89] T. Burrow[90] holds that the home of Finno-Ugrian and the location of Tocharian is the decisive factor to pinpoint the Aryan urheimat in the South Russia. B.K. Ghosh[91] agrees with Nehring and Scharader puts forth his argument that the Aryan home should be some what equidistant between Hither Asia and North West India.

This survey reveals that problem has been dealt with from different angles both inductively and deductively, with the result that the numerous theories have cropped up. It reflects that till today this controversy has not died down on the original home of the Aryans which has been tossed about over a vast tract extending from India and Asia Minor to Arctic ocean and from Scandinavia to Tarim Basin. It must be admitted that every theory has its own merit and demerit. It is also to be honestly accepted that the both continents Asia and Europe present equally strong evidences for the possible home, which bring some scholars to the conclusion that the original home of the Aryans was a large tract falling within the two continent P. Kretschmer[92] claims that it was a narrow strip of land extending from France over middle Europe and the Kirghese steppes to Iran, B. Symons[93] and R. Meringer[94] support it strongly. The same idea perhaps forces Dr. Griswold[95] to believe that the Aryans who were pastoral nomadic, possibly might have roamed over the great "grassy plain" of the Central Asia and Europe.

References

1. Ueber die Sprache and Weisheit der Inder, 1808.
2. Jacobi, *JARS*, pp. 121f (London, 1909).

3. S. Konow, The Indian Gods of Mitanni, Publications of the Christiania Indian Institute, No.1
4. Darmesteter, *SBE*, The Zend Avesta, Vol. I, Introduction.
5. H.K. Bhattacharya, Indian History Congress, Delhi, 24th Session 1961, pp. 6–7.
6. A.C. Das, Rigvedic India, 2nd edition, p. XIII.
7. Ganganath Jha, Aryan Invasion of India: Is it a myth?
8. D.R. Bhandarkar, Some Aspects of Ancient Indian Culture, p. 6
9. The Glory that was Gurjaradesa, Vol. I, pp. 46f.
10. T.N. Ramchandran, Presidential Address to section I of the Indian History Congress, 19th Session, Agra, 1956, pp. 7f.
11. A.D. Pushalkar, The Vedic Age, pp. 194f.
12. 12. K., N. Shastri, New Light on the Indus Civilization, pp. 12–13.
13. Swami Shankarananda, "Mythological Aryans," Indian History Congress, Delhi, 1961, 224th Session, p. 7.
14. Dr. B. Prakash, Rigveda and the Indus Valley Civilization.
15. T.N. Ramchandran, op. cit. pp 7–16.
16. S.D. Giyani, cf. New Light on the Aryan Civilization, op. cit. p–6.
17. F.E. Pargitar, Ancian Indian Traditions, Chapter–1.
18. Ibid.
19. E. Meyer, Geschichte des Altertums, p. 35.
20. Ibid, p. 569.
21. Cf. V.G. Childe, p. 95.
22. A. Moret, From Tribe to Empire, part II, Chap.III.
23. E. Herzfeld Iran in the Ancient East, pp. 191–192.
24. E.G. Syria, IV, pp. 28f.
25. Rostavtseff, The Iranian and Greeks in South Russia (Oxford, 1922) pp. 122 ff.
26. R. G. Harshe, 'Mount Meru' The home land of the Aryans' Vishveshvaranand Indological Journal II (1964) pp. 134.61.
27. W. Schmidt, Rassen and Volker in vorgeschichte and Geschichte des Abendiandes, Vol. I, pp. 274–75.
28. R.N. Dandekar, 'The Antecedents and the Early beginnings of Vedic Period, Proceedings of the Indian History Congress tenth session, Bombay, p., 40.
29. J. De Morgan, Prehistoric Orientals, pp. 172 ff.
30. B.G. Tilak, Arctic Home in the Vedas, pp. 58–60, 453–55.
31. J. Charpentier, The Original Home of Indo-European, Bu. Sch. Or. St., IV, 1936, p. 164.
32. H. Pubert, les Celtes, Paris, 1950.
33. W. Schmidt, Op. cit.
34. Marija Gimbutas, The Prehistory of Eastern Europe: 1 Masolithic, Neolithic and Copper Age culture in Russia and the Baltic Area, Harvard University Bulletin No. 30 Combridge, Moss, 1956.
35. Marija Gimbutas, 'The Indo-Europeans: Archaeological Problems, American Anthropologist, Vol, LXV, No. 4, p. 27. (1963).
36. H. Peake and H.J. Fleure, The Steppes and the Sown.
37. Cf. B. Prakash, op. cit., pp. 131–32.
38. Brandestein, Die erste indogermanische Wanderung (Vienna, 1938; Studien Zur Indogermanische Crundsprache (Vienna, 1952) pp. 23–25.
39. E. Benveniste, "Tokharian et Indo-European" 'Festschrift H. Hirt (Heidelberg, 1936) II, pp. 227–40.
40. R.N. Dandekar, op. cit.
41. Heina Goldern, op. cit. 1936 p. 109; 1956, p. 136–39.
42. A.H. Sayce, The Early Home of Sanskrit, Modi Memorial Volume, pp 68 f.
43. A.H. Sayce, Ramsay studies, p. 393.

44. Dr. Christian, M.A.G.W., LV, p.189.
45. S. Feist, Indogermanen and Germanen (Halle, 1914) pp. 77 et seg Ia question du pays d' origine des Indo–Europeans Scientia (1913), pp. 304–13.
46. A. Stein, The Indo–Iranian Border lands, Their Prehistory in the light of Geography and the recent Explorations, J.R.A.I., 1934, pp. 179–202.
47. E. Forrer, Die acht Sprachen der Boghzkoi–Inschriften, (Berlin, 1919).
48. E. Horowitz, The ARYAN origins , Modi Memorial Volume, pp.16ff.
49. Strzygovski, Hirt Festschrift, 1, p.174.
50. T. H. Engelbrecht, Die Urheimate der Indo-Germanen,Glueckstadt,1933.
51. C. Penka, op. cit., p. 56.
52. K. F. Wolff., Amman Fest gable, Innsbruecker Beitragezur Kulturavessenschaft, Bd.2, 1954, p.191
53. C. Penka, op. cit., p.6.
54. D. Iapouge, L' Aryan, pp. 187 ff.
55. Cf. V.,G. Childe, The Aryans, pp. 159–60.
56. de Ujfalvy, L' Anthropologel (1900, Paris), pp. 23-56 and 193–234.
57. Von Luschen, J.R.A.I., Vol. XLI, pp. 242–43.
58. S. Feist, Kuitur, Ausbreitung and Herkunft der Indogermanen (Berlin, 1913) p. 498.
59. Penka, op. cit.
60. G. Kossinna, Die Indo-Germanen.
61. G. Kossinna, Ursprung and Verberitung der Germanen in Vor-und Fruhfschichtliche Zeit (Leipzing, 1934).
62. H. Hirt, Indo-Germanische Grammatik.
63. E. Sprockhoff, Zur Entstchung Der Germanen, Fests chrift Hirt (Hiedelberg, 1936) pp. 255–74.
64. A. Meillet, Apercudune historie de la langrecque, (2nd ed., 1920) pp. 8–9.
65. P. Kretschmer, Die Vorgriechischen Sprach and Volksschieten, Glota, XXVIII (1940) pp. 84–218.
66. P. Giles, The Aryans, CHI, Vol. I, p.6.
67. Ibid, pp. 66–70.
68. E. de Michelis, L' Origine degli Indo-Europi, esp. cap. IX (1903).
69. De Lapouge , L' Aryan, 1899.
70. H. Krahe, Indogermanisch and Aiteuropaisch, saeculum, VIII (1957), pp. 1–16.
71. P. Bosh-Gompera, Les Indo-European: Problems Archaeologyiques (1961), p. 265.
72. Pittoni, Weiner Bietrage zur Kulturges chichte and Linguistic (1936) p. 531 1954, M.D. Garasanih, Kajesickoj pripadanosti neolistskog prastanovnistva, Balkana, Glasinka Zenaljskog Musga u Sarajevu (1957) pp. 210–16.
73. J. Whatmough, Gaulish, Festschrift F. Zeuss (Dublin,1955) pp.249–55.
74. W. Antoniewicz , Des problem der Wanderungen der Indo-germanischen Uber die Polnischen und Ukrainischen Gebiete, Festschrift, A. Hirt (Heidelberg, 1936).
75. Pokorny, Substrattheorie and Urheimat der Indogermanen, Mitteilungen der Anthropologische en Gesellschaf , IXVI, (1936) pp. 69–91.
76. Nehring , Studien Zur Indo-arischen Kultur und Urheimat, pp. 27, 59–61.
77. F. Schachermeyr, die alteste Kulturen Griechenlands (Stuttgart, 1955).
78. C. Hawkes, The Prehistoric Foundations of Europe (London, 1940).
79. R. Hauschild, Revised edition of Albert Thumb's Handbuch, des Sanskrit (Heidelberg, 1959).
80. G.A. Grierson , linguistic Survey of India. Vol. I, part I, 1927.
81. O. Schrader, Reallexicon der Indogermanische Sprache (1901).
82. Myres, Sprachvergliechung und Urgeschichte (1906).
83. A. Cornoy, Les Indo-Europeans (Louraine, 1921).

84. A.C. Huddon, The Race of Man (Cambridge, 1924).
85. H. Peake, The Bronze Age and the Celtic World (London,1922).
86. V.G. childe, The Aryans (New York, 1926), p. 181.
87. Ibid.
88. Ibid, pp. 188–90.
89. Ibid, pp. 185–86.
90. T. Burrow, The Sanskrit Language, pp. 1-34 (London).
91. B. K. Ghosh, "The Aryan problem," The Vedic Age, pp. 202–17 (1957).
92. P. Kretschmer, Einleitung in die Geschichte der griechischen Sprache, 1896.
93. B. Symons, Het stamland der Indogerman chap. 1898–99.
94. R. Meringer, Indogermanische Sprach Wissenche ft, 1897.
95. H.D. Griwold, The Religion of the Rigveda, p. 18, (London,1923).

Glossary

1. Primate: Pre-human ancestor of man from whom the present man has evolved.
2. Pleistocene: In the geological time scale quaternary period is the last. This is further sub-divided into two viz., Pleistocene which is also recognised as "great Ice Age" having four glacial' and three 'interglacial's' intervals; and Holocene which is recent and current period.
3. Cenozoic: The era of the earth's history which include the Tertiary and Quarternary periods and was preceded by the Mesozoic, Palaeozoic and Pre-Cambrian eras.
4. Glacials : A period of earth's history when large parts of the earth's surface was covered with ice sheets or glaciers. There have been four such periods in the Plistocene epoch and have been named after those parts of the Alps where they were noticed. They are Guntz, Mindel, Riss and Wurm respectively.
5. Genus Homo: The Genus which includes modern man, Neaderthal man and Homo erectus.
6. Hominidae: The family which includes both extinct and modern forms of man.
7. Homo Sapiens: Modern man first appears in the fossil record during the later part of the Upper pliestocene around 35,000 B.C.
8. Interglacial: A warm interlude between two glaciations.

9. Eolithic:	Dawn of the stone Age. A hypothetical period in which natural stone pieces were used as tools.
10. Brachycephals:	The recorded anthropological criteria in man is the shape of skull of man. The index is taken by expressing the maximum bereadth as a percentage of the maximum length. A figure below 75 is called Dolichocephalic, 75 to 80 Mesaticephalic, above 80 branchcephalic.
11. Kafuan Culture:	The earliest pebble tools discovered on a site on the river Kafu in Uganda. But the tools discovered here are no more regarded as man made.
12. Oldowan Culture:	The earliest man made pebble tools comprising scrapers, choppers and hand axes were discovered at Oldowan in Northern Tanganyika.
13. Tortoise Core Technique:	The prepared core with a striking plateform is oval in shape hence it is called "Tortoist Core" from which flakes have been removed by Levallois technique.
14. Levallois:	The flakes removed from a prepared core having striking plateform and making about 90° angle between the under surface and the striking plate form. Such flakes were discovered at levallois near Paris.
15. Victoria West Technique:	The flakes removed after preparing the core as in levallois technique have been discovered at Victoria West in South Africa. In this technique sometime the flakes may ratain in the cortex.
16. Gravettian:	Ia Gravettian, rock-shelter in Couze Velly, Dordogne basin ,South-Western France. An Upper Palaeolithic culture taking root from the Chatelperrocian in Western Europe.
17. Chopper:	It is a massive, large unifacial tool characteristic of the Early Stone Age.
18. Chopping Tool :	It is a large heavy bifacial tool of the Early Stone Age, but tends to be smaller in the middle Stone Age. It is characterized by having a jaggel, wayvy cutting edge and

butt, usually retaining the cortex.

19. Abbevillian: This oldest industry of the Palaeolithic was first discovered at Abbeville on Somme in France, hence termed Abbevillian. It is characterized by crude massive hands axes fashioned by striking with a stone hammer or a stone.

20. Aurignacian: It is a blade and burin culture in the lowest stage of the Upper Palaeolithic and is known after a small rock-shelter in the Pyrenese District.

21. Acheulian: This industry is named after St. Acheul on the Somme in France Where it was first discovered. It is second stage of the lower Palaeolithic and in this industry a wooden hammer was used For controlled flaking. Cleavers and coupde-pong are its characteristic tools. It is an evolved stage from the Abbevillion.

22. Natufian: It is a Mesolithic culture. It originated at Wadi-en-Natuf in Palestine. It occupies a very important place in the history of mankind when food-gathering with static life begins and presents the transitional phase from the hunting to the agricultural economy.

23. Pise: Earth or clay also gravels sometime beaten down until it is solid, and used as building material.

24. Wilton Culture: It is a Mesolithic culture of South Africa flourishing about 4000 B.C. It is characterised by the typical microlithic made in the true tradition of miniature blades and fluted cores. The known tools of this culture are thumb nail and small double ended scrap-ers and crescents. Stone sickles for corn are unique invention of this culture.

25. Blade: It is a flake that was struck-off a core, having almost parallel sides, long, narrow and thin. It usually has a plain or faceted striking plateform.

26. Burin: A type tool found in the Upper Palaeolithic and Mesolithic of Europe. A gnawing tool fashioned by a blow struck at the working point along the length of the flake or blade.

27 Celt: It is a chisel or axe, has straight sides converging towards the butt with ovel section in the middle. The butt end is pointed, having a sharp convex cutting edge. This type of tool was made in the Neolithic culture from certain rocks by the three stages of chipping, grinding and polishing.

28. Clactonian: It is a flint industry of lower Palaeolithic and named after discoveries at Clocton – on sea, Essex. The industry consisted of trimmed flint flakes and chipped pebbles, some of these implements are classified as chopper tools.

29. Microlith: A very small tool made on a blade or flake. These tools commonly occur in geometric shapes. Microliths are characteristic tools of Mesolithic Period.

30. Midrib: A thickening of the centre line of a bronze weapon to add the strength which that material normally lacks.

31. Adze: It is an axe type of implement set at right angles to the haft.

32. Arraw-heads: They were generally made of flint.They were placed in a slot in the shaft, tied, then fixed with the resin.

33. Scraper: An artifact of chipped stone or flint with a semi-circular or convex working edge.

34. Shaft- hole: The perforation running through an implement or weapon to take the haft.

35. Spear-head: A thrusting blade mounted on a long shaft as a weapon for war or hunting.

36. Black-and-red:pottery: A red were with black rim and interior found during the Iron Age in India .It first appeared on the post Harappan sites.

37. Channelled: Decoration with broad incision or grove.

38. Cleaver:- A heavy core or flake tool, with D shaped outline and a straight transverse cutting edge.

39. Combed Ornament: Pottery decoration produced by drawing a toothed instrument across the surface of soft clay. The result is a band of parallel incisions, often wavy.

40. Faience: A substance composed of a sand and clay mixture baked to a temperature at which the surface begins to fuse to a bluish or greenish glass.

41. Flint: A hard but brittle stone found in Chalk or lime stone.

42. Barbed harphoon: A throwing spear whose head usually of bone or antler, consists of a pointed shaft with one or two rows of backward pointing bards.

43. Graver: A tool of Palaeolithic period of a chisel like nature.

44. Lunates: Half moon-shaped flints with the inner edge untrimmed and the thick, rounded edge having small chips removed. They were used as arrow heads.

45. Cire perdue: A technique of casting objects in metal. The object is modelled simply in wax. The model is then coated in clay and baked, vents being left for the molten wax to escape. The cavity thus left is filled with liquid through the vents. The terracotta covering is broken after the metal has cooled. It leaves the metal casting, an exact copy of the original wax figure.

46. Corbel: A stone projecting from a wall to support a beam.

47. Jar burial: An inhuman burial within a pottery vessel. It contrasts urn burial which, being for a cremation, requires a much smaller pot.

48. Incised decoration: Pottery decoration in which the soft surface of the clay is cut with a sharp instrument.

49. Palaeontology: Palaeontology is the study of the origins of man or the study of the fossil remains of animals.

50. Cuneiform: A script developed from the pictographic writing in Mesopotamia (c 3000 B.C.) in order to reduce to angular forms to make

it more suitable for impressing in wet clay with a split reed. This gives the strokes their characteristic (cuneiform = wedge-shaped appearance).

51. Mitanni: A kingdom which arose in the foothills between the Tigris and Euphrates c. 1500 B.C.

52. Gilgamesh: He is the hero of the Sumerian epic. He was half god, half man. As a king of Uruk he abused his position badly. In order to humble him the gods sent the wild man Enkidu. The two fought, and as a result become allies and friends.

53. Ishtar: The Sumerians goddess of the planet Venus.

54. Bel Marduk: The god of Babylon who ousted Enlil, the most prominent god in the Sumerian pantheon.

55. Enki, du: The Sumerian god of sweet water and wisdom. With the help of Anu and Enlil he held the chief power over Sumer.

56. Fata Morgana: The fairy Morgan: in Carlovingian romance the lake-dwelling enchantress overcomed by Orlando. The mirages in the strait of Messina are attributed to her enchantments, and named for her, Fata Morgana.

57. Animism: The belief in souls : the attribution of spirit or personality to physical objects or phenomena: specially, the religious philosophy found universally in mankind which peoples the physical universe with spirits found in animals, plants, stones, weapons, metreological events etc.

58. Manes: The spirits of the dead; the name is probably a euphemism meaning “good spirits”.

59. Tabu: A system of religious and social interdiction and prohibition. Tabu sets apart a person, thing, place, name or an action as an untouchable, unmentionable, unsayable or not to be done for many reasons.

60. Totemism: The term refers to the animal associated

with a clan or gens group, who is either regarded as the mythical ancestor of the group, or a protector and the friend of the group.

61. Charon: In Greek mythology, an old dirty man who ferried the shades of the dead over the styx to the realm of Hades.

62. Tiamat: The primeval dragon of the Mesopotamian cosmological myth, who is believed to be the mother of the gods. When she was killed, from her body the heavens and earth were created.

63. Zoroaster: The traditional founder of the ancient Persian religion.

64. Anthropomorphism: The ascription of human form or qualities to divine beings, particularly to gods; the ascription of human characteristics to the powers of nature or to a natural object animate or inanimate, but especially to animals.

65. Nordic: A race relating to Germanies, Scandinavians and Finland peoples.

66. Upanishads: Philosophical treatises written by Kshatariyas on Vedas.

67. Brahmanas: Treatises of commentaries on the Vedas.

68. Saktism: The cult of the Mother Goddess in which the Mother Goddess is the Supreme deity.

69. Polytheism: Belief or worship of more than one God. The Rigvedic religion is the polytheistic.

70. Monotheism: The doctrine that there is one God. It originated in the Semitic World.

71. Semitic: A member of any of the peoples supposed to be descended from Shem, son of Noah. They include the Jews, Arabs, Assyrians and Phoenicians.

72. Phallus: Male organ, erect penis.

73. Phalli: A miniature model of Phallas used in Mesopotamia as an amulet.

74. India: The turm India is used in this book for Anciant India, which comprises Bharat, Pakistan and Afghanistan.

Cultural Evolution of India & Iran

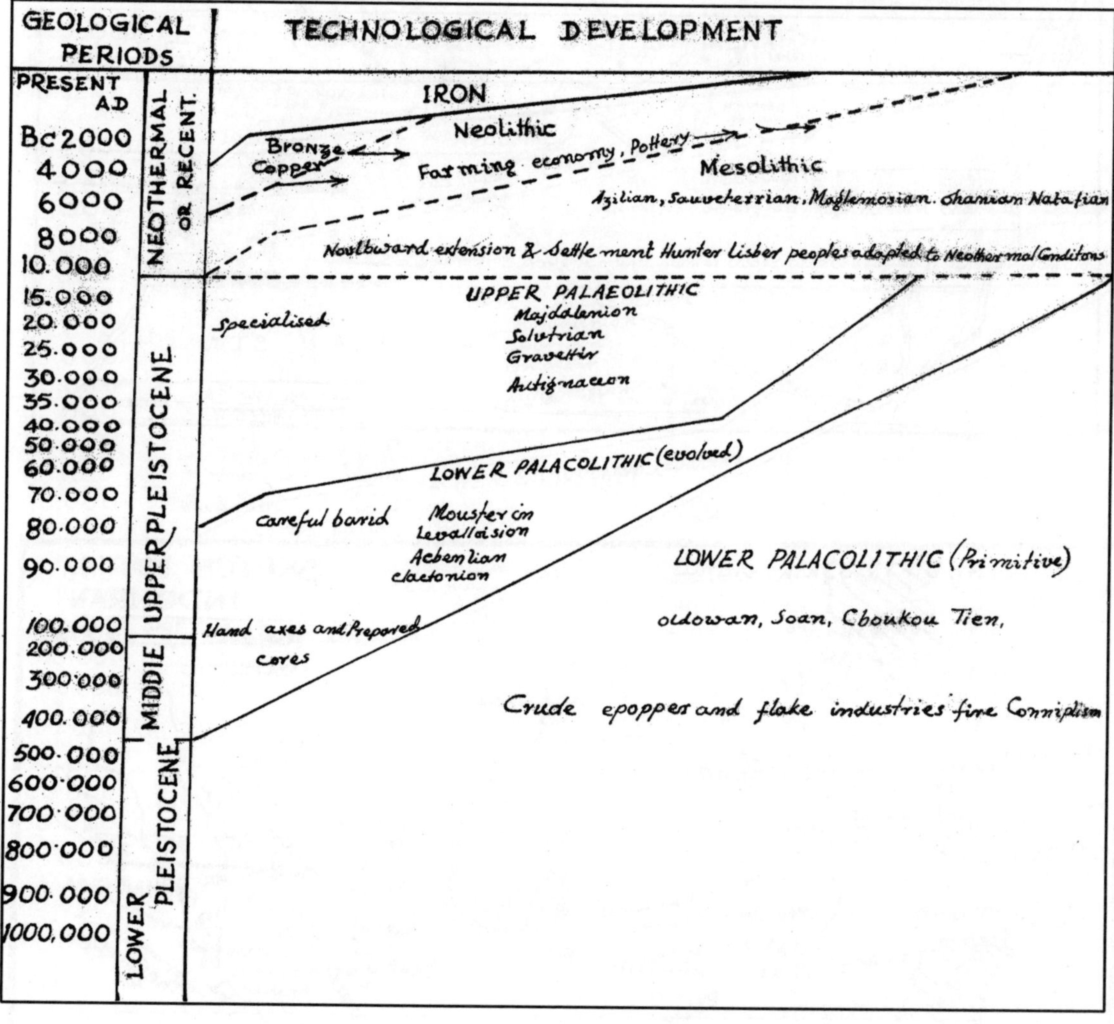

Fig. No. 1

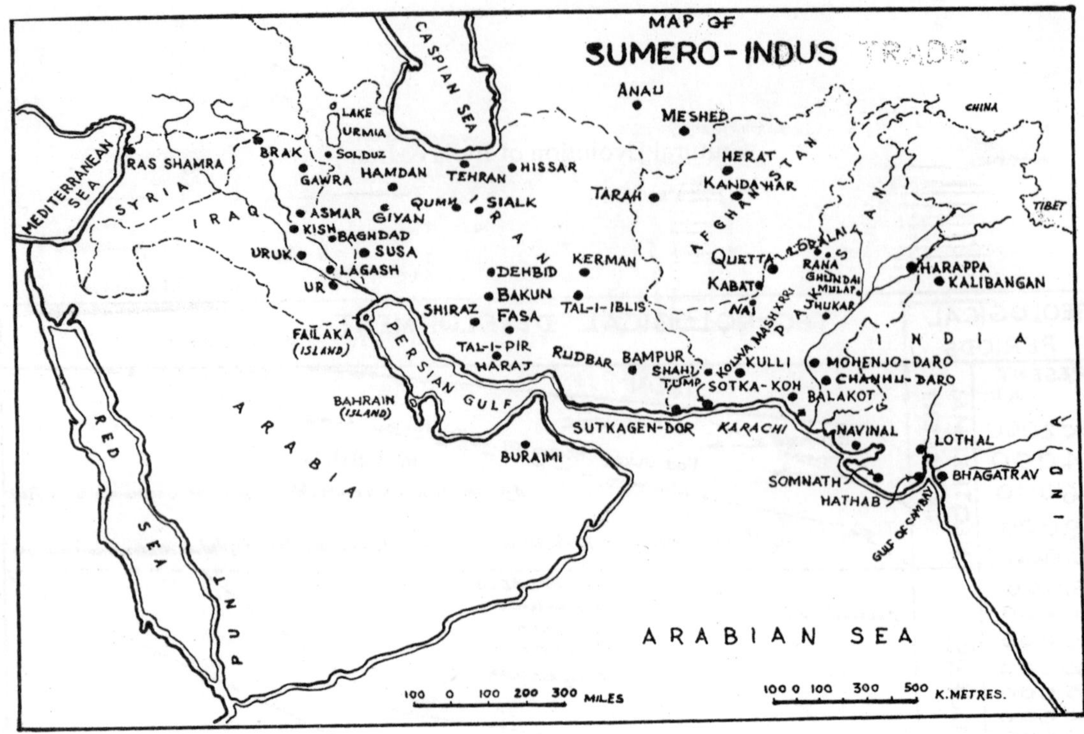

Fig. No. 2

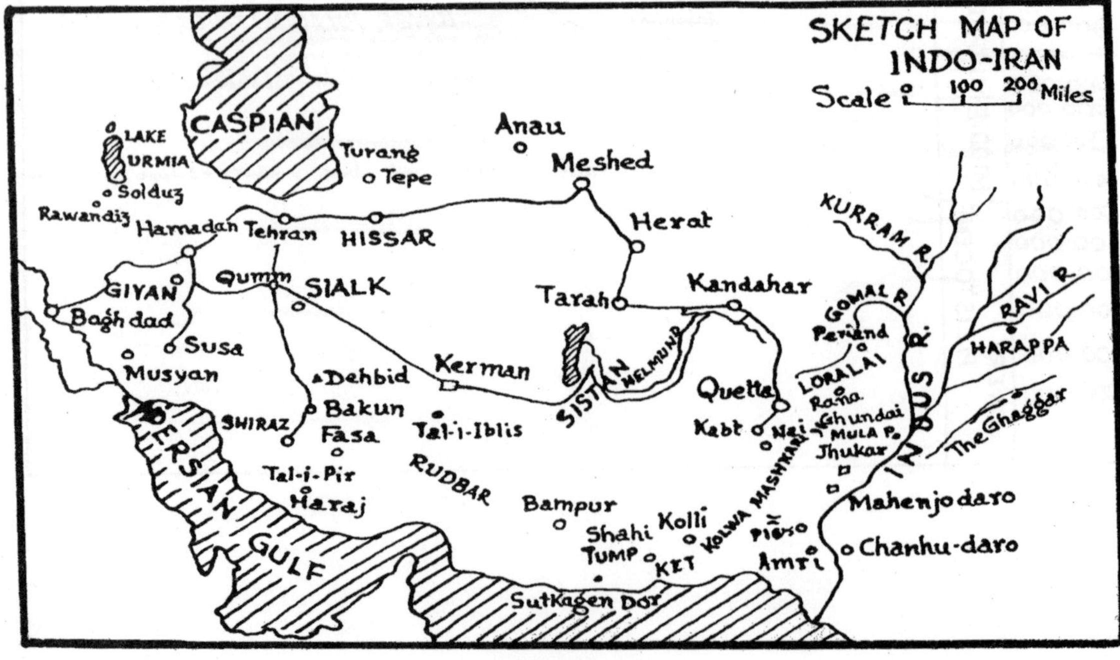

Fig. No. 3

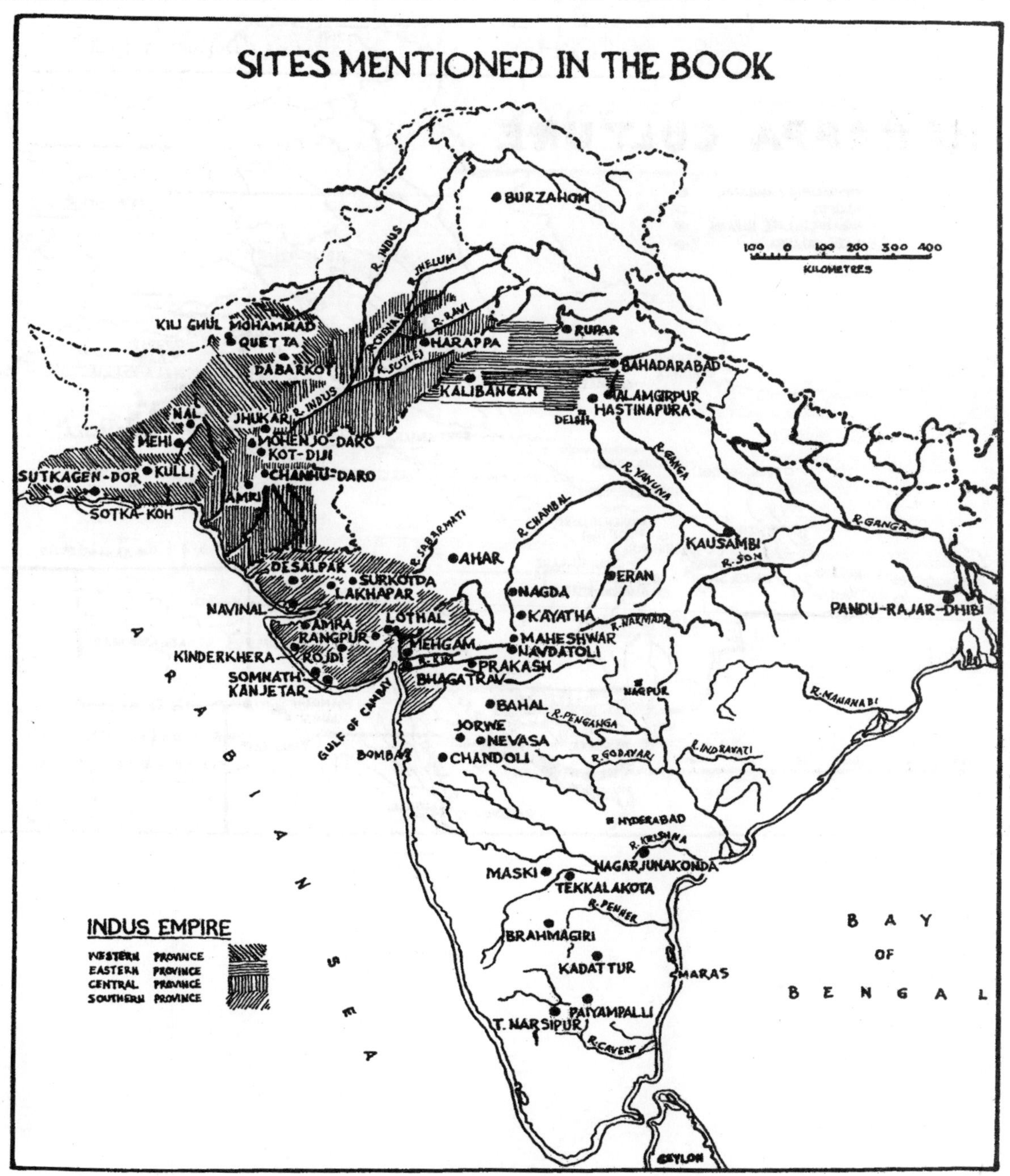
SITES MENTIONED IN THE BOOK
BURZAHOM
100 0 100 200 300 400
KILOMETRES
R. INDUS
R. JHELUM
R. RAVI
R. SUTLEJ
KILI GHUL MOHAMMAD
QUETTA
DABARKOT
HARAPPA
RUPAR
BAHADARABAD
KALIBANGAN
ALAMGIRPUR
HASTINAPURA
DELHI
NAL
JHUKAR
MEHI
MOHENJO-DARO
KOT-DIJI
KULLI
SUTKAGEN-DOR
CHANHU-DARO
AMRI
SOTKA-KOH
R. GANGA
R. YAMUNA
R. CHAMBAL
R. SABARMATI
KAUSAMBI
R. SON
AHAR
DESALPAR
SURKOTDA
LAKHAPAR
NAGDA
ERAN
NAVINAL
KAYATHA
PANDU-RAJAR-DHIBI
AMRA
LOTHAL
RANGPUR
MAHESHWAR
MEHGAM
NAVDATOLI
KINDERKHERA
ROJDI
PRAKASH
SOMNATH
KANJETAR
BHAGATRAV
NAGPUR
BAHAL
R. PENGANGA
R. MAHANADI
JORWE
NEVASA
GULF OF CAMBAY
BOMBAY
CHANDOLI
R. GODAVARI
R. INDRAVATI
ARABIAN SEA
HYDERABAD
R. KRISHNA
MASKI
NAGARJUNAKONDA
TEKKALAKOTA
R. PENNER
INDUS EMPIRE
WESTERN PROVINCE
EASTERN PROVINCE
CENTRAL PROVINCE
SOUTHERN PROVINCE
BRAHMAGIRI
BAY OF BENGAL
KADATTUR
MADRAS
PAIYAMPALLI
T. NARSIPUR
R. CAVERY
CEYLON

Fig. No. 4

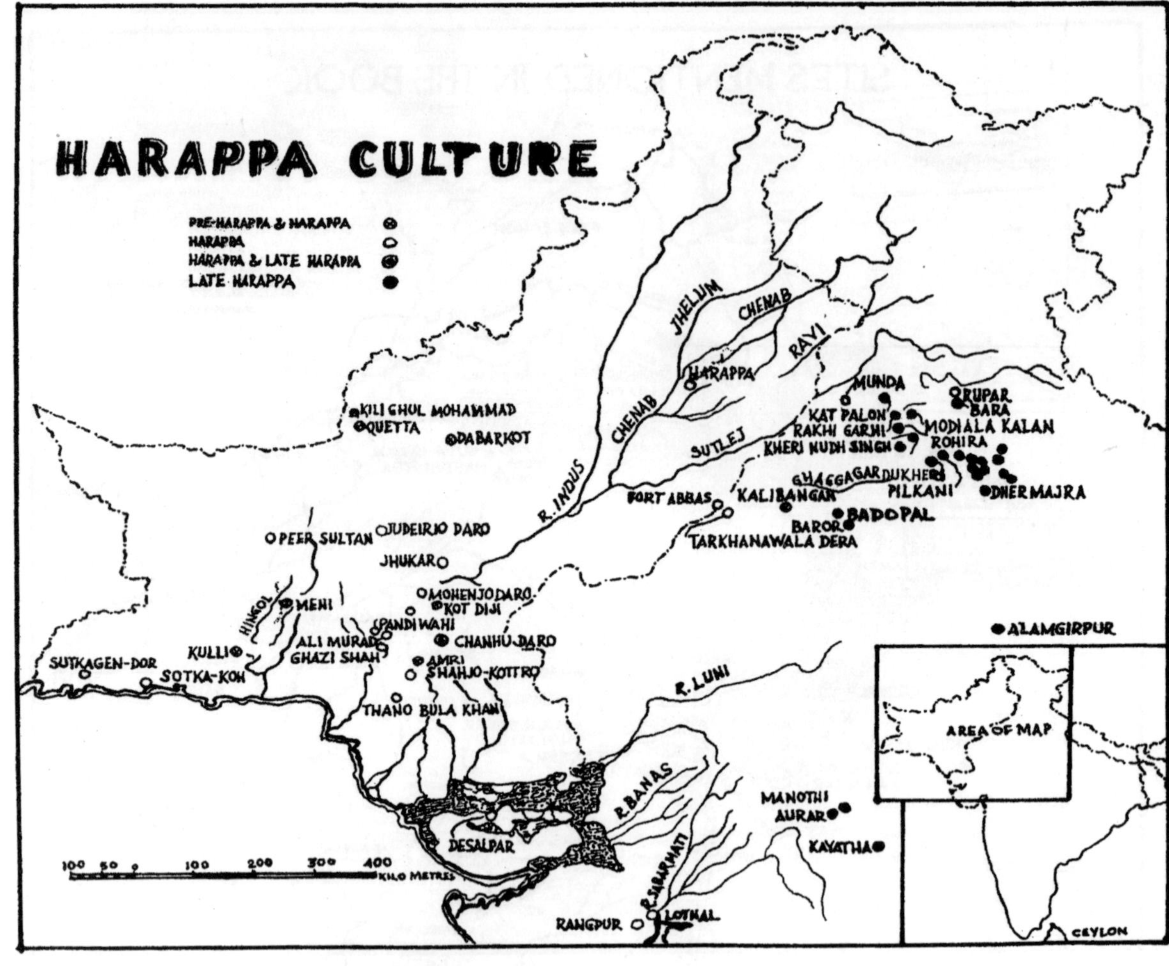
HARAPPA CULTURE
PRE-HARAPPA & HARAPPA
HARAPPA
HARAPPA & LATE HARAPPA
LATE HARAPPA
JHELUM
CHENAB
RAVI
HARAPPA
CHENAB
R. INDUS
SUTLEJ
MUNDA
RUPAR
BARA
KAT PALON
RAKHI GARHI
MODIALA KALAN
KHERI NUDH SINGH
ROHIRA
GHAGGAR
DUKHERI
PILKANI
DHERMAJRA
FORT ABBAS
KALIBANGAN
BADOPAL
BAROR
TARKHANAWALA DERA
KILI GHUL MOHAMMAD
QUETTA
DABARKOT
PEER SULTAN
JUDEIRJO DARO
JHUKAR
MOHENJODARO
KOT DIJI
MENI
HINGOL
PANDI WAHI
ALI MURAD
GHAZI SHAH
CHANHU-DARO
AMRI
SHAHJO-KOTTRO
KULLI
SUTKAGEN-DOR
SOTKA-KOH
THANO BULA KHAN
R. LUNI
ALAMGIRPUR
AREA OF MAP
R. BANAS
MANOTHI
AURAR
KAYATHA
DESALPAR
100 50 0 100 200 300 400
KILO METRES
R. SABARMATI
RANGPUR
LOTHAL
CEYLON

Fig. No. 5

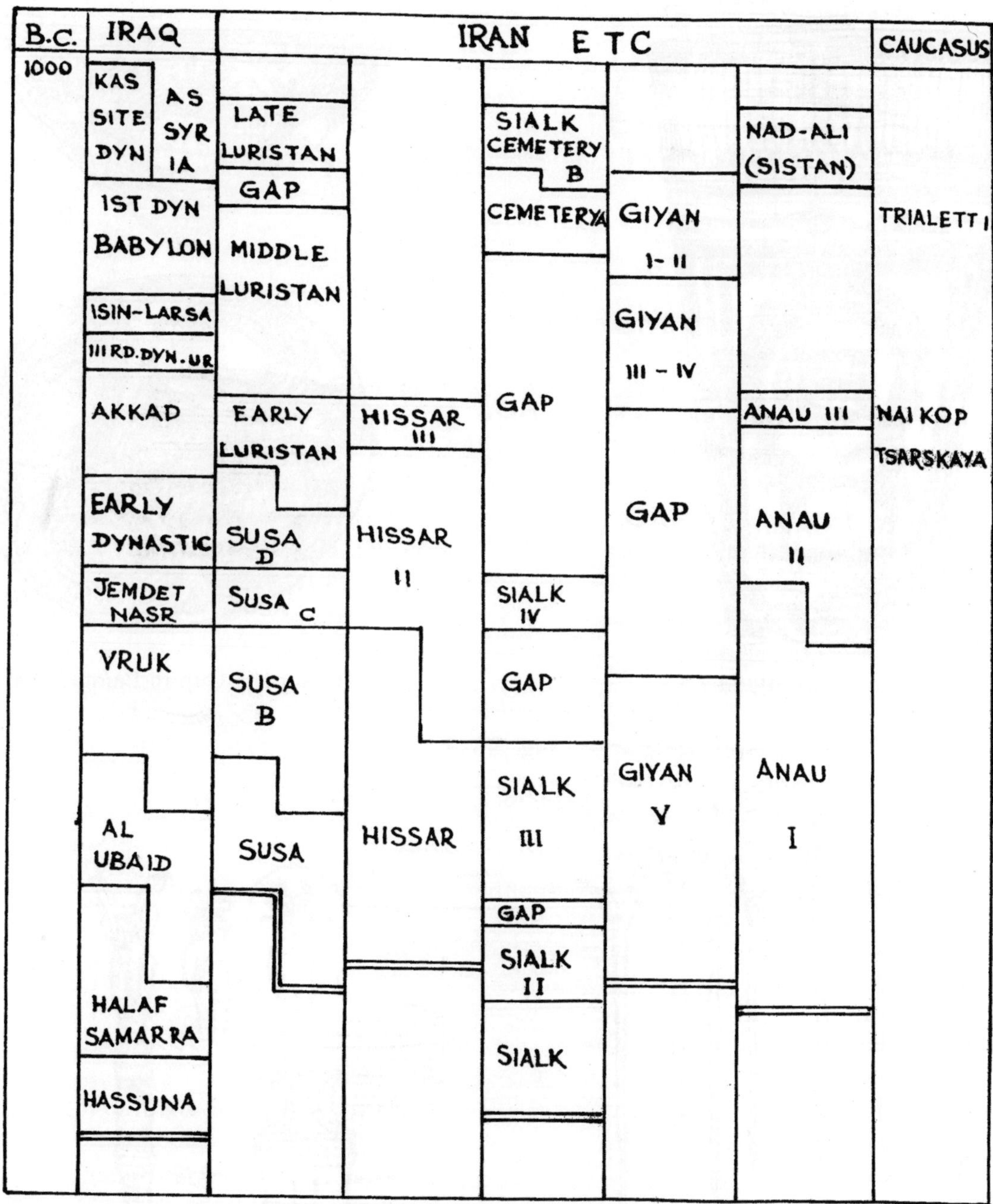

CHRONOLOGICAL TABLE
WEST ASIA

Fig. No. 6

Susa: Goblet of Style I

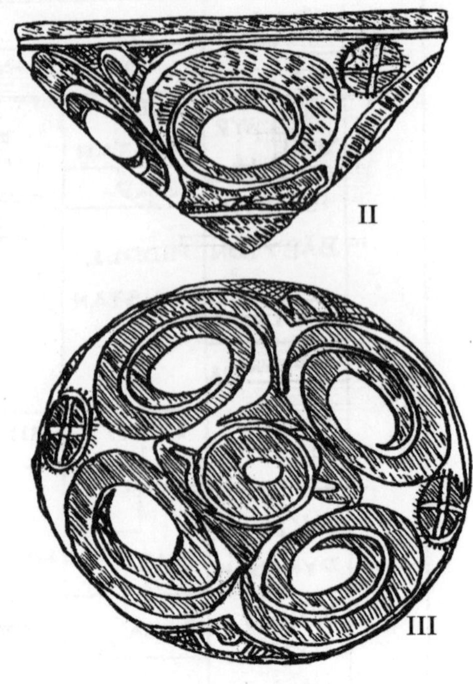

Rersopalis Cup in Painted Ware

Fig. No. 7

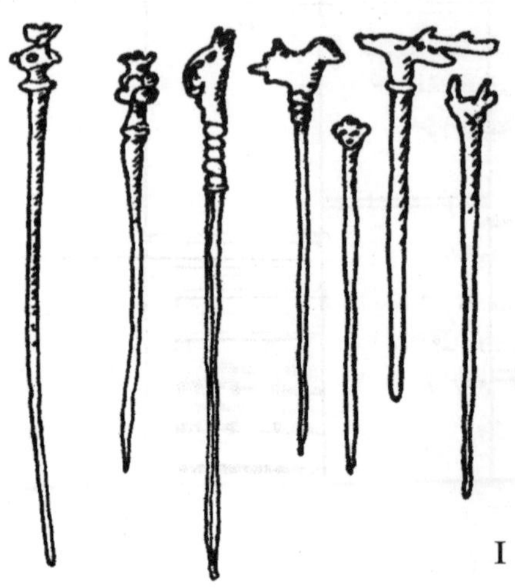

Luristan Bronze Pins

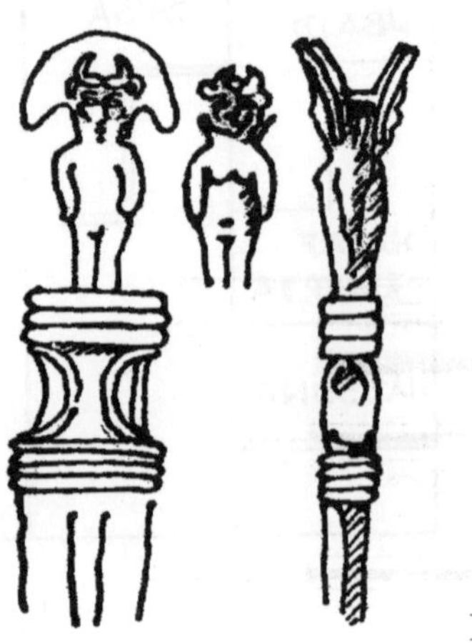

Liristan Bronze Dagger hilt

Fig. No. 8

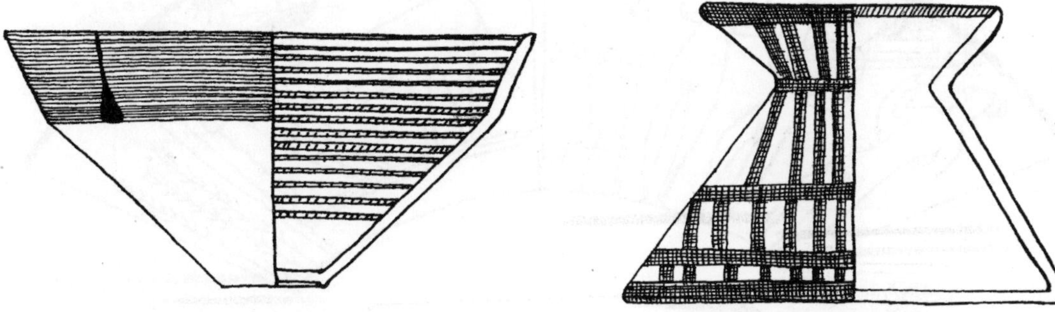

SI5G7

Painted Vases from Sialk 1

Fig. No. 9

Painted Pottery from Sialk II

Fig. No. 10

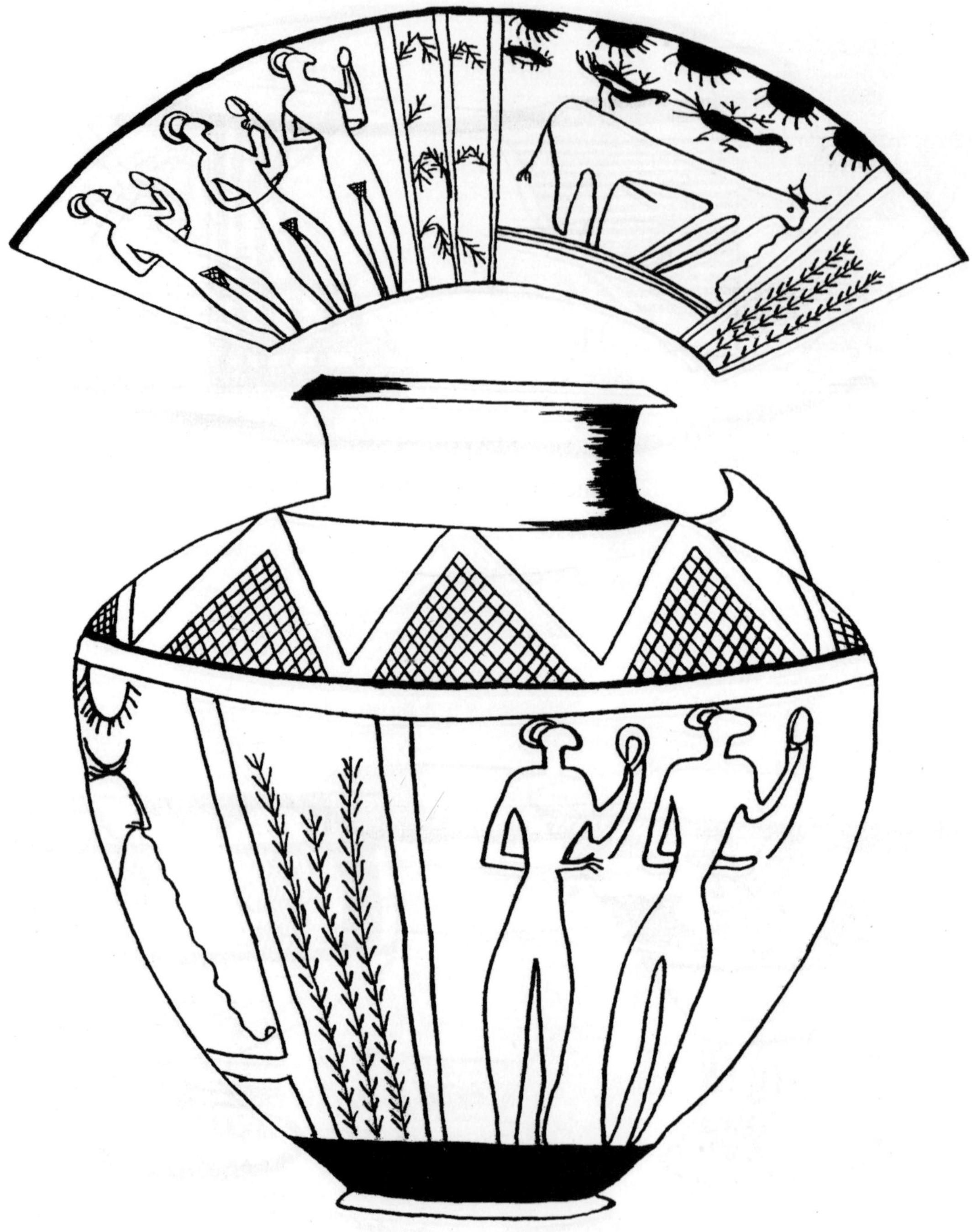

Sialk Painted Pottery

Fig. No. 11

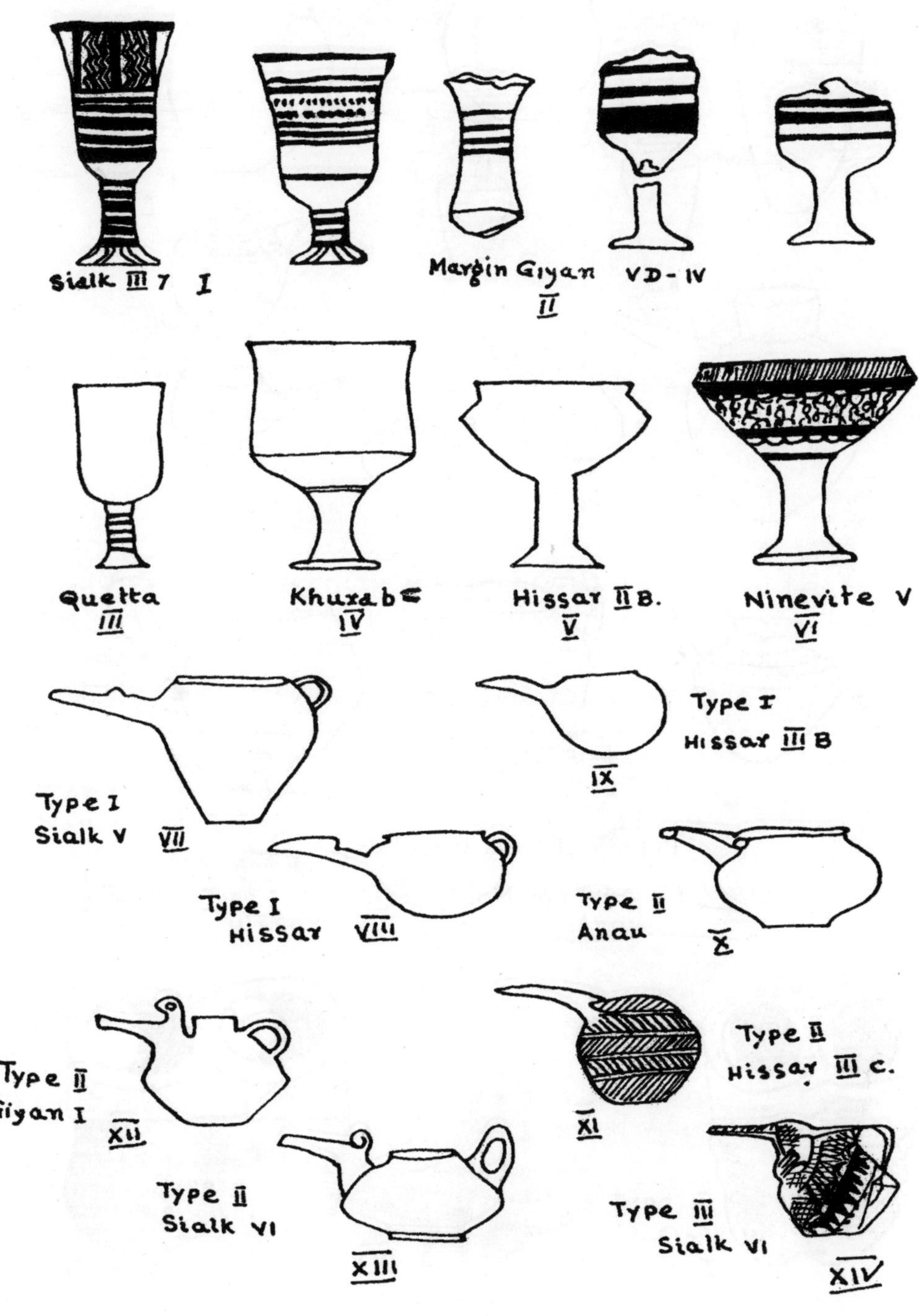
Sialk III 7 I
Margin Giyan VD - IV
II
Quetta
III
Khurab E
IV
Hissar II B.
V
Ninevite V
VI
Type I
Sialk V VII
Type I
Hissar III B
IX
Type I
Hissar VIII
Type II
Anau
X
Type II
Giyan I
XII
Type II
Hissar III C.
XI
Type II
Sialk VI
XIII
Type III
Sialk VI
XIV

Fig. No. 12

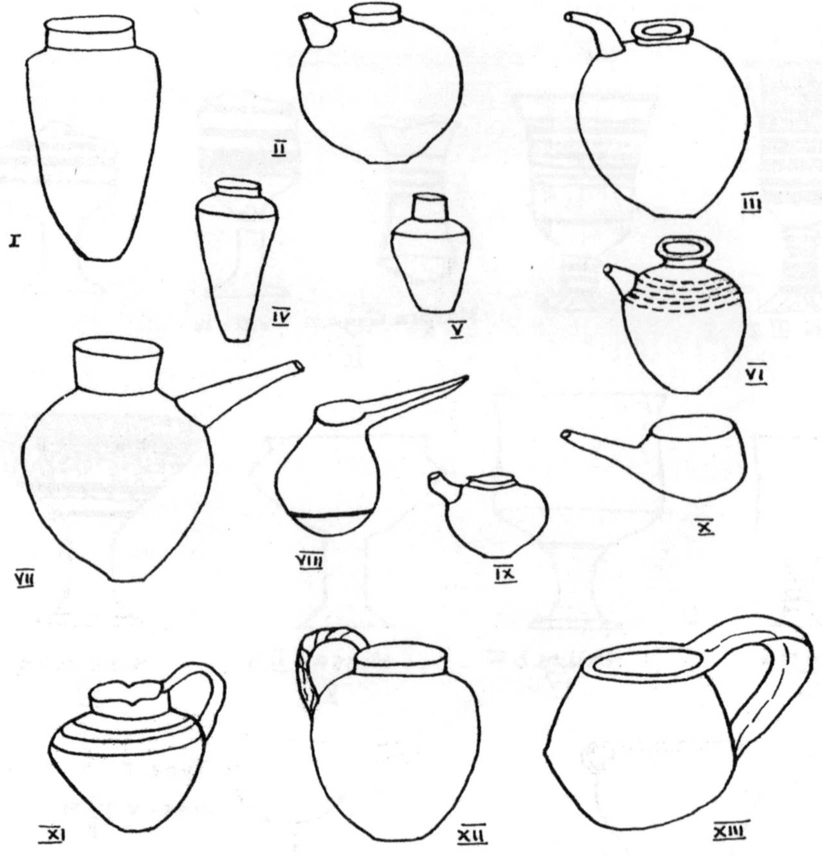

Pottery of Uruk from Susac.

Fig. No. 13

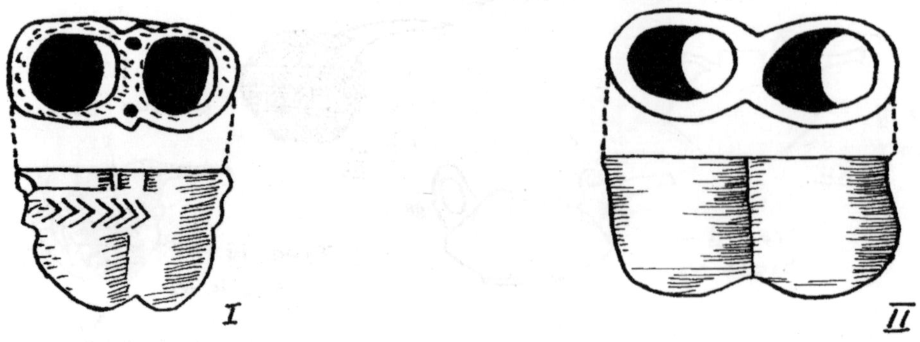

Twin Vases of Alabasteri Susa, D,

Fig. No. 14

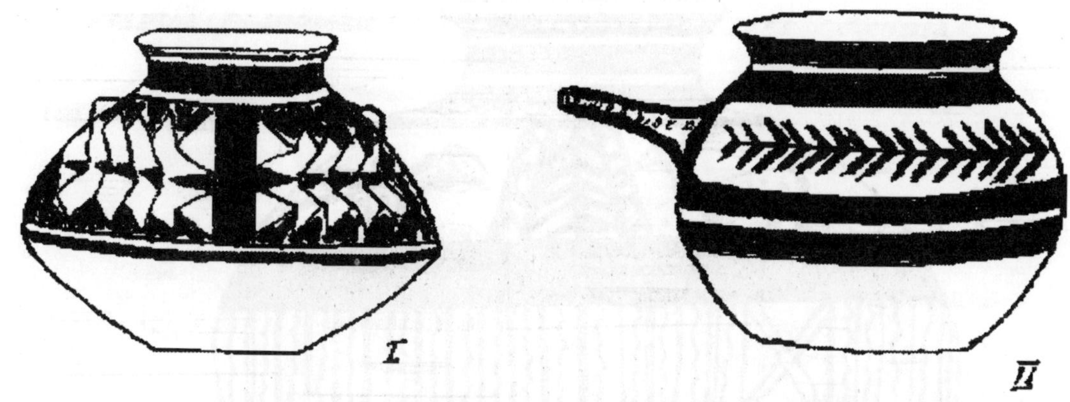

Fig. No. 15 : Carinated pot and Spouted Jug Susa I

Fig. No. 15

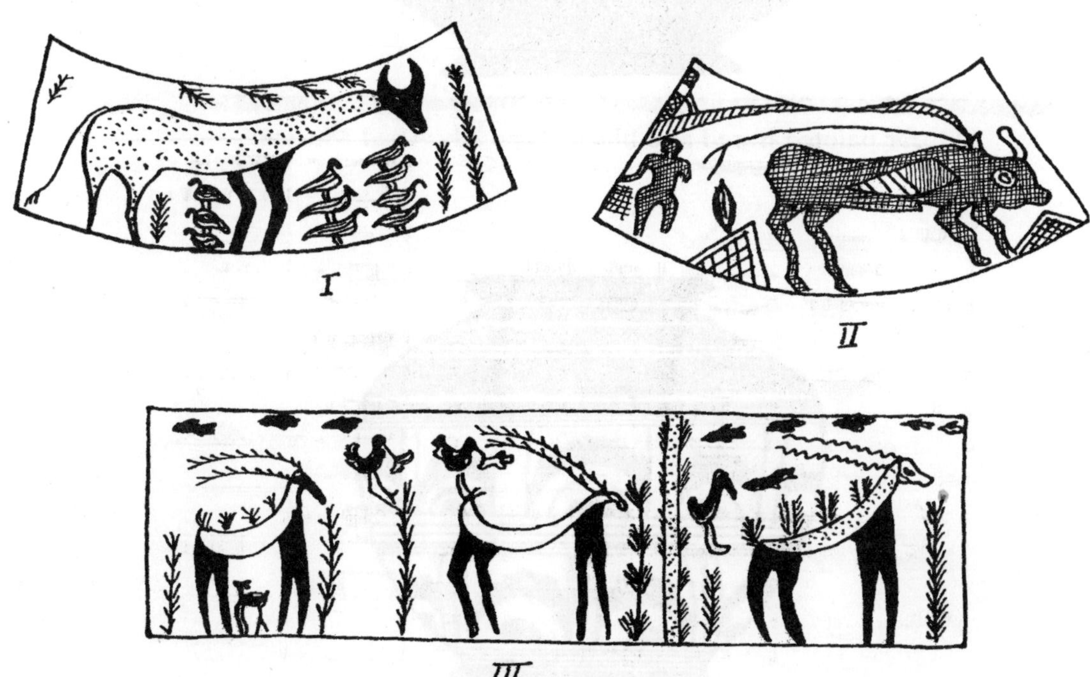

Animals in Lands cape Motif son Early Dynastic
Scarlet ware from susa and the Diyala region.

Fig. No. 16

Jar painted in red and black. Tepe Aly Abad Musyan

Jar Painted red and Black. Tape-C Aly Abad Musyan.

Fig. No. 17

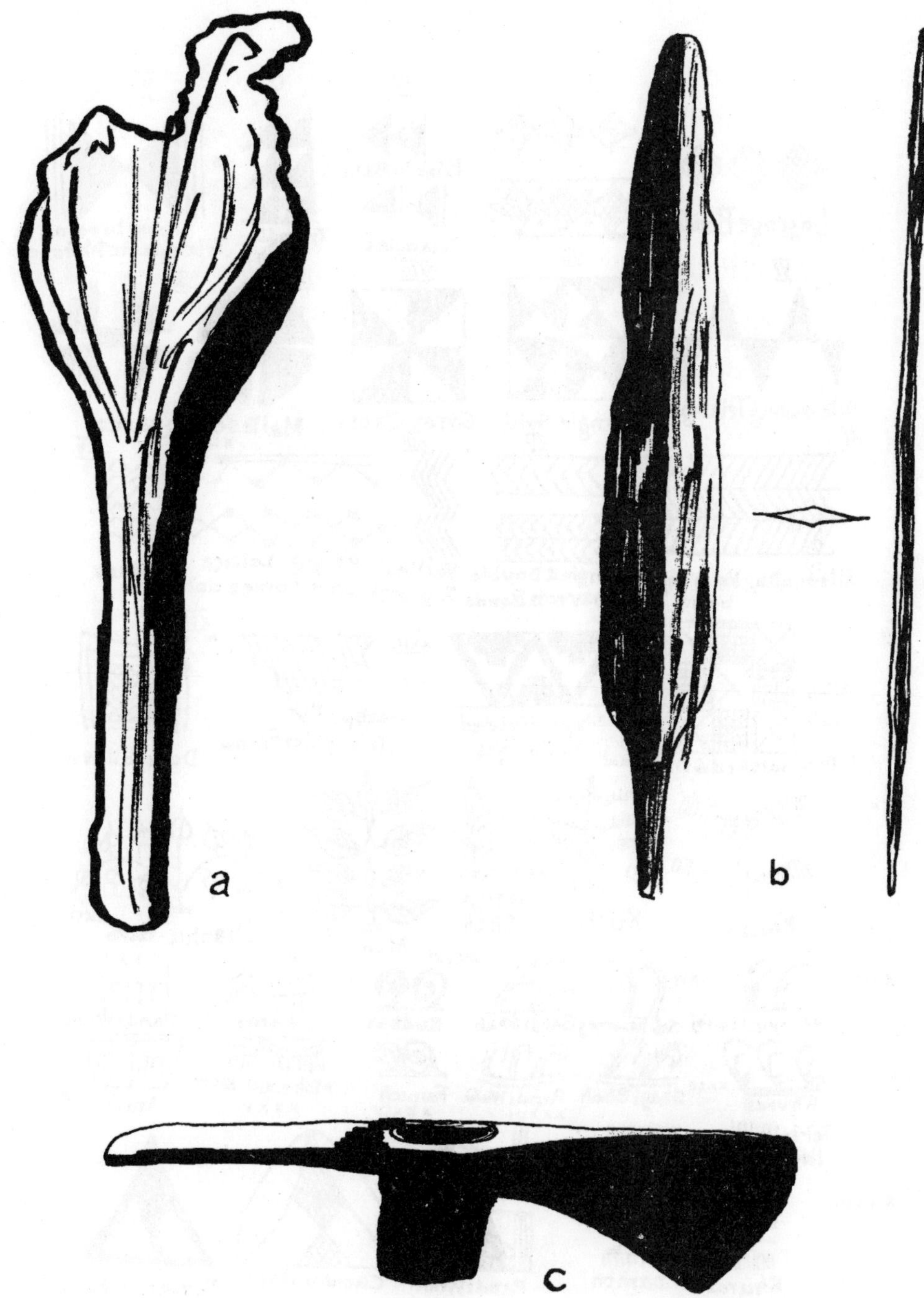

Western type weapons from a. Khurab : b. & c. Mohanjodoro

Fig. No. 18

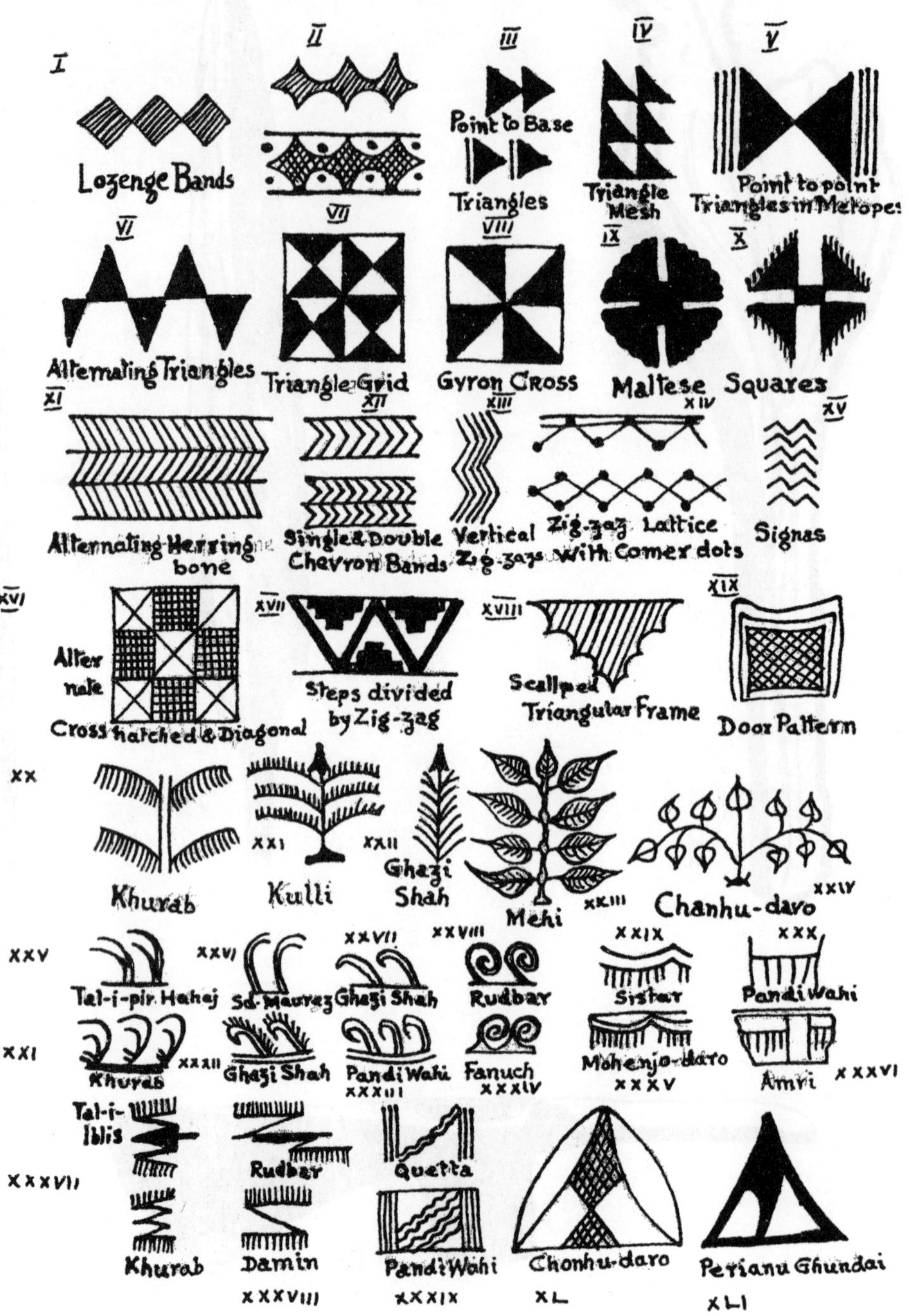
I
Lozenge Bands
II
III
Point to Base
Triangles
IV
Triangle Mesh
V
Point to point Triangles in Metopes
VI
Alternating Triangles
VII
Triangle Grid
VIII
Gyron Cross
IX
Maltese
X
Squares
XI
Alternating Herring bone
XII
Single & Double Chevron Bands
XIII
Vertical Zig-zags
XIV
Zig-zag Lattice With Corner dots
XV
Signas
XVI
Alternate Cross hatched & Diagonal
XVII
Steps divided by Zig-zag
XVIII
Scallped Triangular Frame
XIX
Door Pattern
XX
Khurab
XXI
Kulli
XXII
Ghazi Shah
Mehi
XXIII
Chanhu-daro
XXIV
XXV
Tal-i-pir Hahaj
XXVI
Sd-Maurez
XXVII
Ghazi Shah
XXVIII
Rudbar
XXIX
Sistar
XXX
Pandi Wahi
XXXI
Khurab
XXXII
Ghazi Shah
Pandi Wahi
XXXIII
Fanuch
XXXIV
Mohenjo-daro
XXXV
Amri
XXXVI
Tal-i-Iblis
XXXVII
Rudbar
Quetta
Khurab
Damin
XXXVIII
Pandi Wahi
XXXIX
Chonhu-daro
XL
Perianu Ghundai
XLI

Fig. No. 19

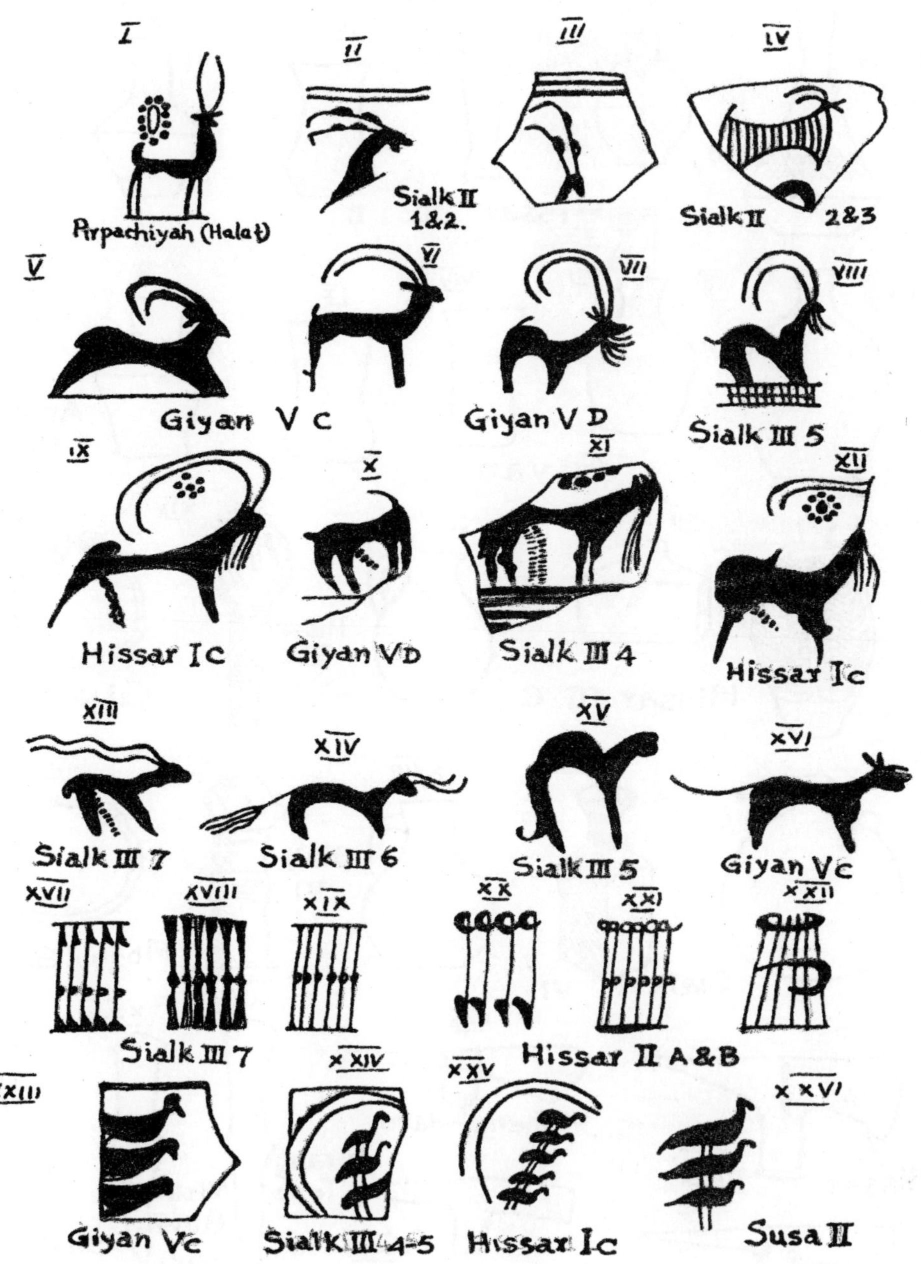
I
Pirpachiyah (Halaf)
II
Sialk II 1&2.
III
IV
Sialk II 2&3
V
VI
VII
VIII
Giyan V C
Giyan V D
Sialk III 5
IX
X
XI
XII
Hissar IC
Giyan VD
Sialk III 4
Hissar Ic
XIII
XIV
XV
XVI
Sialk III 7
Sialk III 6
Sialk III 5
Giyan Vc
XVII
XVIII
XIX
XX
XXI
XXII
Sialk III 7
Hissar II A&B
XXIII
XXIV
XXV
XXVI
Giyan Vc
Sialk III 4-5
Hissar Ic
Susa II

Fig. No. 20

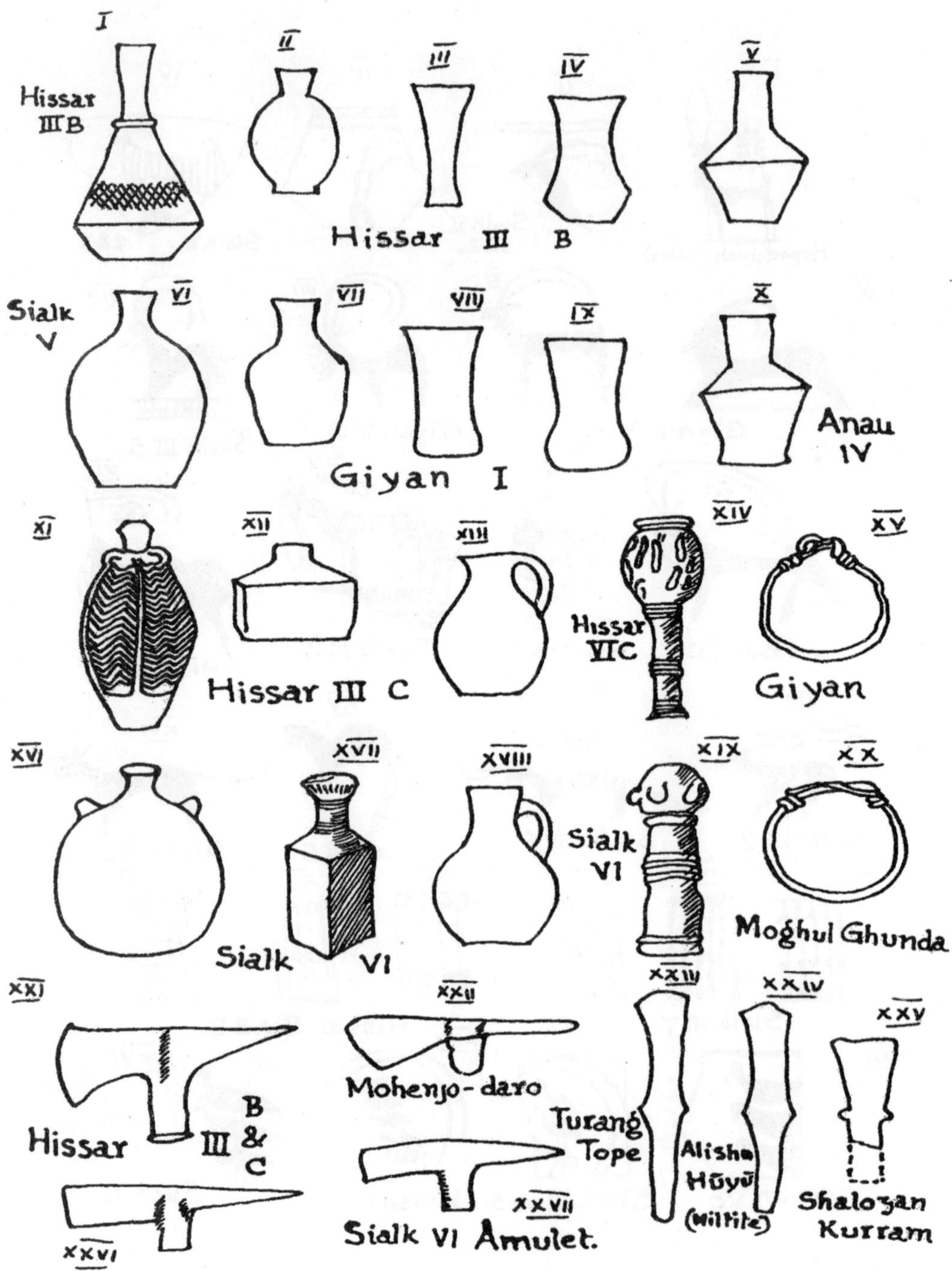
I
Hissar
IIIB
II
III
IV
V
Hissar III B
Sialk
V
VI
VII
VIII
IX
X
Anau
IV
Giyan I
XI
XII
XIII
XIV
XV
Hissar III C
Hissar
VIIC
Giyan
XVI
XVII
XVIII
XIX
XX
Sialk
VI
Sialk VI
Moghul Ghunda
XXI
XXII
XXIII
XXIV
XXV
Mohenjo-daro
Hissar III B & C
Turang Tope
Alisha Hüyü (Hittite)
Shalozan Kurram
XXVI
XXVII
Sialk VI Amulet.

Fig. No. 21

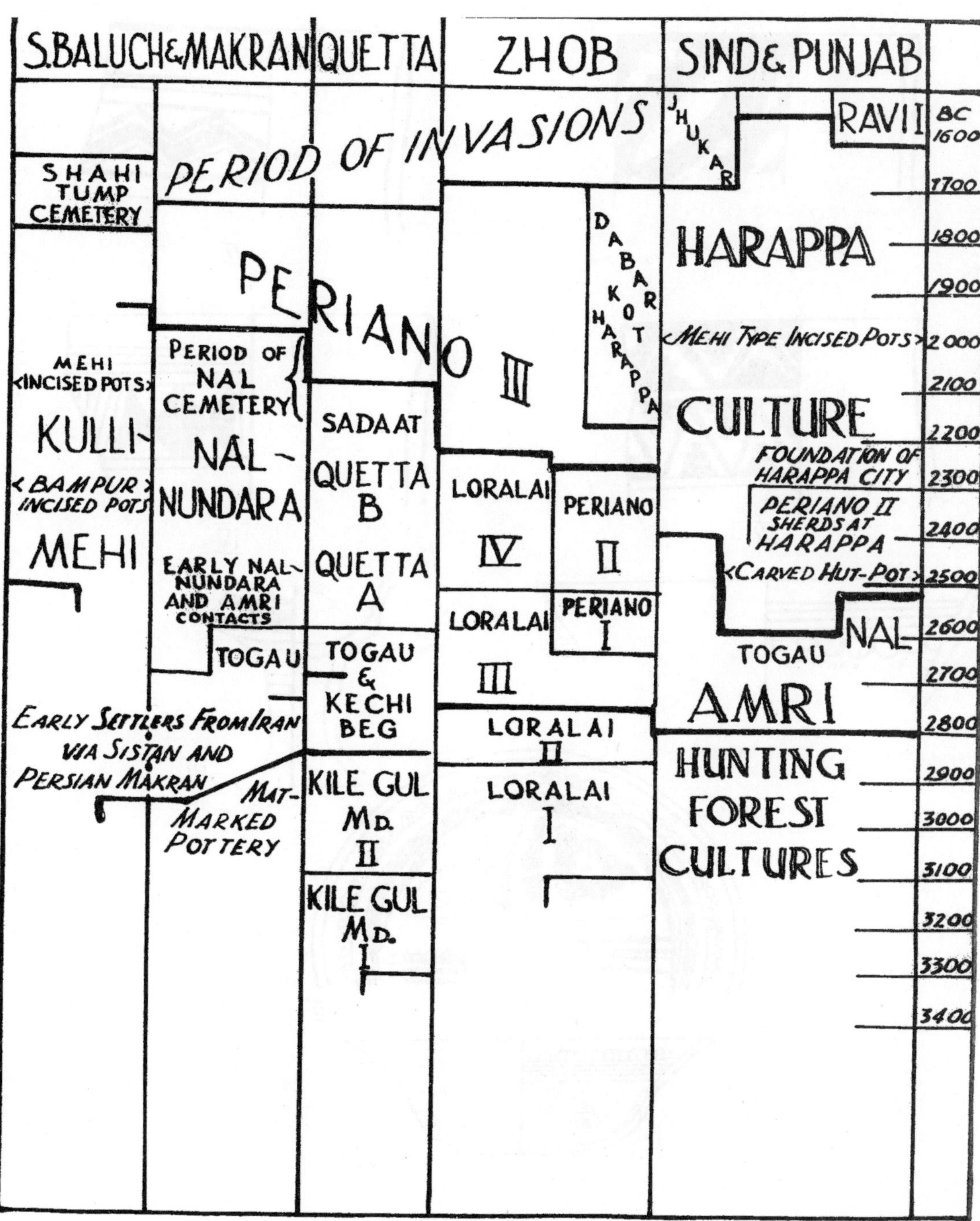

Chronological Table of the early cultures of Baluchistan and Sind.

Fig. No. 22

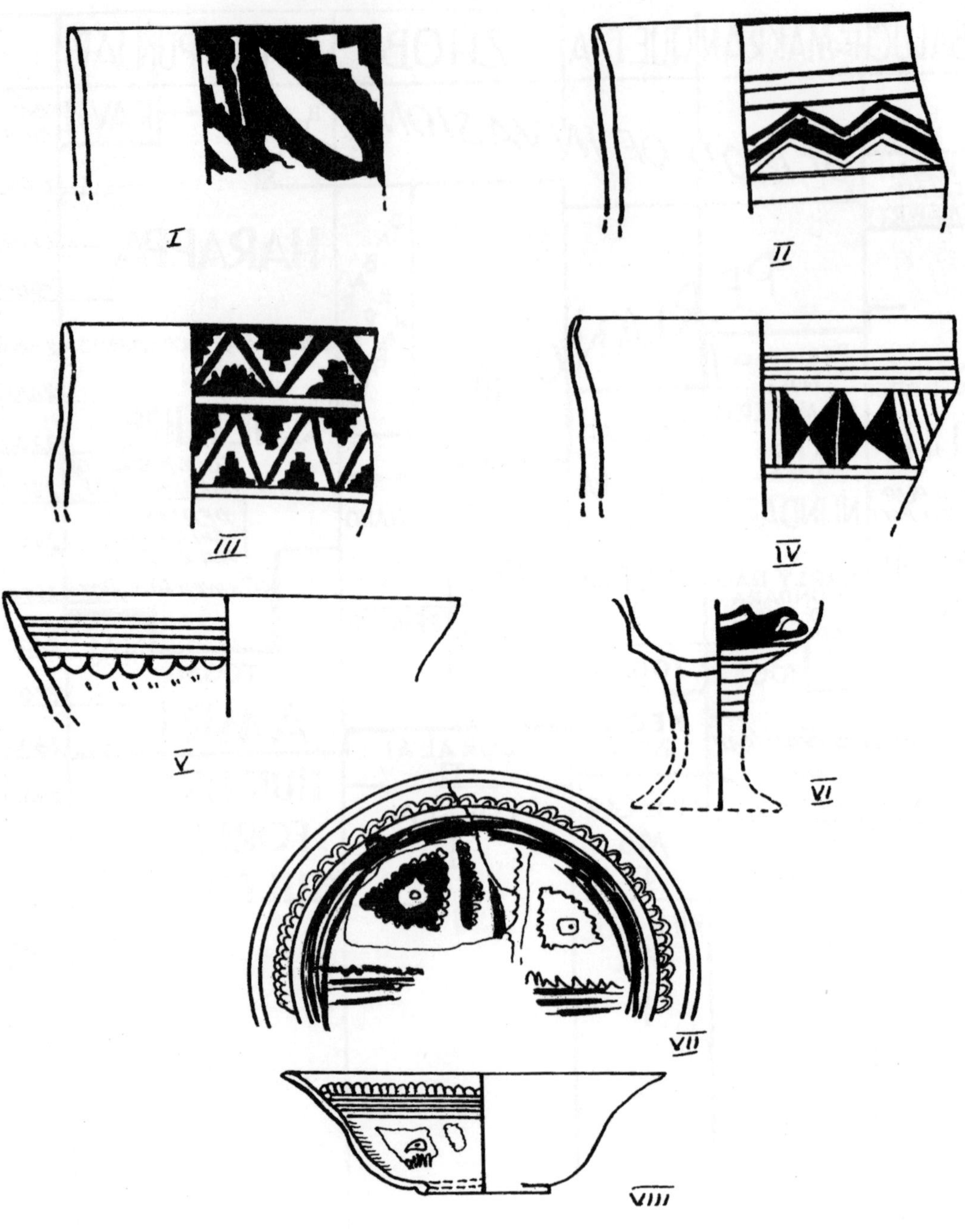

Typical Quetta Ware

Fig. No. 23

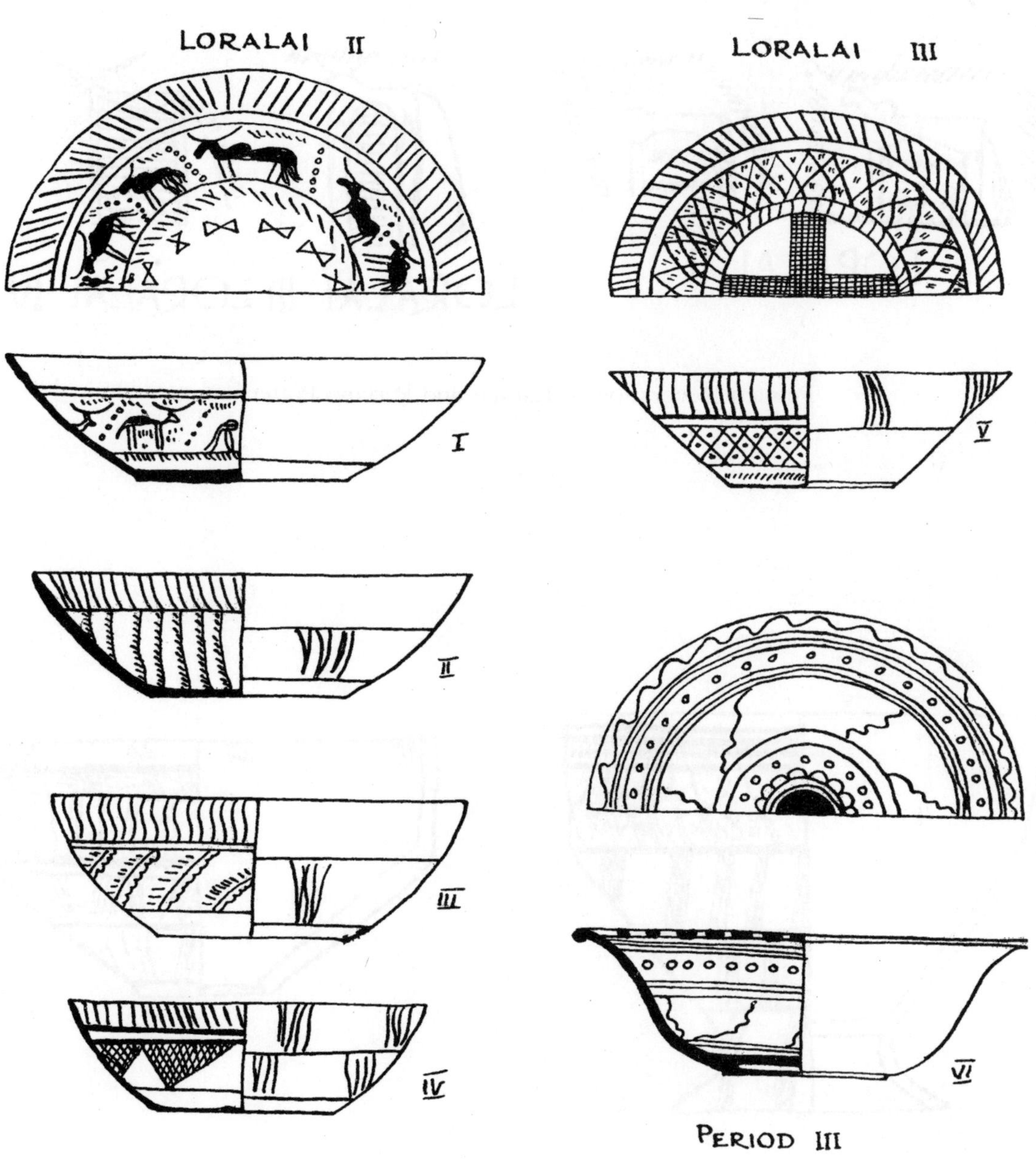

Fig. No. 24

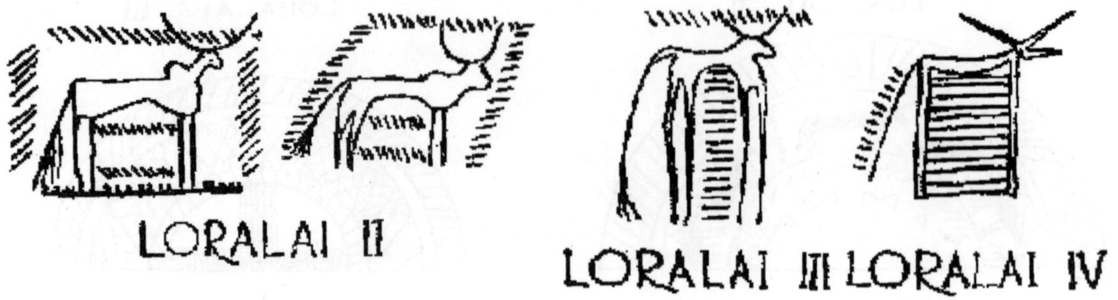

Painted Decoration of Laralai and Periano Pottery

Fig. No. 25

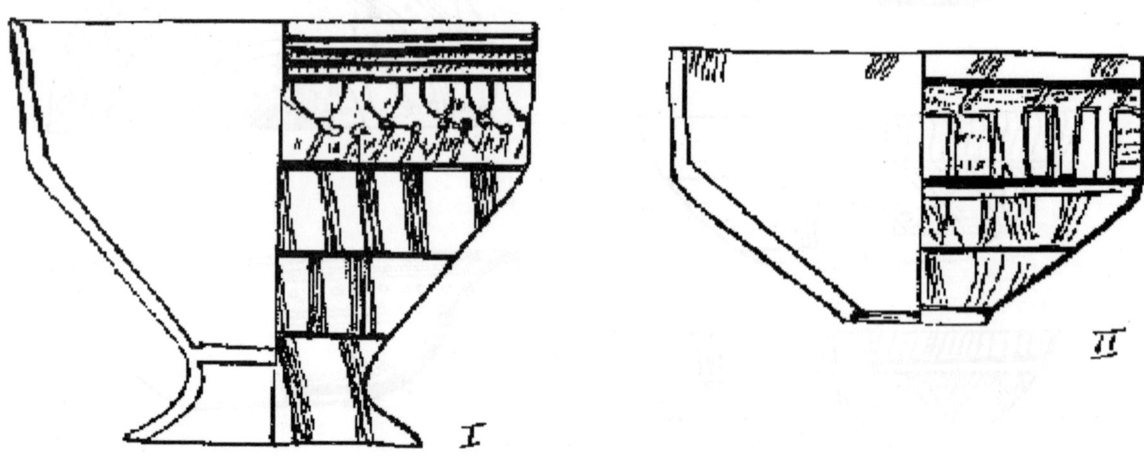

Bowls Painted with Cattle and Black Buck
Rana Ghundai II Phase

Fig. No. 26

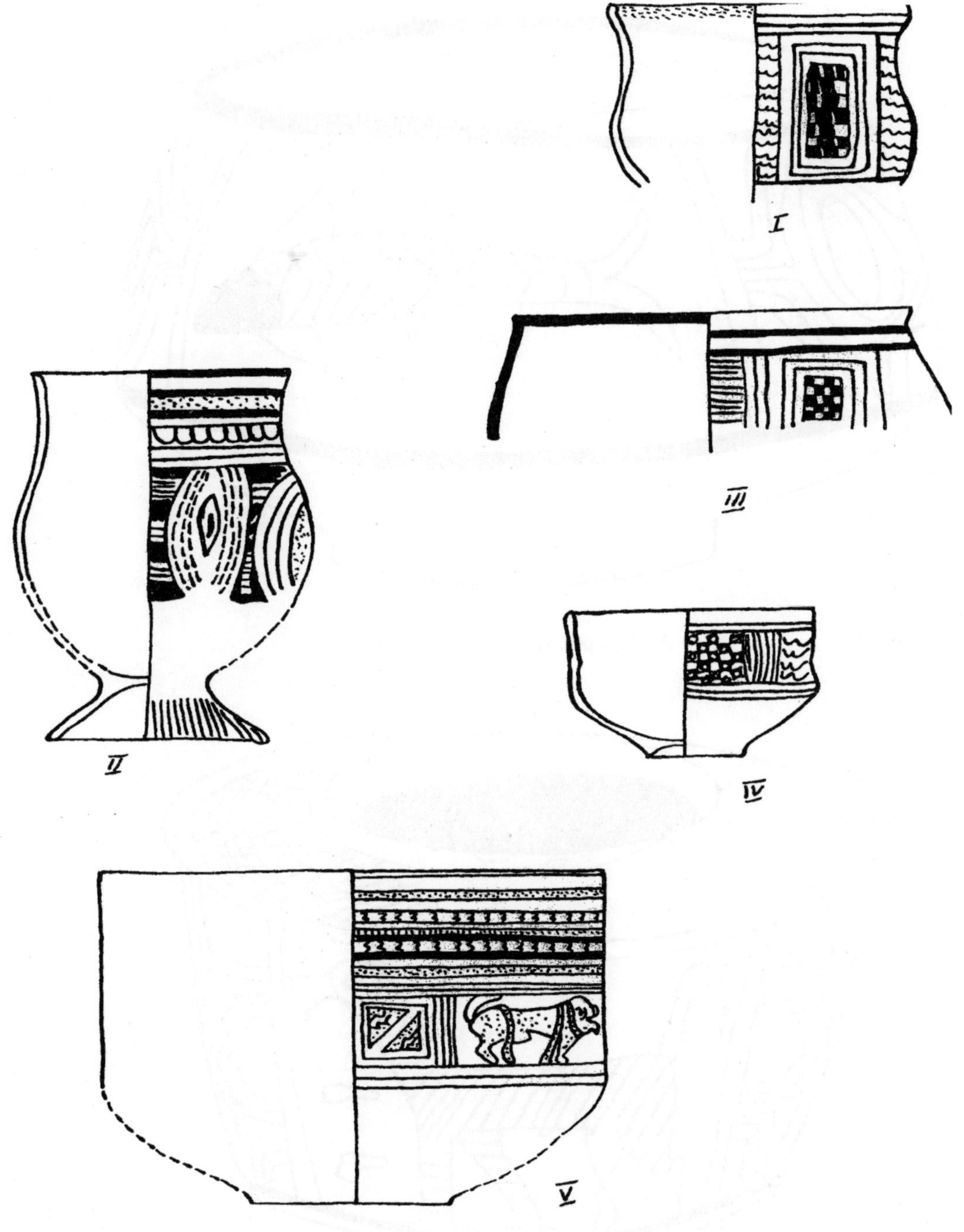

Amri and Nundara beakers and Nundara Bowls
(red paint slippled)

Fig. No. 27

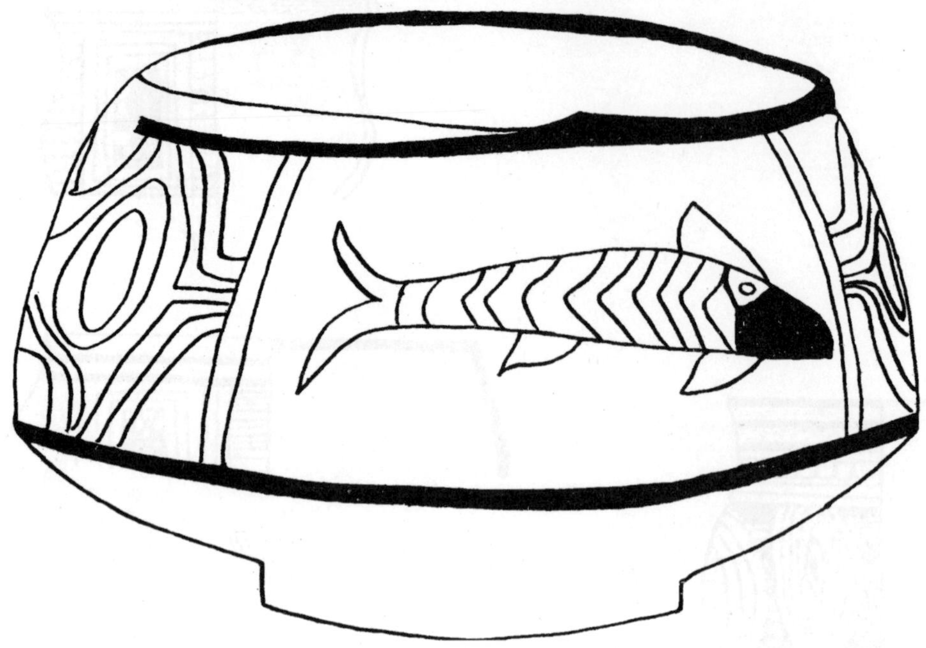

A. Nal pot with Fish design

B. Nal pot with Winged Monster

Fig. No. 28

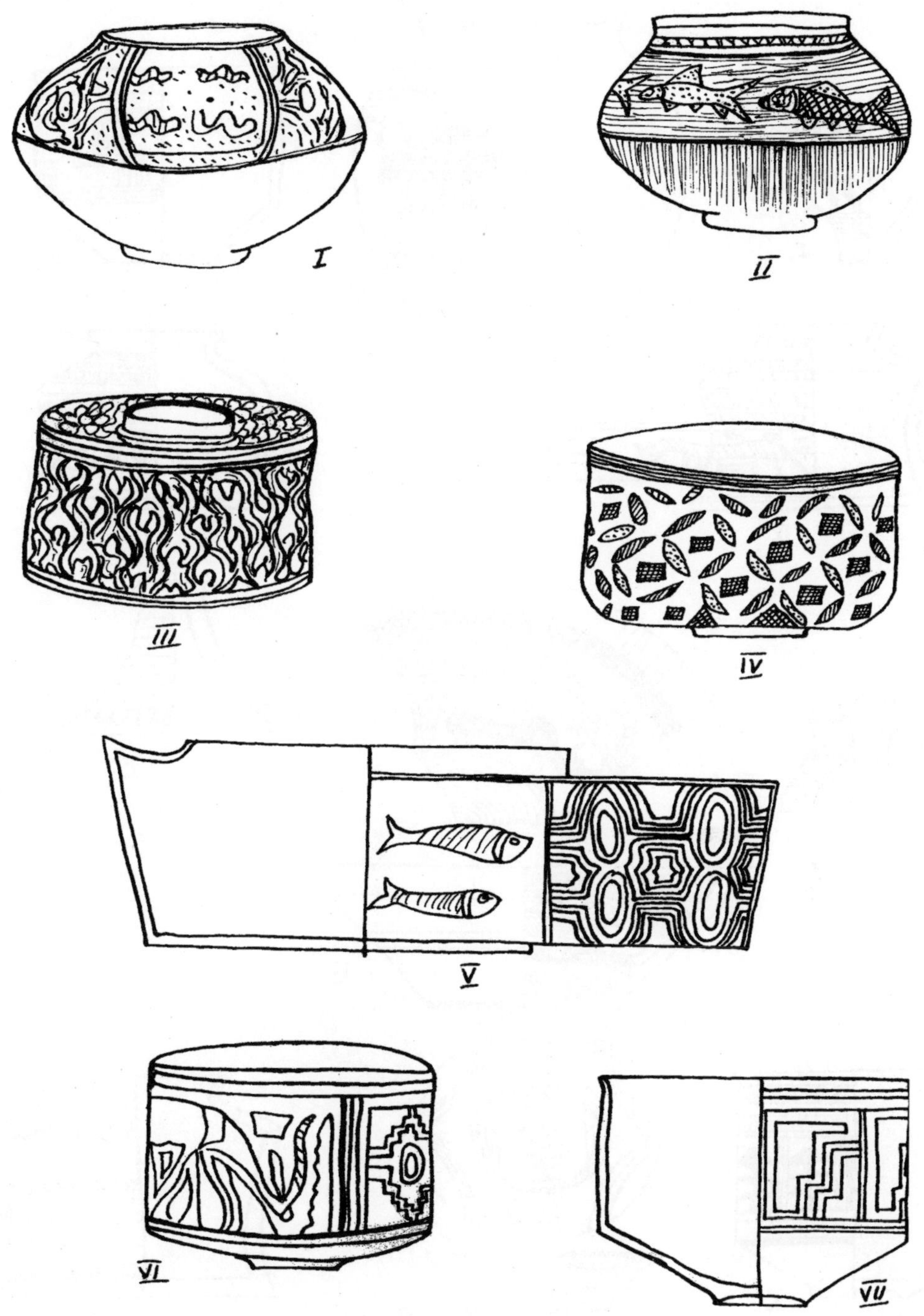

Polychrome nal menal ware (red paint slippled, yellow Horizontal and blue Vertical Shading)

Fig. No. 29

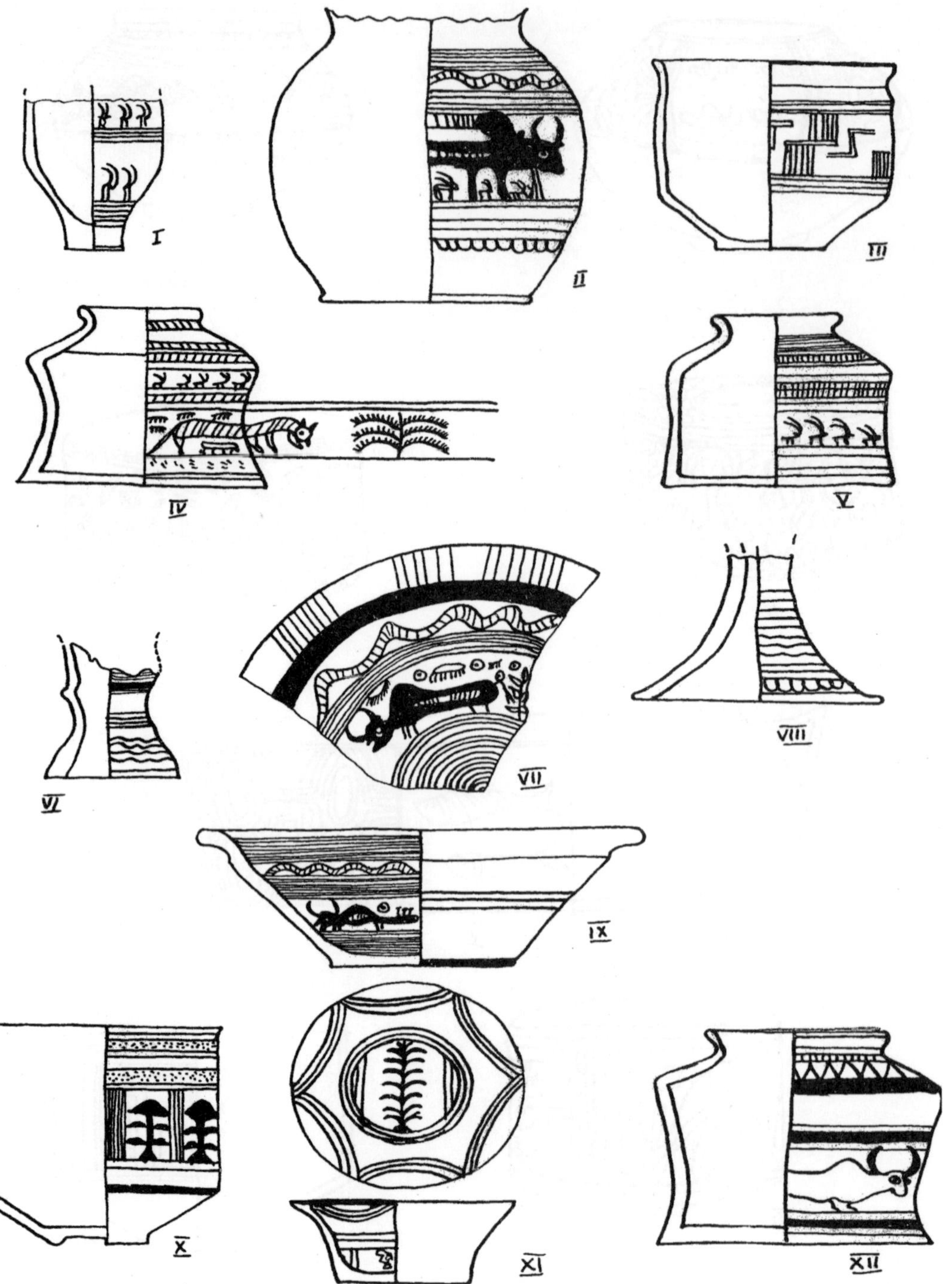

Typical Kulli Ware (read paint slippled)

Fig. No. 30

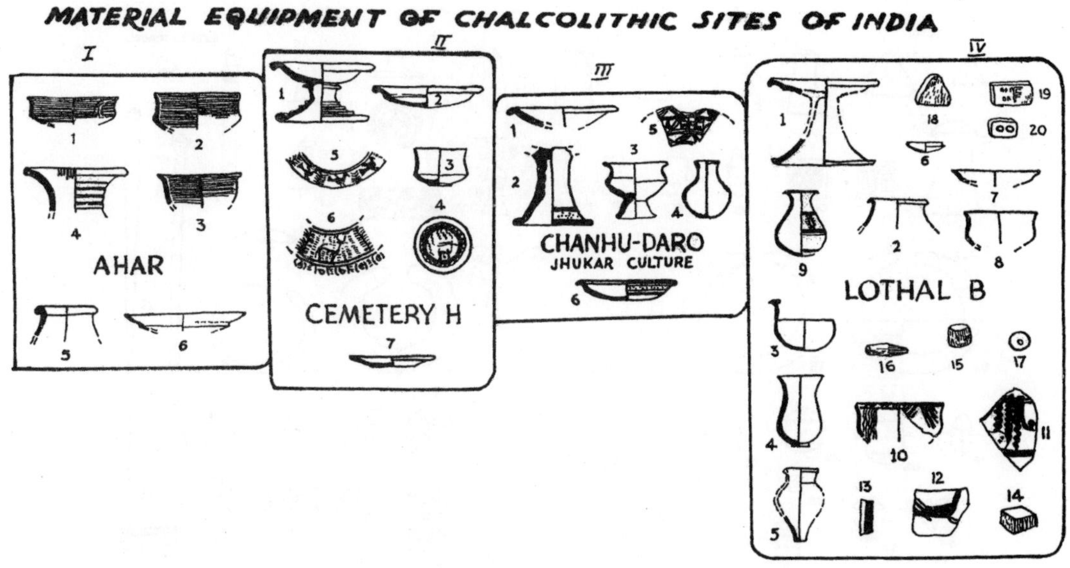

Fig. No. 31

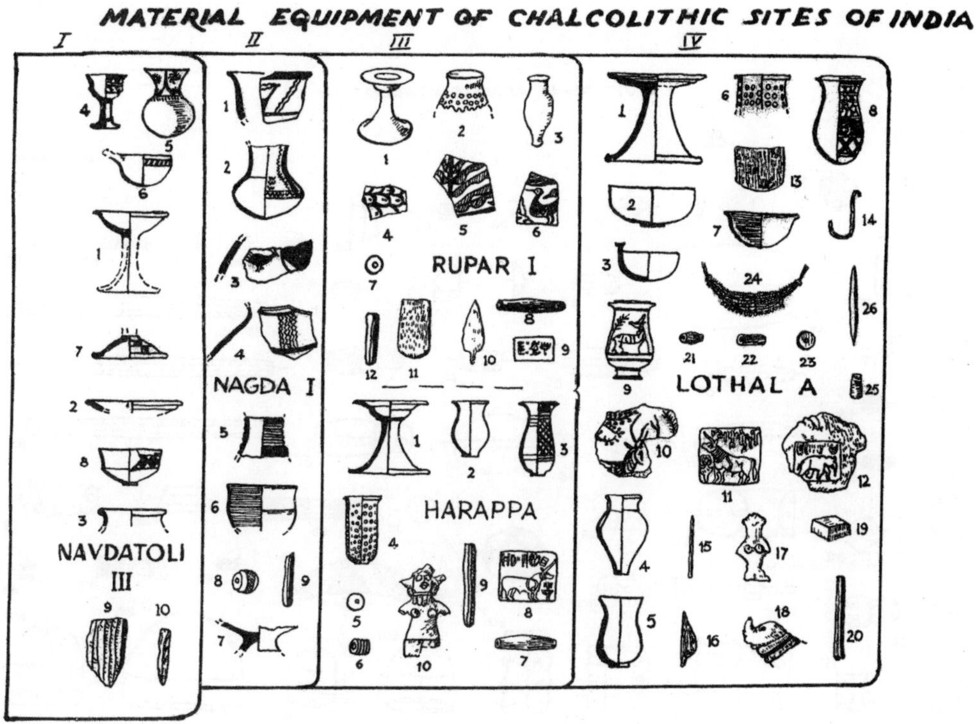

Fig. No. 32

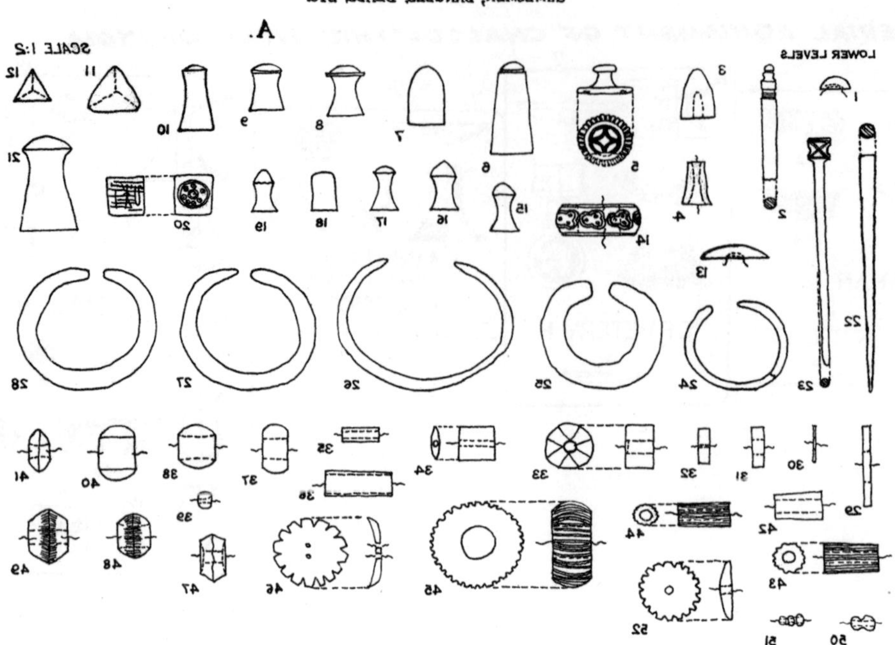

Fig. No. 33

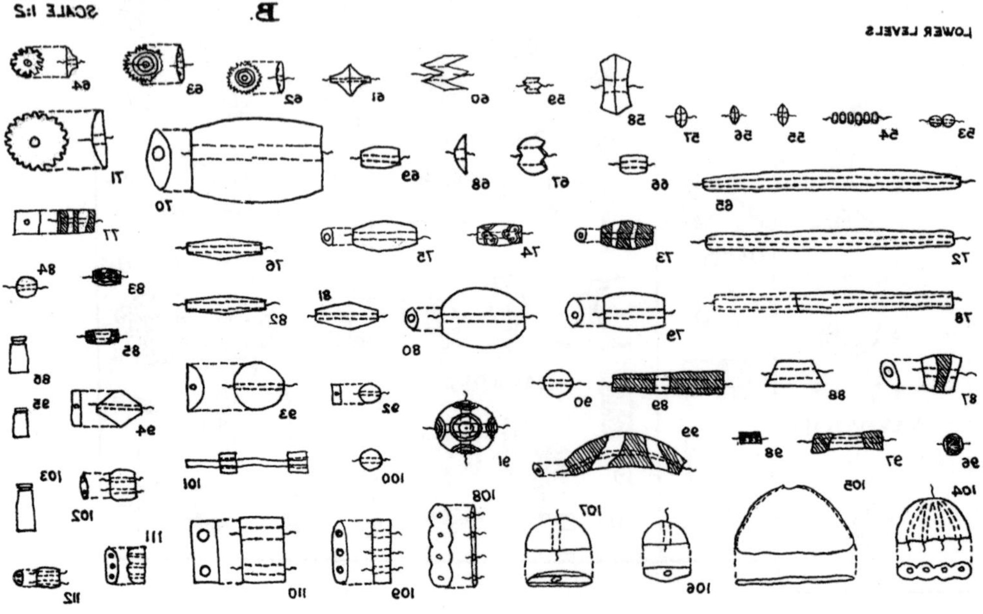

Fig. No. 34

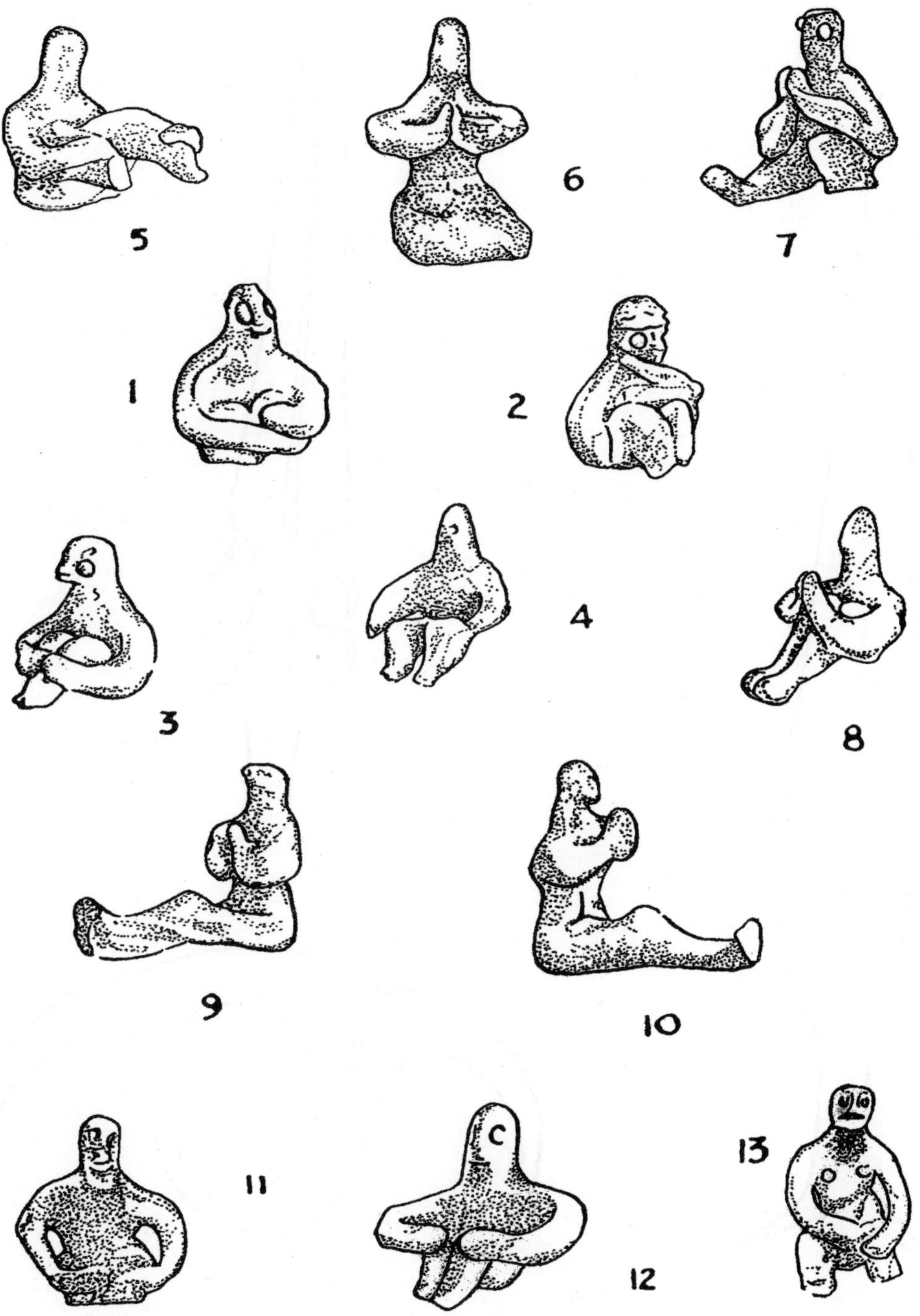

Terracotta figurines in yogic poses from Harappa (1-8) and Mahenjo-daro (9-13).

Fig. No. 35

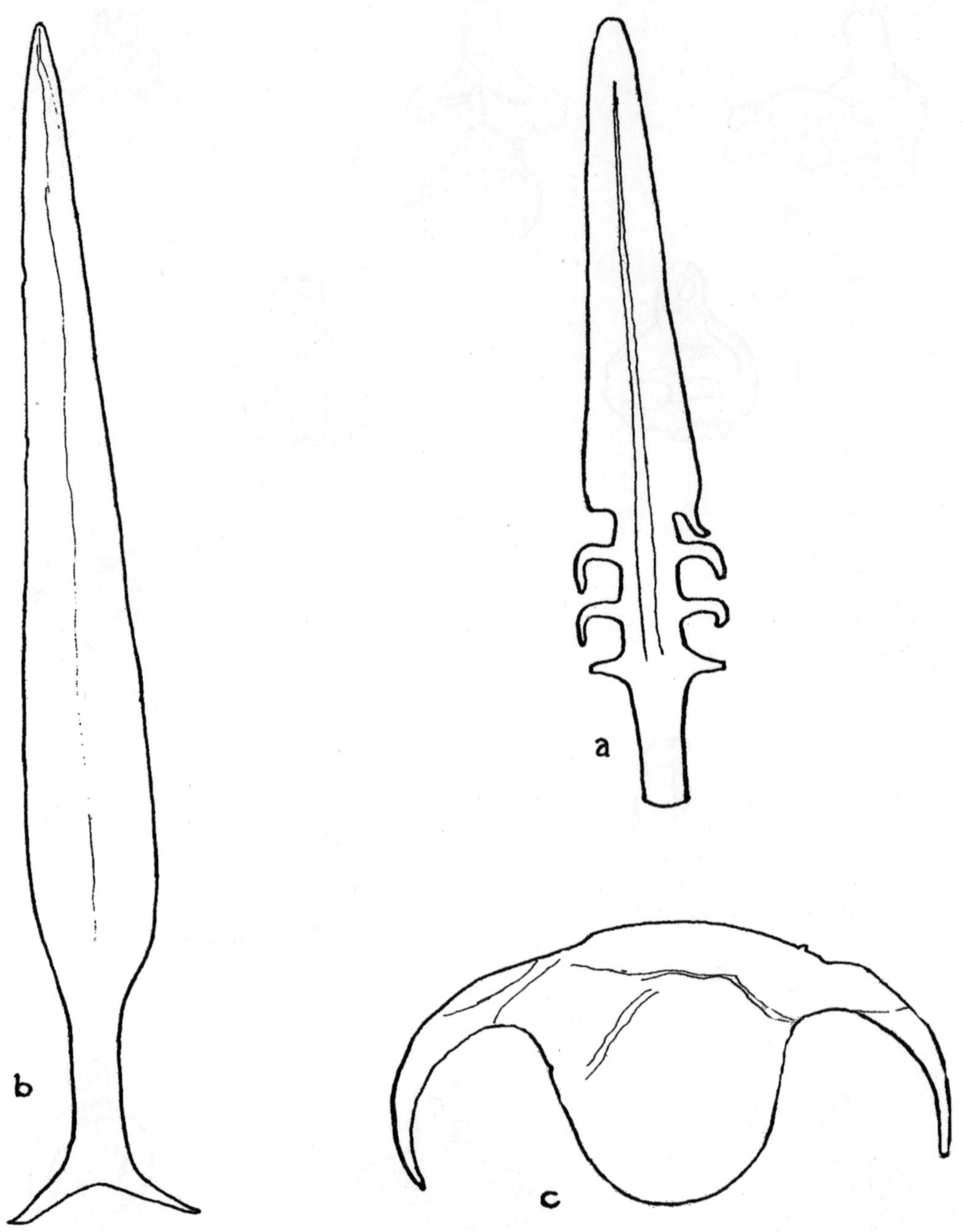

a. Hook-barbed harpoon; b. Antenae sword, Fatehgarh; C. Silver disc with horns, Gungeria

Fig. No. 36

Pl. NO. I – Cylindar Seal - Early Dynastie and Sargonid

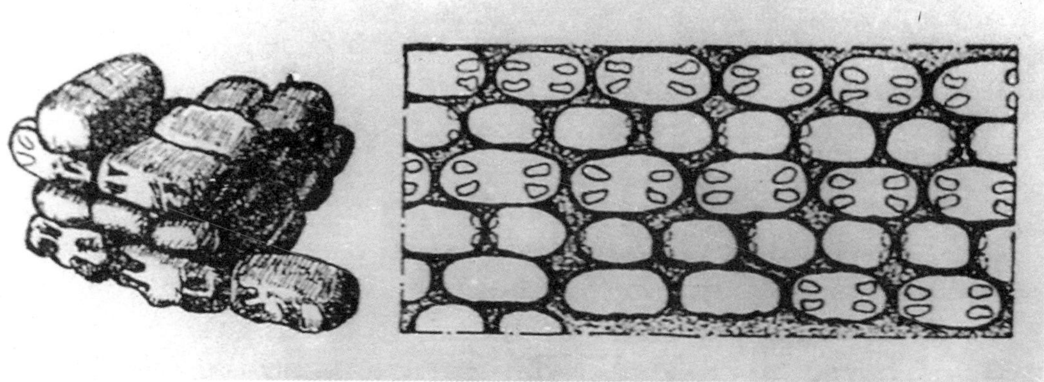

Pl. No. II – Sialk; The earliest form of mud-brick

Fig. No. 37

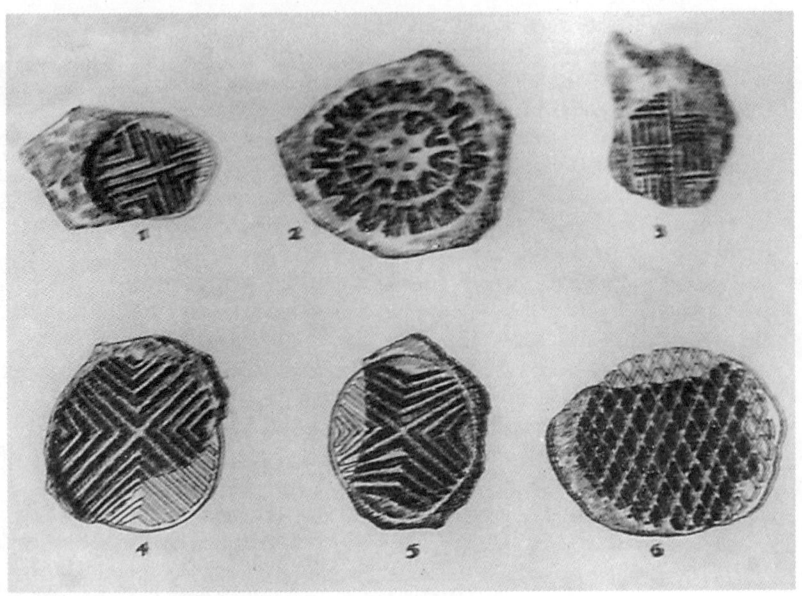

Pl. No. III – Sialk; Seal impressions

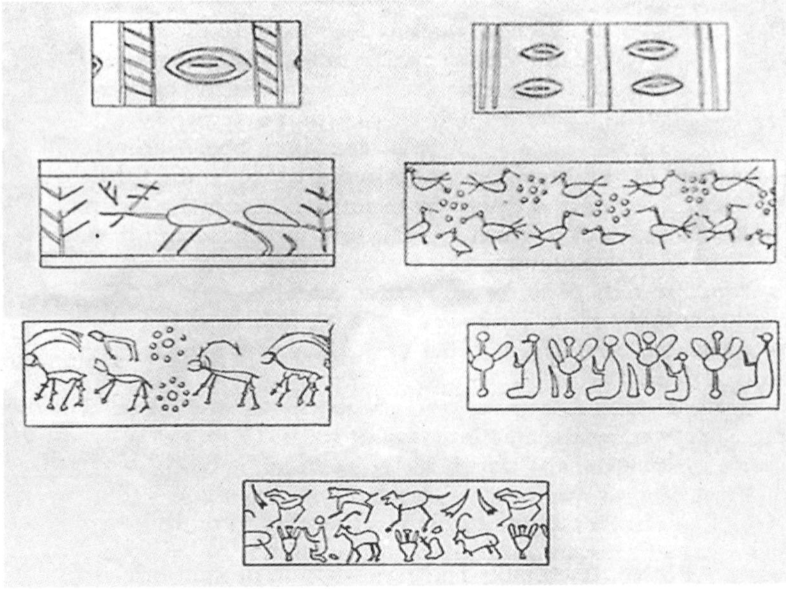

Pl. No. IV – Sialk; Cylinder seals belonging to the period of proto Elamite tablets

Fig. No. 38

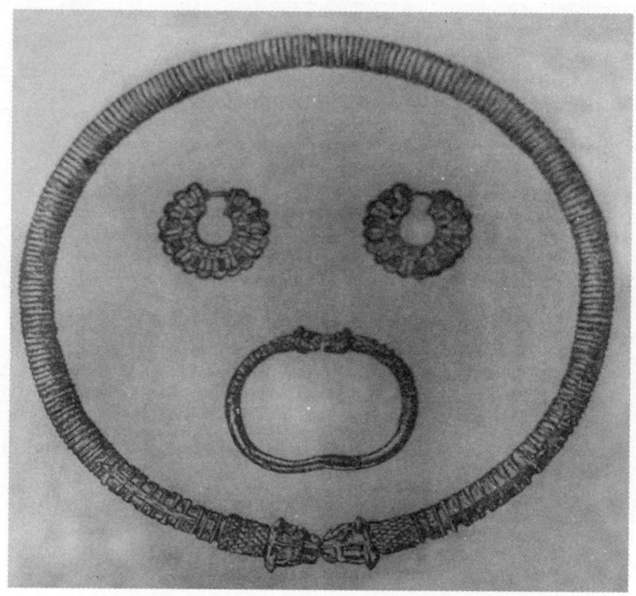

Pl. No. V – Susa; Gold Jewellery from the Achaemenian tomb

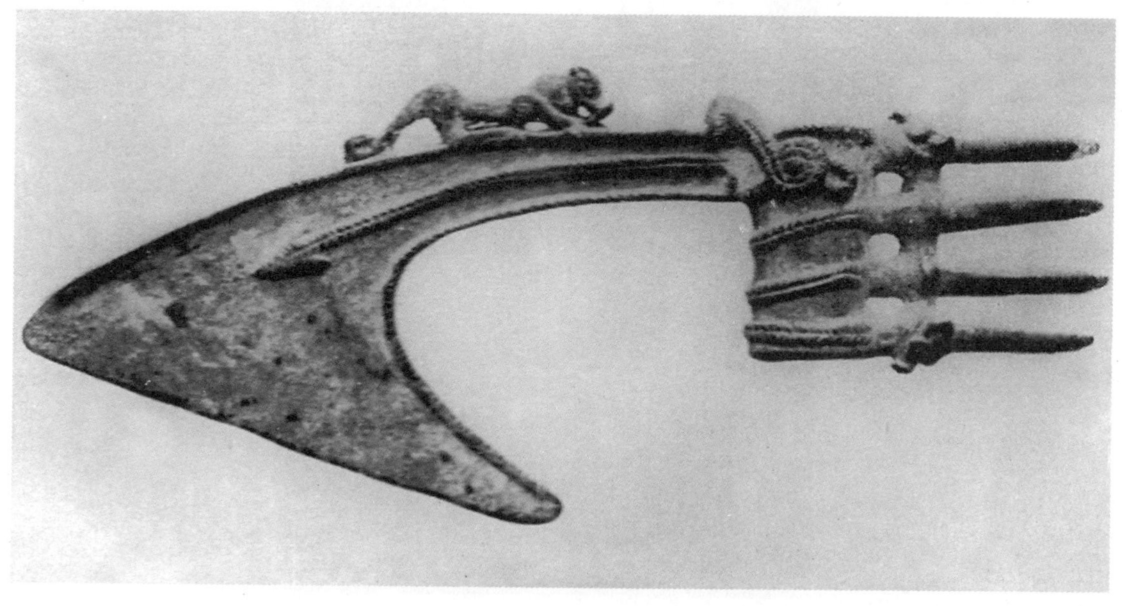

Pl. No. VI – Luristan; Bronze axe.

Fig. No. 39

Pl. No. VII – Painted grey ware - Decean Chalcolithic

Pl. No. VIII – Dish-on-stand and Goblet, I, Navadatoli

Fig. No. 40

Pl. NO. IX – Dish-on-Stand and Goblet, II, Navadatoli

Pl. NO. X – Channel-spouted bowl, Navadatoli

Fig. No. 41

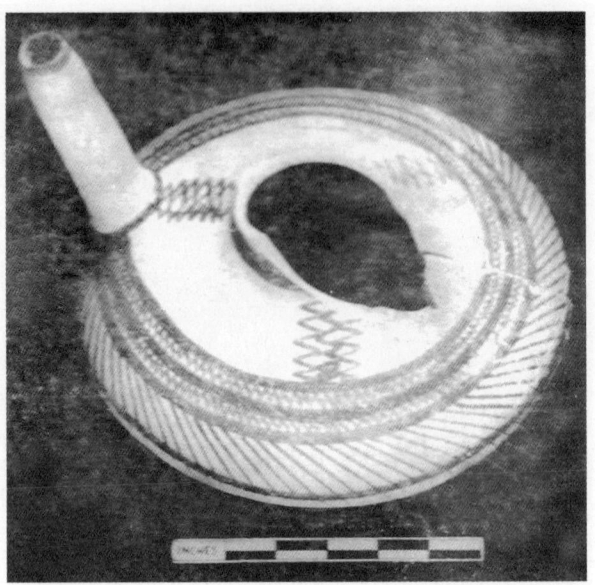

Pl. No. XI – Spouted Pot, Nevasa

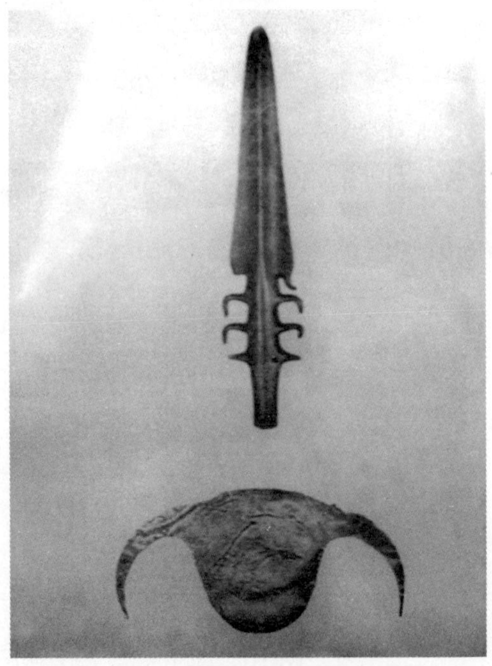

Pl. No. XII – (a) Hook barbed harpoon, Fatehgarh
(b) Silver dish with horn - Gungeria

Fig. No. 42

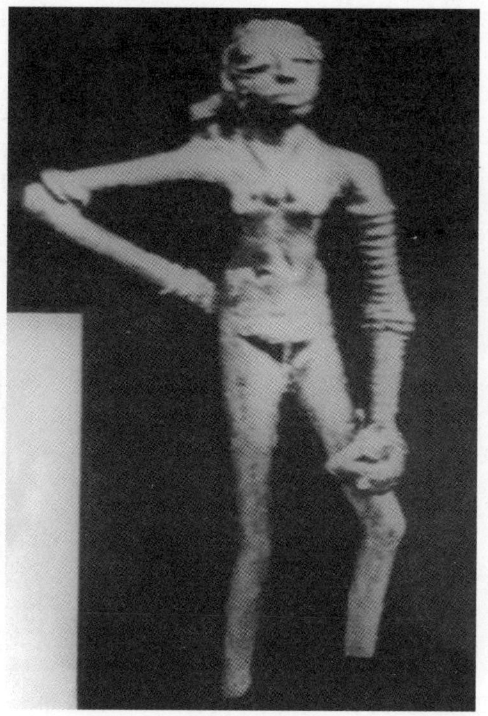

Pl. NO. XIII – Bronze Femal Statuettes - Mohenjodaro

Pl. No. XIV – Painted pots - Harappa

Fig. No. 43

Pl. No. XV – Clay Figurines - Harappa

Pl. No. XVI – Incised Jhangar Ware

Fig. No. 44

Pl. No. XVII – Seal B. Mahenjodaro

Fig. No. 45

Pl. NO. XVIII – Seal C. Mohenjodaro

Pl. No. XIX – Seal D. Mohenjodaro

Fig. No. 46

Pl. No. XX – Seal E. Mohenjodaro

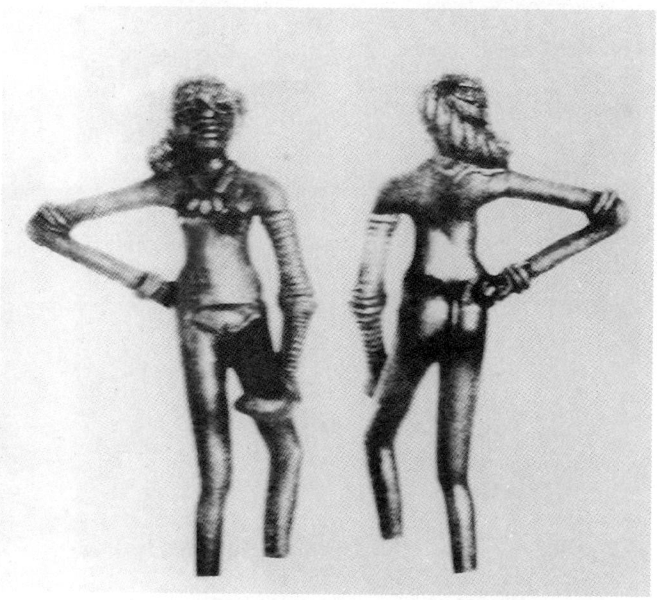

Pl. No. XXI – Bronze dancing Girl, Mohenjodaro

Fig. No. 47

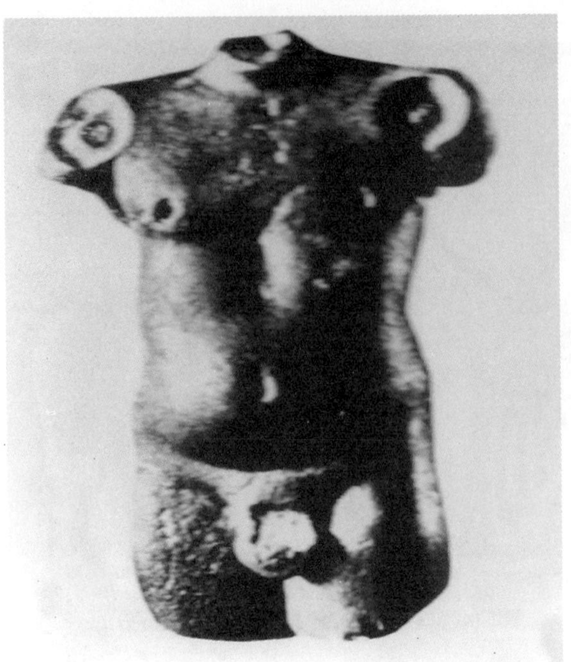

Pl. No. XXII – Standing Youth, Harappa

Pl. No. XXIII – Beard Man, Mohenjodaro

Fig. No. 48

Pl. NO. XXIV – Indus Valley Civilization _ Painted Pottery
(Mohenjodaro Cemetery H) - A

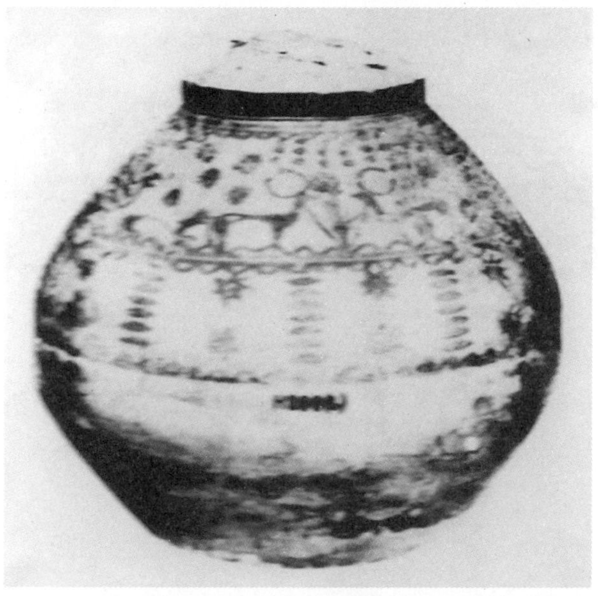

Pl. NO. XXV – Indus Valley Civilization _ Painted Pottery
(Mohenjodaro Cemetery H) - B

Fig. No. 49

Pl. No. XXVI – Indus Valley Civilization Painted Pottery
(Mohenjodaro Cemetery H) - C

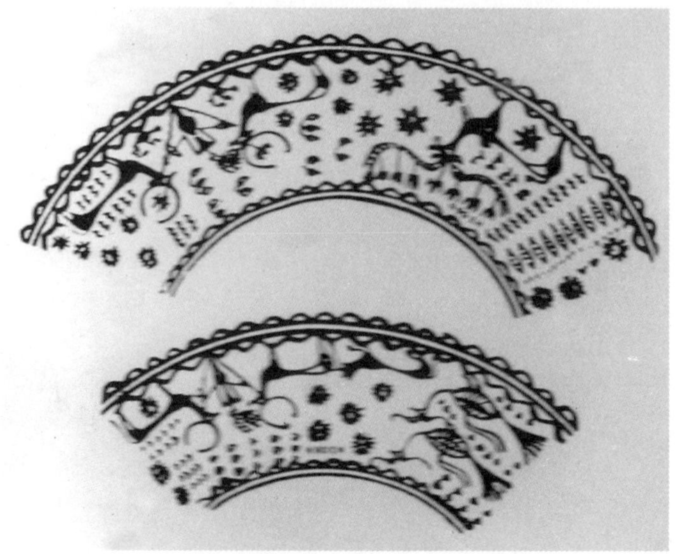

Pl. No. XXVII – Indus Valley Civilization Painted Pottery
(Mohenjodaro Cemetery H) - D

Fig. No. 50

Pl. No. XXVIII – Mohenjodaro; Seal with Pasupati Motif

Pl. No. XXIX – Harappan Culture_Human Figure Fighting with Two tigers.

Fig. No. 51

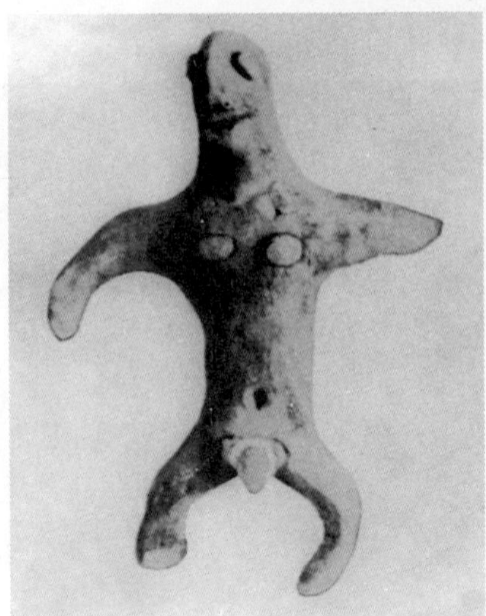

Pl. No. XXX – Harappan Culture, A Human Statue

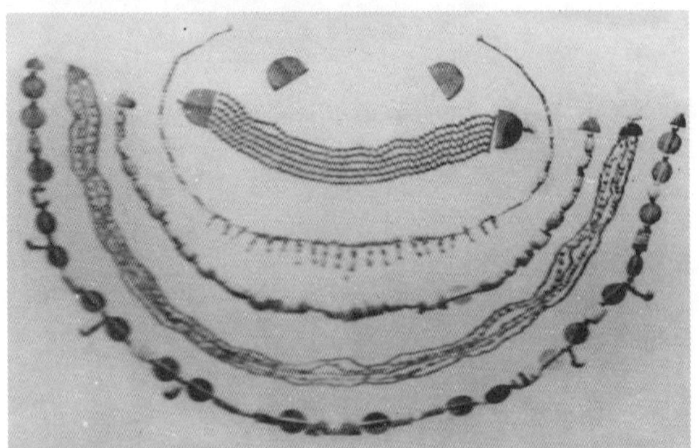

Pl. No. XXXI – Harappan Culture _ Necklaces

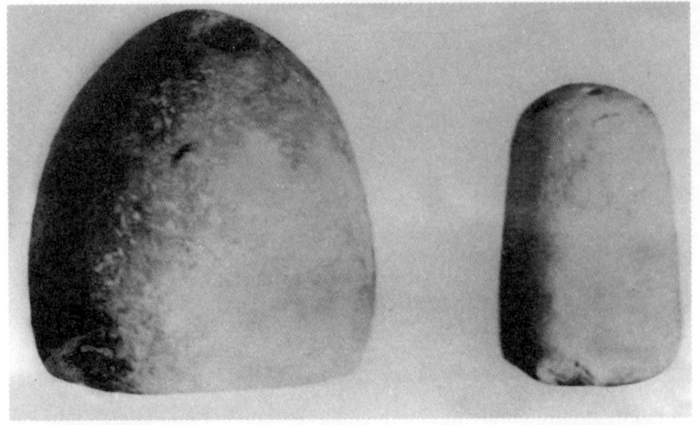

Pl No. XXXII – Harappan Culture - Phallies

Fig. No. 52